WELLINGTON'S FOOT GUARDS AT WATERLOO

THE MEN WHO SAVED
THE DAY AGAINST NAPOLEON

ROBERT BURNHAM AND
RON McGUIGAN

FRONTLINE
BOOKS

WELLINGTON'S FOOT GUARDS AT WATERLOO
The Men Who Saved The Day Against Napoleon

First published in Great Britain in 2018 by Frontline Books,
an imprint of Pen & Sword Books Ltd, Yorkshire - Philadelphia

Copyright © Robert Burnham and Ron McGuigan
ISBN: 978-1-52670-986-8

The right of Robert Burnham and Ron McGuigan to be identified as Authors of this work has been asserted by them in accordance with the Copyright, Designs and Patents Act 1988. A CIP catalogue record for this book is available from the British Library All rights reserved.

No part of this book may be reproduced or transmitted in any form or by any means, electronic or mechanical including photocopying, recording or by any information storage and retrieval system, without permission from the Publisher in writing.

Typeset in India by Vman Infotech Private Limited
Printed and bound by TJ International, Padstow, Cornwall

Pen & Sword Books Ltd incorporates the imprints of Pen & Sword Archaeology, Air World Books, Atlas, Aviation, Battleground, Discovery, Family History, History, Maritime, Military, Naval, Politics, Social History, Transport, True Crime, Claymore Press, Frontline Books, Praetorian Press, Seaforth Publishing and White Owl

For a complete list of Pen & Sword titles please contact:

PEN & SWORD BOOKS LTD
47 Church Street, Barnsley, South Yorkshire, S70 2AS, UK.
E-mail: enquiries@pen-and-sword.co.uk
Website: www.pen-and-sword.co.uk

Or

PEN AND SWORD BOOKS,
1950 Lawrence Road, Havertown, PA 19083, USA
E-mail: Uspen-and-sword@casematepublishers.com
Website: www.penandswordbooks.com

Contents

Acknowledgements vii

Introduction ix

Abbreviations xii

List of Maps xiv

Chapter 1	The Guards Battalions	1
Chapter 2	The Guards Officers	16
Chapter 3	The Enlisted Soldier	25
Chapter 4	April 1814 to March 1815 Inspections, Parades, and Boredom	33
Chapter 5	March to June 1815 War Clouds on the Horizon	43
Chapter 6	16 June 1815 The March To War	65
Chapter 7	16 June 1815 Quatre Bras	76
Chapter 8	17 June 1815 The Retreat to Waterloo	91
Chapter 9	18 June 1815 The Morning of Waterloo	113
Chapter 10	18 June 1815 Waterloo 11.00-13.30 Hours	125
Chapter 11	18 June 1815 Waterloo 13.30-16.00 Hours	137
Chapter 12	18 June 1815 Waterloo 16.00-20.00 Hours	159
Chapter 13	18 June 1815 Waterloo 20.00-21.00 Hours	181
Chapter 14	The Night After Waterloo	198
Chapter 15	The March to Paris, the Siege of Peronné, and the Army of Occupation of France	216
Chapter 16	What Happened to Them After Waterloo?	253

Appendix I	Organization of the Foot Guard Regiments in 1815	277
Appendix II	Monthly Strength Returns for the Foot Guards Battalions in 1815	281
Appendix III	The 1st Division Officers at Quatre Bras (16.00 Hours)	287
Appendix IV	Strength of the Foot Guards Regiments on 18 June 1815	295
Appendix V	The 1st Division Officers at Waterloo (08.00 Hours)	296
Appendix VI	The 1st Division Officers on the March to Paris	304
Appendix VII	Guards Officers on the Staff of Wellington's Army from June 1815 to November 1818	312
Appendix VIII	1st Foot Guards Casualties in the Waterloo Campaign	323
Appendix IX	Coldstream Guards Casualties in the Waterloo Campaign	335
Appendix X	3rd Foot Guards Casualties in the Waterloo Campaign	340
Appendix XI	British Awards	345
Appendix XII	Foreign Awards	349
Appendix XIII	Promotions within the Guards Regiments Caused by Deaths	351
Appendix XIV	Other Officer Promotions in the Guards Regiments in 1815	354
Appendix XV	The Waterloo Dispatch	357
Bibliography		359
Name Index		366

Acknowledgements

This book would not have been possible without the groundwork laid by Gareth Glover. Over the past two decades he has found, edited, and published hundreds of letters, memoirs, and diaries by British soldiers who fought in the Napoleonic Wars. About 75 per cent of the sources that we used can be directly linked to his efforts. He has also been generous with his time and has provided transcripts of yet to be published sources as well as images from his personal collection. Another is Barbara Chambers who spent decades researching the 1st Foot Guards and compiled records on thousands of them who fought at Waterloo. Much of the personal data on the enlisted soldiers was unearthed by her. Rod MacArthur is another whom I cannot say too much about. He is a storehouse of arcane knowledge on the internal workings of the regiments of the British Army. Rod was able to come up with answers to questions on British drill and regulations that had appeared to be lost over the centuries. We spent many hours with Dr. Mick Crumplin, the foremost authority on British military medical practices of the Napoleonic Wars. His insights on casualties in general, but also specifically at Hougoumont, allowed us to come up with some key analysis on what happened to the wounded there. Then there is also Alasdair White, who lives a few kilometres from Hougoumont, who answered many questions on the layout of the complex. And, of course, David Beckford, our cartographer, who drew the map of Hougoumont.

Then there are those of the Napoleon Series Community who are always willing to answer almost any question we pose: Kevin Kiley, our artillery expert; Paul Dawson whose vast files on the French Imperial Guard was instrumental in our being able to provide full names of French officers; Andrew Bamford who provided help in understanding British strength returns; Wu Tian who got us searching in the right direction for Sous-Lieutenant Jeandot; and Steven Smith – who filled in many details on the Siege of Péronne. We thought we had him stumped on this one, but as usual he was able to dig up some of the most obscure sources.

We would be remiss to not thank our long-time friends and supporters who help us with all of our books: Antony Broughton, who once again has opened his personal library of antique books and military prints for us to use; Rory Muir who answered numerous questions on the military politics of the era; and Howie Muir, who gave us his research on how the Foot Guards formed up and manoeuvred at Waterloo.

Several institutions were also generous in their help: the Cavalry and Guards Club for their permission to use the painting on our cover, the Anne S.K. Brown Military Collection at Brown University for several images, and the Huntington Library in San Marino, California. We also need to recognize the importance of the online resources that were so helpful: *London Gazette* online, Google Books, and Hathi Trust Digital Library. It was through them were we able to access so many books that could only be found in a few libraries in the world.

A sincere thank you to John Grehan and Martin Mace, our publishers, who quickly gave approval for the book.

Last but most importantly we need to acknowledge our wives, Denah Burnham and Deb McGuigan. Once again, they have patiently waited while we did our research, wondered when we would get off the computer, even listened to the anecdotes we had found, and not asked too often when we would do some chores. They have definitely made it easy for us.

Robert Burnham and Ron McGuigan,
April 2018.

Introduction

The date of 18 June 1815, is one of the proudest in the history of the British Foot Guards. Their participation in the defence of the Chateau of Hougoumont and the defeat of the French Imperial Guard is long remembered and celebrated. Yet, the Foot Guards contributed much more to the campaign of 1815. This book is an examination of the Foot Guards and their contributions.

The Foot Guards are the Household Troops of the sovereigns of Great Britain and Ireland. They trace their history as Guards from the Restoration of the British Monarchy in 1660 after the English Civil War. The 1st Foot Guards are the former Royalist Guards of King Charles II, while the 2nd Foot Guards are a former Parliamentary Regiment.[1] They were stationed in Coldstream, Scotland, and take their name from there. Although named for a town in Scotland, they are an English Regiment. They are commonly called the Coldstream Foot Guards and are not usually referred to by their number. They existed before the 1st Foot Guards and resent being numbered second. Their motto 'Nulli Secundus' [or Second to None] reflects this. The 3rd Foot Guards were newly raised in Scotland in 1660.

At the time of Waterloo, the regiments were known as: 1st Regiment of Foot Guards, Coldstream Regiment of Foot Guards and 3rd Regiment of Foot Guards. The three Foot Guard regiments never exceeded the combined total of seven permanent battalions. The three regiments exist today as the Grenadier Guards, Coldstream Guards and Scots Guards[2].

As well as their primary function of guarding the sovereign, the Foot Guards were available for active service and made many of the campaigns of the seventeenth, eighteenth and nineteenth centuries. However, before and during the Napoleonic Wars, they did not garrison overseas colonies.

---

1. Parliamentary Regiments fought against the Monarchy during the English Civil War.
2. Known as Scots Fusilier Guards 1831-1877.

The Foot Guards had a number of privileges including rank in the regiment and in the Army known as dual rank. That is, all regimental lieutenants were substantive captains in the Army and all regimental captains were substantive lieutenant colonels in the Army.[3] Officers would be promoted in the regiment by regimental rank but would be promoted in the Army by Army rank. Similarly, officers would exchange regiments based upon their Army rank. Thus, a captain and lieutenant colonel commanding a company in the Foot Guards would become a lieutenant colonel commanding a battalion in a line regiment upon exchange.

To simplify matters, due to this dual rank system, the officer's regimental rank will be used when referring to his service in the regiment and his army rank will be used when he served outside of his regiment.

The term 'Field Officer' is referred to in the text. This is used to identify officers with the rank of major or lieutenant colonel in the regiment and Army. The term 'Company Officer' is used to identify officers serving in a company in the rank of either captain, lieutenant or ensign.

Occasionally we mention brevet rank in the text. This was higher rank in the Army and not in the regiment. Brevet rank carried neither responsibility nor pay in the regiment. It was granted for long service in a rank or for meritorious service. Officers of the rank of captain, major and lieutenant colonel were eligible for brevet promotion. Thus, lieutenants in the Guards with dual rank of captain were eligible for brevet promotion to higher ranks.

Another privilege was that Foot Guard Brigades could only be commanded by Foot Guard officers. Line officers were not allowed to command a Guards Brigade; however, Foot Guard officers could command line brigades. This privilege did not extend to divisions containing a Guards Brigade, but not considered a Guards Division.

During the early French Revolutionary and Napoleonic Wars, the Foot Guards were organized in ad hoc brigades for service. This changed on 26 June 1803, when the seven Foot Guard Battalions were formally organized in three brigades. The First Brigade consisted of the 1st Battalion 1st Foot Guards and the 3rd Battalion 1st Foot Guards. The Second Brigade consisted of the 1st Battalion Coldstream Foot Guards and the 1st Battalion 3rd Foot Guards. The Third Brigade consisted of the 2nd Battalions of the three regiments. It usually served as the depot for the other two brigades, remaining at home and providing drafts of trained men as reinforcements to the battalions on active service.

---

3. Substantive rank was rank for which you received pay and could not be reduced in rank except by court-martial.

INTRODUCTION

Our look at the Foot Guards on the continent in 1815 will start with the regiments already stationed there and follow their active service until the formation of the Army of Occupation in France in late 1815. This will include the formation of the 1st [Guards] Division, the battles of Quatre Bras and Waterloo, the taking of Peronne and the advance to Paris.

After the awarding of the subtitle 'Grenadier' to the title of the 1st Foot Guards, on 29 July 1815, it became acceptable to use either '1st or Grenadier Guards' or just 'Grenadier Guards' and to drop the use of its number.

Short biographies of the principal commanding officers are included. We will also examine in detail the demographics of the three regiments. For officers we will show their average age, average time in service, amount of active service [i.e. combat experience], and whether the officer corps was really drawn from the nobility. For the enlisted soldiers, we also look at the average time they had been in the Army, their combat experience, whether they had served in the militia prior to enlisting, and also a physical description of the typical Guardsman in 1815, such as his age, height, hair and eye colour. We also examine the myth of whether the drummers were boys.

What will become clear is that despite their elite status, the Foot Guards did not recruit the best men from the line battalions, but, recruited at large in Great Britain and Ireland similar to the line regiments. The officers, too, were a mixed lot. Some were peers in their own right, while some were sons and relatives of peers, baronets, landed gentry, and commoners.

Being in the Guards is what made them elite.

Appendices will include the authorized strength of the Guards in 1815, their actual strength during each month of 1815; the command structure of the division, brigades, and battalions; casualties; and awards and promotions granted for the campaign.

This book is a straight-forward re-telling in their own words of what the Guards did and did not do in the Waterloo Campaign. It is not our intent to revisit the controversies surrounding the defeat of the French Imperial Guard. This has been done by others. There is enough glory in that defeat to be shared by all.

With regard to the artillery, at the time, artillery batteries were termed brigades. Each brigade and troop usually consisted of five cannons and a howitzer. The brigade and troop of artillery attached to the Guards Division were each made up of five 9-pounder cannons and a 5 ½-inch howitzer.

For the sake of simplicity, we use Wellington throughout the text instead of his official title and rank of the Duke of Wellington and Field Marshal. We will also use the generic term 'General' regardless of whether the officer is a lieutenant or major general.

Abbreviations

AAG	Assistant Adjutant General
ACG	Assistant Commissary General
ADC	Aide-de-Camp
AG	Adjutant General
AGC	Army Gold Cross
AGM	Army Gold Medal
AOOF	Army of Occupation in France
AQMG	Assistant Quartermaster General
Bde	Brigade
Bn	Battalion
Bns	Battalions
CB	Companion of the Most Honourable Order of the Bath from 1815
cm	centimetre(s)
Cpl/CPL	Corporal
Cpts/CPTs	Captains
d	Pence
DAAG	Deputy Assistant Adjutant General
DACG	Deputy Assistant Commissary General
DAG	Deputy Adjutant General
DAQMG	Deputy Assistant Quartermaster General
Div	Division
DoW	Died of wounds
DQMG	Deputy Quartermaster General
FG	Foot Guards
GCB	Knight Grand Cross of the Most Honourable Order of the Bath from 1815
GCH	Knight Grand Cross of the Royal Hanoverian Guelphic Order

ABBREVIATIONS

GCMG	Knight Grand Cross of The Most Distinguished Order of St. Michael and St. George
G.O.	General Order
HA	Horse Artillery
HEIC	Honourable East India Company
Hon	Honourable
h.p.	half pay
HQ	Headquarters
KB	Knight of the Most Honourable Order of the Bath to 1815
KCB	Knight Commander of the Most Honourable Order of the Bath from 1815
KCH	Knight Commander of the Royal Hanoverian Guelphic Order
KGA	The King's German Artillery
KGL	The King's German Legion
KIA	Killed in action
km	kilometre(s)
KP	Knight of the Most Illustrious Order of St. Patrick
Kt	Knight
LTC	Lieutenant Colonel
LTs	Lieutenants
M	metre(s)
MGSM	Military General Service Medal
MIA	missing in action
MP	Member of Parliament
NPG	National Portrait Gallery
OR	Other Ranks
PTSD	Post Traumatic Stress Disorder
QMG	Quartermaster General
RA	Royal Artillery
RE	Royal Engineers
Rgt	Regiment
RHA	Royal Horse Artillery
S	Shillings
Sgt/SGT	Sergeant
£	Pounds
#	Number

List of Maps

Map 1 The Situation at Quatre Bras   79
Map 2 Position of the Guards on the Morning of Waterloo   124
Map 3 Hougoumont   171
Map 4 March of the 1st Brigade to Paris   215
Map 5 The Storming of Péronne, 26 June 1815   230

Chapter 1

The Guards Battalions

By the end of April 1814, peace had come to Europe. Over the next eleven months the British government began to reduce the military budget and the Foot Guards regiments were not spared. Just paying the salaries of over 11,000 officers and soldiers was an enormous expense.[1] In September 1814, the three regiments were ordered to reduce their numbers. The companies in the 1st Foot Guards had been authorized 147 officers and men, but after September 1814, they were only authorized 132 officers and men. The companies in the Coldstream and 3rd Foot Guard were similarly reduced from 148 officers and men to 132. Furthermore, the Coldstream and 3rd Foot Guards had to disband the additional two companies that had been added to their strength in 1813. The number of lieutenants was reduced by twenty-four in the 1st Foot Guards and by sixteen in the other two regiments. This did not see an overall reduction in the number of officers however. To offset the loss of the lieutenants, an equal number of ensigns were added to the authorized strength of each regiment.[2] The reduction changed the total authorized strength of the regiments from 11,223 to 9,612. How significant of a savings this was is debatable for their salaries still cost the government £309,801 3 shillings 8 pence per year.[3] In salaries alone, it cost the government almost 75 per cent more to pay the two-battalion Coldstream Guards, than it did to pay a two-battalion line regiment.[4]

---

1. In April 1814, the three Foot Guards Regiments were authorized 11,223 officers and soldiers.
2. Appendix I has the authorized strength of each of the Guards Regiments for 1815.
3. *Journals of the House of Commons*, Vol. 70, page 517
4. ibid. Salaries for a two-battalion line infantry regiment was £48,709 9 shillings 2 pence. About 57 per cent of what the Coldstream Guards were paid.

Table 1.1: Losses by the Reduction of the Foot Guards Regiments in September 1814[5]

Regiment	Companies	Captains	Lieutenants	Sergeants	Corporals	Privates	Total
1st Foot Guards	0	0	24	32	32	448	512
Coldstream Guards	2	2	18	56	56	426	558
3rd Foot Guards	2	2	18	56	56	426	558

Note: The above numbers do not add up because in every regiment the loss of lieutenants was offset by a similar increase in the number of ensigns, except for the four ensigns lost when the two companies in the Coldstream Guards and the 3rd Foot Guards were disbanded.

In July 1814, the British Army changed the way they paid their general officers. Prior to that date a general was only paid as a general if he was in a billet that was authorized a general officer. Those who were not were paid the pay of whatever their regimental rank was. For example, in 1813 Captain William Anson of the 1st Foot Guards was also a major general. If he had not been serving in a position that was authorized a major general, he would return to the regiment and serve as a company commander. He would only receive the pay of a captain. A large number of Guards officers were also general officers. Most had not served with their regiment for many years. Yet they were still carried on the regimental rolls and prevented officers who were junior to them from being promoted.

This was a problem throughout the British Army and not just the Foot Guards. In July 1814, the British Army offered every general an option of continuing to serve with their regiment when they were not serving as a general or to give up their regimental commission and become a general officer unattached. Since the pay as an unattached general was more than the regular pay as a regimental officer, almost every general in the Army

---

5. Mackinnon, Daniel, *Origin and Services of the Coldstream Guards*. 2 vols. Cambridge: Ken Trotman, 2003. Vol. 2, p.404. Hamilton, Frederick W., *The Origin and History of the First or Grenadier Guards*. 3 vols. London: John Murray, 1874. Vol. 3, p.363.

chose to do this. All thirty-six generals assigned to the Guards took the option.

Table 1.2: Reduction of General Officers in the Foot Guards 1814-1815

Regiment	Generals	Lieutenant Generals	Major Generals
1st Foot Guards	-	4	11
Coldstream Guards	1	2	9
3rd Foot Guards	-	4	7

This freed up thirty-eight positions[6] that needed to be filled. Normally when there was a vacancy in a rank, the senior officer in the rank below would be offered the opportunity to purchase the higher rank. However, the Army appointed the officers rather than having them purchase the commission.[7]

Table 1.3: Number of Promotions Due to the Removal of General Officers from the Regiments on 25 July 1814.

Regiment	Lieutenant Colonel	1st Major	2nd Major	3rd Major[8]	Captain
1st Foot Guards	1	1	1	1	11
Coldstream Guards	1	1	1	NA	10
3rd Foot Guards	1	1	1	NA	7

Not all the promotions went to officers within the regiment. The Army rewarded eighteen officers from outside the Guards by giving them promotions in a Guard Regiment. The majority of these officers had

---

6. Two generals chose to retire rather than go on half pay as a general officer.
7. For a lieutenant already in the Guards it would cost him £2,000 to buy his next rank. This was quite a windfall for those who were promoted. Burnham and McGuigan, *The British Army against Napoleon*, Barnsley: Frontline, 2010, p.152.
8. The number of majors equaled the number of battalions in a regiment. Only the 1st Guards had three battalions and hence a 3rd major.

distinguished themselves in the Peninsula, most on the Army Staff. There were also a few who may have received the promotions due to Royal influence. All of the promotions from outside the regiment were to the rank of captain.

Table 1.4: Number of Promotions to Captain from outside the Guards Regiments on 25 July 1814.

Regiment	# of Promotions	# Promoted from the Regiment	# Promoted from Outside
1st Foot Guards	11	5	6
Coldstream Guards	10	3	7
3rd Foot Guards	7	2	5

Foot Guards Ranks

The Foot Guards had a number of privileges including rank in the regiment and in the Army. Officers held dual rank. That is, all regimental lieutenants were substantive captains in the Army and all regimental captains were substantive lieutenant colonels in the Army. Substantive rank was rank for which you received pay and could not be reduced in rank except by court-martial. Army rank was rank held when the officer was assigned duties outside of the regiment.

Table 1.5: Foot Guards Ranks and Their Equivalent in Army Rank

Regimental Rank	Army Rank
Ensign	Ensign
Lieutenant	Captain
Captain	Lieutenant Colonel
Major	Lieutenant Colonel
Lieutenant Colonel	Lieutenant Colonel

The Guards Regiments also had only one lieutenant colonel and either two or three majors, depending on the number of battalions in the regiment. Although their regimental rank was either lieutenant colonel or major in reality these positions were held by senior officers. In 1813, for example in the 1st Foot Guards, the lieutenant colonel and the 1st and 2nd majors were lieutenant generals, while the 3rd major was a major general. After the reform of 1814, when most general officers were removed from the regiments, all of the officers in the Foot Guards regiments that held regimental rank of either lieutenant colonel or major, also were senior enough to hold army rank of colonel.

By which rank a Guards officer was referred was situation dependent. Traditionally in the British Army an officer was referred to by the highest rank he ever held, which was usually Army rank. It was not uncommon to see a captain called lieutenant colonel. Until July 1814, all ranks above lieutenant colonel were Army rank including generals.[9] Prior to then, many officers who were regimental lieutenant colonels also held general rank. So they would be called general instead of lieutenant colonel.

Official documents are not consistent on what rank was used. If the officer was serving on the Army staff, he was always called by his Army rank. Yet if the officer was serving with his regiment sometimes he was referred to by his regimental rank and other times by his Army rank. Letters, memoirs, and diaries are not consistent either. An officer could be called by his first name, his rank in the nobility such as Lord, his Army rank, or his regimental rank. To simplify matters, all Guards officers who are mentioned in this book are called by their regimental rank if they were serving with the regiment. For those serving on the Army staff, we refer to them by their Army rank.

Guards officers were promoted in the regiment by their regimental rank. Upon their promotion within the regiment they would automatically be promoted to the Army rank. This did not preclude them from being promoted in Army rank[10] prior to being promoted in the regiment. Similarly, Guards officers could exchange into other regiments based upon their Army rank. Thus, a captain and lieutenant colonel in the Foot Guards would become a lieutenant colonel in the line regiment upon exchange. Should a line lieutenant colonel exchange into the Foot Guards he would become a Guards company commander with the rank of captain and lieutenant colonel, even if he had already commanded an infantry battalion in his old regiment.

When serving outside of the regiment, the Guards officer was considered to be whatever his Army rank was. For example, a Guards lieutenant would be a captain, while a Guards captain would be a lieutenant colonel.

---

9. The exception was those generals who were appointed a regimental colonel.
10. This was also called brevet rank.

When a Guards officer and a line officer of equal rank served together, seniority was based on their Army date-of-rank.

Another advantage this dual rank system gave the Guards officer was that it made him eligible for progressive promotion in the Army via brevet rank faster than an officer in a line regiment. For example, a Guards lieutenant was eligible as an Army captain for brevet promotion while a regimental lieutenant in the line had to be promoted captain to be eligible for promotion to brevet rank. Brevet promotion was usually based upon length of service in a rank but was also granted for merit or an act of heroism. The promotion was always in Army rank and the holder of the rank did not receive any additional pay or privileges unless he was in a position that called for the rank. Regardless of whether his duties were regimental or on the Army staff, a brevet promotion made him eligible for further promotions in Army rank.

Organization of the Battalions

In 1815, the four Foot Guard battalions that served in the Waterloo Campaign were organized the same way, each with ten companies. Furthermore, each battalion had an identical authorized strength, regardless of the regiment. The only exception was that the 2nd and 3rd Battalions of the 1st Foot Guards were authorized two fifers. The authorized strength was 1,333 officers and men for the two 1st Foot Guards battalions and 1,331 officers and men for the Coldstream and 3rd Foot Guards battalions. A full breakdown of the numbers authorized for each rank can be seen in Appendix I. Authorized does not mean the actual number of personnel in each battalion. According to the 25 May 1815 monthly strength report the battalions averaged 1,145 officers and men each or 86 per cent of their authorized strength. The number of officers who were with their battalions and not serving on the staff was only 78 per cent of the total authorized. More importantly only twenty-four (60 per cent) of the forty authorized captains were commanding their companies.[11]

So why were all the battalions understrength? The first reason was because the number of men being recruited did not meet the needs of the regiment. Additionally, when a battalion was deployed on active service, it would not take those men who were either too sick or injured to withstand the rigors of a campaign. To replace those left behind, they took the fittest men available in the regimental depot. Sometimes there were not enough

---

11. The National Archives, WO17-1760.

men available to fill up the ranks. For those battalions already deployed, the battalion in the rear would send drafts of men out to the battalion to replace losses by combat and disease. They would send the available men, but they would not take every man from the battalion left at home. For example, in April 1815, the 2nd Battalion Coldstream Guards, which was stationed in Brussels, received a draft of 258 men from the regiment's 1st Battalion in Knightsbridge. In return, the 2nd Battalion sent fourteen sergeants and one private home. Despite increasing its strength by a third, it still was short 185 privates and corporals.[12]

The officer corps' situation was different. Many of the Guards officers assigned to battalions were serving on the staff of the Army or on the staff in Great Britain and thus not with the battalion in the Waterloo Campaign. Another reason could be the officer was too sick to join the battalion on active service or had been granted leave due to family matters. For example, in June 1815, the 2nd Battalion Coldstream Guards had four officers in these categories: Captain John Walpole and Lieutenant John Drummond were listed on the monthly returns as 'Sick in England', Captain Robert Arbuthnot was on leave, and Lieutenant Windham Anstruther was on his way to join the battalion after being previously listed as sick.[13]

Table 1.6: Number of Officers not Serving with Their Battalion in the Waterloo Campaign

Battalion	Captains	Lieutenants	Ensigns
2nd Battalion 1st Foot Guards	6	3	-
3rd Battalion 1st Foot Guards	1	4	1
2nd Battalion Coldstream	5	1	1
2nd Battalion 3rd Foot Guards	4	1	1
Total	16	9	3

Unlike the line regiments which were authorized a lieutenant colonel and two majors for each battalion, the Guards regiments were different. A Guards regiment was only authorized one officer with the regimental rank of lieutenant colonel and two or three majors, depending on the number of battalions in the regiment. The battalions were commanded by the majors. The senior major, also known as the 1st Major, commanded the 1st Battalion, the next senior was called the 2nd Major and he commanded the 2nd

---

12. TNA, WO17-289
13. TNA, WO17-289

Battalion, while in the 1st Foot Guards the junior major, who commanded the 3rd Battalion, was known as the 3rd Major. In the line regiments the majors had very specific duties while on active service. Because there was not an equivalent position in the Guards the two senior captains in the battalion took over those duties, while the senior lieutenant in their companies commanded it in the field. Within the battalion, every officer would know who these two captains were and would call them by their rank.

Organization and Identification of the Companies

Each battalion were organized the same way. It had a grenadier company, a light company, and eight centre companies. By 1815, the authorized strength of the centre companies was identical with one captain, one lieutenant, two ensigns, six sergeants, six corporals, two drummers, and 114 privates for a total of 132 officers and men. The grenadier and light companies had the same numbers, except instead of one lieutenant and two ensigns, they were authorized three lieutenants. The grenadier companies of the 1st Foot Guards were also authorized two fifers.

The Guards were a law onto their own selves when it came to naming the companies. In the line regiments the companies were named Grenadier Company, 1st through 8th Companies, and the Light Company. In garrison, the companies in the Guards Regiments were named after its company commander. For example, the company returns for 1815 only gave the company commander's name and did not identify which company it was except for the Light Company. The centre and grenadier companies were not identified as such.

Army Regulations concerning drill was specific about how the companies would be named while on active service. The companies were numbered based on the seniority of the captain. For the Centre Companies, the 1st Company would be the most senior captain's company, the 2nd Company would be the second captain's, down through the 8th Company. The Grenadier and Light Companies were excluded from numbering.[14] Furthermore the regulations stated that while in line formation, the Centre Companies would be organized into four divisions, each of two companies. The 1st Company would be paired with the 8th Company and were in the 1st Division, the 2nd Company with the 7th Company in the 2nd Division, the 3rd Company with the 6th Company in the 3rd Division, and the 4th

---

14. *Rules and Regulations for the Formations, Field-Exercise, and Movements of His Majesty's Forces*, p.66.

Company with the 5th Company in the 4th Division. Within the division, the lowest numbered company was on the right. The divisions would line up with 1st Division on the right, next to them would be the 4th Division, followed by the 3rd Division, and the 2nd Division on the left. Thus, the companies in line would be from right to left: Grenadier Company, 1st, 8th, 4th, 5th, 3rd, 6th, 2nd, 7th, Light Company.

The theory behind this formation was to pair the most experienced company commander with the least experienced commander, so that he could provide assistance when necessary. Unfortunately, theory broke down when faced with reality. The Guards battalions would practice this drill while in garrison or in cantonments, however when on active service their company commanders were often assigned to the Army staff. Waterloo was no exception. During the Waterloo Campaign, 40 per cent of the company commanders in the Guards battalions were on the Army staff or in other billets. The other problem was what happened when a company commander became a casualty? The Army's solution to both these problems was that the place of the company in formation did not changed once seniority was established. When a temporary company commander was appointed, he was likely junior to the other company commanders,[15] the company's place in the line was still determined by the original company commander's seniority. This was only changed when the battalion returned from active service or when a campaign ended.

The Individual Battalions

The actual strength of each of the battalions during the Waterloo Campaign is difficult to determine. Army regulations required each regiment in the Army to submit a strength return that showed the status of every officer and soldier in the regiment on the 25th of each month. For those regiments that had battalions serving away from the regiment, the battalion would submit their returns both to the regiment which was at home and to the headquarters of the army or garrison it was assigned to. Often the returns submitted by the regiment were a month behind those submitted by the army because of the time delay caused by obtaining the returns from the deployed battalions. Appendix II is a monthly compilation for each of the

---

15. Many of the Guards companies during the Waterloo Campaign were temporarily commanded by lieutenants.
16. General Orders dated 8 May 1815. Unfortunately, only the return for 17 June 1815 still exists.

Guards battalions that were part of Wellington's army in the Netherlands and France in 1815. These figures are from the returns submitted by the army and not the regiment. Wellington recognized that it would be impossible to have accurate information on the state of his army if he only relied on either the monthly and weekly reports. Beginning on 8 May 1815, he required all units to submit a daily strength report to the Adjutant General. This was to be done whether the army was in its cantonments or on campaign.[16]

There were four Guards Battalions serving in the Waterloo Campaign. They were formed into two brigades and became the 1st or Guards Division in Wellington's Army. This is the first time in their history that the Guards had been formed into a separate division.

The 2nd Battalion 1st Foot Guards

The 2nd Battalion of the 1st Foot Guards served in the Low Countries[17] from February 1793 to December 1794 and then in northern Germany until April 1795. It saw no further active service for fifteen years when it was sent to Cadiz, Spain in March 1810. It fought at Barossa on 5 March 1811 and then returned to England two months later. They did not deploy again until December 1813 when six companies consisting of 16 officers and 800 men were part of the expedition to the Low Countries under General Sir Thomas Graham. In February 1814 the battalion received reinforcements that brought their strength up to over 1,000.[18] The battalion fought at the assault on Bergen-op-Zoom on the night of 8-9 March 1814 and took heavy casualties, including three officers killed, four officers wounded, and nine officers captured; there were twenty enlisted soldiers killed and 275 captured.[19] After Napoleon abdicated in April 1814, the battalion was sent to Brussels where it remained for the next year.

By June 1815, the battalion was not the same battalion that went to the Low Countries eighteen months before. Of the eighteen officers who served in the assault on Bergen-op-Zoom, only one ensign was still with the battalion. Other than him, no ensign had any combat experience. The typical ensign was eighteen-years-old and had been commissioned in the army for thirteen months. The lieutenants were older and more experienced. The average lieutenant was twenty-two-years-old and had

---

17. Present day Belgium and the Netherlands.
18. Hamilton, Vol. 2, pp.485-487
19. Bamford, Andrew, *A Bold and Ambitious Enterprise: the British Army in the Low Countries 1813 – 1814*. Barnsley: Frontline, 2013, p.275.

been an officer for four years. All had served in the Peninsula an average of fifteen months and saw four actions. Lieutenant Charles Allix had spent thirty-four months there and had been in six different actions, but he was not the one with the most combat experience. Although he only served twenty-nine months in the Peninsula, Lieutenant William Moore had fought in ten battles.

As would be expected, the company commanders were older and more experienced. Their average age was thirty-one-years-old, and they had been in the Army for fifteen years. All were veterans of the Peninsular War, with three who had over five years there. Captain Henry Hardinge had sixty-five months in country and fought in seventeen different actions. Captain Lord Fitzroy Somerset served sixty-two months in the Peninsula and was in combat nineteen times. Only Captain Delancey Barclay had no combat experience. What was unique about these captains was that only four of them had any combat experience as a company commander. The rest had served outside the battalion on the staff. This continued during the Waterloo Campaign. Six of the company commanders were serving outside the battalion, while two, Richard Cooke and Francis D'Oyly, were serving as its acting majors.

When the 2nd Battalion went to the Low Countries in December 1813, it was considered the least experienced of the 1st Foot Guards battalions. Many of its soldiers were young and not veterans. By June 1815, the typical soldier was twenty-seven-years-old. The oldest soldier was Private William Alcock who was fifty-two. There were fifty-four soldier who were younger than twenty. The youngest was fourteen-year-old Drummer Robert Mercer. The average time in service for the soldiers was fifty-five months and even though the battalion was considered inexperienced, it had only three soldiers with less than a year's service. The soldier with the least amount of service was Private John Allwright with eight months in the ranks. Only 28 per cent of the soldiers were combat veterans. Among them were 162 Peninsula veterans, but despite the battalion having been in country for eighteen months, only 153 of those who were in the expedition to the Low Countries were still there.

3rd Battalion 1st Foot Guards

Unlike the 2nd Battalion 1st Foot Guards, the 3rd Battalion was the most experienced battalion in the 1st Foot Guards. It had served in Flanders in 1794, Sicily in 1807, and was in the Corunna Campaign from October 1808 to January 1809. After returning to England in February, it was part of the Walcheren Expedition during the summer of 1809. It spent the next eighteen months in England and in April 1811 was sent to Cadiz, Spain. It remained in southern Spain until August 1812 when it marched the length of Spain and joined Wellington's army in Madrid. It would serve with it in Portugal, Spain, and France until Napoleon abdicated in April 1814. By August it returned to its duties in London. It did not go to Belgium until April 1815.

By June 1815, unlike the 2nd Battalion of the 1st Foot Guards, the officers tended to be older and had more experience. The typical ensign was still only eighteen-years-old, but he had twenty-five months as an officer. Of its fourteen ensigns, ten of them were combat veterans, half whom had served with the 2nd Battalion in the Low Countries Campaign the previous year. The veteran with the most experience was Ensign Robert Batty who had served six months in the Peninsula and four months in the Low Countries. During the ten months he saw combat nine times. Temporarily attached to the battalion, was Ensign Rees Gronow of the 1st Battalion. With an average age of twenty-five, the lieutenants were three years older than their fellow lieutenants in the 2nd Battalion, and had average ninety-two months as an officer, almost twice as long as those in the 2nd Battalion. All had served at least a year in the Peninsula, with the minimum time being thirteen months. The average time of active service was twenty-nine months, during which he was in combat seven times. Lieutenant James Lord Hay served fifty-one months there and was in fourteen actions.

All ten captains assigned to the 3rd Battalion were in Belgium at the start of the Waterloo Campaign. Their average age was thirty-two and he had been an officer for fifteen years. All were veterans of the Peninsular War and had spent an average of thirty-two months on active service. The captain with the least amount was George Fead who had only served ten months in the Peninsula, while James Stanhope had forty-nine months of active service. All had been in combat multiple times with Lord Saltoun and James Stanhope having been in nine actions. Nine of the ten company commanders were with the battalion for the Waterloo Campaign. Only Captain Leslie Jones, who was serving as the commandant of Brussels, was absent. Two of them, Captains Horatio Townshend and Edward Stables, would start the campaign as the battalion's acting majors.

In general, enlisted soldiers in the 3rd Battalion were older and more experienced than those in the 2nd Battalion of the regiment. Their average age was twenty-eight and only twenty-four of its soldiers were younger than twenty. The youngest was seventeen-year-old Drummer John Cooke. The oldest was fifty-one-year-old Sergeant Joseph Boulcott. The 3rd Battalion's soldiers were also more experienced than the 2nd Battalion's. Their average time in service being eighty months, over two years more than the soldiers of the 2nd Battalion. Forty-five percent of them were combat veterans, almost all having served in the Peninsular War.

2nd Battalion Coldstream Guards

The 2nd Battalion of the Coldstream Guards had not gone on active service as a battalion during the Napoleonic Wars prior to the Waterloo Campaign. Two companies participated in the Walcheren Expedition in 1809 and two companies also served as part of the garrison in Cadiz, Spain from 1810 to 1811. It was not until the 1813 expedition to the Low Countries did the battalion deployed with more than two companies. But even this was only six companies of less than 600 officers and men.[20] They were part of the assault on Bergen-op-Zoom on the night of 8-9 March 1814, but only took forty casualties.

Like the 2nd Battalion of the 1st Foot Guards, by June 1815 the 2nd Battalion of the Coldstream Guards was not the same battalion that fought in the Low Countries eighteen months before. Only Ensign Henry Gooch had served in that campaign. Two others, Lieutenant Charles Bentinck and Ensign Augustus Cuyler were still in Belgium, but were on the Army Staff.[21] The battalion was short junior officers during the Waterloo Campaign. It was authorized sixteen ensigns, but only eleven were with the battalion on 16 June 1815. These ensigns were young and had little experience. Their average age was eighteen years and they had been an officer for eighteen months. Only the two mentioned previously had any combat experience. Like the ensigns, the battalion was short of lieutenants. It was authorized fourteen, but only eight were with the colours during the Waterloo Campaign. These eight were much older and experienced. Their average age was twenty-five and their average time in service was eight years. All were veterans of the Peninsular War with an average of twenty-six months of active service during which they saw seven actions. Lieutenant Thomas Sowerby had fifty-three months in the Peninsula and fought in ten different actions, while the least experienced was Lieutenant Edward Sumner who had served in the Peninsula for only five months but was in combat two different times.

Only five of the company commanders were serving with the battalion at the start of the Waterloo Campaign. Their average age was thirty and they had been in the army for thirteen years. All were veterans of the

---

20. Bamford, p.267.
21. Mackinnon, Vol. 2, p.207.

Peninsula. They averaged three years on campaign and saw action six times. The most experience was Captain Henry Dawkins with fifty-three months in the Peninsula where he was in combat nine times. The least experienced was Captain Henry Wyndham who had two years in the Peninsula, but even then, he was involved in nine combats. The battalion was short of half of its company commanders and two of its captains, James Macdonell and Daniel Mackinnon, were also the battalion's acting majors. At Waterloo Captain Macdonell would be given command of the defence of Hougoumont.

2nd Battalion 3rd Foot Guards

Like the 2nd Battalion of the Coldstream Guards, the 2nd Battalion of the 3rd Foot Guards saw very little action prior to Waterloo. Two companies went to Walcheren in 1809 and three companies served in Cadiz, Spain in 1810 and 1811. In December 1813 three companies went to the Low Countries but numbered less than 650 officers and enlisted men. The battalion was part of the assault on Bergen-op-Zoom on 8-9 March 1814 and took eighty-four casualties including one officer and thirty-five other ranks captured.[22]

After Napoleon abdicated in April 1814, the battalion went into garrison in Belgium. During the next fourteen months most of the officers were re-assigned to the 1st Battalion in England. Only three lieutenants and two ensigns, who fought with the battalion at Bergen-op-Zoom were still with the battalion in June 1815: Lieutenants William Drummond, Robert Hesketh, and William Stothert, and Ensigns Barclay Drummond and George Standen. The battalion had fifteen of its sixteen authorized ensigns by June 1815.

Like the other Guards Battalions, their average age was eighteen. The typical ensign had been commissioned for two years and only three had combat experience. During the Waterloo Campaign, the battalion had twelve of its fourteen authorized lieutenants serving with it. Their average age was twenty-three and they had an average of sixty-nine months in the Army. All were Peninsula veterans with an average of twenty-two months there during which they saw action five times. The most experienced was

---

22. Bamford, p.274.
23. Their average time on active service was forty months.

Lieutenant John Elrington who had spent twenty-nine months in the Peninsula and had seen combat eight times.

The battalion had only six of its authorized ten captains with it during the Waterloo Campaign. Their average age was twenty-nine, the youngest group of captains in the four battalions. The typical captain had been an officer for 151 months and all had served in the Peninsula for at least twenty-nine months.[23] Among them they averaged having been in combat ten times. The most experienced was Captain Charles Dashwood, the commander of the battalion's Light Company. He had served in the Peninsula for sixty-nine months and had been in combat fourteen times. However, his experience as a company commander was limited because during his time in the Peninsula he was on the staff. Like the Coldstream Guards, although the battalion had six of their company commanders with it at the start of the campaign, the two most senior captains, Douglas Mercer and Charles Dashwood, were serving as the battalion's acting majors. During much of the upcoming campaign, Captain Dashwood would be with the Light Company away from the rest of the battalion. While he was absent, Captain Francis Home served as the other acting major.

Chapter 2

The Guards Officers

By the start of the Waterloo Campaign, 170 Foot Guards Officers were serving in the British Army in Belgium. Although this sounds like a large number, thirty-three of them (19 per cent) were serving on the staff of the army and not with their battalion.

Table 2.1: Number of Guards Officers in Holland in June 1815

Battalion	Majors	Captains	Lieutenants	Ensigns	Staff
1st Battalion 1st Foot Guards	0	1	4	1	0
2nd Battalion 1st Foot Guards	1	10	14	16	4
3rd Battalion 1st Foot Guards	1	9	13	14	1
1st Battalion Coldstream	0	1	1	0	0
2nd Battalion Coldstream	1	7	9	16	4
2nd Battalion 3rd Foot Guards	1	8	14	15	4
Total	4	36	55	62	13

An examination of these officers reveals a similar background. Accepted wisdom about Foot Guards officers is that they were primarily from the upper class and nobility. The Foot Guards were considered to be part of a group of regiments that were known as the fashionable regiments – those whose officers were from the upper levels of society. Their fellow army officers recognized this and during the Peninsular War, nicknamed the 1st Division 'The Gentlemen's Sons'[1] because two of its three brigades were Guards Brigades. It was extremely expensive to join the Guards as an officer, for the cost of a commission as an ensign in a Foot Guards Regiment was

---

1. Cook, John, and Burnham, Robert, 'Nicknames of British Units during the Napoleonic Wars' The Napoleon Series Website, June 2013.

£900, over twice the £400 a commission cost in a line infantry regiment.[2] The cream of society was what they were. Among their ranks at Waterloo were a viscount,[3] three barons,[4] and three lords.[5] In addition, there were nineteen officers, present at Waterloo, known as Honourable, being the sons of Peers and not holding a title. This number did include many of the following who were also in the regiments: two sons of dukes, nine sons of earls, four sons of viscounts, eight sons of barons, three sons of baronets, four sons of knights, and one son of a Count of the Holy Roman Empire. Furthermore, among them were two future earls, two future viscounts and four future barons and baronets.

The ensigns of the four battalions were almost identical in every aspect. One in three came from the nobility, except for those in the Coldstream Guards which included only two. Despite the commonly accepted belief that ensigns in the British Army tended to be very young, often boys, this was not true for the Foot Guards. The average age at commissioning for the ensigns at Waterloo was sixteen years old. The youngest to be commissioned was Ensign William Hamilton of the 3rd Foot Guards, who was only fourteen.[6] However, there were three ensigns who were at least twenty-years-old when they were commissioned.[7] Despite being relatively young when they joined the Army, the average age of the ensigns at Waterloo was eighteen. The oldest was Ensign Robert Batty of the 3rd

---

2. Burnham, Robert and McGuigan, Ron, *The British Army against Napoleon: Facts, Lists, and Trivia 1805-1815*. Barnsley: Frontline, 2010, p.140.
3. Lieutenant Augustus Viscount Bury 1st Foot Guards
4. Captain Alexander Lord Saltoun 1st Foot Guards, Lieutenant Beaumont Lord Hotham Coldstream Foot Guards, and Ensign James Lord Hay 1st Foot Guards. By convention Barons are usually referred to as Lords.
5. Captain Lord Fitzroy Somerset 1st Foot Guards, Lieutenant Lord Charles Fitzroy 1st Foot Guards and Lieutenant Lord James Hay 1st Foot Guards. Lord was a courtesy title of a son of a Marquess or Duke.
6. Among the senior officers, several were commissioned much younger: William Gomm was only ten-years-old, James Stanhope was twelve, while Charles Dashwood and Alexander Woodford were thirteen.
7. Henry Powell of the 2nd Battalion 1st Foot Guards was twenty-years-old, Robert Batty of the 3rd Battalion 1st Foot Guards and Henry Griffiths of the Coldstream Guards were twenty-two-years-old when they were commissioned as ensigns.

Battalion 1st Foot Guards, who was twenty-four.[8] There were six officers under seventeen: Ensigns Thomas Croft, Algernon Greville, and William Tinling of the 2nd Battalion 1st Foot Guards, and Ensigns Whitwell Butler, Andrew Cochrane, and William Hamilton of the 3rd Foot Guards.

Not surprisingly, the ensigns had little time in service. The average ensign had only twenty months with his battalion before Waterloo. Six had less than a year as an officer, while Ensign James Talbot of the 2nd Battalion 1st Foot Guards was still a civilian four months before Waterloo. This was balanced by the six ensigns who had more than three years of service. The most experienced was Ensign William Barton of the 3rd Battalion 1st Foot Guards, who had forty-nine months' time in service.[9] This being said, 60 per cent of the ensigns had less than eighteen months' service. This was important since the Peninsular War ended fourteen months earlier and directly impacted the number of them who served in combat. Of the fifty-six Foot Guards ensigns who served in the Waterloo Campaign, only fourteen (25 per cent) had been on active service. Eight had fought in the Peninsula, but six of them did not arrive in country until the final two months of the war. The only combat they saw was at the French sortie from Bayonne on 14 April 1814, where the Guards were caught by surprise. The other two veterans of the Peninsular War had six months in country during which they both fought in four actions. Six ensigns also served in the 1813-1814 campaign in Holland.

The Foot Guards lieutenants were on the average six years older than the ensigns. The youngest was eighteen-years-old Lieutenant Edward Buckley of the 2nd Battalion 1st Foot Guards, while the oldest was thirty-five-year-old Lieutenant William Stothert of the 3rd Foot Guards. The typical lieutenant had six and-a-half years' time in service. Lieutenant George Bowles of the Coldstream Guards had fourteen and-a-half years of service, while Lieutenant Sommerville Burgess of the 2nd Battalion 1st Foot Guards had only thirty-four months of service. All fifty-five lieutenants had served in the Peninsula, with an average time on active service of twenty-six months, during which they fought in six different actions. Lord James Hay of the 3rd Battalion 1st Foot Guards served fifty-one months

---

8. Robert Batty was a well-known artist and author, who wrote *An Historical Sketch of the Campaign of 1815 illustrated by Plans of Operations & the Battles of Quatre Bras, Ligny & Waterloo* and *Campaign of the Left Wing of the Allied Army, in the Western Pyrenees & South of France, in the Years 1813-1814*
9. Ensign Barton was commissioned in May 1811 in the 87th Foot and transferred to the 1st Foot Guards in February 1813.

in the Peninsula and fought in fourteen actions. Lieutenant Sommerville Burgess was in the Peninsula for only seven months, but during that time he was in combat four times. Like the ensigns, one in three lieutenants were from the nobility.

Thirty-five Foot Guards captains served in the Waterloo Campaign. Their average age was thirty-one. The youngest was Captain John Fremantle, one of the two 1st Battalion Coldstream Guards officers who participated in the campaign.[10] The oldest was thirty-nine-year-old Captain Francis D'Oyly of the 2nd Battalion 1st Foot Guards. The captains averaged almost fifteen years of service. Although Captain William Gomm had been commissioned for 253 months, it is unlikely he served with his regiment until he was older. Captain Francis D'Oyly had 243 months of continuous service. Captain William Miller of the 3rd Battalion 1st Foot Guards, had only eighty-one months of service. Every captain was a combat veteran, except Captain Delancey Barclay of the 3rd Battalion 1st Foot Guards. All others had served in the Peninsula, except for Captain Henry Rooke, who had served in the 1799 Den Helder Campaign and in Holland in 1813-1814. During their time in the Peninsula they served there for an average of thirty-six months and fought in eleven actions. Eight of the veterans had over four years of active service, while two others, both in the 2nd Battalion 1st Foot Guards, over five years in the Peninsula. Captain Henry Hardinge served sixty-five months in the Peninsula and was in 17 actions, while Captain Ulysses Burgh had served sixty-four months and was in combat fourteen times. Half of the captains were from the nobility, with eight being invested as a KCB on 2 January 1815.[11]

The Foot Guards Regiments were authorized only one lieutenant colonel. Additionally, they were only allowed one major for each battalion in the regiment. The majors commanded the battalions. There were four Foot Guards majors in the Waterloo Campaign. Their average age was thirty-six, with the oldest being forty- year-old Major Henry Askew of the 2nd Battalion 1st Foot Guards. The youngest was seven years his junior, thirty-three-year-old Major Alexander Woodford of the Coldstream Guards. All had extensive service averaging 250 months in their regiments. Major Askew had been in uniform the longest

---

10. Captain Fremantle was an ADC to the Duke of Wellington.
11. They were Captains Francis D'Oyly, Henry Bradford, Henry Hardinge, Thomas Hill, and Lord Fitzroy Somerset of the 1st Foot Guards; Captains Colin Campbell and William Gomm of the Coldstream Guards; and Captain Alexander Gordon of the 3rd Foot Guards.

with twenty-two years of service, while Major Woodford at just under twenty years of service. All were combat veterans and had served in the Peninsula. Their average of twenty-seven months of active service was not as much as the captains in their battalions though. Only Major Francis Hepburn, commander of the 2nd Battalion 3rd Foot Guards, with thirty-six months of active service and eight different actions had a similar record as the captains.

Biographical Sketches of Senior Officers in the 1st Guards Division

The Division Commander

George Cooke was born in the year 1768. He entered the army as an Ensign in the 1st Foot Guards on 20 October 1784. All of his service was in the regiment except when on the staff. He was promoted lieutenant and captain on 30 May 1792 and captain and lieutenant colonel on 4 June 1798. Ten years later he became a brevet colonel on 25 April 1808. He was promoted to major general on 4 June 1811, but, remained a member of the 1st Foot Guards until he was removed from the regiment as a general officer unattached on 25 July 1814. He saw active service in Flanders 1794-1795 and in the Helder 1799 where he was wounded on 19 September 1799. He was appointed an AAG in the North West District on the Home Staff 1803-1805. He went with the 1st Battalion to Sicily in 1806 and returned home in 1807. As a colonel, he commanded the 3rd Battalion 1st Foot Guards during the Walcheren Expedition in 1809. He caught 'Walcheren Fever' and was incapacitated for many months.

During the Peninsular War, he served with the 3rd Battalion during the Corunna Campaign, October 1808-January 1809. He went to Cadiz in April 1811 and initially commanded a brigade under Lieutenant General Sir Thomas Graham. While there, he was promoted to major general and took command of the garrison after Graham left in July 1811. Cooke returned to England in 1813.

He served in the army in the Netherlands commanded by General Sir Thomas Graham (later Lord Lynedoch) from December 1813 until the peace in 1814. He commanded the Guards Brigade and then a month later the newly formed 1st Division. He was at the assault on Bergen-op-Zoom 8 March 1814 and made a prisoner of war. Upon his exchange, he was assigned to command the 2nd Division. With the peace in Europe, he remained in the Netherlands to command the 1st Division in the Subsidiary Army under General the Prince of Orange.

The Brigade Commanders

John Byng was born in 1772. He entered the Army as an Ensign with the 33rd Foot on 30 September 1793 and was promoted a lieutenant on 1 December 1793 and then promoted a captain on 24 May 1794. He was promoted a major of the 60th Foot on 28 December 1799 and a lieutenant colonel of the 29th Foot on 14 March 1800. He was appointed a captain and lieutenant colonel of the 3rd Foot Guards on 4 August 1804. He was promoted a brevet colonel on 25 July 1810. He was promoted a major general on 4 June 1813 and was removed from the regiment as a general officer unattached on 25 July 1814.

He served in Flanders in 1794 and was wounded on 5 January 1795 at Geldermalsen. By April he was back in England. In 1797 he was on the staff in Ireland and was wounded during the Irish Rebellion of 1798. He went with his regiment to Halifax, Nova Scotia in 1802 and remained until August 1804. Byng served in the 1st Battalion 3rd Foot Guards during the expedition to Hanover from November 1805 to February 1806. After returning to England he was appointed an AAG on the Home Staff. In 1807 he went with the 1st Battalion to Copenhagen from August to October 1807. In 1808 he was an AAG in the Severn District. He served in the 2nd Battalion during the Walcheren Expedition 1809.

Byng was sent out to serve in the Peninsular War in September 1811. He was immediately appointed a colonel on the staff and given command of a brigade in the 2nd Division on 21 September 1811. He was appointed a brigadier general on the staff on 25 November 1812. He fought at Vitoria in June 1813, in the Pyrenees in July-August 1813, Nivelle in November 1813 and wounded, Nive in December 1813, Orthes in February 1814 and Toulouse in April 1814. He returned to England in June.

Peregrine Maitland was born on 6 July 1777. He entered the Army as an ensign with the 1st Foot Guards on 25 June 1792. All of his service was in the regiment. He was promoted a lieutenant and captain 30 April 1794 and then a captain and lieutenant colonel on 25 June 1803. He was promoted a brevet colonel on 1 January 1812. He was promoted a major general on 4 June 1814 and removed from the regiment as a general officer unattached 25 July 1814.

He served with the regiment in Flanders 1793-1794. He saw action in the raid on the Bruges Canal at Ostend in May 1798 and on the Walcheren Expedition 1809. He went to the Peninsula in 1808 and served with his regiment in the Corunna Campaign and at the battle of Corunna 1809. In July 1811, Maitland was in Cadiz, Spain with the 3rd Battalion. He was at the capture of Seville in August 1812. He was given temporary command of the 1st Guards Brigade in July 1813. He led it at the crossing of the Bidassoa in October 1813, Nivelle in November 1813, Nive in December 1813, the crossing of the Adour in February 1814 and the siege of Bayonne from February-April 1814. He went to the Netherlands and commanded the Guards Brigade in the Subsidiary Army commanded by General the Prince of Orange January 1815.

The Battalion Commanders

Henry Askew was born 7 May 1775. He entered the army as Ensign in the 1st Foot Guards on 19 June 1793. All of his service was in the regiment. He was promoted lieutenant and captain on 18 March 1795 and then captain and lieutenant colonel on 27 August 1807. He was promoted a brevet colonel 4 June 1814. He was promoted to be the 2nd major commanding the 2nd Battalion on 25 July 1814.

He saw active service in Flanders July 1794-May 1795, in the Mediterranean September 1806-December 1807 and on Walcheren in 1809. He went to the Peninsula with the 1st Battalion in September 1812 and served there until the end of the war in April 1814. He fought at the crossing of the Bidassoa in October 1813, Nivelle in November 1813, commanded the 1st Battalion at the Nive in December 1813, the crossing of the Adour in February 1814 and the siege of Bayonne from February-April 1814. He returned to England in June 1814. Askew went to the Netherlands in September 1814 and took command of the 2nd Battalion 1st Foot Guards in the Subsidiary Army commanded by General the Prince of Orange.

Francis Ker Hepburn was born on 19 August 1779. He entered the Army as an ensign in the 3rd Foot Guards on 17 December 1794. All of his service was in the regiment except when he was on the staff. He was promoted lieutenant and captain 28 May 1798 and then captain and lieutenant colonel 23 July 1807. He became a brevet colonel 4 June 1814 and was promoted to be the 2nd major commanding the 2nd Battalion on 25 July 1814.

He saw active service with his regiment in the Irish Rebellion in May 1798. He went with his regiment to the Helder in 1799. He was on the Home Staff at Chelmsford from 1802 until 1805 and then went to Malta in 1805. He then went to serve in Sicily in 1806. He served as a brigade major there; however, being ill, he missed the battle of Maida 4 July 1806.

During the Peninsular War, he was then sent to Cadiz in April 1810 and fought at the Battle of Barossa on 5 March 1811 being severely wounded in the leg. He was sent home to recuperate in May 1811. Hepburn was only able to return to the Peninsula in September 1812 and fought at Vitoria in June 1813, at the crossing of the Bidassoa in October 1813, Nivelle in November 1813 and Nive in December 1813. In February 1814, he left the Peninsula to command the 2nd Battalion in the Netherlands in the army commanded by General Sir Thomas Graham (later Lord Lynedoch) and remained there at the peace, serving in the Subsidiary Army commanded by General the Prince of Orange.

Hon. William Stuart was born on 20 August 1778. He entered the Army as ensign in the 1st Foot Guards on 30 April 1794. He was promoted a lieutenant and captain of the 1st Foot Guards 23 June 1797. He became a major in the 61st Foot on approximately 15 September 1807. He was promoted a lieutenant colonel in the 14th Foot on 26 September 1807 and quickly exchanged back into the 1st Foot Guards as captain and lieutenant colonel on 1 October 1807. He was promoted a brevet colonel 4 June 1814 and promoted to be the 3rd major commanding the 3rd Battalion 25 July 1814.

He saw active service in the Irish Rebellion 1798, in the Helder 1799, in the Mediterranean July 1806-January 1808 and on Walcheren in 1809. He served in the Peninsular War from September 1812 to April 1814 and was in action in the Pyrenees July-August 1813, the crossing of the Bidassoa in October 1813, and Nivelle in November 1813. He commanded the 3rd Battalion at the Nive in December 1813, the crossing the Adour in February 1814 and at the siege of Bayonne from February-April 1814. He returned to England with his battalion in June.

Alexander George Woodford was born on 15 June 1782. He entered the army as a cornet with the 14th Light Dragoons on 6 December 1794. He was promoted a lieutenant of the 115th Foot on 15 July 1795 and appointed a lieutenant in the 22nd Foot on 8 September 1795. He joined the 9th Foot in 1799 and was promoted Captain-Lieutenant 9th Foot 11 December 1799. He was then appointed lieutenant and captain of the Coldstream Foot Guards on 20 December 1799 and then was promoted captain and lieutenant colonel 8 March 1810. He was promoted a brevet colonel 4 June 1814 and the 2nd major commanding the 2nd Battalion on 25 July 1814. He was made an ADC to the Prince Regent 4 June 1814.

Woodford saw active service in the Helder 1799 and was severely wounded and made a prisoner of war on 19 September 1799. He was released by the end of the year. He served with his battalion at Copenhagen in 1807 and then went to Sicily on the staff 1808-1810. He served in the Peninsular War arriving in January 1812. He fought at the capture of Ciudad Rodrigo in January 1812, at the capture of Badajoz in April 1812, Salamanca in July 1812, the siege of Burgos in September-October 1812, commanded the 1st Battalion at Vitoria in June 1813, at the siege of San Sebastian in August 1813, the crossing of the Bidassoa in October 1813, Nivelle in November 1813, Nive in December 1813, the crossing the Adour in February 1814 and siege of Bayonne from February to April 1814.

Chapter 3

The Enlisted Soldier

On 25 May 1815, the 1st Division reported there were 4,355 enlisted soldiers in the four Foot Guards battalions assigned to it. There were 223 sergeants, eighty-three drummers, and 4,049 corporals and privates who were referred to as Other Ranks.[1]

Table 3.1: Reported Strength of the Foot Guard Battalions in the Netherlands on 25 May 1815

Battalion	Sergeants	Drummers	Other Ranks	Total
2nd Battalion 1st Foot Guards	55	22	998	1075
3rd Battalion 1st Foot Guards	55	22	1037	1114
2nd Battalion Coldstream Guards	55	22	1010	1087
2nd Battalion 3rd Foot Guards	58	17	1004	1079
Total	223	83	4049	4355

Barbara Chambers's *The Men of the 1st Foot Guards at Waterloo and Beyond* provides a detailed look at the soldiers of two of the Foot Guards Battalions that fought at Waterloo – the 2nd and 3rd Battalions. The study provides the service records for 2,155 enlisted soldiers in the two battalions. Although the book only covers the men of the 1st Foot Guards, these soldiers are representative of the soldiers in the other two regiments. An examination of the data in the book provides a look at the typical soldier in the regiments.

Unlike the conscripted soldiers in Napoleon's army, all soldiers in the British Army were volunteers. Until 1806, the British soldier enlisted for life or until they were unable to serve due to either age or infirmity. For a typical soldier this usually meant twenty to twenty-five years with the regiment. As the Napoleonic Wars continued, the British Army was

---

1. TNA, WO17/1760.

forced to expand its troops and by 1806, more than 185,000 men were in uniform. As overseas commitments expanded and with them casualties, the Army had to recruit almost 18,000 men to replace the casualties in 1806, almost 10 per cent of the force. This does not include the need to recruit replacements for the soldiers whose enlistment had expired and those needed to fill the ranks of the expanding army. Over the next seven years, the Army needed an average of 29,000 new recruits each year.[2] One way of making service in the army more enticing was that beginning in 1806, a recruit could enlist for limited service of seven years in the infantry, with the option of re-enlisting for further service.[3] Many of these men were still in the ranks in 1815.

Between 1806 and 1809, over 1,500 new recruits were brought into the two battalions of the 1st Foot Guards. Initially the primary source for them was the civilian population with no military experience. In the first four years 236 men were recruited from the population at large, with another fifty-two volunteering from the militia. In 1811, the focus on recruiting changed to obtaining volunteers from the militia. Of the 1,299 men brought into the two battalions, 847 or 65 per cent were militia volunteers.

Recruits were also obtained from soldiers, marines, and sailors who, when their time of service had expired, were allowed to enlist in the regiment. Thirty-four new soldiers were obtained this way. Most were ex-infantrymen, two were ex-Royal Marines, while three were ex-Royal Navy. Perhaps the most unusual recruit was Corporal Peter Hay of the 3rd Battalion, who served ten years in the navy, part of which as a French prisoner-of-war.[4]

By June 1815, the average time in service for a 1st Foot Guard was sixty-five months. Of these soldiers, 522 or 24 per cent were long service soldiers who had enlisted prior to 1806. Only twenty soldiers had less than a year time in the Army. The soldier with the longest amount of service was Sergeant John Smith of the 2nd Battalion with 269 months. The soldier with the least amount of time in service was Private Benjamin Roebuck of the 3rd Battalion, who would die of his wounds in July after having been in the army for less than five months. However, the average time in service varied by battalion.

---

2. Fortescue, John W., *The County Lieutenancies and the Army: 1803 - 1814* London: MacMillan, 1909, pp.291-292.
3. Haythornthwaite, Philip, *Redcoats: the British Soldiers of the Napoleonic Wars*. Barnsley: Pen & Sword, 2012, p.23.
4. Chambers, Barbara, *The Men of the 1st Foot Guards at Waterloo and Beyond*. 2 vols. Letchworth Garden City: Privately Published; 2003. Vol. 1, p.386.

Table 3.2: Average Time in Service in Months by Battalion

	Average	Least	Most
2nd Battalion	55	8	269
3rd Battalion	80	4	267

Not surprisingly, sergeants had the most time in service with an average of 131 months. Sergeant John Horrocks of the 2nd Battalion had only eighteen months. Drummers also had a considerable amount of time in service, because many enlisted as boys. Drummer William Atkins of the 2nd Battalion, joined at the age of thirteen in April 1795 and by June 1815 had 242 months service. The drummer with the least amount of service was John Crooke of the 3rd Battalion who had only eight months service at Waterloo. Privates averaged almost a year more time in service than corporals. This was probably due to the requirement that a soldier had to be able to read and write to be promoted. Of the sixteen soldiers in the two battalions who had more than twenty years in the regiment, twelve, or 75 per cent of them were privates.

Table 3.3: Average Time in Service by Rank in Months in the 1st Foot Guards

Rank	Average	Least	Most
Sergeant	131	18	269
Corporal	55	45	213
Drummer	101	8	242
Private	64	4	267

The typical soldier in the 1st Foot Guards was twenty-two-years-old when he enlisted. Although it varied by year. For those who enlisted prior to 1806, he was twenty-one-years-old, while those joined from 1806 on, the average age was twenty-two. There appeared to be no upper or lower age limit on who could enlist. The oldest was Private Thomas Aldin of the 3rd Battalion who enlisted at the age of forty-seven in 1814. The youngest was Drummer James Perry in the 2nd Battalion, who enlisted as a boy at the age of seven and was sixteen-years-old at Waterloo. Army regulations allowed regiments to enlist boys under the age sixteen.[5] By 1815, the two battalions had forty-eight soldiers who had enlisted as boys.

---

5. De Fonblanque, Edward, *Administration and Organization of the British Army, with Especial Reference to Finance and Supply*. London: Longman, Brown, Green, Longmans, and Roberts, 1858, p.242.

The average age of a 1st Foot Guards soldier at Waterloo was twenty-seven years and five months. Half the soldiers were under the age of twenty-seven. One sergeant and two privates were over fifty-years-old, while more than 300 privates were thirty-five years or older. Sergeants tended to be the oldest, with the average age of thirty-two. The median age for a sergeant was thirty, with the youngest being twenty-one-year-old Sergeant William Cranshaw of the 2nd Battalion. On average, privates were two years older than corporals. Although it would seem that corporals would be older, this is likely caused by the illiteracy of many of the privates. Of the 124 corporals, the oldest was forty-one, while three were only nineteen. Drummers were the youngest, with an average age of twenty-two, while the typical private was twenty-nine-years-old.

Table 3.4: Age of 1st Foot Guards Soldiers in the Waterloo Campaign

Average age	27 years 5 months
Youngest	14-years-old
Number under 20-years-old	78
Oldest	52-years-old
Privates 35 years or older	222
Privates 40 years or older	85

Table 3.5: Age of 1st Foot Guards Soldiers by Rank in the Waterloo Campaign

Sergeant	32
Corporal	27.25
Drummer	22
Private	29

Although the average age of the soldiers were twenty-seven years and five months old, only seventy-eight were younger than twenty years. On 25 February 1813, a new regulation was published concerning boys in the regiment. Previous regulations divided boys into two groups those under seventeen-years-old and those under sixteen.[6] The new regulation defined boys to be under fifteen-years-old. But there was a stipulation for those who were under seventeen. Those who met the minimum age requirement would not be considered fit enough for active service until 'their strength ... be adequate to the management of the firelock ... in no case, to be sent to the

---

6. De Fonblanque, p.242.

West Indies, or to join a Battalion on active service, until they are equal, in every respect, to the performance of their duty, as Soldiers.'[7] This regulation made sense from a management perspective, since soldiers who were not fully developed would in the long run be too weak to keep up on campaign and would end up being a drain on the unit's resources.

Table 3.6: Soldiers under the Age of Twenty in the 1st Foot Guards during the Waterloo Campaign

Age	Number
14	1
15	1
16	1
17	9
18	17
19	49

One of the accepted myths of the Napoleonic Wars is that the British Army used drummer boys. Examination of the drummers in the Waterloo Campaign discredits this myth to a point. Nine of the twelve soldiers under eighteen were drummers. Yet technically, under the 1813 regulations, only one was considered a boy, i.e. Robert Mercer who was fourteen-years-old. There were forty-eight 1st Foot Guards drummers in the Waterloo Campaign.[8] Fifteen or 33 per cent, were under twenty years. The median age of all drummers was twenty-years-old. While young, they were hardly boys.

Physically, recruits entering the 1st Foot Guards were taller than the average recruit in the British Army. Between 1802 and 1812, recruits were an average height of 66 inches (1.68m).[9] The average height for the 1st Foot Guards at Waterloo was 68 inches (1.73m). Although Army regulations stipulated that a recruit had to be at least 63 inches (1.6m), boys under

---

7. *Principles of War, Exhibited in the Practice of the Camp; and as Developed in a Series of General Orders of Field-Marshal the Duke of Wellington.* London: Cadell and Davis, 1815. p.130.
8. Barbara Chambers identified by name forty-eight drummers assigned to the two battalions. However, the Theatre Returns for May and June 1815 only shows them with forty-four drummers.
9. Floud, Roderick and Harris, Bernard, 'Health, Height, and Welfare: Britain, 1700 – 1980', *Health and Welfare during Industrialization.* Chicago: University of Chicago, January 1997, p.102.

the age of sixteen could be 60 inches (1.5m) while those under the age of seventeen had to be at least 62 inches (1.6m).[10] The median height for the soldiers in 1st Foot Guards was also 68 inches (1.73m). The regulation concerning height appeared to be followed, however, in the case of twenty-year-old Private William Walker of the 2nd Battalion, they were overlooked. When he enlisted in 1813 at the age of eighteen, he was only 60 inches (1.5m) tall. Drummer John Crooke of the 3rd Battalion enlisted at the sixteen in 1814 and was only 56 inches (1.4m). Forty soldiers were over 72 inches (1.83m). The tallest was Private Charles Thompson of the 2nd Battalion, who was 75.5 inches (1.9m).

An examination of the heights of the different ranks, shows that the average height for sergeants, corporals, and privates was 68 inches (1.73m), the average height for all soldiers. Drummers were an anomaly, with the average height being 66 inches (1.68m). The tallest drummer was twenty-one-year-old Josiah Ashton of the 3rd Battalion who enlisted as a boy at the age of ten. He was 71 inches (1.8m) tall.

Table 3.7: Heights by Rank in the 1st Foot Guards at Waterloo

Rank	Average	Tallest	Shortest
Sergeant	68 inches	74 inches	65.5 inches
Corporal	68 inches	73 inches	64 inches
Drummer	66 inches	71 inches	56 inches
Privates	68 inches	74.5 inches	60 inches

Another myth of the Napoleonic Wars was that the shorter men were in the Light Companies, since they were often used as skirmishers being smaller would be an advantage. Although there is some logic in this, it did not hold true for the 1st Foot Guards's Light Companies. Their average height was 68 inches, the same as the regiment.

Table 3.8: Heights of the Light Companies Soldiers in the 1st Foot Guards at Waterloo

Light Company	Average Height	Tallest	Shortest	Median Height
2nd Battalion	68 inches	70.5 inches	66 inches	68 inches
3rd Battalion	68 inches	71 inches	60 inches	68 Inches

---

10. De Fonblanque, p.242.

THE ENLISTED SOLDIER

When a soldier enlisted, his physical description was placed in his record. In addition to his height, they listed the colour of his eyes and hair. The most common eye colour was grey, followed by hazel.

Table 3.9: Eye Colour of the Soldiers in the 1st Foot Guards at Waterloo

Eye Colour	Number of Soldiers	Percent
Grey	1002	50 per cent
Hazel	562	28 per cent
Blue	211	11 per cent
Dark	95	5 per cent
Brown	87	4 per cent
Black	19	1 per cent
Green	2	.01 per cent

The soldiers' hair was overwhelmingly a shade of brown. With brown being the most common colour listed.

Table 3.10: Hair Colour of the Soldiers in the 1st Foot Guards at Waterloo

Hair Colour	Number	Percent
Brown	866	40 per cent
Dark Brown	301	14 per cent
Light Brown	284	13 per cent
Dark	246	11 per cent
Light	191	9 per cent
Black	113	5 per cent
Sandy	62	3 per cent
Grey	23	.1 per cent
Red	15	.7 per cent
White	1	.05 per cent
Yellow	1	.05 per cent

The soldiers were recruited from all over the British Isles, mostly from England, but also from Wales and Scotland. Some also came from Ireland.[11] They recruited from a wide range of occupations, but enlisting apprentices was prohibited. The most common occupation listed was labourer, which was a catchall category for recruits with no skills. All boys were listed in this category.

---

11. Chambers, Vol. 1, p.31.

Table 3.11: Top Five Former Occupations of the Soldiers in the 1st Foot Guards at Waterloo

Occupation	Number	Percent
Labourer	954	45 per cent
Weaver	257	12 per cent
Cordwainer / Shoemaker	124	6 per cent
Tailor	55	3 per cent
Framework Knitter	30	1 per cent

Although the 1st Foot Guard Regiment was the senior regiment in the Army, only a third of its soldiers were combat veterans. Its 2nd Battalion was a young battalion, having served in England for much of the Peninsular War. Only 126 of its soldiers were veterans of the Peninsula, however, an additional 130 of its soldiers served in the disastrous campaign in Holland the previous year. The 3rd Battalion had three times the number of Peninsula veterans as the 2nd Battalion

Table 3.12: Percent of 1st Foot Guard Soldiers with Combat Experience

Experience	1st FG Overall	2nd Battalion	3rd Battalion
No Experience	65 per cent	72 per cent	54 per cent
Peninsula	27 per cent	15 per cent	45 per cent
Holland or other service	8 per cent	13 per cent	1 per cent

Table 3.13: Location of 1st Foot Guard Soldiers Combat Service

Experience	1st FG Overall	2nd Battalion	3rd Battalion
No experience	1,353	763	590
Other	3	2	1
Peninsula	580	126	454
Peninsula and Walcheren	40	13	27
Peninsula and Holland	23	20	3
Peninsula, Walcheren, and Holland 1814	5	3	2
Holland 1814	126	124	2
Walcheren	9	4	5
Walcheren and Holland 1814	6	6	0
Total	2,145	1,061	1,084

Chapter 4

April 1814 to March 1815
Inspections, Parades, and Boredom

The abdication of Napoleon in April 1814 found the four Foot Guards battalions already on active service on the Continent. The 3rd Battalion 1st Foot Guards was in Bayonne, France, while the three 2nd Battalions of the Foot Guards were in Steenbergen, a suburb of Antwerp, Belgium. The 3rd Battalion 1st Foot Guards had been in the Peninsula since 1811 and returned to England in early August. The three battalions in Belgium were not so lucky and were assigned to the newly formed British Subsidiary Army in the Netherlands that summer. The Subsidiary Army was a small force of British and Hanoverians kept there to assist with the formation of the new country of the United Netherlands and to guarantee its borders. In late July 1814, its commander was the Prince of Orange, while the Subsidiary Army's second-in-command was Lieutenant General Sir Henry Clinton. The three battalions were ordered to Brussels sometime in late July and entered the city on 4 August.[1] The majority of the troops were housed in the Saint Elizabeth Barracks on Rue Montagne de Sion and other barracks throughout the city. A small number of men were also billeted with local civilians.

Once in their new locations, the three battalions began rebuilding their strength. When the 2nd Battalions deployed to Holland in December 1813, the 2nd Battalion 1st Foot Guards and the 2nd Battalion Coldstream Guards went with only six of their companies and without their Colours. The 2nd Battalion 3rd Foot Guards only sent three companies. All three battalions continued to receive reinforcements and replacements, but by July the numbers were still low:

---

1. Mackinnon, Vol. 2, p.206.

Table 4.1: Number of Effectives in the Three Foot Guards Regiments in Belgium July 1814[2]

Battalion	Number of Effectives
2nd Battalion 1st Foot Guards	737
2nd Battalion Coldstream Guards	589
2nd Battalion 3rd Foot Guards	620

On 8 August the remaining companies of these three battalions were ordered to Belgium. They sailed from Ramsgate on 27 August and arrived in Brussels in early September. For the 2nd Battalion 1st Foot Guards this included 460 men, however as soon as they arrived 200 invalid soldiers were ordered home as well as eleven officers. Five of these officers[3] were in England less than a year, before they returned to Belgium and participated in the Waterloo Campaign. These reinforcements raised the effective strength of the battalions by about 2 per cent.

Table 4.2: Number of Effectives in the Three Foot Guards Regiments in Belgium September 1814[4]

Battalion	Number of Effectives
2nd Battalion 1st Foot Guards	935
2nd Battalion Coldstream Guards	727
2nd Battalion 3rd Foot Guards	763

This would be the strongest the three battalions would be for the next six months.

Not surprisingly, many of the Guards officers in Belgium felt that since the war was over, they should go home. Over the next six months numerous officers returned on leave to England and while there tried to arrange for a transfer to their home battalion. Many would be successful. The number of officers with their battalions was very low in early Autumn and when General Clinton went to a parade of the Guards on 2 October, he wrote that there, 'was no officer above the rank of the adjutant' in

---

2. Theatre Returns dated 25 July 1814.
3. Lieutenants Lonsdale Boldero, Newton Chambers, and Robert Phillimore; and Ensigns William Barton and John Erskine.
4. Theatre Returns dated 25 September 1814.

the three battalions.⁵ This absence of senior officers continued through December when he inspected the three battalions and found two of the three battalions were commanded by a captain. Furthermore, virtually every company was led by a lieutenant. The 2nd Battalion 1st Foot Guards had in addition to Major Henry Askew, only two captains, sixteen lieutenants, and seventeen ensigns. The Coldstream Guards were in worse condition with only twelve officers present for duty: two captains and ten subalterns. The 2nd Battalion 3rd Foot Guards had three captains and twenty subalterns.⁶ This absence of officers was also at the brigade level. Although Major General Peregrine Maitland took command of the Guards Brigade in January 1815, a month later he turned command over to Captain James Macdonell⁷ of the Coldstream Guards and went on leave. Captain Macdonell commanded the Guards Brigade until Major Askew took command on 25 February. General Maitland was back by 8 March.

General Clinton was concerned with the lack of officers and its impact on discipline and training. After watching the Guards march in a parade on 14 October he wrote that, 'the Guard march off without troop or any of the usual ceremonies. From neglecting these troops, officers and soldiers easily accustom themselves equally to neglect of the most important duties & there springs indiscipline, insubordination & all their attendant mischief.'⁸ He began a series of inspections, and his reports were quite detailed.

The first unit General Clinton inspected was the 2nd Battalion Coldstream Guards in a meadow at the Chateau de Laeken in Brussels on 5 September. He found

> Colonel Bouverie⁹ had just arrived from England with a draft & had taken the command of the regiment which for the last 6 months had been under Lt. Colonel Macdonell. . . The previous practise of leaving the instruction of the recruits exclusively to the adjutant and sergeants is in force as it is in general in the Guards

---

5. Clinton, Henry, *The Correspondence of Sir Henry Clinton in the Waterloo Campaign*. 2 vols. Gareth Glover (ed.). Godmanchester: Ken Trotman, 2015. Vol. 1, p.28.
6. ibid, pp.95-96.
7. Captain and Lieutenant Colonel Macdonell was the senior officer in the brigade at the time.
8. Clinton, Vol. 1, p.28.
9. Captain and Lieutenant Colonel Henry Bouverie. He was promoted to brevet colonel on 4 June 1814.

& indeed throughout the army, the almost necessary consequence of it is the utter ignorance of officers in the most simple & at the same time many of the most essential parts of their duty. The most ordinary & obviously necessary movements they knew not how to perform. The men are of good description but ill taught, the accoutrements are not good particularly the pouches many of which do not contain more than 36 rounds of ammunition. The packs are neglected, wanting conformity in shape & size and out of repair. The ammunition is not looked after, no man seemed to know what quantity was in possession or how much was wanting from 60 rounds, had become deficient. This army appears has never been supplied with the camp kettles to be carried by the soldiers but had a proportion of what are called the Flanders kettles issued to them.[10]

General Clinton inspected the battalion again on 12 December. Although things had improved, there were still many deficiencies:

The general appearance of this regiment is superior now to that of the 1st Regiment, the men are more even in age & size, there are fewer objectionable subjects, they are cleaner too & their arms & appointments in better order than at the last inspection. There are however as in the 1st Regiment still several stands of arms, the state of which evinces that the company officers do not look to these matters as they are bound to do & consequently that the commanding officer neglects his duty. Some but not a general attention has been paid to the care of the ammunition, indeed the sort of pouch very commonly in use in this regiment renders it very difficult to have the ammunition in good order. Those furnished with the two tins are much out of order.[11]

The 2nd Battalion 1st Foot Guards was supposed to be inspected in September, but a rain storm caused it to be cancelled. General Clinton did inspect them the same day he did the Coldstream Guards, on 12 December

The flank companies are a stout body of men, but for a battalion of Guards there are several very indifferent subjects. Besides those under arms there are 82 old and unhealthy men selected to be

---

10. Clinton, Vol. 1, p.29.
11. ibid, p.96.

sent to England & 33 batmen & officers servants. Although an amendment is observable since the last inspection, this battalion is still very far short of that order which ought to be found in every regiment in the army & which considering their materials should be far surpassed by every battalion of the Guards., the arms though the locks are not so commonly out of order are dirty, the pouches not clean or taken care of, the ammunition is in better order, The packs better put on, but in the whole there are very evident appearances that if this battalion is regularly inspected the officers do not do their duty at those inspection. There are still some sets of accoutrements the pouches of which do not contain the required quantity of ammunition ... Pioneers tools very deficient.[12]

The 2nd Battalion 3rd Foot Guards was also inspected by General Clinton on 12 December and he found:

As a body of men this is superior to either of the other battalions of Guards, and to the appearance of it in the state of the arms and accoutrements this improvement is still more striking. The ammunition is still not generally properly looked after, the faults in the arms were distance at which the locks are from the barrel. More of the packs are supplied with the useless frame. In the countermarch of the column the mark of good practise of filing was obvious, Lt. Colonel Mercer[13] has lately succeeded to the command of this battalion & by his attention and zeal there is no doubt it will improve.[14]

General Clinton was particularly harsh on the battalion commanders. Of the 2nd Battalion 1st Foot Guards commander he wrote: 'The only movement attempted was the countermarch upon the centre of the battalion by sub divisions, this was ill understood by the commanding officer Colonel Askew, and not well executed by his officers ... unfortunately for this battalion Colonel Cooke[15] was superseded in this command by Colonel Askew.'[16]

---

12. ibid, pp.95-96.
13. Captain and Lieutenant Colonel Douglas Mercer.
14. Clinton, Vol. 1, p.96-97.
15. Captain and Lieutenant Colonel Richard Cooke.
16. Clinton, Vol. 1, pp.95-96.

After meeting the commander of the 2nd Battalion Coldstream Guards, Brevet Colonel Bouverie, on 5 September, General Clinton described him as 'a man of experience & good sense, but his experience is not of that sort which fits him at once for the command of a regiment, in which all is to be taught.'[17] Three months later his opinion of Colonel Bouverie had still not improved. Clinton reported after the 12 December inspection that:

> The only movement attempted to be made by this battalion was the countermarch of the column on its own ground by bringing the rear to the front, this was not at all understood by the commanding officer Colonel Bouverie, & the very indifferent execution of it showed the battalion to be very ill practised in file marching, in short not in a state to go through an ordinary field day ordinary reviewing general; but Bouverie is a colonel in the army & has been many years an Assistant Adjutant General in the army under the Duke of Wellington. The 2nd officer is Colonel Abercromby[18] an officer who after commanding a battalion succeeded to that of a brigade in Portugal & has since been an Assistant Quarter Master General in the same army, but neither of these officers are at all perfect in the movements of a battalion single or as the part of a line & yet the general officers having commissions in the Guards have been removed in order that their places might be filled by efficient regimental officers.[19]

Clinton also had the Guards Brigade go through a series of manoeuvres: 'I saw the Guards exercise by half brigade composed of the right & then the left wing of the several battalions, the commander of the brigade & those of battalions found this an useful lesson, but the soldiers are not sufficiently advanced to derive benefit from exercising in so large bodies.'[20]

After the inspection, General Clinton wrote to Colonel Francis Hepburn, the Guards Brigade commander on 14 December, detailing the problems he found, many of which he attributed to the company officers not doing their jobs:

---

17. ibid, p.29.
18. Captain and Lieutenant Colonel Honourable Alexander Abercromby was promoted to brevet colonel on 4 June 1814.
19. Clinton, Vol. 1, p.96.
20. ibid, p.95.

In the course of the inspection which I have made of the several battalions composing the brigade under your command: although visible improvement has taken place in some aspects since I saw them in detail; I have nevertheless observed several defects, towards the removal of which a great deal is reasonably expected.

The arms in general may be said to be in good order, in the Third Regiment they are particularly so. Those of the First Regiment were not clean, but in the present situation of this army, there is no reason why the arms should not be kept in perfect order, the ordinary failing is in the lock standing at too great a distance from the barrel; and in the screw of the hammer spring being displaced.

I think want of due care is most apparent in the state of the pouches, it seems as if the outside only was attended to, if the pouches were kept in order, and the ammunition in packets as is generally the case in the First Regiment there would very scarcely be any deficiency; at any rate the proportion of ammunition required by the General Orders of this army, to be in the possession of the soldiers; should be kept complete.

The frames of wood with which many of the soldiers continue to keep their packs in shape, are of no use, and should therefore be got rid of by a Brigade Order, and care should be taken that when the troops are ordered to parade in marching order; the whole of the necessaries are stowed in the packs. It is very difficult with men of low stature; to have the pack carried clear of the pouch, particularly when from the blanket being folded in the pack; it is necessary that the greatcoat should be strapped upon it; but it is of so much importance that the pouch be disencumbered; that every attention should be paid to this object, with the lowest men the slings must be lengthened.

The movement which was performed by the Coldstream and the Third Regiments served to show how much both want of practise in file marching; and the officers and non-commissioned officers, particularly of the Coldstream, were very far from being perfect in these parts.

In the double quick march the soldiers must be practised not to swing the arm, a fault which is not uncommon in the quick march, as the company drills should be practised to the double quick march singly and then by single ranks; after the caution, double quick, upon the word march the arms to be sloped; and carried on the halt.

What regards the orders of the arms; ammunition and accoutrements; is very easily to be effected, provided the company officers have clearly signified to them; what they are to attend to at the daily inspections. If a soldier who appears with any of his appointments out of order is required to attend at extra hour; with the necessary repairs made; or deficiencies made good, the defaulters in this respect will be few. With respect to any imperfection in the exercise, a little practise in detail will suffice to cure it.[21]

Life in Brussels

Garrison duty for the three Guards battalions was not too strenuous. They paraded on 18 January in celebration of the Queen's birthday and fired a *feu-de-joie*.[22] On 1 February the brigade fired another *feu-de-joie* to commemorate the entry of allied troops into Amsterdam. The Guards Brigade also took part in a review of the Brussels's garrison to celebrate the Prince of Orange's father becoming the King of the Netherlands on 16 March 1815. This light duty seems to agree with the soldiers' health. One company commander wrote on 6 February that, 'This town is uncommonly healthy, I never remember our sick so few, even in England. In my company, I have only one man out of seventy-five who does not take duty.'[23]

For the officers there was not much of a social scene to keep them entertained after they first arrived in Brussels in the autumn of 1814. Lieutenant George Bowles wrote on 3 October:

> This place is nearly as dull as possible. The plan I mentioned in my last, of taking away our billets and giving us lodging money instead, has just been put into execution. It will be

---

21. ibid, pp.97-98.
22. A *feu-de-joie* is when a unit fires its weapons in the air one soldier at a time to give a continuous sound of gunfire. This sound is similar to that which a machine-gun makes.
23. Bowles, George, *A Guards Officer in the Peninsula and at Waterloo: the Letters of Captain George Bowles, Coldstream Guards. 1807-1819.* Gareth Glover (ed.), Godmanchester: Ken Trotman, 2008, p.94.

about 30/ a year out of our pockets, as, directly the worthy inhabitants of this town found out that we were obliged to take their houses, they doubled their prices; thus you see all arrangements at our cost. However, as we shall be allowed to cook in our houses, and shall not be obliged to live at the coffee houses, it will be a change for the better. We are expecting a pack of hounds from England, which the hereditary Prince has written for. *En attendant*, racing is the order of the day. We had a grand meeting on Monday, at which half Brussels was present. It was certainly a pretty sight. Being a light weight, the Prince constituted me his jockey, and as, luckily, his horse won, I am rather in favour. ... I have had no shooting as yet; when the woodcocks and snipes arrive, I shall commence operations. We are now, however, obliged to get regular leave from the lords of the manor, and, moreover, to take out a license! This you will think quite right, but to us, who have been accustomed to bully a little, it is a rather bitter pill.[24]

The social scene improved over the next three months such that the same officer reported on 30 December: 'Here we are doing nothing but dining and dancing. I never led so dissipated a life in that way before and am beginning to grow rather tired of it.'[25] About the same time rumors also began to spread that they would not remain in Brussels much longer and that the battalions would return to England in April or May.[26]

By February 1815, officers continued to take leave and some of the battalions, especially the Coldstream Guards, were left short of company commanders. This created opportunities for junior officers to gain command experience. Among those who held temporary command was Lieutenant George Bowles, who commanded the Coldstream's Light Company and Lieutenant John Blackman who commanded its 4th Company.

---

24. ibid.
25. ibid.
26. ibid.

Table 4.3: Officers on Leave in March 1815[27]

Battalion	Battalion Commanders	Captains	Lieutenants	Ensigns
2nd Battalion 1st Foot Guards	0	3	2	1
2nd Battalion Coldstream Guards	0	7	3	0
2nd Battalion 3rd Foot Guards	1	1	0	0

The tedium of garrison life caused some officers to re-assess the benefits of peace after being at war for so many years, especially with regards to being promoted. Lieutenant Bowles wrote in October that despite being the second senior lieutenant in the regiment, 'As to promotion, all chance of that is now completely at an end, and I see no possibility of my getting a company[28] under eight or ten years.'[29] Two months later, upon hearing the news of the end of the War of 1812, he wrote: 'Selfishly speaking, I am bitterly grieved at the termination of war, and of consequence at the total extinction of all our hopes of promotion.'[30] Unfortunately he never recorded his feelings about being passed over for promotion to captain in July 1814 when seven officers were brought into the regiment to fill the vacancies created when the general officers were removed from the regimental rolls.

Lieutenant Bowles, however, did not have to endure the boredom much longer.

---

27. Regimental Returns dated 25 March 1815.
28. Getting a company meant being promoted to captain.
29. Bowles, p.94.
30. ibid, p.95.

Chapter 5

March to June 1815
War Clouds on the Horizon

On 9 March 1815, General Henry Clinton, the senior British officer in Brussels, received word that Napoleon had escaped his imprisonment on the Isle of Elba and returned to France on 1 March. Not much was done by the HQ of the Subsidiary Army for several days, but on 13 March preliminary coordination was made with the Prussian Army in Aachen.[1] At first the officers of the Foot Guards were skeptical of the rumours. When the news was officially confirmed their re-actions varied. One veteran, Captain James Stanhope of the 1st Foot Guards, wrote that, 'For the first time I went abroad with rather a heavy heart, it seemed as if all was to begin again & that all our former toils & blood & triumphs had been in vain.'[2] Yet for the young ensigns who had yet to go to war, the attitude was different. Ensign Samuel Barrington, also of the 1st Foot Guards, wrote home that, 'We are all in the highest spirits here and anxious to try our strength with the first who dare oppose us.'[3] Lieutenant George Bowles looked at it as an opportunity and wrote, 'Selfishly speaking I ought to pray for a campaign, as my only chance of promotion'.[4]

---

1. Clinton, Vol. 1, pp.153 & 156
2. Stanhope, James H., *Eyewitness to the Peninsular War and the Battle of Waterloo: the Letters and Journals of Lieutenant Colonel the Honourable James Stanhope 1803 to 1825*. Gareth Glover (ed.) Barnsley: Pen and Sword, 2010, p.157.
3. *Waterloo Archive*. 6 vols. Gareth Glover (ed.). Barnsley: Frontline, 2010 – 2014. Vol. 4, p.133.
4. Bowles, p.95.

The British Headquarters in Brussels notified the Guards on 18 March and according to Lieutenant Bowles, 'Every preparation is made or making for our taking the field at a moment's warning. Our heavy baggage, supernumerary women and children, &c go off tomorrow for Ostend, and a considerable part of the army is actually en route for Mons, where the first point of assembly will be. We shall probably not move from hence until a plan of operations is determined on. We are speculating on the arrival of our old commander-in-chief, and that both this army and that of General Kleist will be placed under his orders.'[5] The possibility of war saw the Guards officers rushing to prepare themselves for a move into France to prevent Napoleon from seizing control of the country. Ensign Joseph St. John of the 2nd Battalion 1st Foot Guards told his parents that: "We have had orders to prepare to march & the officers are obliged to find their own means of conveying their baggage & they won't let us [sic] carts, so I have been obliged to buy a horse & probably must buy another. The one I have now is no expense to me, for I got 15 Napoleons to buy saddles &c. So instead of laying out the money entirely on saddles & bridles, I added 5 Napoleons to it & bought a horse, saddle, bridle & all & I have forage allowed me.'[6] There was some concern among the officers about the condition of their battalions after being in garrison for almost a year. One observed that, 'We have been so long reveling in all the luxuries of Brussels, that I do not think we shall take very kindly to our bivouacs for a little while.'[7]

After the initial notification from Army Headquarters, no decision was made to redeploy the Guards and five days later they still had not received word to march.[8] On 24 March a warning order was sent out to the battalions to be prepared to march the following day. Lieutenant John Blackman of the Coldstream Guards wrote home that, 'We march at 4 o'clock tomorrow morning for Enghien, which place is near twenty miles from here and the next day, I believe, if circumstances allow, to Ath.'[9] The march did not go well. 'at 3 o'clock in the morning & I got my things on my horse and we marched, marching all the way through the town & the

---

5. ibid.
6. St. John, Joseph, 'Letters to His Parents writing during the Waterloo Campaign', various dates. Unpublished.
7. Bowles, p.95.
8. Blackman, John, 'It all Culminated at Hougoumont': the Letters of Captain John Lucie Blackman, Coldstream Guards 1812-15. Gareth Glover (ed.), Godmanchester: Ken Trotman, 2009, p.115.
9. ibid, p.116.

people at the windows crying. By the time that we got 3 miles out of the town I began to feel *ashamed at the Guards*. Half the men were so tipsy that they kept marching into the ditches, but really it was so ridiculous that I could not help laughing. Here & there you saw a fellow rolling in the mud (it was raining very fast) & another on his back in a ditch so tipsy that he could not speak.'[10] After marching the 30km to Enghien the battalions bivouacked for the night and then marched the next day another 20km to Ath, where they went into quarters.[11] Rumours and speculation continued to run amuck in the battalions. One stated that: 'Napoleon is assassinated by Marshal Mortier'[12] and another that they would march into France the next day.[13] On 31 March they received 'an order for us to be ready to march at a moment's notice.'[14]

In London, a decision was made to send a battalion of the 1st Foot Guards to Belgium. General Henry Torrens of the Horse Guards wrote to Wellington, who was on his way to Brussels from Vienna, on 31 March that, 'The Guards will march for embarkation about Tuesday or Wednesday next. They were unfortunately but unavoidably delayed in their preparation, owing to a wish not to weaken London until every symptom of riot was at an end.'[15] On 1 April the 1st Battalion was selected to go and were given orders to march on 4 April. However, its commander, Major Hon. Arthur Upton, had just been appointed the military attaché to the Bavarian Army, with local rank of brigadier general on the Continent. If his battalion went to Belgium, he would not be able to serve as the attaché and would revert back to his regimental rank. The next day, the orders for the 1st Battalion were rescinded and the 3rd Battalion was ordered to go instead.[16]

The day before the 3rd Battalion was notified, Colonel Meyrick Shawe wrote to Wellington: 'In the absence of Major-General Sir Henry Torrens, I have the honour to acquaint your Grace that the third battalion of the 1st Foot Guards, consisting of 1000 rank and file, and as many men as will complete the second battalions of the 1st,

---

10. St. John, letter dated 31 March 1815.
11. Blackman, p.116.
12. *Waterloo Archive*, Vol. 4, p.134.
13. ibid.
14. St. John, letter dated 1 April 1815.
15. Wellington, Duke of, *Supplementary Dispatches, Correspondence, and Memoranda of Field Marshal Arthur Duke of Wellington, K.G.*, Edited by the 2nd Duke of Wellington. London: John Murray; 1860-1871. Vol. 10, p.9.
16. Hamilton, Vol. 3, p.9-10.

Coldstream, and 3rd Regiments to 1000 rank and file each, have been ordered to Flanders.'[17]

The 3rd Battalion 1st Foot Guards spent four days preparing for their deployment to Belgium. Those soldiers who were too injured, sick, or still recovering from their wounds, were replaced by healthy men from the 1st Battalion. Three subalterns from the 1st Battalion were also sent on detached duty to the 2nd Battalion: ensigns Frederick Gould, Seymour Bathurst and George Fludyer. The 3rd Battalion departed its barracks on 9 April and marched through the streets of London, with the Duke of York at the head of the column.[18] They embarked aboard transports at Greenwich the same day and after a fairly calm voyage, they landed at Ostend the next day. On 11 April, the battalion boarded barges and went by canal to Bruges a distance of about 30km. The following day they took the canal to Ghent. Upon arriving in Ghent they mounted guard for King Louis XVIII until they left for Enghien on 14 April.[19] The right wing[20] of the battalion was bivouacked in and around Marcq, while the left wing[21] was in Hoves.[22] Both villages were near Enghien.

Possibly due to the late notification of the battalion's deployment to Belgium, several officers, including its commander, Major William Stuart, did not sail with it on 9 April. The earliest to arrive was Captain James Stanhope, who had sailed from Dover on 7 April. He had hopes of being placed on the staff and went to Brussels to ask Wellington to allow him to serve in the Quartermaster General's Department. His request was denied due to no vacancies and Captain Stanhope spent the next ten days equipping himself for active service. He 'bought a pair of Belgian coach horses & a farm one to carry my baggage, I left Brussels & joined the 3rd Battalion of the 1st Guards at Enghien on the 19th.'[23] Four days later, Major Stuart, Captain John Reeve, Lieutenants James Gunthorpe and Lonsdale Boldero, the battalion's acting adjutant, joined the battalion. The following day, on 24 April, Lieutenants Robert Ellison and Henry Powell, Ensign James Butler, and Surgeon Samuel Watson arrived. Captain Lord Saltoun,

---

17. *WSD*, Vol. 10, p.18.
18. *Waterloo Archive*, Vol. 4, p.141.
19. ibid, Vol. 3, p.89.
20. The Right Wing was made up of the Grenadier, 1st, 8th, 4th, and 5th Companies.
21. The Left Wing consisted of the Light, 3rd, 6th, 2nd, and 7th Companies.
22. *Waterloo Letters*. Herbert T. Siborne (ed.). London: Greenhill, 1993, p.250.
23. Stanhope, p.157.

the commander of the battalion's Light Company, was on his honeymoon and did not reach the battalion until 26 April.[24]

Colonel Shawe was true to his word to Wellington about enough replacements being sent out to bring the Other Ranks strength up to 1000 in the Foot Guards battalions that were already in Belgium. The 2nd Battalion 1st Foot Guards received forty-one replacements; the 2nd Battalion Coldstream 258; and the 2nd Battalion 3rd Foot Guards 262. The 25 April strength returns had the Other Ranks strength for the 2nd Battalion 1st Foot Guards at 998, the 2nd Battalion Coldstream Guards with 1,009, and the 2nd Battalion 3rd Foot Guards at 1,090. It is not recorded which officers escorted the Coldstream Guards replacements to Belgium, but the new men for the 3rd Foot Guards were led by Lieutenant William Scott and Ensign Frederick Keppel. These two officers did not remain in Belgium long and returned to England the following month.

While a decision was being made about reinforcing the Guards, Wellington finally arrived in Brussels on 4 April. His arrival was much anticipated because the officers had great faith in him. Ensign Samuel Barrington wrote on 29 March that, 'If we do but get the Duke of Wellington we are sure to lick them.'[25] Wellington immediately began building his army and one of the issues he had to deal with was the Guards Brigade. With the arrival of the 3rd Battalion 1st Foot Guards in mid-April, the strength of the Guards Brigade was over 4,600 officers and men, almost twice as large as any brigade Wellington had in his Peninsular army. Furthermore, custom of the British Army at the time prohibited him from having any Guards unit being commanded by an officer who had not been in the Guards. Additionally, since the Guards were the senior regiments in the Army, if they were organized into a division, it would have to be the lowest numbered division in Wellington's force.

Wellington announced the formation of the 1st Division[26] in a General Order dated 11 April. Major General George Cooke was appointed its commander. Major General Peregrine Maitland was given command of the 1st Brigade, which consisted of the 2nd and 3rd Battalions of the 1st Foot Guard. The 2nd Battalion Coldstream Guards and the 2nd Battalion 3rd Foot Guards would form the 2nd Brigade. At this time, no general officer was selected to command the 2nd Brigade, so Major Francis Hepburn of the 3rd Foot Guards was given temporary command of it. Also

---

24. Hamilton, Vol. 3, p.10.
25. *Waterloo Archive*, Vol. 4, p.133.
26. It was usually referred to as the Guards Division.

assigned to the division was Captain Charles F. Sandham's Royal Artillery Brigade of 9-pounder guns. The division was assigned to the 1st Corps. Four days later, on 15 April, the Commander-in-Chief of the British Army, ordered that the Guards would be formed into a division. He confirmed Major General Cooke as its commander, Major General Maitland as the commander of the 1st Brigade, and Major General Sir John Byng as the commander of the 2nd Brigade. [27] General Byng was still in England and it was only after he arrived in Belgium was he was placed on the staff of the Army[28] and officially confirmed as the commander of the 2nd Brigade on 3 May.[29]

In keeping with British Army custom, all three of the generals were former Guards officers. Two of the three generals had been in the 1st Foot Guards: General Cooke had thirty years in the regiment, while General Maitland had twenty-two years with it. General Byng had served ten years in the 3rd Foot Guards.

Once the Guards Division had been formed it had to be staffed. Staff positions were sought after and all but three of the military staff were filled by Guards officers, most were from within the division. On the division staff was Lieutenant Colonel Henry Rooke from the 2nd Battalion 3rd Foot Guards as the Assistant Adjutant General. Lieutenant Colonel Henry Bradford of the 2nd Battalion 1st Foot Guards served as the Assistant Quartermaster General and Captain Edward Fitzgerald of the 25th Foot as the Deputy Assistant Quartermaster General. General Cooke's ADC was Captain George Disbrowe of the 3rd Battalion of the 1st Foot Guards and his extra-ADC was Ensign Augustus Cuyler from the 2nd Battalion of the Coldstream Guards. Assigned to the division staff as its artillery commander was Lieutenant Colonel Stephen Adye of the Royal Artillery. Attached to the division was Staff Surgeon Thomas Kidd and Hospital Mate John Walsh. The division staff also had two civilians: John Wood, the Assistant Commissary General, and Reverend George Stonestreet, the chaplain. Rounding out the staff was the Provost Marshal, Sergeant Christopher Garman from Captain James Macdonell's Company of the 2nd Battalion Coldstream Guards.

The brigade staff was limited to the Brigade Major, a Deputy-Assistant Commissary General, and an ADC. If he obtained permission to do so the brigade commander could have an extra-ADC. This extra-ADC

---

27. *Waterloo Letters*. Herbert T. Siborne (ed.). London: Greenhill, 1993, p.250
28. General Order dated 29 April 1815.
29. General Order dated 3 May 1815.

received no allowance and his food and forage expenses was paid by the general. Both Brigade Majors, 1st Brigade's Captain James Gunthorpe and 2nd Brigade's Captain William Stothert were Guards officers. Although Captain Gunthorpe was from the 3rd Battalion 1st Foot Guards, which was in his brigade, Captain Stothert was from the 1st Battalion 3rd Foot Guards, which was still in England. Generals were allowed to select their ADCs and most chose relatives, sons of family friends, or a member of the nobility. Many times, there was also a regimental connection. General Maitland's ADC was eighteen-year-old Ensign James Lord Hay, of the 3rd Battalion 1st Foot Guards, while his extra-ADC was Cornet Lord William Lennox of the Royal Horse Guards. Lord William Lennox was only fifteen-years-old and the fourth son of the 4th Duke of Richmond. His godfather was Prime Minister William Pitt. As importantly for the young lord to getting the position, General Maitland was courting Cornet Lennox's sister Lady Sarah.[30] Neither of General Byng's ADCs were taken from battalions serving in his brigade. His ADC was Captain Henry Dumaresq of the 9th Foot, while his extra-ADC was Ensign Edward Stopford of the 1st Battalion 3rd Foot Guards.

In addition to filling staff positions in the 1st Division and its brigades, there was a need for a large number of officers on the staff of the army that Wellington was building. In 1815, there were very few permanent staff officers in the British Army. When an expeditionary force or army was formed, it was staffed by regimental officers. When it was disbanded, the regimental staff officers usually returned to their regiments. Every infantry division was authorized an AAG, an AQMG, a DAQMG, and an ADC. Each brigade was authorized a brigade major and an ADC. Then there were the Corps and Army level staffs. According to *The Waterloo Roll Call* only seven of the sixty-three staff positions in the army were filled by permanent staff officers. The other fifty-six positions were filled by regimental officers. All of the fifty-eight ADCs and extra-ADCs were regimental officers.[31]

Serving on the staff was very popular for a variety of reasons. Many of the staff positions were filled by officers whose regimental rank was junior to the rank the position was authorized. For example, it was not uncommon for a regimental captain to fill a lieutenant colonel staff billet. Upon taking

---

30. The general eloped with the nineteen-year-old Lady Sarah in October 1815.
31. Dalton, Charles, *The Waterloo Roll Call*. London: Arms and Armour, 1971, pp.1-8.

up the new duties, the officer was promoted to the rank that the position was authorized. This promotion was in Army rank and did not affect his seniority within the regiment. While he was serving in the staff position he would continue to receive his regimental pay, plus staff pay and allowances of that rank. This pay and allowances could be quite significant. Captain John Fremantle of the 1st Foot Guards noted in April 1815 after he had been appointed an ADC to Wellington he received an additional 9 shillings 6 pence to his pay.[32] Reverend Stonestreet wrote that after he was appointed the chaplain of the Guards Division, 'My allowances are no otherwise increased by the reappearance of war, than by the increase of my number of horses from 2 to 4. Calculating all my different receipts & including the excess above my common rate of exchange in which we are paid, I receive in money above £500, my allowance of fuel in the winter (10lbs of wood per day) must have cost the government 3 guineas a week. I draw rations for myself & two servants of meat, bread, spirits, hay, oats, straw, wood & candles.'[33]

Most importantly, however, was that many officers saw serving on the staff as a path to future promotion and recognition. If he did well, the officer was rewarded with a brevet promotion or even a knighthood. In July 1814, eighteen officers from other regiments were brought into the Guards as captains. All but two of them was for meritorious service in the Peninsula. Eleven of them had served on the staff there.[34] Of these, five were already regimental lieutenant colonels (the equivalent to a Guards captain and lieutenant colonel),[35] and four were regimental majors.[36] For

---

32. Fremantle, John, *Wellington's Voice: the Candid Letters of Lieutenant Colonel John Fremantle, Coldstream Guards, 1808-1837.* Glover, Gareth (ed.). Barnsley: Frontline, 2012, pp.200-201.
33. Stonestreet, George G., *Recollections of the Scenes of which I was a Witness in the Low Countries & France in the Campaigns of 1814 and 1815 and the Subsequent Occupation of French Flanders: The Journal and Letters of the Reverend George Griffin Stonestreet 1814-16.* Gareth Glover (ed.). Godmanchester: Ken Trotman, 2009, pp.49-50.
34. In the 1st Foot Guards: Henry Bradford, Henry Hardinge, Lord Fitzroy Somerset, and Ulysses Burgh; in the Coldstream Guards: Alexander Abercromby, Colin Campbell, Robert Arbuthnot, Hercules Pakenham, and William Gomm; in the 3rd Foot Guards: Hon. James Stewart, and James Hope.
35. Lieutenant Colonels Alexander Abercromby, Robert Arbuthnot, Henry Hardinge, Hercules Pakenham, and Hon. James Stewart
36. Majors Henry Bradford, Colin Campbell, William Gomm, and James Hope

the two officers[37] who were regimental captains, this promotion was a jump in two ranks! This lateral promotion into a Guards regiment was significant, because they did not have to purchase the promotion.

The recognition of those eleven officers did not stop with their promotions into the Guards regiments. On 2 January 1815, eight of them[38] were created Knight Commanders of the Bath, while on 4 June 1815, the other three[39] were made Companions of the Bath. Three other Guards officers, who were already company commanders in the Guards, were also created Knight Commanders of the Bath for their Peninsular service on the staff.[40] One of the criteria for being created a Knight Commander of the Bath instead of a Companion of the Bath was how many Army Gold Medals an officer received. An Army Gold Medal was awarded to field officers who served on the staff or as a battalion or brigade commander who had come under fire during a specific battle in which the medal was awarded. Those field officers with at least five Army Gold Medals were created Knights Commanders of the Bath; those who had less than five medals were made Companions of the Bath. To put this in perspective, the four officers[41] who commanded the Guards Battalions in the Waterloo Campaign also commanded Guards battalions in the Peninsula. Although all had received Army Gold Medals for their service there, they did not command their battalions in at least five battles where the Army Gold Medal was awarded. If they had been on the staff, they likely would have seen more action and thus been awarded more Army Gold Medals.

Several other things also made being a staff officer appealing. Being on the staff was a very different world than being a regimental officer. While he was away from his regiment the officer was exempt from the mundane duties of a regimental officer and his position on the staff often allowed him to know what was being planned or going on long before word was filtered down to the regiment. For those who served as either a brigade major or an ADC, they were part of the general's official family. They usually shared the general's quarters and ate what the general was eating;

---

37. Captains Lord Fitzroy Somerset and Ulysses Burgh.
38. Colin Campbell, Henry Bradford, Robert Arbuthnot, Henry Hardinge, Lord Fitzroy Somerset, William Gomm, Ulysses Burgh, and James Hope
39. Alexander Abercromby, Hercules Pakenham, and Hon. James Stewart
40. Henry Bouverie, Francis D'Oyly, and Alexander Gordon
41. Francis Hepburn, Henry Askew, Hon. William Stuart, and Alexander Woodford.

which meant where they stayed and what they ate was much better than if they had remained in the regiment.

Within a few weeks of arriving in Brussels, Wellington was overwhelmed with requests to serve on his staff. Wellington's concern was not that he did not have enough officers to fill the positions but that he had too many unqualified ones already in the job. This prevented him from offering the staff billets to officers who had proven themselves in the Peninsula. On 14 April he wrote to Major General Henry Torrens at the Horse Guards that: 'I am very much distressed about the numerous Staff we have got here. I have begun by turning off all the subaltern officers employed as D.A.A.Gs. and D.A.Q.M.Gs., contrary to regulation; and I propose to strike off all the Barrack masters, Commandants of towns, &c., excepting where we have hospitals. But we have still a good many upon the Staff, whom I must remove to make room for those more capable of doing the duty.'[42]

The situation worsened in the following week, prompting Wellington to write to General Torrens on 21 April:

> I have received your letter of the 17th, regarding my having removed 8 officers from the Adj. Gen.'s and Q.M. Gen.'s Staff; and at the same time I received an official one from you of the 15th, appointing 8 others; and one from Col. Shawe of the 3d, appointing Capt. Cameron of the Guards. The Commander in Chief has a right to recommend, and the Prince Regent to appoint, whom they please to these situations; but I should wish you to take an opportunity of suggesting the following considerations:
>
> 1st; The army, that is, the British part of it, is excessively small, and consists now of only 4 divisions of infantry, including Hanoverian Landwehr, and 4 brigades of cavalry, including the Legion; and it has already a staff more than sufficient for its numbers and organization, and if I could do it without the imputation of harshness and partiality, I would dismiss more.
>
> 2ndly; Supposing the Staff not to be sufficient, and that more will be required hereafter, it has hitherto been His Royal Highness' practice allow those officers who command the troops … to recommend to his notice those officers to be appointed to the Staff …

---

42. Wellington, Duke of, *Dispatches of Field Marshal the Duke of Wellington, During his Various Campaigns in India Denmark, Portugal, Spain, the Low Countries, and France.* (enlarged edition), Edited by Lt.-Col. John Gurwood. London: Parker, Furnivall and Parker, 1844-1847. Vol. 8, p.31.

3dly; I am certain that His Royal Highness would wish to nominate those most capable of serving the army, and those about whom they are placed; and he will admit that the most experienced, that is, those who have been serving in these situations for 5 or 6 years, are of that description. But of the list you and Col. Shawe have sent, there are only three who have any experience at all.

I enclose a list of officers whom I should prefer to all others; and indeed, we shall find it difficult to go on without some of them. [43]

Among those officers Wellington wanted were the Guards officers who had served on the staff of his army in the Peninsula. Initially the Horse Guards refused to give them to him. General Torrens wrote back to Wellington about the officers he wanted, particularly the Guards officers:

The Commander in Chief has observed, that it includes several Officers of the Guards, and H.R.H. is convinced you will concur with Him upon the inexpediency and indeed the impossibility of making too large a draft of Captains (Lt Colonels) from that Corps for employment on the Staff. Many have got their companies in recompense or their Services in the Peninsula, and ought in fairness to the Service, do the duties of their new situation. In this remark, H.R.H. does not include those who served on your own Staff, and whom you naturally and properly require again; But beyond this, He thinks that consideration should be given to the Regimental demands of the Guards for their Officers; which demands gave rise to the measure of appointing efficient Officers in the Room of those who had attained the rank of General. I explained this personally to Lt Colonels Woodford, Gomm and Hope and H.R.H. thinks that the latter, in particular has already received sufficient favour without being placed on the Staff. [44]

This meant that of the eleven Guards officers who were promoted into the Guards because of their service on the Peninsular staff, only Lord

---

43. ibid, pp.36-37.
44. Unpublished letter from Major General Henry Torrens to the Duke of Wellington, dated 25 April 1815.

Fitzroy Somerset, who would be Wellington's Military Secretary, and Ulysses Burgh, who was appointed an ADC, were allowed to join his staff. This prohibition did not include those Guards officers who were not among the eleven mentioned above. These included three of his ADCs: John Fremantle, Charles Fox Canning, and Alexander Gordon. Wellington responded to General Torrens on 28 April:

> I feel no objection to having as many officers on the Staff as His Royal Highness chooses to nominate; and I have directed the list you enclosed should be put in orders and when these officers join they shall be received as officers of the Staff. ... Sir C. Colville yesterday recommend ... Lieut. Col. J. Woodford[45] to be the Q. M. G. of the 4th division; but in consequence of His Royal Highness' orders, the latter shall not be appointed ... I can assure you that scarcely a day passes in which I am not told by officers applying for Staff situations, that they had been informed at the Horse Guards that the selection of officers for these situations had been left to me. Lord James Hay[46] who arrived from England with Gen. Colville and applied to be put on the Q. M. G.'s Staff, told me so yesterday.[47]

Two weeks later, Wellington was still unhappy with his staff. On 8 May he wrote to Lieutenant General Charles Lord Stewart[48] that, 'I have got an infamous army, very weak and ill equipped, and a very inexperienced Staff.'[49] The situation was finally resolved by mid-May. William Gomm wrote to his sister on 25 May that, 'You will be glad to hear that I have succeeded in my application for the staff. The Duke of Wellington appointed me yesterday an assistant quartermaster-general, and although it still requires the Duke of York's sanction.'[50] By the end of May, the Duke of York had lifted his

---

45. John Woodford of the 1st Battalion 1st Foot Guards
46. Lord James Hay of the 3rd Battalion 1st Foot Guards
47. Wellington, Duke of, *Dispatches of Field Marshal the Duke of Wellington ... (enlarged edition).* Vol. 8, p.48-49.
48. Lieutenant General Stewart was Wellington's AG in the Peninsula.
49. Wellington, Duke of, *Dispatches of Field Marshal the Duke of Wellington. . . (enlarged edition).* Vol. 8, p.48-49.
50. Gomm, William M., *Letters and Journals of Field-Marshal Sir William Maynard Gomm from 1799 to Waterloo 1815.* Francis Carr-Gomm (ed.). London: John Murray; 1881, p.348.

ban on Guards officers serving on the staff. By the start of the Waterloo Campaign, thirty-three of them would be serving outside of their regiment. However not every Guards officer who applied to be on the staff was accepted. Despite his early application, James Stanhope was one of those who were affected by the ban.[51] He was quite bitter about the affair and wrote home, 'I had the letters in my hand when the answer arrived from Torrens to the letter in which my name, Woodford's & two other names were placed have a positive veto, but the general tenor was so strong against any captains of the Guards who had been honoured with companies from other regiments, being appointed, that though I am not of that number and though there are ten lieutenant colonels with one battalion, this sad bevue [blunder] has stopped my appointment & the whole list from the Horse Guards is in orders so everything is now filled to choking.'[52] Captain Henry Dawkins, also applied. He had been a brigade major for forty-six months in the Peninsula, but when permission was finally given to use Guards officers on the staff, William Gomm was selected instead.[53] A complete list of the Guards officers appointed to the staff can be found in Appendix VII.

The Guards Division occupied villages in and around Enghien. Life was very comfortable there. General Maitland and his staff were billeted in Duke of Arenberg's Park, which was about 400 acres of land, 'A portion of it was marked off as a cricket-ground, and a green sward that encircled a large sheet of water, backed by a forest of finely-grown trees, made an excellent gallop for those who wanted to test the merits of their horses.'[54] Major Woodford, the commander of the 2nd Battalion Coldstream Guards wrote that: 'We have occupied these quarters near 2 months, it is a nice town with a superb park, & we all prefer it to Brussels, the distance admitting of frequent visits to the city.'[55] Captain Stanhope of the 3rd Battalion 1st Foot Guards wrote home that he was quarters were in a very pretty and comfortable farm among fresh eggs; pigs, poultry & cows before the house, nightingales in every bush behind it, not a bad cuisine & establishment inside.'[56] The other ranks

---

51. He finally got his wish and was appointed the AQMG to the 1st Division after Waterloo.
52. Stanhope, pp.158-159.
53. Gomm, p.348.
54. Lennox, Lord William Pitt, *Fifty Years' Biographical Reminiscences*. 2 vols. London: Hurst and Blackett, 1863.Vol. 1, p.224.
55. *Waterloo Archive*, Vol. 1, p.137.
56. Stanhope, p.158.

were quartered in homes and barns.[57] One sergeant thought that even though they were in barns it was better than being in tents. However, he did not live in the barns, but had a bed in the house occupied by his company commander, Captain Henry D'Oyly. He did note that, 'the people of the house is [sic] very kind.'[58]

Training began soon after the battalions were settled into their quarters. Major Woodford was determined to get his battalion 'on a good footing, & to get the battalions into the best state. I have every reason to hope, it will keep up a high character in every respect & with all my partiality for the 1st battalion. I must own that this is a finer & a more orderly one. They are chiefly young me, & well disposed.'[59] The initial marches were not strenuous, one of the first was only five miles.[60] By mid-May, Wellington ordered 'every division to collect 3 times a week & march en masse some hours on the great roads. We formerly marched & exercised in individual battalions. ... The first took place yesterday.'[61] When they were not marching they often engaged in live fire exercises. Surprisingly, considering the maximum effective range for their muskets was only fifty yards, they 'practiced to fire at targets at the distance of 120 and 130 yards, most of them are tolerable good marksmen.'[62]

On 1 May, Wellington reviewed the Guards Division on the grounds of the Duke of Arenberg's Park in Enghien. The division had about 3500 men in formation at noon waiting to pass in review. After Wellington inspected them by riding past the battalions, they 'marched past by companies and his Grace was pleased to express the highest satisfaction.'[63] Up until this time rumours had been spreading that the 1st Battalion of the 1st Foot Guards would also be joining them. However, after the review this rumour died.[64]

After Reverend George Stonestreet was appointed the Guards Division chaplain in early May, religious services were held every Sunday. Because the division was scattered around Enghien, he would hold two services each Sunday. On 14 May, he 'performed service at nine to Sir John Byng's Brigade, 3 miles from Enghien, at 11 to General Maitland's Brigade

---

57. *Waterloo Archive*; Vol. 4, p.141.
58. ibid, Vol. 3, p.91.
59. ibid, Vol. 1, p.137.
60. Blackman, pp.118-119
61. Stanhope, p.163.
62. Blackman, p.120.
63. ibid.
64. Stanhope, p.159.

(both Guards) in Enghien, afterwards jumped again on my saddle and rode to Brussels in time to do duty to the English families at three.'[65] The chaplain would also visit the division during the week but not hold formal services. Some of the enlisted soldiers, who were not members of the Church of England, held their own services. Sergeant Charles Wood of Captain Miller's company 3rd Battalion 1st Foot Guards, while in their cantonments in Hoves 'opened a place for our religious duties, where many found it their privilege to attend. ... although, when in close contest with the enemy, we are obliged to desist from our public meetings, on account of our duties; yet, we then as often as possible, commune with each other.'[66]

Not all of the time was spent training. There are very few references to what the other ranks did in their spare time. Ensign Samuel Barrington of the 2nd Battalion 1st Foot Guards noted on 15 June, in possibly a prediction of what the weather would be like over the next several days, that their field sports had to be canceled, 'as it rains at all times of the day and night and has done for the last fortnight and promises fair to do the same for another fortnight.'[67] Cricket was very popular among the officers of the 1st Brigade. The Brigade Commander, General Maitland, was an avid cricket player and when he was stationed in London, played for the Marylebone Cricket Club.[68] The general hosted several matches and they turned into social events that brought high society from Brussels to Enghien. One participant wrote that the Duke of Richmond and his family attended several of these events and they would go on for several days. He noted that in early May that: 'we have had cricket matches, collations al fresco[69] etc these three days.'[70]

Horse racing was also popular but did have some unattended consequences. General Maitland's extra-ADC, Lord William Lennox, was challenged to a race around the lake and through the woods at the Duke of Arenberg's Park by Ensign Joseph St. John of the 2nd Battalion 1st Foot Guards. Lennox agreed, but his horse was skittish. The sounds

---

65. Stonestreet, p.50.
66. *Waterloo Archive*, Vol. 6, p.127. Sergeant Wood's letters do not mention what religion he practiced, however from his descriptions he was probably a Methodist, which was popular among enlisted soldiers at the time.
67. ibid, Vol. 4, pp.134-135.
68. McGuigan, Ron and Burnham, Robert, *Wellington's Brigade Commanders: Peninsula and Waterloo*. Barnsley: Pen & Sword, 2017, p.203.
69. Informal meals served outside.
70. Stanhope, p.160.

of the hooves spooked his horse and it bolted through the woods. Lennox was hit by a low hanging branch and was thrown from the horse. He was knocked unconscious and broke his right arm in two places. Two surgeons from the 1st Guards treated him, including trepanning. He did not gain consciousness for seventy-two hours. Twenty-four hours later the attending surgeon said he was well enough to travel. His father, the Duke of Richmond, took him to his home in Brussels. Lennox was blinded in his right eye and was unable to move his right arm for several months. His injuries prevented him from performing his duties as General Maitland's ADC and he missed the Waterloo Campaign.[71]

Brussels was only 30km away from Enghien and many of the officers would ride there when they had time. Madame Angelica Catalani, a very famous opera singer, was touring Europe and was in Brussels in late April. Wellington's senior ADC, Lieutenant Colonel Alexander Gordon, Captain Stanhope, and Lieutenant Blackman were among the Guards officers who attended her first concert on 27 April.[72]

Between 28 April and 15 June, there were six balls held in Brussels, three of which were hosted by Wellington, another by General Thomas Graham Lord Lynedoch, one by Sir Charles Stuart the British Ambassador to the Netherlands, and the last one by the Duchess of Richmond. Because many of the Guards officers were members of society they were usually in attendance. On 28 April, Wellington hosted the first of the balls. It was to honour the newly inducted Knights Commanders of the Bath. Wellington's ADC, Lieutenant Colonel Gordon, was responsible for setting it up.[73] Among the attendees were the King and Queen of the Netherlands. Lieutenant Blackman wrote:

> Wellington gave a most splendid ball and supper in the same room where the concert was the night before, there were a certain number of tickets sent to each regiment of Guards, of which I got one; but I must tell you first of all, there was a grand dinner given by the Duke of Wellington at the Hotel de Belle Vue at 4 o'clock on that day to commemorate the installation of the new Knights of K.C.B., Lord Hill, Sir Sidney Smyth, etc. being of the party.[74] The Duke made his appearance in the ballroom about 9:30, soon

---

71. Lennox, Vol. 1, pp.224-226.
72. Blackman, pp.119-120; Gordon, p.401.
73. Gordon, Alexander, *At Wellington's Right Hand: the Letters of Lieutenant-Colonel Sir Alexander Gordon, 1808-1815*. Rory Muir (ed.). Phoenix Mill: Sutton, 2003. p.401.

after which arrived the King and Queen, an immense number of military, the Duke and Duchess of Richmond, Prince of Orange, Prince Frederick, Lord Uxbridge, etc. Dancing commenced about 10.00, waltzes, country dances, quadrilles, etc. so that everybody was highly amused till supper was announced at 12 o'clock, when the Queen took hold of the Duke of Wellington's arm, who conducted her to the supper room, the Queen being on his right and the King on his left and the dancing continued till 4.00 a.m. when everybody went away, extremely gratified.[75]

Wellington held a ball on 25 May in his own home. It 'was most splendidly and fashionably attended ... they were chiefly military that were present; amongst the first were the Prince of Orange, the Duke of Brunswick, Duke and Duchess of Richmond, Lady George Seymour etc.'[76] One observer found that 'the good Duchess was in a terrible mood at divers flirtations between some of the "Gentlemen of the Guards" and her numerous chicks.'[77]

By the beginning of June, Wellington's army was ready for war, but the balls still continued. Sir Charles Stuart held a large one on 4 June, but it was the last one attended to by the Dutch Royal Family. They left for the Hague soon after and the British civilians in Brussels began 'to ask whether they had better not follow his regal steps.'[78] Captain Stanhope also attended a ball held by Wellington on 7 June. He rightly concluded that it would be the final one hosted by Wellington and that it would be 'the last scene of female society for some time.'[79]

Throughout May and June, Guards officers continued to arrive in Belgium. But others left. Captain William Master,[80] the commander of the

---

74. Unfortunately, the list of attendees cannot be found. However, since it was held in honour of the members of Wellington's army that were awarded a KCB on 2 January 1815, many of those being recognized were from the Guards Regiments, including Henry Bradford, Henry Harding, Lord Fitzroy Somerset, and Ulysses Burgh from the 1st Foot Guards; and Colin Campbell, of the Coldstream Guards.
75. Blackman, pp.119-120.
76. ibid, p.122.
77. Stanhope, p.165.
78. ibid, pp.165-166.
79. ibid, p.168.
80. He was the older brother of Ensign Richard Master of the 3rd Battalion 1st Foot Guards.

2nd Battalion 3rd Foot Guards' Light Company, returned to England for the birth of his son. Lieutenant Colonel Ulysses Burgh, one of Wellington's ADCs, went home on leave to get married. Both officers missed the Waterloo Campaign. Captain William Gomm arrived in early May. As mentioned earlier, he expected to be appointed to the Army staff but it was not until June did he report to the 5th Anglo-Hanoverian Division as the AQMG. About the same time other Guards officers were also pulled out of the battalions to fill staff positions. This created havoc among the command structure of the battalions, especially at the company commander position. Fifty per cent of the company commander would either be on leave or on the army staff during the campaign. In the Coldstream Guards, officers were moved around to fill the vacancies. Captain Henry Wyndham[81] was given command of the Light Company, much to the dismay of Lieutenant Bowles who had temporarily commanded it for many months. On 14 June, he wrote home that: 'I regret bitterly having to slave through this campaign in the ranks, where nothing is to be seen or got in the shape of information, honour, or reward, but I have no alternative but patience and mine is, I own, almost exhausted, more especially as I have just had the mortification of being superseded in command of the Light Company by Lieutenant Colonel Wyndham, who is about two years junior to myself in the Guards and army, and has served abroad about as many months as I have years.'[82]

The numerous vacancies in the 1st Foot Guards caused a shuffling of officers both within the battalion and between battalions. Lieutenant Harry Powell was transferred from the 3rd Battalion to the 2nd Battalion, where he became its senior lieutenant. He replaced Lieutenant Charles Ellis, who moved to the 3rd Battalion. Although Lieutenant Powell was carried on the Light Company's Muster Roll, he would be assigned to the 2nd Battalion's Grenadier Company. Lieutenant Lonsdale Boldero of the 1st Battalion was the 2nd Battalion's acting adjutant.[83] Ensigns Seymour Bathurst and George Fludyer were temporarily attached to the 2nd Battalion in April, but by May their move became official. At the same time this was occurring, Ensign Frederick Gould was sent to the 3rd Battalion. They replaced Ensigns Francis Needham and Thomas Cary Askew who went to England to be in the 1st Battalion. Ensign Bathurst's father was Earl Bathurst, the Secretary of State for War and the Colonies.

---

81. Captain and Lieutenant Colonel Henry Wyndham
82. Bowles, pp.97-98.
83. Lieutenant Boldero arrived in April.

The most curious case was Ensign Rees Gronow, who was assigned to the 1st Battalion 1st Foot Guards. He did not want to miss out on the action. In early June he met General Sir Thomas Picton in London, who was going to Belgium to take command of the 5th Anglo-Hanoverian Division. General Picton's extra-ADC was Captain Newton Chambers, a friend of Ensign Gronow. General Picton told him that he had no vacancies on his staff, but it was likely his ADC would be killed so, 'he could go over with me if he could get leave.'[84] Ensign Gronow never bothered to ask for permission from his regiment, thinking he could go to Belgium, fight in the upcoming battle, and return to London in time to mount guard at St James Palace, before anyone noticed he was missing. He did not have enough money to outfit himself properly for campaigning, so he went to 'Cox and Greenwood's, those stanch friends of the hard-up soldier. ... I there obtained £200, which I took with me to a gambling-house in St James's Square, where I managed, by some wonderful accident to win £600; and having thus obtained the sinews of war, I made numerous purchases, amongst others two first-rate horses at Tattersall's for a high figure, which were embarked for Ostend, along with my groom.'[85] He met General Picton in Ostend and went to Brussels with him. They arrived there on 15 June. He was not permitted to stay on with General Picton, who already had two ADCs, and was ordered to join his regiment in Enghien.

The commander of the 1st Corps, the Prince of Orange, ordered a final review of the Guards Division be held on 31 May. They left Enghien at 02.00 hours and marched over 20km to Bruyère de Casteau, located about 7km south of Soignies along the Mons Road and 1km west of it. Some believed that this was unnecessary harassment of the men, however others felt that this was a good test to see how quickly the army would be able to concentrate should the French cross the border. Despite bad weather, the Division acquitted itself well and after being reviewed by the Prince in the morning, returned to its cantonments in the vicinity of Enghien. General Cooke passed on the Prince's approval in a message the next day:

> Major-General Cooke has great pleasure in communicating to the division the entire satisfaction of H.R.H. the Prince of Orange at

---

84. Gronow, Rees Howell, *The Reminiscences and Recollections of Captain Gronow: being Anecdotes of the Camp, Court, Clubs, and Society 1810-1860.* 2 vols. London: Smith, Elder, 1863. Vol. 1, pp.64-65.
85. ibid.

their appearance yesterday morning, and the warm approbation that he expressed at the steadiness and discipline with which the several corps performed their movements. The Prince of Orange was pleased to remark also to the other officers, that, although he had been many years with the British army, he never before had seen so perfect a body of men.[86]

Training of the battalions continued, and final preparations were made for war. By the beginning of June, the Guards were issued tents.[87] In anticipation of the upcoming campaign, Major Woodford stepped up the training for his battalion. After noticing how long his battalion's baggage train was, he decided to reduce it. 'At first folks persevered in keeping carts, but only the high roads are paved, & in wet the cross roads & even the sides of the high roads, are impassable. I established a regular peninsular train under General Carter, from the first & now all carts & carriages are strictly forbidden, a very proper measure, I am convinced; though many are unreasonable & stupid enough to grumble.'[88]

On 7 June Wellington added Captain [Brevet Major] Henry Kuhlmann's Troop of King's German Horse Artillery to the Guards Division. It was equipped with 9-pounder guns.[89]

Despite the increasing chance that the army would be marching soon, one last ball was held. It was given by the Duchess of Richmond on 15 June and destined to go down in history. Thirty-eight Guards officers or officers from the Guards Division were invited. There is some question regarding how many of the invitees actually attended the ball. Tensions were high and based on rumours, many officers believed they would be marching off to war in a few days. Captain James Stanhope thought it would be imprudent to go.[90] In all likelihood, the Guards Division commander, General Cooke, as well as the two brigade commanders – Generals Maitland and Byng – were at the ball. Their ADCs, would have accompanied them, except for General Cooke's extra-ADC, Ensign Augustus Cuyler, who had not received an invitation.

The following is a list of Guards and 1st Division Officers who were invited. Those who were known to attend are indicated in bold. Those

---

86. Hamilton, Vol. 3, pp.13-14.
87. Bowles, p.98.
88. *Waterloo Archive*, Vol. 1, p.138.
89. General Order dated 7 June 1815.
90. Stanhope, p.172.

who were invited and were known to not have attended are in italics. All others on the list were invited but there is no record stating whether they attended or not.

Army Staff	
Lieutenant Colonel Hon. Alexander Abercromby	2nd Battalion Coldstream Guards
Lieutenant Colonel Delancey Barclay	2nd Battalion 1st Foot Guards
Lieutenant Colonel Sir Colin Campbell	1st Battalion Coldstream Guards
Lieutenant Colonel John Fremantle	1st Battalion Coldstream Guards
Lieutenant Colonel Hon. Sir Alexander Gordon	2nd Battalion 3rd Foot Guards
Lieutenant Colonel Sir Thomas Noel Hill	2nd Battalion 1st Foot Guards
Lieutenant Colonel Lord Fitzroy Somerset	2nd Battalion 1st Foot Guards
Major Chatham Churchill	1st Battalion 1st Foot Guards
Captain Francis Dawkins	2nd Battalion 1st Foot Guards
Captain Lord Charles Fitzroy	3rd Battalion 1st Foot Guards
Captain Hon. Orlando Bridgeman	1st Battalion 1st Foot Guards

Guards Division	**Position**
Major General George Cooke	Commander
Lieutenant Colonel Sir Henry Bradford	AQMG
Captain George Disbrowe	ADC

1st Brigade Guards Division	
Major General Peregrine Maitland	Commander
Captain James Gunthorpe[91]	Brigade Major
Ensign James Lord Hay	ADC

2nd Battalion 1st Foot Guards
Lieutenant Charles Allix   Adjutant
Ensign Hon. Seymour Bathurst
Ensign George Fludyer
Ensign Algernon Greville

3rd Battalion 1st Foot Guards
Captain Alexander Lord Saltoun
Captain Hon. James Stanhope

---

91. Robinson, p.82.

2nd Brigade Guards Division
Major General Sir John Byng   Commander
Captain Henry Dumaresq   ADC
Ensign Hon. Edward Stopford   Extra-ADC

2nd Battalion Coldstream Guards
Major Alexander Woodford   Commander
Captain Hon. Edward Acheson
Captain Henry Wyndham
Lieutenant George Bowles
Lieutenant John Stepney Cowell[92]
Ensign Hon. James Forbes
Ensign Hon. John Montagu

2nd Battalion 3rd Foot Guards
Captain Edward Bowater
Lieutenant Hon. Hastings Forbes
Lieutenant Robert Hesketh
Ensign David Baird
Ensign Hon. Ernest Edgcombe
Ensign Hon. Henry Montagu

---

92. Harrison, Robert, *Some Notices of the Stepney Family*. London: Privately published, 1870, p.92. Lieutenant Cowell was not on any list of the invitees, but he claims he was there.

Chapter 6

16 June 1815
The March To War

Early on the morning of 12 June, Napoleon rode from Paris to join his army along the Belgian border. He arrived at the army headquarters at Avesnes the next day, having travelled over 200km in less than thirty-six hours. His plan was to attack into Belgium on 14 June, but after arriving at the army, he found it not ready to march. The attack was postponed until the following day. His goal was to march quickly and get between the British and Prussian armies to prevent them from uniting. To do this he would then attack one of them with most of his army while pinning the other with a smaller force. Once he defeated one, he would turn the might of his army onto the other.

Napoleon's Armée du Nord had 125,000 men organized into five infantry corps, four cavalry corps, and the Imperial Guard. His plan called for, 'Speed, surprise, and massive local superiority.'[1] The army would advance north along an axis of Beaumont – Charleroi-Quatre Bras – Brussels. Opposing them were the 106,000 men of Wellington's Anglo-Allied Army which was in cantonments to the west and northwest of the axis of advance; while the 116,000-man Prussian Army under the command of Field Marshal Prince Gebhard Blücher was to the east. Watching the border to the east of the axis of advance was the 30,000 men of the 1st Prussian Corps. It was deployed in a 40km long screen along the border, while the rest of the army was to the northeast. Along the border to the west was the 2nd Netherlands Light Cavalry Brigade command by Major General Jean, Baron van Merlen.

On the evening of 14 June, Napoleon wrote to Marshal Davout, his Minister of War that: 'I shall pass the Sambre [River] tomorrow, the 15th.

---

1. Hussey, John, *Waterloo: The Campaign of 1815.* 2 vols. Barnsley: Greenhill, 2017. Vol. 1, p.334.

If the Prussians do not abandon it we shall have a battle'.[2] He also told his army that: 'We have forced marches to undertake, battles to fight ... the moment has come to conquer or die.'[3] The French would advance on Charleroi in three prongs each consisting of two corps: one from the southwest, one straight up the middle from Beaumont, and the third from the southeast.

The invasion of Belgium began at 04.30 hours on 15 June when elements from Lieutenant General Honoré Reille's 2nd Corps attacked the town of Thuin, 5km from the border. By noon, the French had taken Charleroi, about 30km from the border. The French continued to advance north but was encountering increasing Prussian resistance. Four hours later the advance elements of General Reille's corps were on the outskirts of Gosselies which laid along the main road to Brussels. By 17.00 hours the French had advanced another 8km and had taken the town of Frasnes. By this time, the French had marched 40km and fought a series of skirmishes and combats. They were less than 50km from Brussels and 7km from the key crossroads of Quatre Bras, which was being defended by Lieutenant General Hendrik Baron de Perponcher Sedlnitsky's 2nd Netherlands Division. The Prussians were falling back to the northeast, while the British had yet to be seen.

By 15 June, word had reached the Guards Division that Napoleon had arrived at the border of France and Belgium.[4] This did not prevent much of the division's chain-of-command from attending the Duchess of Richmond's Ball in Brussels that night. In all probability they would have left on 14 June, so that they would not have to ride the 45km and go to the ball on the same day. Around 14.00 hours on 15 June, an orderly dragoon arrived from the 1st Corps alerting the Guards Division to be ready to move. The battalion commanders, except for Major Woodford of the Coldstream Guards who was at the ball, began to prepare their battalions for movement. About 17.00 hours, Wellington sent orders to the 1st Corps HQ at Braine-le-Comte to have the Guards Division to be ready to move at a moment's notice.[5] Around 20.00 hours another dragoon orderly arrived at the Guards Division Headquarters and informed them that the French were across the Sambre River near Charleroi, less than 60km away. At 22.00 hours Wellington's message reached the division.[6] About the time it

---

2. ibid, p.340.
3. ibid.
4. *Waterloo Archive*, Vol. 6, p.113.
5. Hussey, Vol. 1, p.422.
6. Robinson, Mike, *The Battle of Quatre Bras 1815*. Stroud: Spellmount, 2008. p.82.

arrived Wellington sent another message to the 1st Corps HQ, telling them if Nivelles was attacked, to have the Guards move to Braine-le-Comte.[7] There is no evidence that any effort was made to recall the officers who were attending the Duchess of Richmond's Ball in Brussels.

The 2nd Battalion 1st Foot Guards began to prepare to move as soon as it received notification. Its right division was ordered from its cantonments in Marcq and join the left division in Hove, where they were linked up with the rest of the battalion.[8] The battalion's baggage was also packed. The 2nd Battalion 1st Foot Guards could only muster thirty-nine officers. It was missing eight officers, including six of its ten company commanders. All six of the absent captains were on the army staff. They were captains Henry Bradford, Henry Hardinge, Thomas Hill, Delancey Barclay, Lord Fitzroy Somerset, and Ulysses Burgh.[9] Although the battalion was authorized fifteen lieutenants, only twelve were serving with it. Lieutenants Augustus Viscount Bury and William Moore were on the staff, while Lieutenant Philip Perceval was on his way to join the battalion. He arrived too late to fight in the campaign. It had sixteen ensigns present for duty on 15 June,[10] plus five of its staff officers.[11]

Among the enlisted ranks in the 2nd Battalion 1st Foot Guards were fifty sergeants, twenty-three drummers, and 965 other ranks. Another sixty soldiers were in the hospital and unable to march with the battalion, while five sergeants and twelve other ranks were on command and not with the battalion. The battalion marched that night with 1,077 officers and men, 81 per cent of its authorized strength.

The 3rd Battalion 1st Foot Guards was quartered in Enghien and also made arrangements to move. The companies that had been billeted in the outskirts of the town were ordered back to the town. It had thirty-six officers present. In addition to its battalion commander, it had nine of its ten company commanders, only Captain Leslie Jones, who was the Commandant of Brussels was missing. Although the battalion was only authorized fifteen lieutenants it had sixteen on its rolls. Regardless of the number authorized it had only nine lieutenants serving with the battalion. Those missing were Lieutenants William Cameron, George Disbrowe, Lord

---

7. Hussey, Vol. 1, p.422.
8. *Waterloo Letters*, p.250.
9. Captain Burgh was on the staff but was in England getting married.
10. The battalion was only authorized fifteen ensigns but had Ensign Bathurst attached to it.
11. For some reason its quartermaster was not with the battalion.

Charles Fitzroy, James Gunthorpe, and Lord James Hay who were serving on the staff. James Lindsay was sick in England. John Hely-Hutchinson was supposed to be with the battalion but did not participate in the Waterloo Campaign. He was probably too sick to go on campaign. The battalion did have thirteen of fifteen authorized ensigns. The two missing ensigns were James Lord Hay who was serving as General Maitland's ADC and Frederick Gould who was assigned to the battalion and was reported as being with it in Belgium. He did not participate in the Waterloo Campaign. He too was most likely too sick to march. Furthermore, Ensign Henry Vernon would not march with the battalion. He would remain in Enghien in charge of the battalion's baggage guard.[12] Ensign Edward Pardoe, who had been wounded in both arms and taken prisoner at Bergen-op-Zoom in March 1814, arrived at Enghien late on 15 June. His fellow ensigns were surprised to see him and immediately had him join their company mess.[13] Although it reported that it had five of six staff officers, like the 2nd Battalion, it too was missing its quartermaster and had Lieutenant Charles Allix of the 1st Battalion serving as its acting adjutant.

The 3rd Battalion could muster fifty sergeants, twenty-three drummers, and 987 other ranks. It left forty-two soldiers who were too sick to march in Enghien, while another eight were on command. The battalion would march with 1,097 officers and men, 82 per cent of its authorized strength.

In the 2nd Brigade, the 2nd Battalion Coldstream Guards received word of the French movements about the same time as the other battalions. It was told, 'to be ready to move at a moments [sic] notice'.[14] With the battalion and several of the company commanders in Brussels, the senior officer with the battalion was Captain James Macdonell. The battalion had thirty-one officers present for duty, but was missing half of its company commanders. Captains Alexander Abercromby and William Gomm were serving on the staff of the army, Robert Arbuthnot was on leave, while Hon. John Walpole and Hercules Pakenham were on sick leave in England. Furthermore, the battalion was reporting that it had all 14 of its authorized lieutenants present, but in fact had only eight. Those lieutenants who would not make the campaign were: John Rous who fell from his horse that morning and broke his leg; Thomas Chaplin who despite being in Belgium was still incapacitated due to wounds

---

12. *Waterloo Archive*, Vol. 1, p.135.
13. Master, Richard, 'An Ensign at War: the Narrative of Richard Master, First Guards'. David Fraser (ed.). *Journal of the Society for Army Historical Research*. Vol. LDVI Number 267 August 1988, p.137.
14. Blackman, p.122.

he received in the siege of San Sebastian in 1813; William Grimstead who was sick; John Drummond who was so sick he had to return to England; Windham Anstruther who had been severely wounded at Nivelle in November 1813 and was still in England; and Charles White who was serving as the ADC to the Duke of Cambridge[15] in Hanover. Only thirteen of the battalion's sixteen ensigns were available to march. Ensigns Frederick Fitz Clarence and James Buller were in Enghien, both too sick to go on campaign, while Ensign Augustus Cuyler was serving as the extra ADC to General Cooke. The battalion had only four of its staff officers.[16] It was missing its adjutant, Lieutenant Charles Bentinck, who was serving as a DAAG to the 2nd Division. His duties were performed by Lieutenant William Walton.

The 2nd Battalion Coldstream Guards was top-heavy with sergeants, having on its roster five more than the sixty it was authorized. However only fifty-five were available to fight. Of the others, one was in the hospital, three were carried as present but were too sick march with the battalion and rode with the battalion baggage, and six were on command. The battalion was also over-strength in drummers having twenty-two while only being authorized twenty. Like the sergeants though, not all were available. Six were absent on command, and though fifteen were being reported as present, one was sick and rode with the baggage. The battalion had 1,003 other ranks, but only 939 were available to fight. Forty-nine other ranks were present but sick, nine were in the hospital, and eleven on command. The battalion had 1,039 officers and men ready to march – 78 per cent of its authorized strength.

Major Hepburn, the commander of the 2nd Battalion 3rd Foot Guards was dining with Ensign Charles Lake and was eating dessert, when Lieutenant Robert Hesketh came into the room and told him, 'I just left the Prince of Orange's quarters, and have gallop'd over to tell you that the French have suddenly moved towards us on the Nivelle [sic] road.' Hepburn said, 'Hesketh, may I depend upon this news being correct?' 'You may.' 'Will you then tell the Adjutant to immediately come to me, as it will enable me to have the Regiment in readiness to move as soon as orders arrive from Head Quarters.'[17] Major Hepburn's battalion had thirty-six officers with the battalion, but were missing half

---

15. Field Marshal Prince Adolphus, Duke of Cambridge Regimental Colonel of the Coldstream Guards was the seventh son of King George III.
16. The Quartermaster, the Surgeon, and the two Assistant Surgeons.
17. Lake, Charles, 'Waterloo Reminiscences of Ensign Charles Lake, Third Guards'. *Scots Guards Magazine*. 1961, p.66.

its company commanders, including captains Charles Fox Canning, Alexander Gordon, William Keate, and Henry Rooke who were on the staff. Also absent was Captain William Master, the commander of the Light Company, who was on leave. Due to his absence, Major Hepburn appointed Captain Charles Dashwood the commander of the Light Company. The battalion had thirteen of its fifteen lieutenants present, missing only Lieutenant William Stothert, who was the 2nd Brigade's Brigade Major and Lieutenant James Rodney, who was on leave in England. The battalion had seventeen ensigns assigned to it, two more than were authorized. Only Ensign Henry Paxton, who was sick, was unable to march. The battalion had three staff officers with it, but was missing Assistant Surgeon Warde, who was on leave in England, and its paymaster who never went to Belgium with it. Lieutenant William Stothert had been the battalion adjutant and he was replaced by Ensign Barclay Drummond as the acting adjutant.

Although the 2nd Battalion 3rd Foot Guards had sixty-seven sergeants assigned to it, only sixty-five were available to march and fight. Two were with the baggage train too sick to march. It was authorized twenty drummers, but only had nineteen because one was sick. Out of the 1,061 other ranks assigned to the battalion, it was only able to muster 1,001 men. They brought thirty-four sick men with the baggage but left six in the hospital. The total number of officers and enlisted men with the battalion who were ready to fight was 1,120 or 84 per cent of its authorized strength.

Word was late in reaching Captain Henry Kuhlmann's 2nd Horse Artillery Troop of the King's German Artillery. It was stationed in Ghislenghien, about 13km west of Enghien. It was not until the evening did they received word to be on 'stand by and be ready for an immediate departure.'[18] It is unknown when word reached Captain Charles Sandham, the commander of the Royal Artillery Brigade attached to the Guards Division. Since they were cantoned in Enghien it was probably around 14.00 hours.

On the morning of 16 June, between 01.00 hours and 01.30 hours orders were received by the battalions to march to Braine-le-Comte, where the headquarters of the 1st Corps was located, starting at 03.00 hours. Where they were to go after that was not known. General Cooke arrived from Brussels before the march began and he rode towards Nivelles to find out where they were supposed to go.[19]

---

18. *Waterloo Archive*, Vol. 3, p.42.
19. *Waterloo Letters*, p.250.

For the 2nd Battalion 1st Foot Guards, at 'half-past one a.m. Drums beat to arms, the Battalion and baggage ready to move at two. At three the order came for the Brigade to assemble at Hove. Heavy stores and hospital ordered to Brussels.[20] About this time some of the officers who had been attending the Duchess of Richmond's ball began to arrive. Major Woodford, the commander of the Coldstream Guards, showed up just before the march began still dressed for the ball.[21] Lieutenant Bowles however did not leave the ball until after 02.00 hours. Unfortunately, he never said when he linked up with his battalion.[22]

At 04.00 the division began to march. The 1st Brigade led the division and started along the Nivelles Road preceded by the advance guard of at least one company. It was likely because the division would encounter the French sometime that day, the advance guard consisted of the brigade's two light companies under the command of Captain Alexander Lord Saltoun, the commander of the 3rd Battalion's Light Company. It was followed by the 2nd Battalion 1st Foot Guards and then the 3rd Battalion 1st Foot Guards. The 2nd Brigade, which was marching from Enghien, followed behind the 1st Brigade. It was led by the brigade's light companies under the command of Captain James Macdonell of the Coldstream Guards. Behind the light companies came the 2nd Battalion of the Coldstream Guards, followed by the 2nd Battalion 3rd Foot Guards. Behind them was the artillery and then the division's baggage train. Bringing up the rear was the division's Provost Marshal, Sergeant Garman of the 2nd Battalion Coldstream Guards.

When it left Enghien on the morning of 15 June, the 1st Division had about 4,200 officers and men present. The infantry marched in columns of four abreast. Each battalion averaged about 1,000 officers and enlisted men. In a typical battalion, one in eight of a battalion's strength were officers, sergeants, and drummers; or about 124 men. The 876 other ranks would be in the column marching four abreast. According to Army Regulations the length of the column must not exceed the length of the battalion when it stood in a two-deep line. A two-deep line of 876 men would have a frontage of 438 men. The regulations stated that each soldier would take up twenty-four inches while standing in line. Therefore the 438 men would have a frontage of 876 feet or about 250m.[23]

---

20. ibid.
21. *Waterloo Archive*, Vol. 4, p.14.
22. Bowles, p.98.
23. *Rules and Regulations for the Formations, Field-Exercise, and Movements of His Majesty's Forces*. London: War Office, 1792. pp.35, 282 & 368.

The regulations also stipulated that when a brigade stood in line there should be about six paces (about 5m) between the battalions. Thus, a brigade stretched along the road for about 500m. As they marched, the infantry of the Guards Division stretched down the road about 1km. Captain Sandham's Royal Artillery Brigade and Captain Kuhlmann's 2nd Horse Artillery of the King's German Legion Artillery each had six artillery pieces and nineteen limbers, caissons, and various other waggons. Each of these vehicles with their horses took up a space about 11m in length. If there was 5m distance between each gun or waggon, then each troop or brigade occupied 300m of space in column. Thus, the artillery portion of the column would add another 650m to the column. By the time the division's baggage train followed, the column would be about 2km long.

Because the division did not know where it was going and how fast it had to get there, it marched at a speed that could be maintained for a long period of time. This was known as Ordinary Pace which was seventy-five paces per minute. The British soldier's pace was thirty inches (.76m) and in an hour they would cover 3.4km (2.14 miles).[24] The soldiers began their march with sloped arms until the order was given to 'March at Ease.' The first halt was made after marching for thirty minutes to allow stragglers to catch up. During this time the soldiers would get a quick bite to eat and arrange their 'accoutrements, pack, haversack, and canteen, so as to sit well.'[25] After this short break they marched for an hour before stopping again for another short break of at 'least five minutes after the men had piled their arms'.[26]

The division marched along the Nivelles road through Hove for 12km to Steenkerque. From there it was 7km to Braine-le-Comte, where the lead elements arrived at around 07.30 hours. The 2nd Battalion 1st Foot Guards averaged 3.4km per hour during this stage of their march. The streets were packed with the baggage and waggons of the 1st Corps Headquarters that blocked progress through the town. By 09.00 hours the division had made it through the town and halted in the fields on its eastern side. Rations were distributed and there they waited for further orders. About noon, General Cooke arrived from his reconnaissance to the south. The division still had not received any orders, so he ordered them to march to Nivelles about 17km away.[27]

---

24. Nafziger, George. *Imperial Bayonets: Tactics of the Napoleonic Battery, Battalion and Brigade as Found in Contemporary Regulations*. London: Greenhill, 1996. p.297.
25. Gurwood, John, *The General Orders of Field Marshal the Duke of Wellington in the Campaigns of 1809 to 1818*. London: W. Clowes, 1837. p.xxxiv.
26. ibid.
27. *Waterloo Archive*, Vol. 4, p.139; *Waterloo Letters*, p.250.

The 1st Brigade moved out and despite the excessive heat and heavy backpacks by 15.00 hours they were within 1km of Nivelles. Because of the lack of orders, the officers and men assumed that after marching almost 40km in twelve hours that their day was done. They began to set up a bivouac in woods on the west side of the town.[28] Although they could hear firing in the distance, they continue to set up camp, sent out watering parties, and began to cook their food.[29]

The Strategic Situation

On the morning of 16 June, the French army split into two wings. Napoleon marched northeast with 70,000 men in an attempt to catch the retreating Prussian army. The lead elements of the Prussians were falling back so they could re-unite with the main part of the army. Blücher met with Wellington about 11.00 hours and they agree to unite their forces if possible. The Prussians would stand at Ligny and once the British concentrated their forces, they would march south from Quatre Bras and attempt to strike the French in the flank.

Napoleon's goal was to defeat the two armies separately and to do this he had to prevent them from uniting. He left Marshal Michel Ney with 30,000 men and ordered him to take Quatre Bras which was 15km north of where his forces were that morning. Quatre Bras sat across the main north-south road from Charleroi to Brussels. It was bisected by another good road that ran from the British cantonment area in the west to where the Prussians were concentrating their army 15km to the east at Ligny. If Marshal Ney could seize the crossroads at Quatre Bras he would prevent the British with linking up with the Prussians.

The village of Quatre Bras was on a small ridge that overlooked the land to the south. About 600m south of it was another ridge that was 10m lower and the terrain continued to gently slope southward. To the east of the Brussels-Charleroi road the fields were planted with rye and wheat. The crops were up to 2m in height and concealed any troops in them. This was a mixed blessing, since they also reduced the visibility of the infantry in them to see any movement to their front. To the west of the road were more fields but after 150-200m there was a forest called the Bois de Bossu.

---

28. *Waterloo Letters*, p.250; Master, p.137.
29. Clay, Mathew, *Narrative of the Battle of Quatre Bras & Waterloo with the Defence of Hougoumont*. Gareth Glover (ed.). Godmanchester: Ken Trotman; 2006. p.6.

These woods stretched for 1.2km southeast from Quatre Bras and at its widest point was about 300m wide. Along its eastern edge was a sunken lane. The woods eventually thinned out in the south near a farm lane that ran east-west. There are three different descriptions by Guards officers of how dense the woods were. Unfortunately, none of them corroborate the other. Sir William Gomm of the Coldstream Guards, who was the AQMG for the 5th Anglo-Hanoverian Division, described them as being 'passable everywhere for light cavalry'.[30] Lord Saltoun of the 1st Foot Guards wrote in 1838 that they were a 'large and in some parts thick wood'.[31] Lieutenant Henry Powell, also of the 1st Foot Guards, noted in his journal that: 'the thickness of the underwood soon upset all order'.[32]

Crossing the battlefield from the east to the west was the Gemioncourt Stream. It entered the woods about 1km south of Quatre Bras. At the southern part of the woods was the Odomiant Stream.[33] Neither Lord Saltoun nor Lieutenant Powell remember the most southern stream, but both comment on the Gemioncourt Stream. Lord Saltoun considered it an obstruction, while Lieutenant Powell called it small.[34] One kilometre south of Quatre Bras was Gemioncourt Farm, which consisted of several large brick buildings connected by a high brick wall.

The Fight at Quatre Bras: 06.30-18.00 Hours

Around 06.30 hours on 16 June, the Prince of Orange, commander of the 1st Corps, had arrived in Quatre Bras. As the senior officer present, he took command and begun placing the arriving Dutch troops. At first it was quiet, but as the morning wore on the advance elements of the French troops under Marshal Ney began skirmishing with the Dutch who were covering the approaches to Quatre Bras. Wellington arrived at 10.00 hours and checked out the Dutch positions. Around 11.00 hours he rode east for a meeting with Marshal Blücher at Brye. Marshal Ney was slow to move his forces toward Quatre Bras but by 14.00 hours, he had the 18,000 men of General Reille's 2nd Corps and General Adrien Wathiez's Brigade of lancers in position to attack the 8,000 troops of the Prince of Orange. Marshal Ney opened the battle by bombarding the

---

30. Gomm, p.353.
31. *Waterloo Letters*, p.246.
32. ibid, p.251.
33. Robinson, p.104.
34. *Waterloo Letters*, p.246 & 251.

Dutch positions and then sent in his infantry. Under heavy pressure from three French infantry divisions the Dutch began to move back after taking heavy casualties. They continued to defend the Bois de Bossu, but as the centre fell back towards Quatre Bras, the units in the woods also pulled back. Wellington, who at 14.00 hours was still in Byre 12km away, heard the artillery fire coming from the west and raced back to Quatre Bras. He arrived there by 14.30.

The first battalions of Lieutenant General Sir Thomas Picton's 5th Anglo-Hanoverian Division[35] began arriving around 15.00 hours and Wellington directed them into the positions that were most threatened. The fighting continued for an hour as both commanders continued to feed troops into the fight. The Black Brunswickers arrived about 15.30 and were placed between the Bois de Bossu and the Charleroi-Brussels road. About 16.30, Marshal Ney committed General Wathiez's Brigade of lancers, who charged General Pack's Brigade. The high crops concealed their approach until the last moment and they caught the British attempting to form into squares. The British were mauled and took heavy casualties.

The first British units of the 1st Corps, Lieutenant General Sir Charles Baron Alten's 3rd Anglo-Hanoverian Division,[36] began arriving in Quatre Bras around 17.00 hours. They deployed directly behind the Brunswickers and to the left of General Picton's 5th Anglo-Hanoverian Division. With their arrival, Wellington's forces out-numbered the French. But all was not lost for the French. Wellington's Army had been hit hard. On Wellington's left and in the centre, the Dutch units were spent and the 5th Anglo-Hanoverian Division had taken heavy casualties. On his right, General Prince Jérôme Bonaparte's 6th Division had battered the Brunswickers and almost cleared the Bois de Bossu. Backing up the Brunswickers was the 3rd Anglo-Hanoverian Division, but they were tired, having been up since 01.00 hours and had been marching most of the day. The fighting began to slowly die down until the arrival of the Guards Division.

---

35. The 5th Division consisted of Major General Sir James Kempt's 8th Brigade, the 9th Brigade commanded by Major General Sir Denis Pack, as well as Colonel Charles Best's 4th Hanoverian Brigade which was attached.
36. It consisted of Major General Sir Colin Halkett's 5th British Brigade, Colonel Christian Baron Ompteda's 2nd King's German Legion Brigade, and Major General Friedrich, Graf von Kielmansegge's 1st Hanoverian Brigade.

Chapter 7

16 June 1815
Quatre Bras

'Now men let us see what you are made of"
Captain Charles Dashwood Light Company 3rd Foot Guards[1]

Shortly after the division halted for the night 1km west of Nivelles, Colonel Felton Hervey, the AQMG assigned to the 1st Corps rode up and said that, 'the French were advancing and we were immediately to move up to the front, being at that time about 12 miles from the enemy.'[2] General Cooke responded immediately and ordered the division back on the road and to 'move with all speed as there was a severe action in which the Belgians had suffered considerably.'[3]

While the men of the 2nd Brigade were waiting to move the married men, whose wives had followed them on the march and 'were permitted to take farewell of them; they being ordered to the rear, and going a short distance apart from the throng; in the open field were joined by others, who delivered to them for security of their watches, with various other small articles they held in esteem, also others whose families were absent desired that their expressions of affection might be communicated to their absent wives and families; now the parting embrace although short was sincere and affectionate and expressed with deep emotions of grief as though a state of widowhood had suddenly come upon them, while the loud thunder of the destructive cannon was sounding in their ears.'[4]

---

1. Clay, p.8.
2. *Waterloo Archive*, Vol. 4, p.139.
3. ibid, Vol. 6, p.114.
4. Clay, p.7.

The troops moved out at 'Quick Pace', which was 108 paces a minute, and would allow them to cover 5km in an hour.[5] They were in high spirits even with the heat and not having the opportunity to eat. Ensign Richard Master of the 3rd Battalion 1st Foot Guards reported that they had no stragglers, despite having already marched 40km, and they began to sing. One of the songs they sang was, 'All the World's in Paris' sung to the tune of 'Yankee Doodle'.[6]

It wasn't long before they began to meet the wounded from the battle. Captain James Stanhope of the 3rd Battalion 1st Foot Guards reported that there were 'a good many wounded men going to the rear with ten times their number to take care of them, which did not strike me as a good specimen of the first trial of our allies. A little further on I met Colonel Dick of the 79th who was also wounded and who told me they had been rode in upon by the French cavalry and suffered dreadfully.'[7]

After marching 7km, a halt was made at Hautain-le-Val, about 8km from Quatre Bras to let stragglers catch up and for the artillery to move to the front of the column. The officers who were not riding with their companies were sent back to them and the men were ordered to 'untie ten rounds of ammunition[8]... to see the flints in order ... and fix bayonets.'[9] The new order of march was the artillery, the 1st Brigade's Light Companies under the command of Lord Saltoun, the 1st Brigade, and then the 2nd

---

5. Nafziger, p.297.
6. Master, p.138. Ensign Master records the words they were singing as 'Lunnon is out of town, the world in Paris', however there were two other versions of the song, 'The Corsican Drover' and 'Boney's Return to Paris' all with similar lyrics and sung to 'Yankee Doodle'. What he probably heard was:

London now is come to town,
Who in England tarries?
Who can bear to linger there,
When all the world's in Paris?

7. *Waterloo Archive*, Vol. 6, p.114. Captain Stanhope was mistaken about which regiment Brevet Lieutenant Colonel Robert Dick was in. He was wounded at Quatre Bras, but was in the 42nd Foot, not the 79th Foot.
8. A British infantryman carried sixty rounds of ammunition. These rounds came in packs of ten and were tied together. Thus the order to 'untie ten rounds of ammunition'.
9. *Waterloo Letters*, p.251.

Brigade. Many of the wounded continued to come down the road and among them was Major John Jessop of the 44th Foot, who was the AQMG for the 3rd Anglo-Hanoverian Division. He had been shot in the foot, but 'urged us to get on as the Action was going on badly'.[10]

The closer the division got to Quatre Bras the heavier the firing was. Ensign Robert Batty of the 3rd Battalion 1st Foot Guards wrote five days after the battle about the anxiety they felt about the approaching fight:

> We marched up towards the enemy, at each step hearing more clearly the fire of musquetry; and as we approached the field of action we met constantly waggons full of men, of all the various nations under the Duke's command, wounded in the most dreadful manner. The sides of the road had a heap of dying and dead, very many of whom were British: such a scene did, indeed, demand every better feeling of the mind to cope with its horrors.[11]

The time the Guards Division arrived at Quatre Bras is open to much confusion. Many sources give the time as 17.00 hours while an equal number state it was 18.00 hours. Ensign Charles Short, of the Coldstream Guards states that it was even later, not having arrived until 19.30 hours.[12] Several factors affected the speed of the march.

1. The men were tired, hot, and hungry. They had been up since 01.00 hours and had already marched 40km (twenty-five miles) through the heat of the day. They had not eaten since mid-morning.
2. The roads were crowded with the wounded leaving the battlefield. They would have to move out of the way for the column to pass them.
3. The column halted at Hautain-Le-Val to allow the artillery to move to the front of the column. Up until this point the artillery was at the rear of the column about 2km behind the lead battalion.

The infantry marched at 'Quick Pace' or 5km an hour. Because of the urgency for them to reach the battlefield, they might have been started out at even a faster pace, possibly 6.4km (four miles) per hour but it was unlikely they could have maintained that pace for any length of time

---

10. ibid.
11. Jones, George, *The Battle of Waterloo, with Those of Ligny and Quatre Bras, Described by Eye-Witnesses*. London: L. Booth, 1852, p.37.
12. *Waterloo Archive*, Vol. 4, p.14.

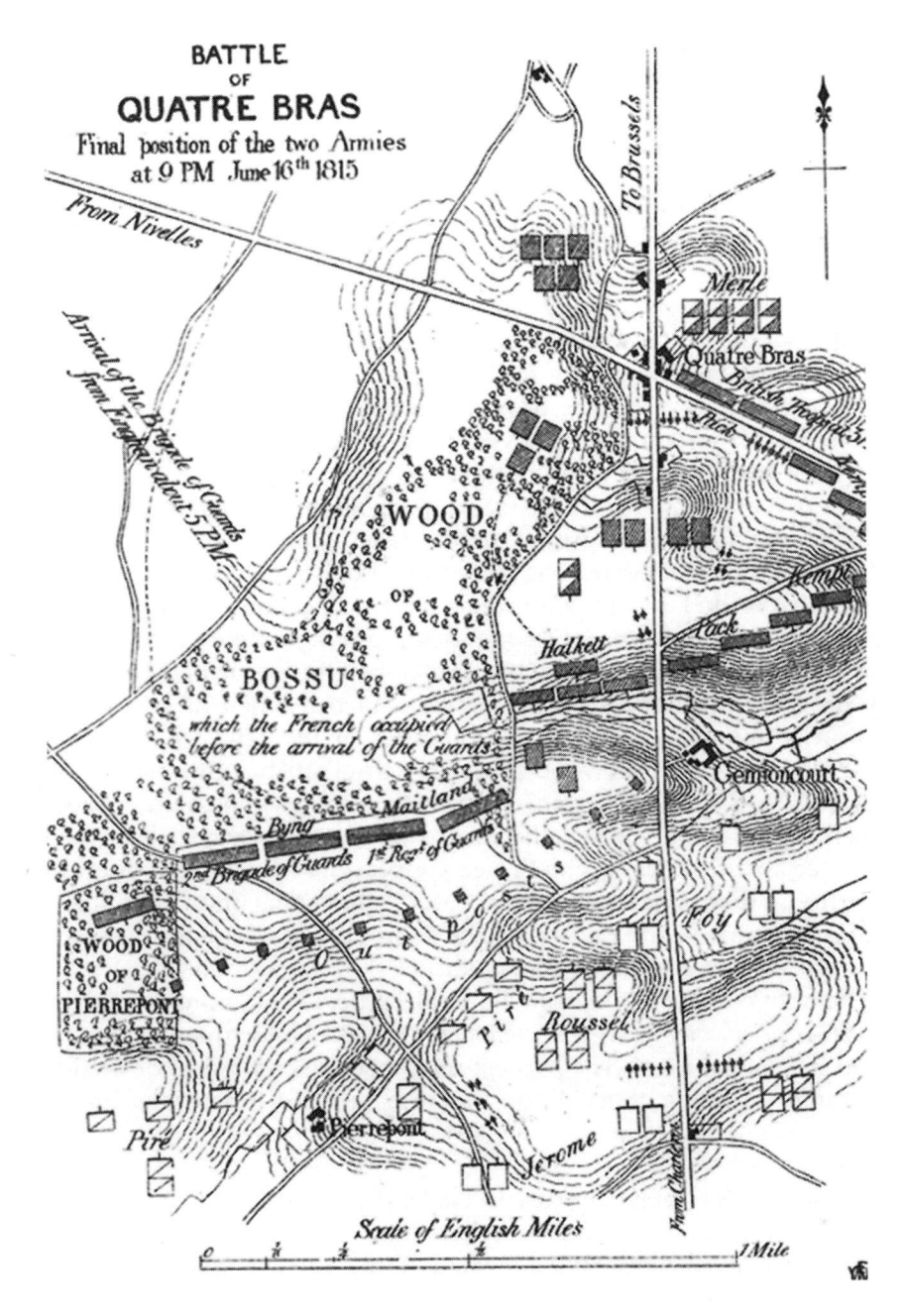

The Situation at Quatre Bras
Derived from a map in *The Origin and History of the First or Grenadier Guards*

because of the factors above. However, if they marched at Quick Pace for three hours, the earliest they would have arrived in Quatre Bras was 18.00 hours.

The division stopped before it reached the Bois de Bossu and began to prepare to go into battle. Although being told to hurry, General Cooke had not received any orders regarding where he was supposed to deploy on the battlefield. The Guardsmen took the time to check their equipment and fix bayonets. The officers dismounted and in the 3rd Battalion 1st Foot Guards, Ensign Richard Master, the senior ensign in the battalion, unsheathed the King's Colours, while Ensign James Butler did the same for the Regimental Colours.[13] As soldiers tend to do, two of Ensign Master's friends, lieutenants Thomas Brown and Edward Grose approached him, and said with an attempt at levity they 'would not give a 6d for your chance' of surviving the coming fight.[14]

The Advance Guard of the 1st Brigade, under the command of Lord Saltoun, was about 500m from Quatre Bras and almost to the outskirts of the Bois de Bossu. Legend has it that Lord Saltoun saw a finely dressed rider, surrounded by an entourage of officers, come galloping down the road from Quatre Bras. As the group got closer they recognized the commander of the 1st Corps, the Prince of Orange. It had been a long day for the Prince and he was less than tactful when he ordered Lord Saltoun to take his two Light Companies of the 1st Foot Guards into the western edge of the wood and drive the French southeast out of the woods. Allegedly Lord Saltoun, who was also tired, and could not see any French in the woods, asked the Prince where the French whom he was supposed to attack were. The Prince supposedly lost his temper and told him: 'If you do not like to undertake it, I'll find some one who will.' Lord Saltoun remained calm and asked the Prince again where the enemy was. This time he received better information.[15]

The above anecdote is from General Frederick Hamilton's *The Origin and History of the First or Grenadier Guards*. Unfortunately, he never stated his source for it. The earliest reference we could find of the Prince of Orange ordering the Guards into the Bois de Bossu was on pages

---

13. Master, p.138. Each company in the 1st Foot Guards had a set of King's Colours. During the Waterloo Campaign, the 3rd Battalion carried the 1807 Major's Colour. What Ensign Butler carried for the Regimental Colour is unknown.
14. ibid.
15. Hamilton, Vol. 3, pp.17-18.

153-154 in Volume 1 of Captain William Siborne's *History of the War in France and Belgium in 1815*, which was first published in 1844. But like General Hamilton, Captain Siborne never stated where he obtained the information. Few eyewitnesses state it was the Prince of Orange who gave the order. It is possible that the Prince of Orange did give the order, however, it was more likely relayed to General Maitland by Colonel Hon. Alexander Abercromby of the 2nd Battalion Coldstream Guards who was serving as the AQMG of the 1st Corps. Captain James Stanhope, left the only known account of the order being given. But even he got it incorrect, when he wrote:

> We had hardly arrived opposite of the wood when Colonel Abercromby Quarter Master General of the 1st Corps rode up to us in great haste & said 'The French are close to you, a battalion must go into the wood and happen what will you must maintain it'. The 2nd Battalion wheeled into line, entered the wood and in an instant were engaged & we followed also in line.[16]

Regardless of who gave the order, Lord Saltoun quickly deployed his two companies into the woods. It did not take long for the 200 men of the 1st Foot Guards to find the French. The woods were swarming with the six voltigeur companies of the 1st and 2nd Line Infantry regiments of General Jean-Louis Soye's Brigade of the French 6th Division, which was commanded by Napoleon's brother, General Prince Jérôme Bonaparte. Supporting them were the three voltigeur companies of the 3rd Line Infantry Regiment and the six companies of the 2nd Battalion of the 1st Light Infantry Regiment, both from General Pierre-François Bauduin's Brigade, also of the 6th Division. There were about 1,000 French light troops in the woods.[17] General Maitland, the commander of the 1st Brigade of the Guards Division, quickly found that his light infantrymen had bitten off more than they could chew. He decided to reinforce the outnumbered light troops by sending in the rest of the 2nd Battalion 1st Foot Guards. The heavy underbrush and numerous trees would limit the effectiveness of advancing in the normal two-rank line that British infantry usually fought in. So instead of forming the battalion into a line and advancing it into the woods, he began to feed two companies at a time into the melee.

---

16. Stanhope, p.172.
17. Field, Andrew, *Prelude to Waterloo: Quatre Bras-The French Perspective.* Barnsley: Pen & Sword, 2014, pp.131-132.

While they were waiting for their turn to go in, the officers and men started seeing the wounded filtering out through the woods. This had to be unnerving for some of the young officers who were in combat for the first time. Ensign Hon. Samuel Barrington, who was just seventeen, turned to his friend, sixteen-year-old Ensign Thomas Croft and said to him, 'Croft we are likely to have warm work, suppose you and I say our prayers.' They left the line for a few minutes and found a quiet area and prayed together. Shortly afterwards they went into the fight with their company.[18] Eventually the whole 2nd Battalion was fighting in the woods. The soldiers were enthusiastic about attacking but the fatigue from being up since three hours before dawn[19] and having marched over 50km began to become a major factor. Soon they began to fall out, too exhausted to move on. As they laid there, they cheered on their friends as they moved through the woods.[20]

Soon it was the 3rd Battalion's turn and General Maitland ordered them to enter the woods to support the 2nd Battalion on their right. He rode with them as they advanced. Because of the thickness of the woods and the piecemeal commitment of the forces, the fight quickly disintegrated into company and smaller firefights between the Guardsmen and the French. Ensign Robert Batty, who at the age of twenty-five was the oldest ensign in the division, wrote shortly after the battle: 'The trees were so thick, that it was beyond any thing difficult to effect a passage. As we approached, we saw the Enemy behind, taking aim at us: they contested every bush, and at a small rivulet [the Gemioncourt Stream] running through the wood, they attempted a stand but could not resist us.'[21]

The fighting was intense, and all cohesion was lost. The companies who went into the battle after Lord Saltoun's companies started fighting, lost touch with them and were not able to determine where they were located. It became very difficult to distinguish between friend and foe. The newly arriving companies heard firing to their front and assumed it was the French. Lord Saltoun began to take so many casualties from this friendly fire that he sent Lieutenant Charles Ellis to the rear to let them know they were shooting at their own troops. Lieutenant Ellis was unsuccessful in his mission and the Light Companies continued to be shot

---

18. *Waterloo Archive*, Vol. 4, p.139.
19. Dawn on 16 June was at 03.45 hours, *Sunrise and Sunset Calculator*
20. Near Observer. *The Battle of Waterloo Containing the Series of Accounts Published by Authority, British and Foreign*. London: J. Booth, 1815, p.52.
21. ibid.

by their friends until they reached the far side of the woods and the firing died down.[22]

In Captain Milnes's Light Company of the 2nd Battalion, a small group of soldiers led by Corporal Philip Hogg was surrounded. They fought hard and four of them, all wounded, were taken prisoner. Corporal Philip Hogg and Privates James Crofts, John Delbridge, and John Ford were initially listed as killed, but were eventually returned to their battalion. Private John Hood, also of Captain Milnes's company, may have been part of this group. He was initially listed as missing, but he never returned and his status was changed to killed.[23]

At times the fighting turned vicious and neither quarter was given nor received. Sergeant Charles Wood, the Colour Sergeant who stood next to Ensign Master as he carried the King's Colours of the 3rd Battalion into the fight reported that the 'French behaved very ill to our prisoners. ... several of our wounded the blood thirsty cowards ran through with their bayonets and swords.'[24] Sergeant Wood also wrote of a rumour that one French officer who was wounded and, 'unable to make his escape, he ripped out his bowels with his own sword, and beat his head on a gate rather than be taken prisoner.'[25]

Yet there were some humourous moments during the fighting. Ensign St. John of the 2nd Battalion reported that: 'A sergeant of the French came up with his bayonet fixed to one of our officers[26] who is a very little fellow & told him that he must surrender himself prisoner, no says our officer, you forget that you are a Frenchmen and I an Englishman, so you are my prisoner, "*Eh bien*", says the Frenchman "*Chacun son lot, et je me rends votre prisonnier*".'[27]

Drummer William Blake, who enlisted in 1807 at the age of nineteen, was assigned to Captain Miller's Company of the 3rd Battalion. After eight years of service he was the senior drummer in the battalion and thus the battalion's drum major.[28] Even though he was with the battalion headquarters group, he too was in the thick of the fighting. He wrote: 'our

---

22. *Waterloo Letters*, p.279.
23. Chambers, Vol. 1, pp.241, 265, 314, 403 & 410.
24. *Waterloo Archive*, Vol. 6, p.131.
25. ibid.
26. Unfortunately, Ensign St. John did not say which officer had been captured.
27. *Waterloo Archive*, Vol. 6, pp.106-107.
28. Chambers, Vol. 1, p.142.

regiment marched into the wood without the slightest suspicion, when we were attacked on all sides by the enemy who had lain in the ditches on each side of the wood where hundreds of brave fellows fell without an opportunity of defending themselves.'[29]

Even with their heavy casualties the overwhelming numbers of the British began to tell, and the French began to slowly withdraw south through the woods. After an hour of fighting, the Guards reached the southern edge of the woods. They were still disordered and more of a mob than a formation. General Maitland and his officers quickly tried to get them into some semblance of order. On the brigade's extreme left were remnants of Lord Saltoun's two companies. In the middle was the 2nd Battalion and on the right was the 3rd Battalion. The two battalions soon attracted the attention of two French guns on a hill about 300m to their front and three battalions of French infantry in the woods on their flank.[30] The enemy fire got to be so heavy that General Maitland ordered them to retreat into the woods back to the Odomiant Stream. Lieutenant Henry Powell of the 2nd Battalion's Grenadier Company found that even though they were no longer visible to the French gunners, they continued to fire into the woods and a 'great many men were killed and wounded by the heads of the trees falling on them as cut off by cannon shot.'[31] Even after being almost an hour under heavy fire, some officers were still mounted. Captain James Stanhope was thrown from his horse when a branch that was knocked from a tree by a cannonball landed on it.[32]

The division's artillery, which led it during the last 7km of the road march, had just halted near the Bois de Bossu when a staff officer hurried up. Captain Charles Sandham and his six guns were ordered to continue down the road and stop in fields to the northwest of Quatre Bras. They would be part of the reserve and see little action. Captain Henry Kuhlmann and the six guns of his King's German Legion Horse Artillery were sent into Quatre Bras. A section of two guns under the command of 1st Lieutenant Theodore Speckmann were sent about 250m south of Quatre Bras and just north of La Bergerie Farm,[33] while the other four guns went with Captain

---

29. Fletcher, Ian and Pouler, Ron, *'Gentlemen's Sons' the Guards in the Peninsula and Waterloo, 1808-1815.* Tunbridge Wells: Spellmount, 1992, p.197.
30. *Waterloo Archive*, Vol. 4, pp.131-132.
31. *Waterloo Letters*, p.251.
32. *Waterloo Archive*, Vol. I, p.133.
33. Some British sources refer to this farm as the Quatre Bras farm.

16 JUNE 1815 QUATRE BRAS

Kuhlmann about 700m to the east along the road to Namur. Lieutenant Speckmann's guns were positioned to enfilade any force moving up the road.[34] To the immediate left of his two guns was Lieutenant Colonel Ludwig von Ramdohr's Luneburg Landwehr Battalion of Colonel Charles Best's 4th Hanoverian Brigade that had been attached to General Picton's 5th Anglo-Hanoverian Division. The guns would spend the next thirty minutes firing at the French artillery 1km to the south.[35]

After the 1st Brigade deployed into the Bois de Bossu, the 2nd Brigade was ordered to continue to march towards Quatre Bras. It stopped short of the town and moved into the fields north of the Nivelles Road. Around 19.00 hours, the Light Companies of the 2nd Brigade under the command of Captain James Macdonell were given orders to go through Quatre Bras and move south along the road to Charleroi towards the Gemioncourt Farm, about 1200m south of the crossroads. While they were moving through Quatre Bras, they came under fire from the enemy guns. Captain Macdonell moved them into a farmyard to avoid the enemy fire. In this farmyard were the bodies of French cavalry troopers. While there the two guns from Captain Kuhlmann's Horse Artillery Troop moved past them.[36]

Before Captain Macdonell's Light Companies could move from the protection of the farm, French cavalry attacked the British lines in front of them. In a final effort to break Wellington's line, Marshal Ney ordered General François Kellermann to have the recently arrived cuirassiers of General François Guiton's Brigade charge the Brunswickers and the 3rd Anglo-Hanoverian Division which were deployed on either side of the Charleroi Road, about 400m south of the crossroads. The cuirassiers broke the 33rd Foot and the 2nd Battalion 69th Foot of General Halkett's Brigade and forced the rest of the battalions into squares or to flee into the Bois de Bossu.

The lead squadron of the 11th Cuirassiers saw the two 9-pounder guns of Captain Kuhlmann's troop sitting in the open and continued their charge. The gunners stood by their guns and fired canister at the threatening cuirassiers. To the left of the two guns was the Luneburg Landwehr Battalion, which was standing in a ditch that had once been held by the 1st Battalion 92nd Foot. Instead of trying to form square the battalion held its fire until the last moment. The heavy fire from the

---

34. Siborne, William, *History of the Waterloo Campaign*. London: Greenhill, 1990, p.181.
35. *Waterloo Archive*, Vol. 2, pp.42 & 119.
36. Clay, p.7-8.

artillery and muskets inflicted many casualties and broke the charge of the cuirassiers. The survivors quickly retreated leaving behind their dead and wounded, some within a handful of paces of the guns and infantry.[37]

Once the cuirassiers had cleared out, Lieutenant Speckmann's two 9-pounder guns were joined by their commander, Captain Kuhlmann, who brought with him two more guns. He had just received orders to wait until Captain Macdonell and his light troops arrived as support and to move four of his guns south to the west side of the Charleroi Road and just north of the Gemioncourt Stream. At the same time, Captain Macdonell began moving his two companies out of the farmyard. Private Clay and his company[38] passed 'singly through a gap in the hedge, at the extremity of the garden nearest the enemy, we immediately formed in the field into which we had entered.'[39] The two companies marched south over a

> considerable distance through the rye (that was trampled down) and passed over numerous bodies of the slain, more particularly near to a fence enclosing a house and garden,[40] which clearly shewed there had been a very severe contest for the possession of it: (I particularly noticed a young officer of the 33rd Regiment laying among the slain, his bright scarlet coat and silver lace attracted my attention when marching over his headless body), for the most part English, Brunswickers, and Highlanders, more especially of the latter; we halted for a short time whilst our brigade of guns which, a little further to the left exchanged shots with the enemy.

While they were waiting, Captain Charles Dashwood, the commander of Private Clay's light company, moved through the line and stood in front of his and told them, 'Now men let us see what you are made of.'[41]

By 19.30 hours, General Maitland had finally got his brigade under control and into a line. To help replace some of his casualties, he took survivors of the 33rd and 92nd Foot who had fled from the French cuirassiers into the woods and placed them in the 2nd Battalion's line.[42]

---

37. *Waterloo Archive*, Vol.2, pp.43 & 119.
38. The Light Company of the 2nd Battalion 3rd Foot Guards
39. Clay, p.8.
40. La Bergerie Farm.
41. Clay, p.8.
42. Robinson, p.346; *Waterloo Letters*, p.252.

Although the French skirmishers had been pushed out of the woods, as soon as the Guards retreated to the safety of the Gemioncourt stream to reform, the French voltigeurs returned and brought them under fire. The brigade also continued to receive fire from their right front from two French guns and three battalions of French infantry. Towards the 1st Brigade's left were another two French Infantry battalions. General Maitland decided to once again clear the woods of the French, but also to force their guns and battalions away from the Charleroi Road.[43]

The Guards immediately came under heavy fire from the French artillery and the five battalions that opposed them. They made multiple attacks on the guns to force them back, but to no avail. Captain Stanhope wrote that the brigade 'suffered severely from the fire of the enemy's grape and round shot from a battery on the hill and still more from partial and I think imprudent attempts to attack it. We should have contented ourselves with maintaining the wood and covering our men. It was an unpleasant sort of battle, for we were very much in air and only supported by one battalion and if the French had moved a strong column round our right we should have been very uncomfortably situated.'[44] It was during this fighting Major Henry Askew was severely wounded and had to be evacuated to the rear.

Around 20.00 hours Marshal Ney made one final effort to break the British line. He sent forward General Cyrille Picquet's 2nd and 7th Dragoons, which were supported by lancers. What lancer regiments they were is unknown. Some sources state it was the 2nd Lancer Regiment of the Imperial Guard[45] while others state that it was 5th and 6th Lancers from General Wathiez's Brigade.[46] The dragoons attacked north up the Charleroi Road while the lancers charged the Guards. Rather than attempting to form square the Guards ran back to the road. The 2nd Battalion stopped at the sunken wood and formed into a line, while the 3rd Battalion and Lord Saltoun's two companies ran further into the trees. The 2nd Brunswick Line Battalion, which was to the left of the brigade, formed square instead.

Lieutenant Powell of the 2nd Battalion wrote in his journal that: 'The hollow way now covered us from the Cavalry, and from it the men threw in so destructive a fire as to nearly annihilate them, whilst the Brunswickers

---

43. *Waterloo Archive*; Vol. 4, pp.131-132.
44. Stanhope, p.173.
45. Dawson, Paul L., *Au Pas de Charge! Napoleon's Cavalry at Waterloo*. Stockton-on-Tees: Black Tent, 2015, p.85.
46. Field, *Prelude to Waterloo*, p.148.

(whose front became uncovered by our retreat into the wood) formed square beautifully, and did their part most effectively in their destruction.'[47]

The trees and underbrush prevented the lancers from catching the rest of the brigade and soon they retreated. But the Guards were not out of danger. Following closely behind the lancers as they went into the woods were a swarm of French skirmishers and the French artillery fire resumed. The 2nd Battalion, was protected by the sunken road, however the 3rd Battalion and Lord Saltoun's men were exposed. Major William Stuart, the commander of the 3rd Battalion was seriously wounded, and Private Swann of Captain William Miller's company of the 3rd Battalion was knocked down by a musket ball that went through his knapsack and blanket and grazed his shoulder. He continued to fight. After the lancers retreated, Captain Miller ran forward to mark the position where he wanted his company to form on. Private Swann was on the very left of the line when the captain, who was standing next to him, was shot and was sent to the rear.[48]

Captain Stanhope, who was behind Captain Miller's company saw an officer being carried in a blanket by several soldiers. He asked the soldiers who it was and Captain Miller, who was still conscious, called him over and 'embraced me and bade me an affectionate farewell.'[49] The small party soon came to the battalion's colours and Captain Miller asked that the colours of the battalion be brought to him because he would 'like to see the colours of the Regiment before I quit them for ever.'[50]

In the centre of the line Lord Saltoun's men were firing at the French when General Maitland and his ADC, Ensign James Lord Hay of the 3rd Battalion 1st Foot Guards rode up. The seventeen-year-old Lord Hay, was the oldest son of the 16th Earl of Errol. He was a superb rider and during the battle rode a horse called Abelard. Having come straight from the Duchess of Richmond's Ball he still wore his dress uniform. As General Maitland was talking to Lord Saltoun, a French skirmisher fired at their party, killing Lord Hay. The young ensign fell across Lord Saltoun's horse and then on to the ground. One of the British light infantrymen saw who shot the young lord

---

47. *Waterloo Letters*, p.252.
48. *Waterloo Archive*, Vol. 4, p.141.
49. ibid, Vol. 6, p.116.
50. Jones, p.292 Captain Miller's death notice stated that: 'He sent for Col. Thomas, and said, "I feel I am mortally wounded; but I am pleased to think it is my fate rather than yours, whose life is involved in that of your young wife."' Captain Stanhope never mentioned Thomas being there.

and shot him in return. Afterwards there was speculation that the French skirmisher saw the ensign in his finery, mistook him for a senior officer, and shot him instead of General Maitland and Lord Saltoun. Lord Hay had a premonition of his impending death. At the ball the night before, he approached his friend, the fifteen-year-old Lord William Lennox,[51] and told him that he would be killed during his first battle. Furthermore, he believed that his body would never be found and all his personal possessions would be lost. Lord Hay gave Lennox a gold chain to give to a young woman with whom he was enamoured and his sword and sash to give to his family.[52]

While the 1st Brigade was fighting the French lancers, the two light companies of the 2nd Brigade formed a square with their officers in the centre because of the danger of being charged by the French dragoons. Although the French cavalry eventually withdrew they still remain close enough to be a threat. Captain Macdonell kept his two companies in a square and manoeuvred them closer to the Bois de Bossu. Private Clay noted with pride that:

> The enemy's artillery would alternately annoy us with their shells which were skilfully [sic] directed, but were equally skilfully [sic] avoided, through the tact of our commander. ... we escaped the destructive effects of the well directed shells of the enemy, who no doubt having observed our repeated escapes from the galling fire of their artillery. Their cavalry now menaced us more daringly and prevented our taking fresh ground until their artillery had thrown their shells amongst us, by this means we had a more narrow escape than before, being compelled to remain longer in our position to resist cavalry. I being one of the outward rank of the square, can testify as to the correct aim of the enemy, whose shells having fallen to the ground and exploded within a few paces of the rank in which I was kneeling, a portion of their destructive fragments in their ascent passing between my head and that of my comrade next in rank; its force and tremulous sound causing an unconscious movement of the head not to be forgotten in haste.[53]

---

51. Lennox had been General Maitland's extra-ADC until April, when he seriously injured himself from a fall from his horse. See Chapter 5 for more details.
52. Hamilton, Vol. 3, p.23; Fraser, Vol. 1, p.258; Lennox, Vol. 1, pp.246-247.
53. Clay, pp.9-10.

Although under artillery fire for almost an hour, the 2nd Brigade's Light Companies took few casualties. Private Clay attributes this to his commander, Captain Macdonell, who remained mounted on his horse in the middle of the square and 'could undoubtedly from his elevated position distinctly see the preparation of the enemy for the renewal of attack on us by the united force of the infantry, cavalry, and artillery being foiled by the timely movements of our square ever obedient to the commander.'[54]

By 22.00 hours, night began to fall and the sporadic firing between the two forces slowly died down. Despite his prayers, Ensign Barrington was shot through the head and died a few moments before all firing ceased.[55]

---

54. ibid.
55. *Waterloo Archive*, Vol. 4 pp.137 & 140.

Chapter 8

17 June 1815
The Retreat to Waterloo

The fighting eventually tapered off as the French pulled back from the Bois de Bossu. Their campfires could be seen on a ridgeline about 1km south of the woods. The 1st Brigade was exhausted but still sent out picquets to guard against a surprise attack.[1] About 23.00 hours the 2nd Brigade moved up through the woods and relieved the 1st Brigade. The men of the 1st Foot Guards went back through the woods where they had fought for four hours and then camped in the fields on the other side.[2] The 1st Brigade's picquets were replaced by those of the Coldstream Guards and the 3rd Foot Guards. The 2nd Brigade's Light Companies, under the command of Captain Macdonell, also had to provide picquets even though they had been fighting for several hours. This caused a bit of resentment for Ensign George Standen of the 3rd Foot Guards who felt he and his men had done enough that day.[3]

Seventeen-year-old Ensign Charles Short of the Coldstream Guards, was nervous when he was given the outpost duty for his battalion. He had only been in the Army for eight months and it would be the first time he might be in combat. He and his men were on their own in the forward outposts and he had no senior officer he could turn to for advice. He wrote to his mother a few days later that: 'I kept a sharp look out and did the best I could by placing my sentries to give the alarm in case any attack should be made. The night, however, passed off very well.'[4] He might

---

1. *Waterloo Archive*, Vol. 4, p.140.
2. *Waterloo Letters*, p.252.
3. ibid, p.279.
4. *Waterloo Archive*, Vol. 4, p146.

have been trying to reassure his mother that he had not been in much danger, however, Ensign Standen wrote that the French would fire at them throughout the night, whenever they heard movement coming from the British lines.[5] This caused several casualties among the British.[6]

The woods and fields were covered with the dead and wounded of both armies. Throughout the night, the quiet was broken by the moans, screams, and crying of those who were too seriously wounded to make their way on their own to the aid stations behind their lines. The wounded were not only from the British, but from French, Dutch, Nassau, and Brunswick soldiers who had fallen there before the Guards arrived. Private Clay of the 3rd Foot Guards Light Company was manning a two man post on a picquet line. Both he and his friend had been out of water for some time and were quite thirsty. The cries of the wounded for help and also for water reminded them of how thirsty they were. The other soldier, who was older than the twenty-year-old Clay, suggested he would keep watch, while Clay went and found water:

> I went (in the dark) in search of water – having groped my way about among the sufferers and placed them in as easy a position as I could; many having fallen in very uneasy postures, and being altogether helpless, increased their sufferings – some having fallen with their legs doubled under them, others, with the weight of the dead upon them, and the like – having afforded them all the ease that lay in my power, and all being quiet around us, and taking a camp kettle from off the knapsack of a dead man, wended my way a short distance to the rear of our posts, (where I had observed the appearance of water when advancing after the enemy on the afternoon previous,) and finding a narrow channel of water in a ditch, which I traced into the wood, (from where our brave comrades the 1st Guards had driven the enemy in the evening) – there was a pond from which I filled my kettle and drank freely from its contents, enjoying it much, whilst in the dark I found my way back to my post, where my comrade and the poor sufferers from wounds gladly partook of the contents of the same.[7]

---

5. *Waterloo Letters*, p.279.
6. Clay, p.11.
7. ibid, pp.10 – 11.

Private Clay eventually returned to his position and stayed there until,

> just before the dawn of morning,[8] my comrade wished me to go again for water, which I did; on my arriving at the pond, the light of day just enabled me to see that in and around lay the bodies of those who had fallen in combat in the evening previous, and the liquid we had partaken of was dyed with their blood, for so I saw the remainder. I do not remember whether I returned with a further supply, although I am quite aware that I lost all relish for any more of it; having hastened back to my post being just in time to fall in and stand in column as the light disclosed us to the view of the enemy.[9]

Ensign Short was also relieved of his outpost duties about this time. He went back to his company and slept.[10]

The sight that greeted the soldiers when the sun finally rose was ghastly. Private Clay reported that the 2nd Brigade's Light Company occupied the ground 'where the Grenadier Guards met with such a severe reception from the enemy, when in pursuit of them from the wood on entering the corn field; on the slope from the field to the hollow track within the wood, the dead bodies of the same regiment were laying very thick on the ground.'[11]

After the morning stand-to,[12] the 1st Brigade began to realize how bad the fighting was the previous day. Casualties were quite heavy and because the fight covered almost a km of woods the number of killed and wounded was not known. A roll call was done to see who was still present. The full extent of their casualties became apparent. Lieutenant Henry Powell, who was the temporary commander of the Grenadier Company, reported that he could only muster forty-three men out of the eighty-four who left Enghien the night before.[13] Many were listed as missing or

---

8. According Paul Dawson in *Au Pas de Charge!* Sunrise on 17 June 1815 was at 03.57 hours. Dawson, p.12.
9. Clay, pp.10-11.
10. *Waterloo Archive*, Vol. 4, p.146.
11. Clay, p.12.
12. Stand-to is the period when units are formed up and ready to fight in case the enemy uses the cover of night to attack them at dawn. Units would stay in formation, 'Until you can see a white horse a mile off.' Surtees, William. *Twenty-five Years in the Rifle Brigade*. London: Greenhill, 1996, p.13.
13. Unpublished letter to Sir Henry Martin dated 20 June 1815.

captured, but their true status was unknown. Parties were sent out to find their wounded and have them collected in one spot, 'with the blankets of the dead (made into a sort of bed) under the shade of the trees in the wood, in the hope of their being safely taken to the hospital.'[14]

While the sergeants supervised the finding and gathering of the wounded, the officers went looking for their fellow officers who were missing. Ensigns Charles Lake and David Baird of the 3rd Foot Guards found the body of Lord Hay, lying bootless and wearing blue striped stockings, having come straight from the Duchess of Richmond's Ball without having the time to change them.[15] Ensign Samuel Barrington's body was recovered but not before scavengers stripped it of valuables. His sword was missing, but the thieves did not take his sash.[16] Lieutenants Edward Grose and Thomas Brown, who had jokingly told Ensign Master that he no chance of surviving the battle, unwittingly predicted their own demise. Both were killed, while Ensign Master came through the battle unscathed.

The four 1st Foot Guards officers who were killed were buried under a hollow oak, 'the largest tree on the right of the wood nearest towards Nivelles.'[17] Captain James Stanhope of the 3rd Battalion reflected afterwards that: 'There is nothing more awfully impressive than this sublime service, affecting at all times, at a moment when the bearers feel the decisive hour is not yet come, when the enemy is still marshalled before their eyes and when perhaps before one night has passed, they may themselves require the aid, their affection and piety are now bestowing on their friends.'[18]

No effort was made to bury the dead enlisted soldiers.

In addition to the four officers killed, the brigade had another thirteen officers wounded, eleven so severely they were sent to the rear. In the 2nd Battalion, besides its commander, Ensign George Fludyer was severely wounded, as well as Ensign Thomas Croft who was shot in the foot. Lieutenant James Simpson the acting commander of Captain Barclay's company was also severely wounded. Lieutenant James Nixon, the acting commander of Captain Somerset's company, was slightly wounded by a contusion in the instep of his right foot and was cut by the bayonet of one of his soldiers. Lieutenant Francis Luttrell was also slightly wounded, but

---

14. Clay, p.12.
15. Lake, p.67.
16. *Waterloo Archive*, Vol. 4, p.135.
17. ibid, Vol. 6, p.116; *Waterloo Letters*, pp.252-253.
18. *Waterloo Archive*, Vol. 6, p.116.

the extent of his wound was unknown. Both of these lieutenants would continue to serve with their companies in the coming days.

The 3rd Battalion also had its commander wounded, as well as six other officers. Captain William Miller, who asked to see the battalion's colours, survived the night and was sent to Brussels. Lieutenant Robert Adair of Captain Stables's company was hit by a cannonball which shattered his thigh. Legend has it that the battalion's assistant surgeon did a field amputation that night:

> His sufferings during the amputation were dreadful; the shot had torn away the flesh of the thigh, and the bones were sticking up near the hip in splinters. The surgeon, Mr. [Frederick] Gilder, had much difficulty in using his knife, having blunted it, and all his other instruments, by amputations in the earlier part of the battle. Poor Adair during the operation had sufficient pluck to make one last ghastly joke, saying, 'Take your time, Mr. Carver.'[19]

Captain Horatio Townshend and Lieutenant Thomas Streatfield, both of the Grenadier Company, were severely wounded, as well as Lieutenant Charles Ellis of the Light Company and Ensign William Barton of Captain D'Oyly's company.

Lieutenant Colonel Henry Hardinge of the 2nd Battalion, was not at Quatre Bras. He was attached to the Prussian Army as a liaison officer. He was severely wounded at the battle of Ligny the same day. His left hand was amputated and after the surgery he laid 'in a wretched hut with his amputated left hand lying by his side'.[20]

The number of casualties among the enlisted soldiers was very heavy. In the 1st Foot Guards, the 2nd Battalion lost Sergeant John Ford of Captain Francis D'Oyly's company, two corporals, and twenty-three privates killed.[21] Another ten privates were listed as missing.[22] Appendix VIII provides the names of every officer and soldier from the 2nd Battalion who died at Quatre Bras. According to this list the number of sergeants

---

19. Gronow, Vol. 2, p.22. This story was told by Ensign Rees Gronow, who did not join the battalion until the next day.
20. Dalton, p.101. Lieutenant Colonel Hardinge had local rank of brigadier general, while he was serving as the liaison to the Prussian Army.
21. The official returns give the 2nd Battalion's killed as one sergeant and twenty-two rank and file. *The London Gazette*, 8 July 1815, p.1358.
22. The ten missing soldiers would eventually be listed as killed.

and other ranks who died was forty-five. The number of wounded is open to some debate. A return was submitted by the battalion on the morning of 18 June which listed eight sergeants, one drummer, and 276 other ranks as 'Sick Absent', for a total of 285 not present with the colours.[23] This figure includes all soldiers who were in the hospital for any reason. It would include those who were too sick or injured to march when the battalion left Enghien, soldiers who fell out from the march due to exhaustion, sunstroke, or injury, as well as the wounded. The official numbers reported by Wellington on 30 June, gave the number as six sergeants, 250 rank and file wounded.[24] In her exhaustive study of the 1st Foot Guards in the Waterloo Campaign, Barbara Chambers provides a named listing of the wounded and gives the number at four sergeants, nine corporals, and eighty-five privates for a total of ninety-eight wounded.[25]

In the 3rd Battalion 1st Foot Guards, Sergeant Benjamin Verity, a nineteen-year veteran, was killed as well as two corporals, a drummer, and sixteen privates.[26] Appendix VIII lists the name of every officer and soldier from the 3rd Battalion who died at Quatre Bras. According to this list the number of sergeants and other ranks who died was thirty-five. Like the 2nd Battalion, none of the sources agree on how many wounded the battalion had. A return was submitted by the battalion on the morning of 18 June listed eight sergeants, two drummers, and 255 other ranks as 'Sick Absent', for a total of 265 not present with the colours.[27] Wellington's Dispatch of 30 June 1815 gave the number of wounded as nine sergeants, one drummer, and 225 rank and file for a total of 235.[28] Barbara Chambers has identified by name 124 enlisted men wounded: six sergeants, seven corporals, one drummer, and 110 privates.[29]

---

23. Wellington, Duke of, *The Dispatches of Field Marshal the Duke of Wellington ...* Edited by Lt.-Col. John Gurwood. London: John Murray; 1834-9. Vol. 12, p.486.
24. *The London Gazette*, 8 July 1815, p.1358.
25. Chambers, Vols. 1 and 2
26. The official returns give the 3rd Battalion's killed as two sergeants, one drummer, and seventeen rank and file; *The London Gazette*, 8 July 1815, p.1358.
27. Wellington, Duke of, *The Dispatches of Field Marshal the Duke of Wellington ...* Vol. 12, p.486.
28. *The London Gazette*, 8 July 1815, p.1358.
29. Chambers, Vols. 1 and 2.

No killed or wounded were reported by the 2nd Battalion Coldstream Guards. The 2nd Battalion 3rd Foot Guards reported seven rank and file wounded.[30]

Most of the soldiers were hungry and thirsty, not having eaten since they stopped in Braine-le-Comte the morning before. What water could be found in the streams and ponds was often contaminated with blood. After the fighting had died down, Ensign Master was fortunate to be standing with his friend Ensign Pardoe, when much to their surprise, his corporal 'arrives, presenting me his shako full, saying "here Sir, is water; I fetched it for you a mile off."'[31] Ensign Short after coming off picquet duty woke up about 05.30 and was happy to find that his servant Whittaker, who was with the battalion's baggage in the rear, had sent him bread, meat, and brandy.[32] Some of the men in the Light Company of the Coldstream Guards were still in their outposts when one of their wives found them, 'having fearlessly passed over the slain bringing a supply of provisions for her husband and companions'.[33] Even the senior officers were not immune to hunger. Major Hepburn, commander of the 2nd Battalion 3rd Foot Guards had no food. He ended up asking Ensigns Lake and Baird if they had any. Baird gave him the last of their food to him, a bologna sausage.[34]

Many of horses of the slain French lancers were still in the woods and those Guards officers, who had lost their mounts, took them as replacements.[35]

Both battalions of the 1st Foot Guards had lost their commanders. Major Askew of the 2nd Battalion was evacuated to Brussels and was replaced by the senior company commander, Captain Richard Cooke of the Grenadier Company. His company was taken over by Lieutenant Henry Powell, who commanded it when Captain Cooke was the acting major. Captain Edward Stables, took command of the 3rd Battalion, after its commander, Major Stuart, was wounded in the arm. After the death of Lord Hay, General Maitland needed a new ADC and chose Ensign Seymour Bathurst of the 2nd Battalion.

---

30. *The London Gazette*, 8 July 1815, p.1358.
31. Master, p.138.
32. *Waterloo Archive*, Vol. 4, p.146.
33. Clay, p.7.
34. Lake, p.67.
35. *Waterloo Letters*, p.252.

After the officers were buried and the wounded were cared for, the officers and men waited for orders on what to do next. Captain Stanhope of the 3rd Battalion 1st Foot Guards took the opportunity to ride around the other parts of the battlefield. He later wrote:

> The highlanders were cut up from having been too slow in throwing themselves into squares. As I passed the spot where a heap of the French cuirassiers were laying, a figure covered and clotted with blood so that his face was indistinguishable rose up from the heap and with a swift but staggering pace went across the country towards the Guards. I returned and sent 2 drummers after him, but he was too far and the retreat commenced. I never knew who he was or heard of him more, but it was like an apparition, so rising from the mound of the dead.[36]

Lieutenant Bowles of the Coldstream Guards was with his company in the vicinity of the Gemioncourt farmhouse, when Wellington rode up:

> Being personally known to him he remained in conversation for an hour or more, during which time he repeatedly said he was surprised to have heard nothing of Blucher. At length a staff officer arrived, his horse covered with foam, and whispered to the Duke, who without the least change of countenance gave him some orders and dismissed him. He then turned round to me and said. 'Old Blucher has had a damned good licking and gone back to Wavre, eighteen miles. As he has gone back we must go too. I supposed in England they will say we have been licked. I can't help it, as they are gone back we must go too.' He made all the arrangements for retiring without moving from the spot on which he was standing, and it certainly did not occupy him five minutes.[37]

Word began to spread through the division that the Prussians had been beaten at Ligny and had withdrawn, leaving the British to face the might of the French Army alone. Orders were sent to the 1st Division by 09.00 hours to be ready to march north, but they had to wait until the 3rd and 5th Anglo-Hanoverian Divisions had marched before they could start. By

---

36. *Waterloo Archive*, Vol. 6, p.116.
37. Bowles, p.100.

11.00 hours the 1st Brigade began marching. The soldiers were not happy at having to withdraw because they felt they had beaten the French and had held the field at the end of the battle. The hot weather and intermittent rain did not improve their disposition.[38] As they marched north, they could hear artillery fire against the cavalry of the rear guard.[39]

Lieutenant Powell of the 2nd Battalion 1st Foot Guards wrote about the march in his journal:

> The day was excessively hot and the road very much crowded, but yet there was but little confusion and the stoppages but short. The only material one was from the narrowness of the bridge over the Dyle at Genappe. After a march of perhaps eight miles we were ordered to take along a cart track to the left, which soon brought us behind a country chateau and farm with a garden and orchard but separated from us by a deep hollow way (the continuation of the cart road). Here we halted supposing we were fixed for the night. However, orders came shortly afterwards to order us to move to our right over the standing corn up the rise, and on to the next rise till we got to the chaussée from Nivelles to Mont-St.-Jean.[40]

Because it was on the front lines and only a few kilometres from the French, the 2nd Brigade's withdrawal north was more complicated and dangerous than the 1st Brigade's. The order came to withdraw through the Bois de Bossu. The 2nd Battalion 3rd Foot Guards lost its way and exited the woods when an ADC rode up to its commander to warn him that:

> We were approaching the enemy's lines, they being concealed beyond a distant hedge; we immediately brought our left shoulders forward, and stepped in double quick time until we reached the woods side, and continued to move on quickly until we were more concealed from the enemy … We now proceeded along a footpath across a field, the situation being higher than the lane, and from whence we could distinguish at a distance to our right a body of English cavalry dismounted standing by their

---

38. *Master*, p.138-139.
39. *Waterloo Archive*, Vol. 6, p.117.
40. *Waterloo Letters*, pp.252-253.

horses. We had now arrived at a brook, which crossed our path, and being extremely thirst, for the moment forgot the danger we were in and drank most eagerly from it, being a little refreshed, we passed on until we had overtaken some of our returning troops when we halted for a short time by the road side near Genappe. We then proceeded until near the plains of Waterloo; we then passed along a path through some fields to our left, where we again halted for a short time.[41]

The 1st Division had not been able to evacuate all of its seriously wounded by the time it came to march and it was forced to abandon them. A party of light dragoons led by a sergeant was sent to carry the wounded to the rear.[42] The number they were able to rescue is unknown, however twelve privates from the 2nd Battalion 1st Foot Guards and a sergeant and two privates from the 3rd Battalion were left behind. Their battalions initially carried them as missing, but they were never found and were eventually listed as dead.

The 1st Division's artillery under the direct command of Lieutenant Colonel Stephen Adye,[43] was attached to the army's reargaurd. The French pursued the retreating British so vigourously, that the guns were force to deploy and, 'to assist our troops with a few shots. These had the desired effect in that the enemy now let up on his determined pursuit. The fire of the enemy's guns, which was then directed against us, did very little damage.'[44]

Although the day's march was only 25km they had little rest from the grueling march of the day before and the four hours of combat after they arrived at Quatre Bras. The heat and fatigue began to take its toll on the soldiers as well as the officers as they retreated north. Lieutenant John Stepney Cowell, the acting commander of Captain William Gomm's company of the 2nd Battalion Coldstream Guards, was hit with a severe case of dysentery and had to ride in one of the baggage waggons. Around 19.00 hours, he reached the village of Mont St. Jean, where he met his battalion's assistant surgeon, George Smith. The doctor provided him

---

41. Clay, p.12-13.
42. ibid, p.13.
43. Captain Charles Sandham's Foot Brigade and Captain Henry Kuhlmann's 2nd King's German Legion Horse Artillery Troop
44. *Waterloo Archive*, Vol. 2, p.43.

with some medicine that revived him enough, so he could rejoin his company.[45] Captain James Stanhope of the 3rd Battalion 1st Foot Guards was also having difficulty with the wound he received at the assault on San Sebastian on 25 August 1813. He had been shot in the chest and it broke his shoulder blade. The musket ball lodged in his back and was too deep to remove. Part of it was removed sixteen months later, but the surgeon was unable to get it all and the wound never properly closed.[46] It was still bothering him in June, but he marched anyway. By the night of 17 June, he 'had been getting worse every day, could eat nothing, was in wretched spirits at the idea of being obliged to give it up, for my back was now so swelled I could not button my coat, etc.; this completely overcame me. All my friends and the surgeons had urged me to go to Brussels from the 16th when we marched. I agreed that board should inspect the wound on the morning of the 18th and determined to go to Brussels that night if the French did not attack.'[47]

Eventually all four battalions were on a ridge overlooking the Hougoumont chateau. The enemy could be seen in the distance, so the battalions had to stay on high alert. Shortly after their arrival it began to rain, and it continued through the night. An officer in the 3rd Battalion wrote later that they 'laid down again on wet ploughed field. I am in a rut of water where my mackintosh was anything but waterproof! We were not allowed to light fires until daylight.'[48] The much-suffering Captain Stanhope noted: 'such a night was hardly passed before; for the ground was of such a spongy nature that it soon became a bog and torrents of rain fell without intermission till the morning, the wind driving it along with prodigious force and peals of thunder filling up the intervals of the lightnings [sic]. We could get no wood that would burn and we were all miserable enough, but the thoughts of the morrow superseded all others.'[49] The 3rd Foot Guards were fortunate that their quartermaster, John Skuce, was able to send forward some spirits which was well received by the tired men. Ensign Lake traded his ration for fresh water. The men could see the fires of the French on the ridge about 2km away and this did not

---

45. Harrison, p.63-64.
46. Stanhope, p.122 & 125.
47. *Waterloo Archive*, Vol. 6, p.117.
48. Master, p.139.
49. *Waterloo Archive*, Vol. 6, p.117,

put them in the best of moods because they assumed they were using the fires to cook their food.[50]

The night was not quiet and was filled with false alarms. Ensign Charles Short of the Coldstream Guards wrote to his mother two days later that: 'We were under arms the whole night expecting an attack and it rained to that degree that the field where we were was halfway up our legs in the mud. Nobody of course could lie down and the ague got hold of some of the men. I with another officer had a blanket, and with a little more gin, we kept up very well. We had only one fire and you cannot conceive of the state we were in. We formed a hollow square and prepared to receive cavalry twice but found it was a false alarm both times.'[51]

Even the general officers were not able to find shelter from the rain. General John Byng, the commander of the 2nd Brigade, spent the night with the 3rd Foot Guards and had to rough it with the rest of his men. He, 'slept close to us, covered with nothing but straw, and hollowed lustily at one of our officers accidentally treading on him!'[52]

The light companies of the 2nd Brigade, which were still under the command of Captain Macdonell, halted upon reaching the ridge. The men were allowed to take off their knapsacks and make camp. The men:

> were ordered to pitch our blankets (they having been prepared for such purpose, having six button holes with loops of small cords, and lined with pieces of duck at each corner, also, on each side of the centre). The company having been previously told off in fours, cast lots to see which two of each four should unpack their knapsacks and pitch their blankets, myself being one of the unlucky two; we fixed our muskets perpendicular at each end of the blanket, passing the knob of the ramrods through the two button holes at the corresponding corner of each blanket, then slipping the loop of the cord round the muzzle of both muskets, keeping them upright at the full stretch of the blankets and pegged down the bracing cords at the opposite ends, whilst the other two men, first at one end, then at the other end tightened and pegged down the lower corners of the blankets, the upper edges being kept close; all four creeping under the cover taking the remainder

---

50. Lake, p.67.
51. *Waterloo Archive*, Vol. 4, p.146.
52. Lake, p.68.

of our equipment – the storm still continuing with equal force, our covering became very speedily soaked with wet.[53]

In the meanwhile, the divisional artillery had arrived and began firing on the French on the ridge opposite of them. Around 19.00 hours, Private Clay and the men of his light company were rousted out of their tents and all four of the 1st Division's light companies were ordered down to the Hougoumont chateau. The 1st Brigade's light companies occupied the orchard, the 3rd Foot Guards' Light Company moved into the formal garden, while the Coldstream Guards garrisoned the chateau itself.[54] Captain Macdonell, being the senior British officer, was given overall command of the four light companies.

Those men who provided their blankets to form the tents were left behind to pack them up and proceed down the hill on their own. Private Clay found this very difficult to do, for 'the blankets being exceedingly wet, and the buff straps of the knapsacks being very slippery, were (when open to so heavy a storm) very difficult to pack and slip on the shoulders, the straps becoming quite or nearly useless.'[55]

On his way to join his company in Hougoumont Private Clay came across a flooded ditch and while trying to jump across it fell into the neck deep water barely avoiding drowning. He had trouble climbing out of the ditch due to his sodden knapsack but eventually found his company on the other end of the orchard behind a hedge and in a ditch. The French were close, so they spent the night on alert. Lord Saltoun, who was still mounted, rode along the positions in the orchard to ensure the men were staying vigilant.[56]

Twenty-five-year-old Lieutenant Robert Ellison, the acting commander of the Light Company of the 3rd Battalion 1st Foot Guards, had picquet duty that night and noticed once it got dark, the French placed outposts in the woods near the hedge that the 3rd Foot Guards' Light Company was behind. Despite the proximity of the two forces both sides chose to not fire on the other and night past in relative quiet.[57]

---

53. Clay, pp.13-14.
54. Paget, Julian and Saunders, Derek, *Hougoumont: the Key to Victory at Waterloo*. Barnsley: Pen & Sword, 2001, p.32.
55. Clay, p.14,
56. ibid, p.15.
57. *Waterloo Letters*, p.249.

The battalions on the ridge also sent out picquets to provide warning of any French approach. Lieutenant James Nixon, the acting commander of Captain Somerset's company in the 2nd Battalion 1st Foot Guards, was in command of his battalion's picquet. He was not happy with having the duty and described it as 'a miserable wet picquet bivouac for me, the rain falling in torrents'.[58] Who commanded the 3rd Battalion's outposts, is not known. In the 2nd Brigade, a section from the 3rd Foot Guards' Light Company under the command of Ensign George Standen initially had the duty. Who relieved them after the company was sent to Hougoumont is also unknown.

Lieutenant Cowell, who had recovered from his bout of dysentery, took command of the Coldstream Guards' picquets, which were to the east of Hougoumont. Ensign Walter Forbes was with the most forward outpost when he sent word back that there was cavalry to their front. Lieutenant Cowell, accompanied by a sergeant and two privates, crawled through the crops to his position. He too heard the movement of horses but ordered his men not to fire until they could determine whether or not they were the enemy. He went forward on his own and soon heard officers giving commands in French. The lieutenant was able to recognize that they were speaking with Belgian accents and thus identified them as friendly cavalry who had lost their way in the dark.

The heavy rain continued through the night and Lieutenant Cowell had a relapse. Major Woodford, the Coldstream Guards's commander, decided to visit the outposts and found the lieutenant in bad shape. He relieved him on the spot as being unfit for duty and sent him to the rear. In a coincidence that is stranger than fiction, he came upon a hut behind the lines, which was occupied by his company commander, William Gomm along with Guy Campbell,[59] both of whom were serving as staff officers in General Picton's 5th Anglo-Hanoverian Division. He laid on the mud floor by a large fire for the rest of the night. The next morning, despite being very weak, Lieutenant Cowell attempted to re-join his company. Instead he was intercepted by his battalion surgeon, William Whymper, who reiterated the battalion commander's order to go to the rear. Surgeon Whymper helped the lieutenant onto a baggage waggon that was returning to Brussels. The waggon had not gone far when rumours spread that French cavalry had been sighted. The waggon rushed off as fast it could go. In its effort to escape, the waggon collided with another waggon

---

58. *Waterloo Archive*, Vol. I, p.135.
59. Brevet Lieutenant Colonel Sir Guy Campbell of the 6th Foot, AAG

and turned over, throwing Lieutenant Cowell into a ditch. His troubles did not end there. He had barely pulled himself out of the ditch, when a party of cavalry came galloping by and knocked him over.

Lieutenant Cowell was able to flag down the baggage cart of General Fredrick Adam, who commanded the 3rd Brigade of the 2nd Anglo-Hanoverian Division. The waggon was moving at a smart clip when a wheel came off. He then got a ride on an artillery ammunition waggon that was heading north and made it to within three miles of Brussels when it was ordered back to Waterloo. Lieutenant Cowell had had enough and collapsed along the side of the road and slept for five hours. He did finally make it to Brussels where he was bed-ridden for a week.[60]

Ensign Rees Gronow of the 1st Battalion 1st Foot Guards had attached himself to General Picton's Headquarters hoping to be appointed as an extra-ADC. He rode with the general to Quatre Bras on 16 June and spent the day following him. General Picton, who had just assumed command of his division, had better things to do than deal with a wayward ensign but chose to ignore the fact that Ensign Gronow was not supposed to be there. The next day his friend Captain Newton Chambers, who was also from the 1st Battalion 1st Foot Guards and General Picton's ADC, advised him to go find his regiment since they had taken heavy casualties and, 'as you have really nothing to do with Picton, you had better join your regiment, or you may get into a scrape.' He took his friend's advice and went looking for his regiment. He came upon Captain Charles Thomas of the 3rd Battalion who was astonished to see him and asked: 'What the deuce brought you here? Why are you not with your battalion in London? Get off your horse, and explain how you came here!' By the tone of the questions, Ensign Gronow began to realize that he might have got himself into trouble. He was rescued by the Brigade Major, James Gunthorpe, who said: 'As he is here, let us make the most of him: there's plenty of work for every one. Come, Gronow, you shall go with Captain Clements[61] and a detachment to the village of Waterloo, to take charge of the French prisoners.'[62]

Realizing he was back with his regiment and would have no need for two horses, Ensign Gronow sold his extra horse to Ensign Edward Stopford who was serving as an extra-ADC to General Byng. He proceeded with Lieutenant Clements and the detachment ahead of the division to Waterloo.

---

60. Harrison, pp.64-65.
61. Lieutenant Hon. Robert Clements of the 3rd Battalion 1st Foot Guards.
62. Gronow, Vol. 1, p.67.

There he found several hundred prisoners in the barn and courtyard of a farm. Neither he nor Lieutenant Clements were very diligent in their duties and only placed sentries at the entrance to the farm yard. On the far side of the enclosure was a waggon placed against the rear wall. While the guards were not looking, several enterprising prisoners took the opportunity to use the waggon to jump over the wall and escape. Their absence was noted and a section of guards were placed on the other side of the wall. When night fell, more prisoners attempted to escape the same way, however the guards on the other side of the wall were more alert and open fire on them, killing and wounding about a dozen. This firing so close to the village, and at such a late hour, roused some staff officers in the other buildings. Among them was Ensign Gronow's friend, Captain Chambers, who invited him back to his billet for supper. There they dined on a meal of cold meat and some wine. At dawn Ensign Gronow and Lieutenant Clements were relieved by a detachment from the 3rd Foot Guards, led by Lieutenant Richard Wigston and Ensign George Anson. Before Ensign Gronow had left London, he was approached by Lady Anson, George's mother, who gave him a Barwise silver watch[63] to give to her son.[64]

As dawn broke over their bivouac, the men of the 1st Division began to take stock of their situation and prepared for battle. Foremost on everyone's mind was drying out and finding food, since they were wet and had not been fed in two days. Finding dry wood was a priority, since it would be impossible to start a fire without it. Once the fires were started, the men huddled around them with 'shaking and clappering of teeth! The steam rising like smoke out of a chimney'[65] trying to get warm. Some of his men brought Captain Stanhope some dry wood and straw and he was able to buy a bottle of champagne from a sutler. However, he had no food. He had given his servant his horse and sent him back to the baggage train to get some mutton, but he rode off and did not return for three days.[66] The quartermaster for the Coldstream Guards, Benjamin Selway, sent up gin, and some enterprising soldier found a cask filled with loaves of rye bread. Despite being soggy, the bread was welcomed. The cask was broken up and used to start a fire.[67]

---

63. The Barwise family were one of several watchmakers in London.
64. Gronow, Vol. 1, p.185.
65. Master, p.139.
66. *Waterloo Archive*, Vol. 6, p.117.
67. ibid, Vol. 4, p.146.

The Light Companies in the Hougoumont chateau were a little better off, having a wide variety of wooden objects to use for firewood. Inside the farm there were pigs and cows. Soon the word was passed among the companies anyone who had been a butcher to come forward. Lord Saltoun's company had had two butchers in its ranks, but only Private John Southgate[68] was still with the company. The other butcher, Private Thomas Minchell, had been seriously wounded at Quatre Bras when he was shot in the left hand.[69] The 3rd Foot Guards also provided one, but it is unknown if the Coldstream Guards had one in their ranks. While they were waiting for the butchers to finish the job, the sergeants passed out a small piece of bread to each soldier. The meat was divided among the companies, and Private Clay received a pig's head. The soldiers immediately began cooking their share. Clay placed the head directly on the fire and after it was black on the outside and warm on the inside he removed it from the fire and started to eat it. He found that it was still raw and tasteless, since he had no salt to season it with.[70] He decided to eat it later.

Once the troops were fed and warmed up, they began to clean their weapons and personal equipment. Wet cartridges had to be removed from the muskets and their flints replaced. Rather than having each individual shoot off his musket whenever he was ready, the battalions were placed in line and fired a volley starting with the company on the right. One officer described it as being similar to a *feu-de-joie*.[71] For the Light Companies, the cleaning of the muskets was less organized. Private Clay left a detailed description on the steps he took to ensure his weapon was ready for the coming battle:

> Taking my musket to put in order for action, (which having been loaded the day previous and the enemy not having disturbed us during the night), I discharged its contents at an object which the ball imbedded in the bank where I had purposely placed it as a target, while so employed we kept a sharp look out on the enemy (who were no doubt similarly employed) at the same time having well attended to those things usual for a soldier to do, (in the presence of the enemy) when not actively engaged, viz., examining the amount and state of ammunition after previous engagements,

---

68. Chambers, Vol. 2, p.695.
69. His hand was crippled, and he was discharged with a pension nine months later, on 6 March 1816, Chambers, Vol. 2, p.534.
70. Clay, pp.15-16.
71. Lake, p.67.

also putting his musket in fighting trim, well flinted, oiled, &c. (bye the bye the flint musket then in use was a sad bore on that occasion, from the effects of the wet the springs of the locks became wood-bound and would not act correctly, and when in action, the clumsy flints became also useless; the shortest way of amending these failures which were very disheartening, was to make an exchange from those that were laying about amongst the slain).[72]

After putting everything in order, the waiting began. Ensign Short of the Coldstream Guards found some dry straw and went back to sleep.[73] In the Hougoumont chateau, the 1st Division Light Companies continued to prepare their positions. The Coldstream Guards dug loopholes in the chateau walls and built a firing step so they could shoot over the walls. The 3rd Foot Guards' Light Company which was stationed in the gardens, began to make holes in the thick hedge they were hiding behind so they could shoot at the enemy without exposing themselves. While others in his company were doing this, Private Clay, took the opportunity to change his underclothes, having found a clean set on a dead German the day before. He noted that they were homemade and still wet from being recently washed.[74] He then went exploring the grounds of the chateau. After passing through its gates into the farmyard, he saw a large haystack upon which some troops from the Coldstream Guards were still sleeping. He grabbed an armful of straw to sit on and returned to his mates. He had not been there long when his company was ordered through the chateau and occupy the ground on the west side of the chateau[75]

Around 09.30 hours reinforcements arrived in the orchard. They consisted of the 800-man 1st Battalion of the 2nd Nassau Light Infantry Regiment, commanded by Captain Moritz Büsgen and three Hanoverian Feld Jäger Companies from the 1st Hanoverian Brigade under the command of Captain August von Reden.[76] Captain Büsgen was accompanied by an unidentified British staff officer, who ordered Lord

---

72. Clay, p.16.
73. *Waterloo Archive*, Vol. 4, p.146.
74. Since he was thoroughly soaked by the rain and falling into the ditch up to his neck the night before, I am not sure how he could come to this conclusion and not assume their wetness was caused by the weather.
75. Clay, pp.16-17.
76. Adkin, Mark, *The Waterloo Companion*. Mechanicsburg: Stackpole, 2001, pp.40-41.

Saltoun to turn his position over to the Nassau captain and take his two companies back to the 1st Brigade.[77] As he and his two companies moved up the hill, Wellington, his Military Secretary,[78] and Major General Carl von Müffling, the Prussian liaison officer to Wellington's Headquarters, rode up. Wellington called out: 'Hallo, who are you? Where are you going?' Lord Saltoun halted his men, had them order arms, and then lay down. He then told Wellington that he had received orders to turn his position over to the Nassau troops and return to his brigade. This caught Wellington by surprise who said: 'Well, I was not aware of such an order; but, however, don't join the brigade yet; remain quiet here where you are until further orders from me.' Lord Saltoun remained in the exposed position on the slope of the ridge for about an hour when an ADC arrived and told him Wellington said to rejoin his brigade. He quickly moved them the rest of the way up the hill and each company returned to its battalion.[79]

A final roll call was done by each battalion around dawn. The results were forwarded by the brigades to the division, which sent it up the chain-of-command to the Army Headquarters.[80] The 1st Division reported that it had 3,742 officers, sergeants, drummers, and other ranks under arms that morning. The figures below do not include the artillery, which was reported separately, nor the four civilians assigned to the division.[81]

Table 8.1: Strength of the 1st Division on 18 June 1815

	Div HQ	1st Brigade Bde HQ	2nd Bn 1FG	3rd Bn 1FG	2nd Brigade Bde HQ	Coldstream	2nd Bn 3FG	Total
Officers	5	3	29	29	5	36	35	142
Sergeants	-	-	43	40	-	55	55	193
Drummers	-	-	21	20	-	15	9	65
Other Ranks	-	-	688	758	-	939	957	3342
Total	5	3	781	847	5	1045	1056	3742

---

77. *Waterloo Archive*, Vol. 4, p.156.
78. Lord Fitzroy Somerset, a captain in the 2nd Battalion 1st Foot Guards.
79. Hamilton, Vol. 3, pp.29-30.
80. See Appendix IV for the actual return.
81. The four civilians were: ACG John Wood and Chaplain George Stonestreet, who were assigned to the Division HQ; DACG Robert Cotes attached to the 1st Brigade; and DACG John Henry Edwards in the 2nd Brigade.

Although the above figures for the enlisted soldiers is likely accurate, the number of officers reported with the colours is not. This will be explained below.

The 2nd Battalion 1st Foot Guards was involved in the heaviest fighting at Quatre Bras and it took a huge toll on its command structure. After its commander, 2nd Major Henry Askew was seriously wounded, the battalion was commanded by its senior captain, Richard Cooke. Only three other captains were present on the morning of 18 June. Two of them, captains Francis D'Oyly and Goodwin Colquitt were serving as the acting majors. This left the Light Company, led by Captain William Milnes, as the only company with a captain commanding it. Eight of the other companies had lieutenants leading them, except for Captain Colquitt's company, which was commanded by sixteen-year-old Ensign William Tinling. In Captain Hill's company, the only officer present when it left Enghien two days before, Ensign Henry Lascelles, had been wounded at Quatre Bras. Who commanded it now is unknown. However, as the senior ensign, eighteen-year-old Donald Cameron was probably given command of it. The Grenadier and Light Companies were authorized three lieutenants. The Grenadier Company had Lieutenant Henry Powell, who commanded it, and Ensigns Samuel Hurd and Fletcher Norton. The Light Company still had its commander, Captain Milnes, but instead of three lieutenants there were only Lieutenant Francis Luttrell and Ensign Algernon Greville. The eight Centre Companies had six lieutenants and two ensigns to command them. Four of these companies still had an ensign, while Captain D'Oyly's company had two. It is likely one of its ensigns were temporarily assigned to one of the companies that had only one officer. Which officer was moved and to what company he went is unknown.

Among the enlisted ranks, the 2nd Battalion 1st Foot Guards had lost seven sergeants, two drummers, and 277 other ranks since they left Enghien on the early morning of 16 June. It started the march with 1,077 officers and men but on the morning of 18 June could only muster 781. It had lost 28 per cent of its men in one battle. It would fight at Waterloo with only 59 per cent of its authorized strength.

The 3rd Battalion 1st Foot Guards also fought at Quatre Bras and was in not much better shape than the 2nd Battalion. It was now commanded by its second senior company commander, Captain Edward Stables, since 3rd Major William Stuart, and its senior acting major, Captain Horatio Townshend, had been seriously wounded. Captain Lord Saltoun was commanding the brigade's Light Companies. Three of its companies still had captains commanding them, while three had lieutenants in command. Three of the remaining four companies were commanded by ensigns. Captain D'Oyly's had none of its subalterns and he was serving as the senior acting major. It is likely either Lieutenant Robert Phillimore of Captain Stanhope's company or Ensign Thomas Swinburne of Captain Reeve's company was temporarily moved to command it. After Ensign Gronow returned from guarding the prisoners in the Waterloo farmhouse he was assigned to the 3rd Battalion and placed in the Grenadier Company. Although he was the senior ensign in the regiment at Waterloo, it is unknown if he commanded it. He never mentioned doing so in his *Reminiscences*. Surprisingly, the information on officers in the morning returns for 18 June that was reported up to the Army HQ even included him. The total officers present for duty was twenty-nine.

When the 3rd Battalion 1st Foot Guards left Enghien in the early hours of 16 June, it marched with thirty-six officers, fifty sergeants, twenty-three drummers, and 987 other ranks. On the morning of 18 June, it reported forty sergeants, twenty drummers, and 758 other ranks with the colours. This was 818 enlisted soldiers, which when combined with the twenty-nine officers gave the battalion a strength of 847. In the past two days it had lost eight officers, ten sergeants, three drummers, and 229 other ranks through combat and fatigue. This loss of 250 men was 23 per cent of its personnel it started with. The battalion would fight with only 64 per cent of its authorized strength.

The 2nd Brigade, took very few casualties and reported only ten men in the hospital and another ninety with the battalions too sick to fight. Most of those with the battalions were incapacitated from exhaustion due to the grueling marches from the previous days. The Coldstream Guards reported on the morning of 18 June that it had one major, five captains, twenty-five subalterns, and five staff officers for a total of thirty-six officers. As noted in Chapter 6, the battalion had only thirty-one officers present for duty when it left Enghien. On the morning of 18 June only thirty officers were with the colours. Lieutenant Cowell had been sent to the rear with dysentery the previous night. Three of its companies were commanded by captains, five by lieutenants, and two by ensigns. Although carried as being with the battalion, Captain Macdonell and the Light Company were in the Hougoumont chateau. The battalion had fifty-four sergeants,[82]

---

82. Sergeant Christopher Garman from Captain James Macdonell's company was on command serving as the Guards Division Provost Marshal.

fifteen drummers, and 939 ranks for an enlisted strength of 1,009 men. Total strength of all men in the battalion was 1,039.

The situation with the 2nd Battalion 3rd Foot Guards was similar to that of the Coldstream Guards. After doing a roll call on the morning of 18 June it reported it had one major, five captains, twenty-six subalterns, and three staff present with the colours. In reality, it had thirty-three officers present for duty. There were one major, five captains, twelve lieutenants, twelve ensigns, and three staff. Lieutenant Richard Wigston and Ensign George Anson were on command as well as ten sergeants, six drummers, and fifty-seven other ranks. Most were guarding prisoners taken at Quatre Bras.[83] Ensign William James was in the rear in charge of the baggage guard.[84] Four of its companies were commanded by captains, while five were led by lieutenants. The senior ensign in the battalion, Charles Lake, led Captain Gordon's Company. Most companies had two officers, except Captain Rooke's Company which only had Lieutenant Hasting Forbes commanding it. Captain Charles West's 8th Company had its authorized lieutenant and two ensigns, while the Grenadier Company had all three of its lieutenants. One of Captain West's ensigns was probably sent to Lieutenant Forbes to assist him during the battle. The Light Company, commanded by Captain Dashwood, had two lieutenants and an ensign. Captain Dashwood also served as one of the acting majors, but on 18 June he was with his company at Hougoumont. His place as the acting major was filled by the next senior captain, Francis Home, who commanded the Grenadier Company. On the morning of 18 June, the 2nd Battalion had fifty-five sergeants, nine drummers, and 937 other ranks for a total of 1,001 enlisted men with the colours. The total strength of the battalion was 1,031 men available to fight.

An explanation of the command structure and a list of the names of officers in every company for each battalion can be found in Appendix V.

---

83. Mackinnon, Vol. 2, p.221; Gronow, Vol. 1, p.67.
84. Mackinnon, ibid.

Chapter 9

18 June 1815
The Morning of Waterloo

The strategic situation left Wellington few options. Anglo-Allied and Prussian strategy was based on mutual support. Napoleon was strong enough to defeat either the Anglo-Allies or the Prussians but would be outnumbered by almost two to one if they could combine against him. After stopping the French at Quatre Bras, Wellington was forced to retreat because the Prussians had been beaten at Ligny and had marched north. Wellington had two options. He could march northwest and secure his line of retreat to Antwerp, where he could evacuate the army if necessary, or he could march north towards Brussels and try to link up with the Prussians. The Prussian commander, Marshal Blücher, had promised Wellington that if he chose to fight before Brussels, he would do everything possible to join him in the battle. Wellington chose to march north to Brussels and hoped that the Prussians would arrive in time.

By early morning on 18 June, Wellington's Anglo-Allied army was in place on a ridgeline that was halfway between Brussels and Quatre Bras. By occupying the ridge, Wellington was able to block two of the three major roads that led to Brussels from the south. Furthermore, it was the last defensible position before the Bois de Soignes, a large forest that was on the outskirts of Brussels. Wellington had to stop there or abandon Brussels. The battlefield was mostly farmlands that was cultivated with crops of rye, wheat, barley, and oats. Unlike at Quatre Bras two days before, the fields had been trampled on the night of 17 June by thousands of men and horses as they moved into position. On the far right of the battlefield was the village of Braine-l'Alleud, which sat astride the road from Nivelles. A few kilometres to the east was the Charleroi-Quatre Bras-Brussels Road, which bisected the position. To the east of the road was Frichermont. A few hundred metres south of the ridge was the Hougoumont chateau on the right and alongside the Charleroi Road was a walled farm called La Haye Sainte. The position was about 5km wide by 4km deep.

The Anglo-Allied position was quite good. The ridgeline on which Wellington deployed his army, dominated the valley that the approaching French would have to cross. It was high enough that by placing his forces on its reverse slope it prevented Napoleon from seeing their exact deployment; and also kept the French from bringing effective artillery fire on them. His right was anchored by the village of Braine-l'Alleud while deep, wooded valleys would keep the French from trying to out-flank him on his left. To his front center, the farm complex of La Haye Sainte farm would break up any advance, while the Hougoumont chateau on the right was a natural strongpoint that could not be ignored by the French if held by the Allies.

To defend the 5km front, Wellington had 53,850 infantry, 13,350 cavalry, and 157 guns. On the far right, in Braine-l'Alleud, was Lieutenant General David Baron Chassé's 3rd Netherlands Division. To their left was the Guards Division which also had responsibility for defending Hougoumont chateau. To the left of the Guards and just to the other side of the Charleroi-Quatre Bras-Brussels Road was the 3rd Anglo- Hanoverian Division led by Lieutenant General Sir Charles Baron Alten. Holding the left half of the position, about 2.5km in length, was the 2nd Netherlands Division under Lieutenant General Hendrik Baron de Perponcher-Sedlnitsky. Infantry was also deployed in a second line. Behind the Guards Division was the 2nd Anglo-Hanoverian Division commanded by Lieutenant General Sir Henry Clinton. To the left of the Charleroi-Brussels Road was Lieutenant General Sir Thomas Picton's 5th Anglo-Hanoverian Division. Interspersed between and behind the infantry was the cavalry and the artillery. Lieutenant General Rowland Lord Hill commanded the forces on the right, General William the Prince of Orange commanded the centre, and Lieutenant General Sir Thomas Picton commanded those on the left. Lieutenant General Henry Earl of Uxbridge commanded the cavalry, while Colonel Sir George Wood commanded the army's artillery.

About 20km away to the northwest in the town of Hal,[1] were another 17,000 men under the command of Lieutenant General Sir Charles Colville. This force consisted of General Colville's own 4th Anglo-Hanoverian Division,[2] and Colonel Albrecht von Estorff's 1st Hanoverian Cavalry Brigade; as well as, Lieutenant General John Stedman's 1st Netherlands

---

1. This town is known as Hal in French and Halle in Flemish.
2. The 4th Anglo-Hanoverian Division was minus its 4th British Brigade which was attached to the 2nd Anglo-Hanoverian Division.

Division and Lieutenant General Karl Baron Anthing's Netherlands Indian Brigade both under the command of Lieutenant General Prince Frederik of the Netherlands. This force was to protect the army from any French attempt to out-flank its position on the right.[3]

Although Napoleon decisively beat the Prussians at Ligny on 16 June, they had successfully withdrawn from the battlefield. The French were slow in pursuing them and the Prussians were able to break contact. By the evening of 17 June Napoleon knew they were heading north, but did not know if they were retreating back towards the Rhine or to Brussels to link up with Wellington. Napoleon sent Marshal Emmanuel de Grouchy with about 30,000 men to find the Prussians.[4] At first his orders were quite specific. The marshal was told to 'Get off in pursuit of the Prussians, complete their defeat by attacking them wherever you find them and never let them out of your sight.'[5] Napoleon later amended the orders to 'You are to reconnoiter in the direction of Namur and Maastricht, and you should pursue the enemy, scout his march and inform me of his intentions.'[6]

On the morning of 18 June, Napoleon still had no idea where the Prussians were. However, he had caught up with Wellington's army and he now had the opportunity to bring it to battle. He had to do it quickly, since there was a possibility that Blücher and his Prussians might arrive to support Wellington. Napoleon had few options on how he could attack. The first would be to try to outflank him by moving around the left wing of the Anglo-Allied army. This was impractical because of the rough terrain and the very real possibility that the Prussians might appear in his rear. The second option was to move against the right wing of Wellington's army. This was possible, but it would take time for him to get his forces in position. Furthermore, as the Prussian liaison officer[7] to Wellington's Headquarters noted, there was a real danger that, 'Wellington could make the whole of this right wing wheel back on its left, and as soon as the Prussians arrived, simultaneously assume the offensive from the left

---

3. Adkin, pp.37, 118 and 119.
4. The exact number of men that Marshal Grouchy had is unknown. Andrew Field, on page 290 in *Grouchy's Waterloo* states, 'it is impossible to give accurate strengths for formations or units'. Mark Adkin on page 51 gives the number at 30,000.
5. Field, Andrew, *Grouchy's Waterloo: the Battles of Ligny and Wavre*. Barnsley: Pen & Sword, 2017, p.252.
6. ibid, p.253.
7. General Carl von Müffling

wing.'[8] The need to decisively beat Wellington's army before the Prussians arrived left Napoleon no real choice. He had to attack them head-on.

To do this Napoleon had about 77,000 men and 246 artillery pieces organized into the Imperial Guard, three infantry corps, and two cavalry corps. On the French left flank were the 20,000 men and thirty-eight guns of General Honoré Reille's 2nd Corps. It consisted of three infantry divisions and one cavalry division. In the centre, just west of the Charleroi Road was General Georges Mouton, Comte de Lobau's 6th Corps of, 10,000 men and forty-two guns. It had two infantry and two cavalry divisions. To the right of the Charleroi Road was General Jean Baptiste Drouet, Comte d'Erlon's 1st Corps of 20,000 men and forty-six guns, organized into four infantry divisions and a cavalry division. In a second line behind the infantry – from left to right – were the two divisions[9] of General François Kellerman's 3rd Cavalry Corps, the Imperial Guard, and General Edouard Milhaud's 4th Cavalry Corps of two cuirassier divisions.[10]

The initial deployment of the British Guards Division was on the ridge on the right flank of the Anglo-Allied army. Hougoumont chateau was about 200m to the southwest of the ridge. Captain John Reeve of the 3rd Battalion 1st Foot Guards wrote that their position was covered with clover but the valley they overlooked south of the ridge had been sown with crops which had been trampled down.[11]

During the Peninsular War, the British Army did not number its brigades. Instead they were referred to by its commander's name – i.e. General Smith's Brigade. The brigades would march and deploy by order of the brigade commander's seniority. The senior brigade commander's brigade would be in the position of honour on the right of the line, while the next senior commander's brigade would be to their left. If there were more than two brigades, this would continue down the line until the junior commander's brigade would be on the left.

When the Anglo-Allied army was organized in the spring of 1815, every British, King's German Legion, and Hanoverian Brigade was given

---

8. Müffling, Carl von, *The Memoirs of Baron von Müffling: a Prussian Officer in the Napoleonic Wars*. London: Greenhill, 1997, p.243.
9. The 11th Cavalry Division had two dragoon and two cuirassier regiments. The 12th Cavalry Division had two carabinier and two cuirassier regiments.
10. Adkin, pp.51, 55-64, 118 & 119.
11. *Letters from the Battle of Waterloo: Unpublished Correspondence by Allied Offices from the Siborne Papers*, Gareth Glover (ed.), London: Greenhill, 2004, p.150

a unique number. The Guards Division's were the 1st and 2nd Brigades. General Maitland was appointed commander of the 1st Brigade in April, while General Byng, who was senior to General Maitland, was appointed to command the 2nd Brigade the next month. One of the Guards' privileges was that whenever possible they would only be commanded by a general officer who had served in their regiment. Because they were the senior battalions in the Army, the 2nd and 3rd Battalions of the 1st Foot Guards were placed in the same brigade and it was given the honour of being the 1st Brigade. Its commander, General Maitland, had served in the 1st Foot Guards. As the next senior battalions in the Army the 2nd Battalion Coldstream Guards and the 2nd Battalion 3rd Foot Guards were placed in the 2nd Brigade. General Byng, who commanded them, had served in the 3rd Foot Guards.

Because General Byng was senior to General Maitland, tradition called for the 2nd Brigade to be in the place of honour on the right when the division was in line. They deployed this way on the ridge on the morning of 18 June. Tradition also called for within a brigade the senior battalion would be on the right. Battalion seniority was based on its regimental number. The lowest number being the senior. For some reason that morning the 2nd Brigade did not follow tradition. Instead, the 2nd Battalion 3rd Foot Guards was on the right and the Coldstream Guards on the left. To their left, the 1st Brigade did keep with tradition and had its senior battalion, the 2nd Battalion 1st Foot Guards on its right, while the 3rd Battalion was to its left.

This morning the four Guards Battalions formed in columns of grand divisions. Each battalion had four divisions each composed of two centre companies. They were on the reverse of the ridge, however this did not prevent them from seeing the French forming up across the valley. The total frontage of the Guards Division was about 500m, which was about half the distance it would have occupied if it was deployed with its soldiers standing shoulder-to-shoulder in its normal formation of a two-deep line.

In front of the Guards Division was its supporting artillery. Captain Henry Kuhlmann's 2nd Horse Artillery KGA was posted at the crest of the ridge and he wrote that the 'terrain, on which we stood, was slightly elevated, sloping downward both in front and in back, thus forming a kind of plateau. The ground consisted of clayey soil and had been softened by the rainfalls lasting throughout the night to the extent that the 9-pounder cannon [sic] and the 5½-inch howitzers [sic] could hardly be moved by the men.'[12] To his left was Captain Charles Sandham's five 9-pounder guns and his 5½-inch howitzer.

---

12. *Waterloo Archive*, Vol. 2, p.43.

Detached from the Guards Division were the two Light Companies of the 2nd Brigade, which were part of the force defending Hougoumont chateau to the division's right front. The chateau was a large complex built in the late seventeenth century but continued to be expanded into the early eighteenth century. Including the fields, orchards, and woods, the farm covered an area of about 500m by 500m. As seen from the ridge, on the right were the farm buildings with a tall brick wall between each. These occupied a space about 90m by 50m. The complex was split into two parts. The northern section consisted of low buildings for housing animals and what was known as the Great Barn, a large two-storey structure. All of these buildings surrounded the Lower Courtyard. Entrance to this part of the farm was through a gate in the northern wall. This gate consisted of two large doors and was wide enough for waggons and carts to pass through. At the southern end of the courtyard was the owner's two-storey house. A gateway connected it with the Great Barn to the left. On the south side of the house was the Upper Courtyard. It was smaller than the courtyard to the north, but it too had sheds and low buildings along its perimeter. At the southern end of the courtyard was a large building that was a combination of stables and living quarters. The western third of the building were the stables, while the eastern part was known as the Gardener's House, a two-storey building that had windows overlooking the southern approach. Where the Gardener's House joined the stables was a covered double gate big enough for carriages to pass through into the courtyard. This gate was known as the South Gate. Access to the courtyard could also be made through a small doorway in the eastern wall that led to the formal gardens, and another small doorway in the low barn along the western wall.[13]

To the east of the buildings were the formal ornamental gardens that measured approximately 200m long from the east to the west and 80m wide. These were surrounded by a wall about 3m high to the south and east,[14] while a thick, quickset hawthorn hedge protected its northern perimeter.[15]

---

13. White, Alasdair, 'Of Hedges, Myths and Memories – A Historical Reappraisal of the Château/Ferme de Hougoumont'. Project Hougoumont Online. 13 September 2017, p.1; Fosten, Bryan, *Soldiers of the Napoleonic Wars: British Foot Guards at Waterloo June 1815.* 4 vols. New Malden: Almark, 1967. Vol. 1, pp. 11-15; Glover, Gareth, 'Defence of Hougoumont'; Paget, pp.37-42.
14. White, p.11.
15. A quickset hedge was made by planting cuttings along its length.

To the east of the formal gardens was a large orchard about three acres in size. It was about 200m long and 220m wide.[16] What kind of trees were in the orchard is unknown, however, Private Richard MacLaurence, who was in the Light Company of the Coldstream Guards claimed, 'the tempting ripe cherries drew their attention and the soldiers were to be seen plucking them off the wall trees by the handful quite regardless of the shot and shells which were incessantly pouring amongst them.'[17] Private William Pritchard of 3rd Foot Guards claims it was an apple orchard.[18] The trees in the orchard were planted far enough apart so that carts would have been able to drive between them. Surrounding the orchard on the north, south, and east was another large hawthorn hedge. This hedge was built on a small dike and gave the impression that there was a ditch between the hedge and the orchard. At the southwestern corner, where the hedge connected to the wall of the formal garden there was a gate that permitted access to the orchard from the road. At the southeast corner of the hedge there was a large opening in the hedge. Along the northern boundary of the farm was a sunken road.[19] According to Captain Moritz Büsgen, the commander of the Nassau troops that defended the orchard at the beginning of the battle, there was no door or gate between the orchard and the formal gardens.[20]

Immediately south of the farm buildings was a small vegetable garden that was also enclosed by the wall. South of the farm, gardens, and orchard was an open space about 25m wide. On the other side of this area was a five-acre wood. Its trees were mostly hardwood and were between seventy-five and 150 years old. They were mature trees and probably not much bigger than a metre in diameter.[21] Lieutenant Robert Ellison, who commanded the Light Company of the 3rd Battalion 1st Foot Guards at Hougoumont and actually fought in the woods,

---

16. The measurements of the formal gardens and the orchard are taken from William Siborne's map in *Waterloo Letters* and W.J. Craan's map of Waterloo done in 1816. The measurements are from the collection of Gareth Glover.
17. *Waterloo Archive*, Vol. 6, pp.140-141.
18. ibid, p.148.
19. White, pp.21-22 & 27; Fosten, Vol. 1, pp.11-15; Glover, 'Defence of Hougoumont'; Paget, pp.37-42; Clay, p.15. *Letters from the Battle of Waterloo*, pp.172-173.
20. *Waterloo Archive*, Vol. 2, p.156.
21. *Waterloo Letters*, p.262. White, p.27.

described them as having 'no underwood, and was easily traversed in all parts by Light Infantry, and the communication of files kept up with the greatest facility.'[22]

The hedges that surrounded much of the property were an incredible obstacle. One of the British defenders wrote that the 'stems of the quick were thicker than the arm of a strong man, at least ten or twelve feet high, and so close that nothing larger than a cat could pass between them. Immediately behind the hedge was a deep ditch enough to shelter the troops employed, thus offering a natural and secure stockade, stronger than any artificial fortification.'[23] In most places the hedge was at least 3m tall.

Along the west side of the chateau were the kitchen gardens that ran the length of the wall. Bordering it along the western edge was a hedge and on its eastern side a low fence. Between this fence and the chateau's wall was a narrow lane that was higher in elevation than the garden. The low fence also ran along its southern edge, where there was a large haystack. There was a tree line along the northern side of the garden. On the other side of the tree line was a road, another haystack, and a pond.

The Guards spent the night fortifying the chateau. Each Guards battalion was authorized eleven pioneers and Captain James Macdonell brought with him those from the Coldstream Guards. Considering the importance that Wellington had placed on holding the chateau, it was likely that the other battalions provided their pioneers also. Additionally, Major Georg Baring of the 2nd King's German Legion Light Battalion was ordered to send his battalion's pioneers there to help with the fortifications. How much assistance they were able to provide is unknown, but probably not much since the battalion's entrenching tools were lost during the retreat to Quatre Bras when the mule carrying them disappeared.[24] Loopholes were dug in the brick walls, firing platforms were built so that the men could shoot over the high walls without exposing too much of themselves, shingles were knocked off the roofs, and holes were made in the hedges to fire through. The gate in the northern wall that allowed access into the

---

22. ibid, p.249.
23. *Waterloo Archive*, Vol. 6, p.143.
24. Fosten, Vol. 3, p.80; *Letters from the Battle of Waterloo*, p.243. Ironically Major Baring led the defence of La Haye Sainte, another farm complex. He was unable to fortify it due to among other things the lack of tools and not having any pioneers.

Lower Courtyard was left open, as well as the door that allowed access into the Great Barn from the west. The South Gate was barricaded and blocked.

Although they did a very good job in fortifying the farm complex, nothing was done to make the woods to the south impassable. One officer wrote later that: 'either from the want of entrenching tools and axes, or from some other cause, not a tenth part was done of that which might have been done, and which would have added greatly to the security and certainty of the defence. Not a spadeful of earth was moved; and although the wood in front presented very great facilities, no attempt to form an abattis, or oppose any impediments to the rush of an enemy by the felling of a few trees, was made, although this could have been done within thirty yards of the defences of the place.'[25]

The same British officer noted that although the walls and hedges made the position strong, what made it virtually impregnable were the woods to its south which 'screened the house, garden, and offices from the sight and operation of the enemy's artillery; rendering mud cemented walls,[26] through which their shot would have passed like brown paper, thus equal for the purposes of defence, to the strongest fortifications. Owing to the existence of this wood, the troops occupying the house and garden enjoyed a complete exemption from the storm of shot and shells which fell with such fury on the other parts of the position.'[27]

When Wellington visited the Guards Division and Hougoumont, he gave General Byng the overall responsibility for the defence of Hougoumont, telling him that he was 'to keep the house to the last moment, relieving the troops as they required it.'[28] Command of the forces defending the chateau was given to Captain Macdonell of the Coldstream Guards. There was some question about the extent of his authority. If another officer arrived with reinforcements and that officer was senior to him, was he still in command? And then there were the Allied units defending the woods, the orchard, and the formal gardens. Was he in command of them also? This appeared to be an oversight for Captain Moritz Büsgen, commander of the Nassau troops, later wrote that: 'Neither upon my being detached, nor

---

25. *Waterloo Archive*, Vol. 6, pp.142-143.
26. His description of the walls is incorrect. They were made of brick.
27. *Waterloo Archive*, Vol. 6 pp.142-143.
28. ibid, Vol 3, p.143.

during this entire period, was a commander named to me under whose orders I was to operate.'[29]

By 11.00 hours the forces defending Hougoumont were:

- Light Company 2nd Battalion Coldstream Guards commanded by Lieutenant Robert Moore, with a strength of 93 officers and men.[30] It was stationed in the buildings around the Lower Courtyard and the North Gate.
- Light Company 2nd Battalion 3rd Foot Guards commanded by Captain Charles Dashwood. It had 124 officers and men,[31] and was to defend the lane and kitchen garden along the southwest corner of the chateau
- From Colonel Prince Bernhard von Saxe-Weimar's Brigade: 1st Battalion of the 2nd Nassau Regiment commanded by Captain Moritz Büsgen with 800 men in six companies:
One company in the Orchard
1st and 3rd Companies in the formal gardens
The Grenadier Company in the buildings of the Upper Courtyard guarding the South Gate
The Light Company in the woods in a line with the Hanoverian jägers
One company in the woods behind the Light Company, acting as its support[32]
- From Major General Friedrich, Graf von Kielmansegge's 1st Hanoverian Brigade: the Feld Jäger Corps of 130 men under the command of Captain August von Reden, the Feld Jäger Companies of the Lüneburg and Grubenhagen Feld Battalions were all in the woods south of the chateau.[33]

After reviewing the arrangements for the defence of Hougoumont with Wellington, General Carl von Müffling voiced his concerns to the Duke that the chateau was vulnerable to a determined enemy assault.

---

29. ibid, Vol. 2, p.158.
30. Company Muster Roll. *Waterloo Medal Roll*, pp.148-149. The Light Company had three officers, four sergeants, four corporals, one drummer, and eighty-one privates.
31. Company Muster Roll. *Waterloo Medal Roll*, pp.149-150. The 3rd Foot Guards' Light Company had four officers, six sergeants, five corporals, two drummers, and 108 privates.
32. *Waterloo Archive*, Vol. 2, p.157; ibid, Vol. 5, p.115.
33. ibid, Vol. 5, pp.115 & 198.

Wellington disagreed based on the way it had been fortified and because 'I have thrown Macdonell into it.'[34]

Once it became apparent that Wellington would fight at Waterloo, Lieutenant General Colville, whose 4th Division was located in the vicinity of Hal, 20km to the west of Waterloo, sent his AQMG, Lieutenant Colonel John Woodford of the 1st Battalion 1st Foot Guards, to the Army's HQ. General Colville was not happy with his command only being given the mission of guarding the army's right flank. He was hoping that Wellington would give it a more active role. Wellington ignored his request and instead of sending Lieutenant Colonel Woodford back to Hal, he kept him on as an additional ADC.

---

34. Müffling, p.243.

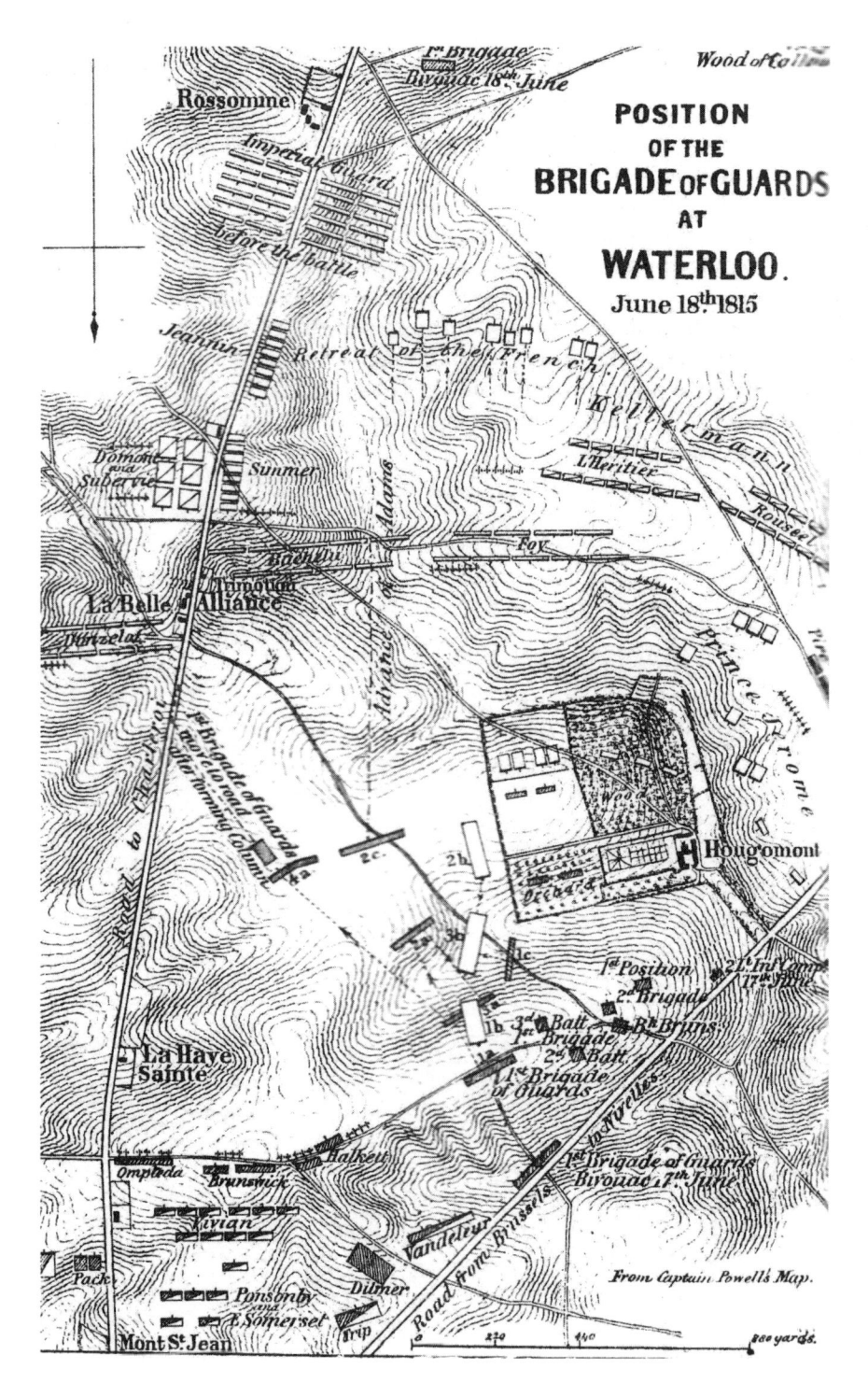

Position of the Brigade of Guards at Waterloo, June 18th 1815

Chapter 10

18 June 1815
Waterloo 11.00-13.30 Hours

Around 10.30 hours the French began to mass their regiments on the ridgeline about 1km south of where the Guards Division stood. Captain Stanhope, of the 3rd Battalion 1st Foot Guards, could see on the 'hills on which we had seen but small bodies the night before was now black with clustered troops & large masses of infantry'.[1] Ensign Rees Gronow, who was now attached to the same battalion as Captain Stanhope, could hear music being played by several bands coming from the French lines as the regiments moved up.[2] On the ridge were the three divisions of Lieutenant General Honoré Reille's 2nd Corps. On the French left and masked by Hougoumont and its woods, was the 6th Division commanded by Lieutenant General Prince Jérôme Bonaparte. In the centre and to the southeast of Hougoumont, was Lieutenant General Maximilien Foy and his 9th Division. On the 2nd Corps's right, in full view of the British officers standing on the ridge, was Lieutenant General Gilbert Bachelu's 5th Division.

The artillery of both armies remained silent until the French began moving down the ridge towards the British lines. Sources vary on the time this occurred. Lieutenant Powell, the acting commander of the Grenadier Company of the 2nd Battalion 1st Foot Guards noted in his journal that he checked his watch when the first cannon fired and it was 10.45 hours.[3] Ensign Daniel Tighe, also of the 2nd Battalion, said it was about 11.00 hours.[4] Ensign Thomas Wedgewood of the 2nd Battalion 3rd Foot Guards

---

1. Stanhope, p.17.
2. Gronow, Vol. 1, p.188.
3. *Waterloo Letters*, p.253.
4. *Letters from the Battle of Waterloo*, p.168.

gives the time as 'about ½ past eleven'[5] while Captain Francis Home, an acting major of the same battalion, states that it was 'exactly ½ past eleven'[6] when the British artillery opened fire. The first shots were fired by Captain Kuhlmann's 2nd KGA Horse Artillery, which was assigned to the Guards Division. Unfortunately, he did not record the time. Most sources give the time the battle opened as 11.30 hours.[7]

The Duke of Wellington had rode down the lines earlier that morning and had stopped and talked with the artillery overlooking Hougoumont. He specifically ordered them to never fire at the French artillery.[8] Supporting the Guards at this time were Captain (Brevet Major) Norman Ramsay's RHA Troop of 9-pounders, which was directly in front of the Coldstream Guards, Captain (Brevet Major) George Beane's RHA Troop of 6-pounders, Captain Kuhlmann's 2nd KGA Horse Artillery Troop, and Captain Sandham's RA Brigade. All three of the latter were to the left of the 3rd Battalion 1st Foot Guards. There were fifteen 9-pounders, five 6-pounders, and four 5 ½-inch howitzers.[9]

Both Wellington and the Prince of Orange were present when the first salvoes were fired, however there is no indication that either gave the order to fire. Instead Captain Kuhlmann opened fire on the advancing French force, 'As soon as it was within effective firing range'.[10] Captain Stanhope noted that 'The 1st shot, the signal of such slaughter was fired from our front, it fell short, the second plunged into the middle of the column and in an instant a blaze burst from the range of the hill, which roared from 100 mouths'.[11] Captain Home wrote that the effect of the artillery was almost immediate: 'Large openings were instantly formed in the column into which almost every shot fell, and before the guns could be re-laid it had halted and retired under a rising ground for shelter, thus breaking the order of this first attack'.[12] Wellington appeared to be pleased with these initial results remarking that it was a 'Very pretty practice indeed,'[13] while

---

5. *Waterloo Archive*, Vol 1, p.146.
6. ibid, p.141.
7. The variations in time is probably due to the inaccuracy of the watches of the period.
8. *Waterloo Archive*. Vol. 2, p.43.
9. Adkin, pp.157 & 274.
10. *Waterloo Archive*, Vol. 2, p.43.
11. Stanhope, p.176.
12. *Waterloo Archive*, Vol. 1, p.142.
13. ibid.

the Prince of Orange complimented the artillery for their 'well-aimed and effective fire'.[14]

The French 1st Battalion 1st Light Regiment of General Pierre Bauduin's Brigade in the 6th Division was on the far right of its division protected by a fold in the ground from the fire. The regiment's 2nd Battalion was in a sunken road to the right of the 1st Battalion when it was ordered to leave its covered position. This exposed it to fire from the British guns. Chef-de-Battalion Pierre Jolyet, the commander of the 1st Battalion, observed that: 'Hardly had the first division got into position than the English batteries established in front of their line, opened a lively fire which knocked over 20 men of the second battalion, and more balls followed so rapidly that it was obliged to drop back down into the shelter of the lane'.[15] The rest of the 1st Light Regiment did not appear to come under fire. Much of the artillery fire struck General Foy's 9th Division.

It was not long before the French artillery opened up. Captain Kuhlmann and the other commanders had to avoid the temptation of conducting counter-battery fire because of their orders forbidding it that they had received from Wellington earlier. Beside which it would have been foolhardy to do so while Wellington was present. An estimated four French batteries began firing and at first it was ineffective. However, once they got the range, the shots began to tell on the guns and the British infantry which were in columns of grand divisions on the other side of the ridge.[16] Wellington ordered the Guards to change formation into squares and to lay down in order to reduce their casualties.[17] They would remain in these squares for several hours.

The artillery bombardment continued until about noon, when General Bauduin was ordered to send the light companies of his five battalions to clear the Hougoumont Woods. They were quickly engaged by the Hanoverians under the command of Captain von Reden. His troops belonged to battalions that were raised to fight the French in the newly liberated Hanover in late 1813. All were volunteers and most had little military experience.[18] In the Grubenhagen Feld Battalion was Sergeant Mann, who during 'the most

---

14. ibid, Vol. 2, p.44.
15. Field, Andrew, *Waterloo: the French Perspective*. Barnsley: Pen & Sword, 2015, p.64.
16. *Letters from the Battle of Waterloo*, p.167.
17. *Waterloo Letters*, p.256; Stanhope, p.176.
18. When the Hanoverian battalions were first formed, the British sent officers and sergeants from the King's German Legion to form their cadre.

heavy skirmishing, he made his young men use the terrain most skillfully, while maintaining good order. He had already proven himself a master of this kind of fighting at Quatre Bras where he had served as an outstanding example.'[19] Soon the fighting bogged down and General Bauduin ordered the 1st and 2nd Battalions of the 1st Light Regiment into the woods. Chef-de-Battalion Jolyet, stated that this occurred about 13.00 hours, but it was probably closer to 12.30 hours.[20] It was during this fighting that General Bauduin was killed and Colonel Amédée Louis de Despans-Cubières, of the 1st Light Regiment assumed command of the brigade.

The fighting was intense and before long the German light troops fell back before the onslaught of the French. The German unit cohesion began to disintegrate and soon the skirmish became a fight between small groups of individuals. Captain von Reden and a few of his jägers, including Julius and Wilhelm Brinkmann, were soon surrounded. Wilhelm Brinkmann escaped, but was shot as he went back for help. Julius stayed with his captain but was also wounded. Wilhelm returned with reinforcements and they rescued the captain.[21]

Captain von Reden and his troops fell back to the orchard. After passing through the Nassau troops defending the hedge, they continued through the orchard and stopped in the sunken road that bordered it on the north. There they waited, re-organizing their companies, re-distributing ammunition, and dressing their wounds. The French followed the retreating Germans but halted when they came to the northern side of the woods and found in their way the large brick walls and hedges of Hougoumont. They were brought under fire by the Nassau troops in the buildings and the orchard. After taking heavy casualties, the men of the 1st Light Regiment retreated into the woods.

General Byng could hear the increase in the tempo of the firing and gave orders to Major Hepburn to send reinforcements to the chateau. Captain Douglas Mercer, the senior officer in the battalion after Major Hepburn, was sent with the Grenadier and 3rd companies.[22] The captain was an

---

19. *Waterloo Archive*, Vol. 5, p.198.
20. Field, *Waterloo: the French Perspective*, p.66.
21. *Waterloo Archive*; Vol. 5, p.198. The anecdote is taken from the citation for the Guelphic Medal that he received. The source states that the British Guards also were involved in the rescue, but no British source mentions it.
22. The exact time they left the ridge is unknown, however they were in the chateau prior to the French assault on the north gate, since at least one of their men, Sergeant Ralph Fraser, was involved in the closing of the gate.

experienced officer with over twelve years with the regiment and had served forty months in the Peninsula, virtually all as an ADC. But during that period, he was in combat at least ten times. The Grenadier Company, was commanded by twenty-six-year-old Lieutenant Robert Hesketh since the night before. He assumed command of the company when Captain Home took over the responsibilities of one of the battalion's acting majors, normally held by Captain Dashwood who had gone down to the chateau with his Light Company. The Grenadier Company had 100 officers and men on the morning of 18 June. Captain Mercer's own company, the 3rd, was temporarily commanded by Lieutenant Joseph Moorhouse and had a strength of 105.[23] The detachment was short of experienced officers, having only four lieutenants and one ensign of the eight subalterns they were authorized. Whitwell Butler, the only ensign, was just sixteen-years-old. The lieutenants were older and more experienced. Lieutenant Hesketh had been in the regiment since 1806 and had served thirty-two months in the Peninsula, while the other lieutenants averaged seven years of service and twelve months in the Peninsula. Upon arriving at Hougoumont, Captain Mercer was able to get his two companies into the chateau during a lull in the fighting. After consulting with Captain Macdonell, they decided to leave the 3rd Company in the lower courtyard, while Captain Mercer would take the Grenadier Company into the formal gardens.

About this time, the other brigade of Lieutenant General Prince Jérôme Bonaparte's 6th Division, under the command of General Jean-Louis Soye, was committed to the fight. It advanced through the woods and attacked the southern side of the chateau. The 1st and 3rd Companies of the 1st Battalion 2nd Nassau Regiment defended the formal gardens to the east of the buildings. Early in the morning the buttresses on the interior of the garden's wall had been demolished and the rubble was used to build a firing platform for the men to stand on so they could shoot over the wall. There was not enough rubble to use for a firing platform on the east wall that bordered the orchard. Instead they used farm implements, barrels, and anything else they could find. In some places there was an embankment that was high enough for the soldiers to stand on and fire over the walls. Loopholes were also cut in the wall where the firing platforms did not reach.[24]

---

23. The Grenadiers had three officers, six sergeants, seven corporals, one drummer and eighty-five privates. The 3rd Company had two officers, seven sergeants, eight corporals, one drummer and eighty-seven privates, *Waterloo Roll*, pp.152-155. Company Muster Rolls.
24. Cotton, Edward, *A Voice from Waterloo*. East Ardsley: EP, 1974, p.28.

The Grenadier Company defended the large building that formed the southern wall of the chateau. Although it was only one building, it contained stables, the south gate, and the gardener's house. There were no windows or openings in the southern wall of the stables, so loopholes were dug into it. The south gate went through the two-storey gardener's house, which had four windows that looked out over the southern approach to the chateau. The flooring above the gate had been torn up to allow the defenders to fire down onto any attackers who made it through the gate. Four loopholes had also been cut into the doors of the gate.[25]

When they occupied the southern part of the chateau, the grenadiers place their battalion colours on the roof of the gardener's house. Each of the Grenadier Company's four sergeants were given a specific part building to defend. Sergeant Andreas Buschieb was placed in charge of the gate and given eight men to hold it with. The initial assault on the gate was met with heavy fire that caused the French to pause and then run back to the protection of the woods. The Grenadiers continued to fire at them. The French realized that the gates were barricaded so while they were re-organizing for the next assault a couple of trees were cut down for battering rams. During the initial lull in the fighting Lieutenant Andreas Harth was concerned that the battalion colours would be lost if the French broke through the gate. He ordered Sergeant Buschieb to take them down and protect them. The next French assault was better organized and with the use of the improvised battering rams, they were able to stove in the gate and enter the courtyard. Sergeant Buschieb and his men retreated into the house, where they fired into the mass of French soldiers as they ran through the gate. They began to take so many casualties that French soldiers began to trip over the bodies as they entered the courtyard. A counter-attack forced the French back through the gate and Sergeant Bushieb and his men quickly barricaded the gateway again. During the counter-attack, Lieutenant Harth was shot in the head and killed.[26]

During the attack on the South Gate, the French also attacked the orchard which was defended by two companies of Nassau troops. Faced by overwhelming numbers, the Germans pulled back and joined Captain von Reden's troops in the sunken road on the north side of the orchard. Six intrepid French soldiers scaled the wall of the formal garden and found 200 men of the 1st and 2nd Companies of the 1st Battalion 2nd Nassau Regiment waiting for them. The French were unable to retreat back over

---

25. ibid.
26. *Waterloo Archive*, Vol. 5, pp.115-116.

the wall and chose to fight rather than surrender. The one-sided firefight lasted fifteen minutes before the last French soldier died.[27]

While General Soye's Brigade attacked the southern part of the chateau, Colonel Cubières ordered his men to clear the British out of the kitchen gardens which were along the western walls of the chateau. The gardens were occupied by the 3rd Foot Guards's Light Company under command of Captain Charles Dashwood. The men were posted along the hedge that bordered the garden on the west and south. Captain Dashwood remained mounted on his horse on the path that was next to the wall. This position was slightly elevated and allowed him to see over the hedges. During this time, the French brought up some artillery and began firing on the western walls of the chateau. Many of the shots fell short and some struck the light infantrymen hiding behind the trees. Private Clay claimed that, 'their small shots rarely escaped contact with our knapsacks and accoutrements, even the heels of our shoes (whilst kneeling) were struck by them'.[28]

The swarming French light infantry not only were in the hedge line on the west side of the kitchen garden but they also began moving to the small orchard on the north side of the chateau. Captain Dashwood realizing that they would soon be surrounded with no way of retreating, ordered the company back into the chateau via the north gate. He, Lieutenants George Evelyn and John Elrington, and most of the company manage to extract themselves from the fighting and make it to safety. The left section of the company, led by Ensign George Standen, covered them as they withdrew. He and his men, including Private Clay, slowly retreated up the path towards the north gate. In a desperate attempt to buy time for the rest of the company, Ensign Standen, waving his hat with one hand and with his sword in the other, led his small band of men in a charge back down the path. This unexpected charge stopped the French for a few moments. The few men still with the ensign made it back to the southwest corner and took cover behind the large haystack there.[29]

---

27. Du Fresnel, Henri, *Un Régiment à Travers l'Histoire: le 76e, ex-ler Léger*. Paris: E. Flammarion, 1894, p.274. Du Fresnel claims that the soldiers were from the 1st Light Regiment, but Charras on page 257 clearly states they were from General Soye's Brigade. Their last stand is memorialized in Eugene Chaperon's painting *Six Contre Deux Cents* which was unveiled in the 1892 Paris Salon.
28. Clay, pp.17-18.
29. *Waterloo Letters*, pp.268-269; Clay, p.18.

Ensign Standen and his men did not stay there long and took the momentary lull to get his men back up the path and into the chateau via the north gate. Once inside, Captain Macdonell gave the order to shut the gate. Unfortunately, Private Clay and his mess mate Robert Gann were so absorbed in firing at the French skirmishers that they did not hear the order to withdraw and were left behind. It was not long before the two realized that they were all alone and began to retreat up the lane, using the fence for cover and halting occasionally to fire at the advancing French. Private Clay, hoping for a better shot, stood on the higher ground near the wall but quickly found that his red coat made him a target. His musket became jammed and not being able to clear it he dropped it and took one that was lying on the ground. Private Gann, who was an older and more experienced soldier, stayed near the fence rather than exposed himself. They eventually made it to the northern perimeter of the farm and found some cover.[30]

Inside the chateau the situation was chaotic. Prior to this time, the north gate had been kept open since it was easiest way for reinforcements to enter and for the resupply of ammunition. No efforts had been made to barricade or block it should the French assault it. There was a real danger that the French, who were hot on the heels of Captain Dashwood and his men as they scrambled for the safety of the chateau might follow them in. At this time, the only organized troops there were the men from Captain Henry Wyndham's Light Company of the Coldstream Guards, which had been augmented with another officer, Ensign James Hervey. During the fighting in the kitchen garden, the company manned the western perimeter of the chateau, and provided supporting fire from the great barn and the building immediately north of it. As Captain Dashwood's Light Company moved into the chateau the sections under Lieutenants Evelyn and Elrington were kept in the centre of the courtyard near the well. Ensign Standen and his men were sent to the house on the opposite end, where they occupied the lower floor, including the parlour. The company had taken heavy casualties during the fight in the garden and could muster less than half its strength.[31]

The French troops under the command Colonel Cubières swarmed after the retreating Guardsmen and almost made it through the north gate

---

30. Clay, pp.18-19.
31. *Waterloo Archive*; Vol. 3, p.111. *Waterloo Letters*; pp.268-269.

before it was closed. A small group of soldiers, led by Sous-Lieutenant Pierre François Legros of the 1st Company of the 3rd Battalion of the 1st Light Regiment, approached the gate and broke the west panel of the gate with an axe. It was not long before he and his men were inside.[32] They were surrounded on three sides by the British Guardsmen and a short, vicious firefight ensued. When the smoke cleared, all the French were either killed or wounded.[33] The firefight was not all one sided. Among those seriously wounded was Lieutenant Evelyn of the 3rd Foot Guards. He was shot in the arm and fell to his knees from the pain. His men rallied around him and told him that they would defend him with their lives. Someone gave him a drink of beer from a canteen and then moved him into the house for protection.[34]

Although the French who had entered courtyard were all casualties, the crisis was not over. The gate had been breached and a large number of French were approaching it. Captain Macdonell saw the danger and called for the officers nearby to follow him. He and the three officers of the Coldstream's Light Company, Captain Henry Wyndham, and Ensigns James Hervey and Henry 'Vigorous' Gooch[35] charged the gate. They reached the gate a few seconds before the French and a desperate struggle to close it began. They were joined by two Irish brothers from County Monaghan, Corporals James and John Graham both in the Coldstream's Light Company. Sergeant Ralph Fraser of the 3rd Company of the 3rd Foot Guards saw the fight at the gate and rushed in support of Captain

---

32. The number of the French soldiers who made it through the gate is unknown but was probably twenty to thirty men.
33. Field, *Waterloo: the French Perspective*, p.243. There is some debate regarding who actually led the French attack on north gate. The most commonly accepted name was Sous-Lieutenant Legros. However, there are no known surviving French accounts of the assault. Colonel Auguste Petiet, a staff officer assigned to the French Army's HQ, states that it was Sous-Lieutenant Bonnet. According to Aristides Martinien's study, the 1st Light Regiment did not have an officer named Bonnet killed or wounded at Waterloo. The regiment did have a Sous-Lieutenant Legros who was killed at the battle (Martinien, p.387). One source says the British spared a French drummer boy but we have found no other source that can corroborate this.
34. *Waterloo Archive*, Vol. 3, p.111.
35. Gronow, Vol. 1, p.77.

Macdonell with Sergeants Brice McGregor and Joseph Aston,[36] as well as an unknown private, all from the 3rd Foot Guards.[37]

One soldier described Sergeant Fraser as a giant, while a fellow Guards officer described Captain Macdonell as having a colossal stature.[38] The two of them pressed their shoulders to the gate, while the others tried to keep the French from entering. The Guardsmen fired their muskets and used their bayonets to clear room to shut the gate. Eventually they were able to place a cross beam in the brackets to close it. The French were not done though. Being denied passage through the gate, they tried going over the walls, two soldiers hoisting a third high enough up to get on the top of the wall. They were harassing the Guardsmen trying to block the gate up with beams and debris, by shooting at anyone approaching. Captain Wyndham was targeted by one French grenadier on top of the wall. The captain was holding John Graham's musket while the corporal carried a heavy beam to the gate. He quickly passed the musket to the corporal who shot at the same time as the grenadier. Corporal Graham did not miss and the French soldier fell off the wall onto his comrades below.[39]

During the fighting at Hougoumont, the Guards Division on the ridge was subjected to a continuous artillery bombardment. Despite being on the ridge's reverse slope, they began to take casualties. Ensign Gronow of the 3rd Battalion 1st Foot Guards wrote later that: 'as you looked

---

36. There is some confusion about Sergeant Aston's name. The June 1815 Light Company Muster Roll lists a Sergeant John Aston. The December 1815 Light Company Muster Roll does not a list an Aston. The December 1815 Muster Roll for Captain Mercer's company has a Sergeant Joseph Aston, but the June 1815 does not. After Waterloo, Sergeant Joseph Aston became a quartermaster sergeant and in 1833 was promoted to be a regimental quartermaster. Clearly the June 1815 Company Muster Roll was incorrect.
37. On page 51 of *Hougoumont*, Julian Paget gives the name of the unknown private as Joseph Lester, however there is no one by that name in the 2nd Battalion 3rd Foot Guards Muster Rolls for June 1815. There was a Private Joseph Liester in Captain Home's company. Wellington, in a letter dated 15 August 1815, refers to him as Joseph Lister. To confuse matters, the National Archives at Kew, has a Joseph Lester who served in the 3rd Foot Guards from 1807 to 1827.
38. *Waterloo Archive*, Vol. 6 p.141; Gronow, Vol. 1, p.76.
39. Cotton, p.48.

along our lines, it seemed as if we formed a continuous wall of human beings ... we could hear the shot and shell whistling around us, killing, and wounding great numbers'.[40] As the shells began to land among the troops, one officer wrote that: 'though many men were blown up and horribly mangled I never saw such steadiness. As the poor wounded wretches remained in the square it was a horrid sight in cold blood'.[41] The 2nd Battalion 1st Foot Guards lost its second battalion commander in forty-eight hours when Captain Richard Cooke was wounded in the shoulder.[42] Despite lying down, Ensign Charles Simpson of the 3rd Foot Guards was hit by a bouncing cannonball and was severely injured. He was 'dreadfully lacerated, he however remained perfectly sensible and aware of his situation. His only request then was to be put out of his pain but lived till the evening'.[43] Two other officers besides Lieutenant Simpson were also hit by artillery. One was Captain Edward Bowater who was still mounted on his bay horse when a ball grazed his foot and broke his big toe.[44]

---

40. Gronow, Vol. 1, p.6.
41. Stanhope, p.176.
42. Booth, John, *The Battle of Waterloo: Containing the Accounts Published by Authority, British and Foreign*. London: J. Booth, 1815, p.xlix; *Waterloo Archive*, Vol. 1, p.137.
43. *Waterloo Archive*, Vol. 1, p.142.
44. ibid, Vol. 3, p.108.

WELLINGTON'S FOOT GUARDS AT WATERLOO

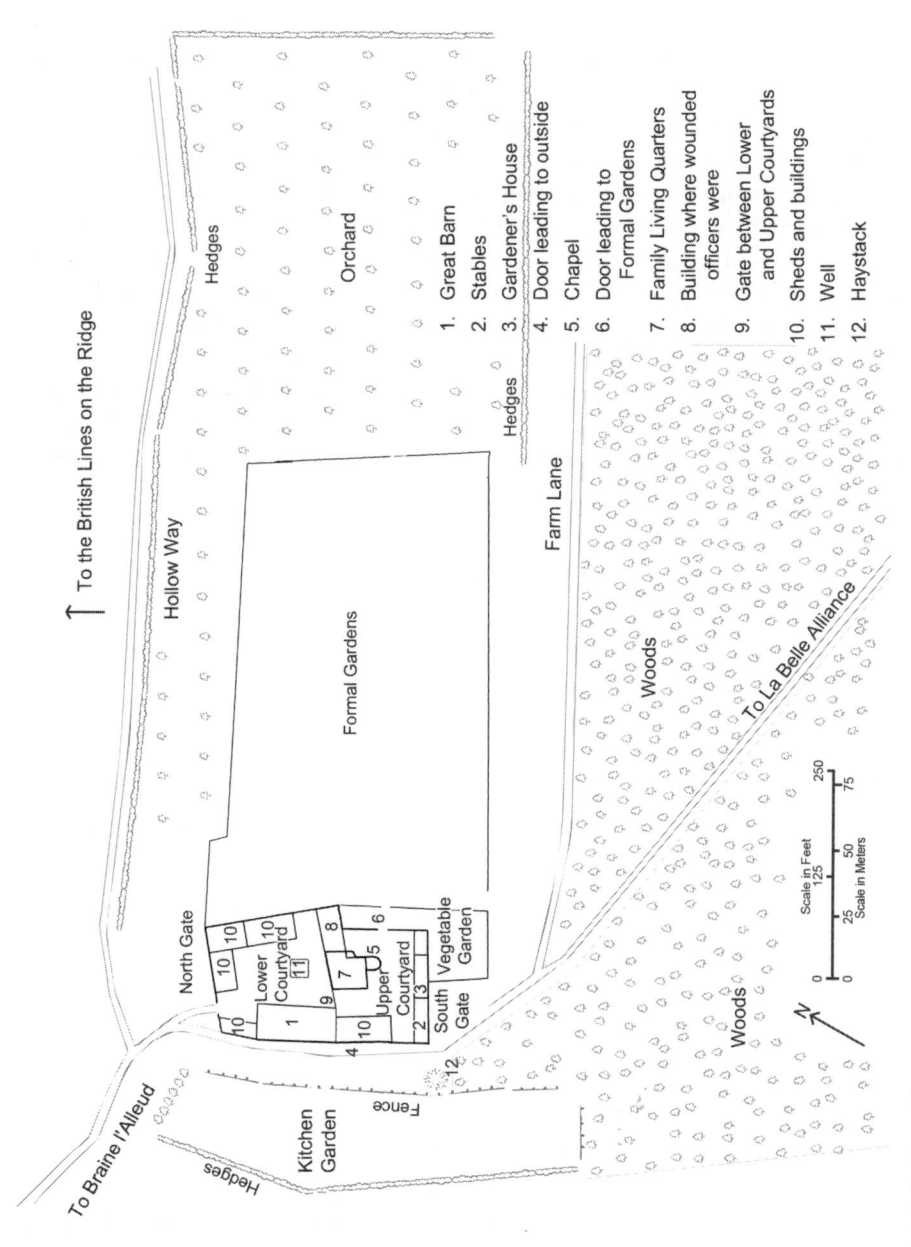

1. Great Barn
2. Stables
3. Gardener's House
4. Door leading to outside
5. Chapel
6. Door leading to Formal Gardens
7. Family Living Quarters
8. Building where wounded officers were
9. Gate between Lower and Upper Courtyards
10. Sheds and buildings
11. Well
12. Haystack

Hougoumont

Chapter 11

18 June 1815
Waterloo 13.30-16.00 Hours

Since the battle began that morning, Wellington stayed on the ridge in front of General Maitland's Brigade. From there he could see much of battlefield, and it also provided a clear view of the fighting for Hougoumont. The French reinforcements moving towards Hougoumont combined with the crescendo of the gunfire coming from chateau and orchard gave him a good idea on the intensity of the firing. Of concern was the appearance around 13.00 hours of Nassau and Hanoverian troops withdrawing from the orchard. Lieutenant John Bloomfield, Royal Horse Artillery, was on the staff of Colonel Sir George Wood, the commander of the British artillery and was part of Wellington's entourage on the ridge. He saw 'the Nassauers retiring in skirmishing order from the orchard, up the hill towards us, not running away, but retiring steadily, fighting in good order, and very fine and picturesque they looked'.[1]

Orders were given to Lord Saltoun to take the two light companies of the 1st Foot Guards that he had been commanding and move back down the hill to ensure the orchard did not fall. Who gave the order is not known. General Byng, had the overall responsibility for holding the defence of the chateau, however Lord Saltoun and the two light companies were not in his brigade and they had been released that morning back to General Maitland. Lord Saltoun would have had to been given the orders and the men from the two battalions would have had to be gathered together. Legend has it that Wellington himself said to the troops, 'There, my lads, in with you – let me see no more of you', and Lord Saltoun took them down the hill. The anecdote was first recorded in Frances Lady Shelley's diary on 18 September 1815. She claimed to be touring Waterloo with the

---

1. Fraser, Vol. 1, p.261.

Duke of Richmond who told her that he was there when Wellington said it. Unfortunately, no other eyewitness confirms this. Furthermore, Cornet Lord William Lennox, the Duke of Richmond's son was also there, having been General Maitland's ADC before his accident two months before. He writes about meeting General Maitland and then riding on with his father to see Wellington but does not mention the Duke saying anything to Lord Saltoun and the light troops.[2]

Regardless of who gave the order, Lord Saltoun had to gather the two companies and explain what they would be doing to their commanders. By 13.30 hours, the two light companies were moving off the ridge to the orchard in columns of march four abreast. The 2nd Battalion's Light Company was commanded by twenty-seven-year-old Captain William Milnes, from the Peaks District in Derby. He was commissioned in the 1st Foot Guards in 1804 and had served twenty months in the Peninsula. Captain Milnes had commanded his company for less than a year. Although heavily engaged at Quatre Bras, the company had taken only four killed and two wounded. Corporal Philip Hogg and three privates were reported missing and assumed dead.[3] The casualties were disproportionate among the officers. Lieutenant Thomas Brown had been killed and Lieutenant Francis Luttrell had been lightly wounded. Despite his wound, he continued to serve with the company. The company's strength was down to eighty-eight officers and men, i.e. three officers, five sergeants, four corporals, three drummers,[4] and seventy-three privates.[5]

Lord Saltoun's Light Company of the 3rd Battalion was commanded by twenty-five-year-old Lieutenant Robert Ellison, of Hebburn Hall, Tyne and Wear, Durham. He was commissioned in 1807 and had served twenty-eight months in the Peninsula, during which he saw little action. He was popular with his men. On the morning of 18 June, he had not

---

2. Shelley, Frances, *The Diary of Frances, Lady Shelley*. Richard Edgecombe (ed.) New York: Charles Scribner, 1912, p.169; Lennox, Vol. 1, p.242.
3. Privates John Delbridge and John Ford had been wounded and taken prisoner. Corporal Hogg and Private James Crofts were not wounded but were captured, Chambers, Vol. 1, pp.241, 265, 314 & 403.
4. Although only authorized two drummers, Captain Milnes's company had three drummers assigned to it: William Clarke, John Jepson, and John MacKenzey, Company Muster Roll dated 24 June 1815.
5. Chambers, ibid; Company Muster Roll dated 24 June 1815; *Waterloo Medal Roll*, pp.121-122.

shaven in three days and had a heavy beard. It was so dark it earned him the nickname of Black Bob.[6] The company took heavy casualties at Quatre Bras, especially among its leadership. All three subalterns were casualties. In addition to Lieutenant Edward Grose being killed, Ensign William Barton was severely wounded and Lieutenant Charles Ellis severely contused. Despite the bad bruise, probably caused by a spent musket ball, Lieutenant Ellis was still present with the company. Of the ten sergeants and corporals in the company, Colour Sergeant Francis Dixon was shot in the left leg and Sergeant John Stone in the thigh. Corporal John Stable had been hit in the right thigh. Seven privates and a drummer were killed, while sixteen privates had been wounded.[7] The company had only ninety-two officers and men as it marched down from the ridge: two officers, four sergeants, two corporals, one drummer, and eighty-three privates.

Once Lord Saltoun reached the northern border of the orchard he met with Captain Mercer, who turned over command to him. The captain, who had been overseeing the defence of both the formal gardens and the orchard, returned to the gardens. Lord Saltoun began to organize the forces in the orchard. They included not only his own Guardsmen, but the Grenadier Company of the 3rd Foot Guards, and the Hanoverian and Nassau Companies. This force was about 450 men. His orders were to clear the orchard of the French and then to hold it. They would have to fight their way through 200m of trees to get to the other side. Lord Saltoun could have tried to form his multi-national force into a line but getting it through the hedge combined with making his orders understood to the Germans who made up most of his force would have made this almost impossible to accomplish. Furthermore, the line would have been broken up very quickly by the numerous trees. It had been a long day for the soldiers, especially for the German and Nassau troops. They had taken numerous casualties and the thought of going back across the killing field was not something they wanted to do. Lieutenant Hesketh's grenadiers were also reluctant to leave the safety of the hedge. Private Joseph Lister was the first to step forward. He turned to speak to his comrades. What he said is unknown, but when the order came to move they followed him into the maelstrom. The sheer weight of this multi-national force pushed the French out of the orchard and back to the woods. During the charge, Lieutenant Hesketh was knocked to the ground and was about to be bayonetted. Private Lister saw his lieutenant go down and saved him

---

6. Gronow, Vol. 1, p.211.
7. Private William Halliday died of his wound.

by shooting the French soldier.[8] Once the hedge had been re-taken, Lord Saltoun sent the remnants of the Hanoverian companies back up the ridge to rejoin their battalions.

While Lord Saltoun was clearing the orchard, Major Woodford was ordered to send support to Captain Macdonell and his men defending the North Gate. Captain Mackinnon who was riding a grey horse, formed the Right Wing of the battalion – the Grenadier, 1st, and 4th companies – into a line and marched down the ridge. The pond near the northwestern corner of the chateau forced them to angle to the right. According to Lieutenant Colonel Lord Fitzroy Somerset, Wellington's Military Secretary, who watched as they marched off the hill, they moved in line along the Nivelles Road as they approached Hougoumont.[9] This small force of less than 300 men[10] struck the French 1st Light Regiment in the flank about the time it was forced out of the North Gate. An intense firefight began, and the French contested the ground for a considerable time. The Coldstreamers slowly cleared the French from the tree-line into the kitchen garden. Captain Mackinnon and his men pushed through the trees and were soon out of sight of General Byng and Major Woodford.

Captain Mackinnon and Captain Edward Acheson, the commander of the 4th Company, were both on horseback and became prime targets for the French light infantrymen. It was not long before Captain Mackinnon was shot in the knee and had his horse killed. Mackinnon family legend tells that he dropped his sword when he fell from his horse and landed on top of a wounded French officer. Unable to find his own weapon, he apologized to the wounded Frenchman and took the man's sword. He then mounted his dun coloured horse that was brought forth by his orderly.[11] Captain Acheson's horse was also shot and he was unable to jump off the horse as it fell. Stunned by the fall, he laid trapped under it. While unconscious,

---

8. Wellington, Duke of, *Supplementary Dispatches* ... Vol XI, p.121.
9. Somerset, Lord Fitzroy, 'Somerset's Account of the Battle of Waterloo'. Gareth Glover (ed.). *Waterloo Association Journal*. Spring 2007, p.11.
10. The Grenadier Company had four officers, four sergeants, four corporals, four drummers, and eighty-five privates. The 1st Company had two officers, seven sergeants, four corporals, two drummers, and eighty-one privates. The 4th Company was the weakest, with three officers, four sergeants, three corporals, and eighty-one privates. For some reason the company had no drummers, Company Muster Rolls and *Waterloo Medal Roll*, pp.139-141, 143-144.
11. *Waterloo Archive*, Vol. 4, p.145.

Captain Acheson was passed by French soldiers several times during the ebb and flow of the fighting. Fortunately for him, the French either thought he was dead or had no time to take him prisoner. During a lull in the fighting, Captain Acheson awoke and was able to extract himself from beneath his horse by pulling his leg out of the boot.[12]

On the ridge, General Byng, needing to know what was happening, sent Captain Henry Dumaresq, his ADC, down to the chateau to find out. The captain discovered that the Coldstream's counter-attack had kicked over a hornet's nest. Captain Mackinnon and his men were in danger of being overwhelmed. Captain Dumaresq raced back to General Byng with the news, who ordered him to find Wellington and tell him about what he saw. General Byng ordered Major Woodford to send the rest of the Coldstream Guards into the fight, minus the 7th and 8th companies, which were to be left in reserve with the battalion's colours.

Major Woodford took down the ridge the 2nd, 3rd, 5th, and 6th companies, about 400 Men.[13] This force was short officers, having only ten, including the battalion commander and adjutant. The French continued to resist, despite the British reinforcements. But eventually the fresh troops were enough to turn the fight in the favour of the British and the French withdrew into the woods. When General Byng committed the Coldstream Guards to the fight, he ordered two companies be kept as a reserve. The 7th and 8th companies, as well as the battalion colours, came off the ridge but were ordered to lay down in the road a few hundred metres away. General Byng and his command group went with the Coldstream Guards but stayed with the 7th and 8th companies when the battalion went in. General Byng, once again, sent Captain Dumaresq forward to ascertain what was going on. He arrived as the French were pulling back southward to the woods. While he was watching them withdraw, he was

---

12. Near Observer, p.28; Thomson, Thomas, *A Biographical Dictionary of Eminent Scotsmen*. 9 vols. London: Blackie, 1855. Vol. 9, p.424; Mackinnon, Donald, *Memoirs of Clan Fingon*. London: Lewis Hepworth, 1899, p.153.
13. The 2nd Company had one officer, five sergeants, three corporals, two drummers, and eighty privates. The 3rd Company was the strongest with two officers, six sergeants, five corporals, two drummers, and ninety-four privates. The 5th Company had three officers, six sergeants, five corporals, a drummer, and eighty-seven privates. The 6th Company had two officers, five sergeants, seven corporals, a drummer, and eighty-three privates, Company Muster Rolls and *Waterloo Medal Roll* pp.141-146.

shot. Captain Dumaresq realized that the Coldstream Guards had retaken the garden, rode back to General Byng. Not telling the general that he was wounded Captain Dumaresq rode back up the ridge to let Wellington know that the French had withdrawn. After telling Duke the news, he passed out from the loss of blood.

Captain Dumaresq was helped off his horse and the extent of his wound was discovered. In an interview with Surgeon George Guthrie he said: 'I was wounded by a musket-ball, which passed through the right scapula, penetrated the chest, and lodged in the middle of the rib of the axilla [armpit], which was supposed to be broken. When desired to cough by the medical officer who first saw me, almost immediately after receiving the wound, some blood was intermixed with the saliva'. Captain Dumaresq rested for about an hour and a half and feeling a little better, mounted his horse and rode to the main British hospital at Waterloo about 5km away. He had severe pain in his neck, chest, and right side, plus had trouble breathing. A surgeon bled him which helped with his breathing and alleviated some of his pain.[14]

Despite being behind the front line, the General Byng and his entourage, as well as the 7th and 8th companies, attracted the fire of the French. Ensign Charles Short, who was carrying the King's Colours, wrote that the 'musket shots flying over us like peas. An officer next to me was hit on the cap but not hurt as it went through, and another next to him was also hit on the plate of the cap, but it went through also with hurting him. Two sergeants that lay near me that were hit in the knapsacks, and were not hurt, besides several other shots passing as near us as possible. I never saw such luck as we had'.[15] Ensign Short and his comrades might have been lucky, however General Byng and his brigade major were not. The general, who was standing about 3m from Ensign Short, was hit by a spent musket ball and received a severe contusion, while Captain William Stothert was hit by a cannon ball which tore his arm off and killed his horse.[16]

Among the French casualties was Colonel Cubières, the acting brigade commander, with his arm in a sling, he coolly sat on his horse on the path that privates Clay and Gann had recently ran up to escape the advancing

---

14. Crumplin, Michael, *Guthrie's War: a Surgeon of the Peninsula & Waterloo.* Barnsley: Pen & Sword, 2010.p.150; Near Observer, p.28; Scott, Walter, *Paul's Letters to His Kinsfolk.* Edinburgh: Archibald Constable, 1816, p.174.
15. *Waterloo Archive*, Vol. 4, pp.147-148.
16. ibid, Vol. 1 p. 4; Vol. 4, p.148.

French. The colonel quickly became a target for the Guardsmen. He was shot in the right shoulder,[17] knocked off his horse, and passed out. By the time he got to his feet, his men had retreated from the garden and he was surrounded by the British. In an act of chivalry, the British officers held their men's fire and let him return to the woods. Colonel Cubières confirmed this seventeen years later when he met Major Alexander Woodford, the commander of the Coldstream Guards.[18]

Over the next hundred years two legends arose about this incident. The first that has been re-told many times is that while the Light Company of the 3rd Foot Guards was retreating back to the North Gate, Sergeant Ralph Fraser, one of the men who helped to close the gate, saw that they were about to be cut off and 'while his comrades made for the gate, rushed forward into the thickest throng of the enemy, alone and at great personal risk, and attacked the mounted officer whom he saw urging his charger forward with the obvious intention of preventing the heavy gates from being closed. With a powerful thrust of his sergeant's halberd he pulled the officer, who was no other than Colonel Cubières himself, from the saddle; and then, with a swiftness which utterly disconcerted the Frenchmen around him, he "rode into the courtyard on the Frenchman's horse before the surprised assailants had realised his daring design"'.[19]

The second is a Mackinnon family legend. It is aside to the story of Daniel Mackinnon losing his sword after he fell off of his horse and having to take one from a wounded French officer. One of his relatives was at the spa in Baden-Baden when he met an old French general. He said was in the fight at Hougoumont and 'was knocked down but being only stunned he recovered his senses after surviving comrades had retired and then standing up among the dead and dying around him, he of course expected to be taken prisoner instead of which all the British men and officers when

---

17. Du Fresnel, page 274.
18. *Waterloo Letters*, p.262; Field, *Waterloo*, p.69.
19. Macbride, Mac Kenzie, *With Napoleon at Waterloo and Other Unpublished Documents of the Waterloo and Peninsular Campaigns*. London: Francis Griffiths, 1911, p.127. This story appeared several times in journals and magazines in the early 1900s before it was published in *With Napoleon at Waterloo*. It is now accepted by many modern histories of the battle as having occurred. Unfortunately, the author of the story, Edward Bruce Low, never cited his source for the anecdote. We have found no eyewitness account of it having happened and Colonel Cubières never mentioned it in his conversation with Major Woodford.

they saw him, gave him three hearty cheers upon which he saluted them with a low bow and quietly walked back to join the corps to which he belonged. The old General mentioned that this incident took place before the gates of Hougomont [sic] and that he had to surrender his sword to a British officer who had lost his own in the mélèe.'[20]

Once the French had retreated into the woods and the battalion had secured the kitchen garden area, the Coldstreamers took time to assess their casualties. It was likely during this fight that Lieutenant Edward Sumner of the 5th Company and Ensign Henry Griffiths of the Grenadier Company were severely wounded. The ensign was hit in the arm. Ensigns John Montagu of the 1st Company and Henry Vane of the 3rd Company were also wounded.

After the Coldstream Guards had secured the kitchen gardens, Captain Macdonell ordered the North Gate to be opened so that the wounded could be evacuated. Privates Clay and Gann took the opportunity to go into the chateau. They passed several wounded soldiers, included their company commander, Captain Dashwood, who were heading towards the British lines on the ridge to get medical help. Private Clay noticed the entrance of to the gate was covered with dead and wounded French soldiers that had been trampled during the fighting and covered with blood-tinged mud. While passing through the gates he saw that it was filled with bullet holes. Upon entering the courtyard Captain Macdonell came up carrying a heavy plank that would be used to block the gate. His face bloody, but whether it was his or someone else's Private Clay did not say. Laying in the courtyard was the captain's dead horse. Private Clay and other soldiers who had been locked out of the chateau when the French attacked were taken by Ensign Henry Gooch of the Coldstream's Light Company to the southern end of the upper courtyard, where they were sent to the second storey of the chateau's family quarters. From there they could see over the lower courtyard and out into the woods.[21]

While the Coldstream Guards was re-organizing itself, Major Woodford entered the chateau through a small door in the west wall of the lower courtyard. He met up with Captain Macdonell. Being the senior officer on the site, he could have taken command of the chateau, but instead he deferred since Captain Macdonell had been placed in command of the chateau by Wellington. The two of them inspected the defences and

---

20. Mackinnon, Donald, *Memoirs of Clan Fingon*, p.153.
21. Clay, p.26.

then went to the formal gardens.[22] There they found Captain Mercer and Lord Saltoun, who was the junior of the four officers. Between them they agreed upon how they would defend Hougoumont. The 3rd Company of the 3rd Foot Guards would be left in the lower courtyard to help Captain Macdonell, while its Grenadier Company would stay with Lord Saltoun in the orchard.

After receiving the news that the situation had stabilized around the chateau from Captain Dumaresq, General Byng ordered Major Hepburn to send them more reinforcements. Captain Francis Home, took the 1st Company led by Captain Edward Bowater who had a broken toe, and the 5th Company commanded by Lieutenant John Ashton.[23] Captain Bowater's 1st Company had 103 officers and men, while the 5th Company mustered 107.[24] Captain Home's orders from Major Hepburn were 'to occupy the debouches of the wood, to cover and defend the right flank of the post, and put himself in communication with and report his arrival to the officers in the chateau and garden'.[25]

Upon reaching the kitchen garden, Captain Home halted his two companies. He sent a sergeant into the chateau to find Major Woodford and Captain Macdonell, to let them know of his arrival and to find out where they wanted them. The sergeant returned a short time later and reported he could not find the two senior officers. Eventually word got to the senior officers in the formal gardens and they revised their plans. Captain Home and his two companies had responsibility for the kitchen garden and the western approaches to the chateau. The 3rd Company of the 3rd Foot Guards would move to the orchard. Major Woodford would defend the formal gardens with his seven companies.[26] Captain Macdonell would hold the upper courtyard of the chateau, while Captain Büsgen would continue to hold the lower courtyard. Lord Saltoun with his two companies of the 1st Foot Guards and the Grenadier and 3rd companies

---

22. *Waterloo Letters*, p.261.
23. *Waterloo Archive*, Vol 1, p.147.
24. The 1st Company had two officers, seven sergeants, seven corporals, and 103 privates. They did not have a drummer with them. The 5th Company had three officers, five sergeants, eight corporals, one drummer, and ninety privates, *Waterloo Medal Roll*, pp.156 -158, Company Muster Rolls.
25. *Waterloo Archive*, Vol. 6, p.146.
26. The Grenadiers, 1st, 2nd, 3rd, 4th, 5th, and 6th companies, *Waterloo Archive*, Vol. 1, p.139.

of the 3rd Foot Guards, under the command of Captain Mercer, would defend the orchard. The much reduced four Nassau companies that were in the formal gardens and the orchard were sent to help defend the lower courtyard.

French Skirmishers continued to fire at the defenders from the woods and Lord Saltoun felt the need to do something about it. He sent Lieutenant Robert Ellison and the Light Company of the 3rd Battalion to clear them from the edge of the woods. The French were tired and did not offer much resistance. They quickly broke contact and withdrew further into the woods. Lieutenant Ellison and his men followed on their heels until they were on its southern edge. The Guards were about to continue their pursuit when the lieutenant noticed 'three French Columns, which were posted at the bottom of the hill outside the wood, ready to move up and renew their attack upon the farmhouse, two of these Columns just beginning to move, the third unpiling arms and falling in to the support'.[27] Lieutenant Ellison, thinking discretion was the better part of valour, immediately ordered his men back to the orchard.

The troops Lieutenant Ellison saw were those of the French 93rd Line Regiment of the 1st Brigade of General Maximilien Foy's 9th Division of the French 2nd Corps. They and the 92nd Regiment would attempt what the General Prince Jérôme Bonaparte's troops could not – take the formal gardens and the orchard. The French 2nd Line Regiment of General Soye's Brigade would attack through the kitchen garden and try to break in from the west. This time the attack was better planned. An artillery battery would move up to the west and provide support against the chateau. Another gun would accompany the right regiment to give them direct fire support. The French regimental commanders knew what their soldiers would be facing and ordered that the regimental eagles not be sent forward, but to be kept in the rear. This order was ignored by the sergeant majors of the regiments.[28]

About 14.30 hours, the French advanced in skirmish order and began to take heavy fire from the troops protected by the walls and the hedges. An artillery piece, probably a 6-pounder, was dragged forward with them to batter the walls. Lord Saltoun sent the Grenadiers and 3rd companies of the 3rd Foot Guards to capture it, but the French fire was too great for them to get near it.[29] The French troops initially had trouble making it through the

---

27. *Waterloo Letters*, p.249.
28. Field, *Waterloo*, p.124.
29. *Waterloo Letters*, p.246; Mackinnon, Vol. 2, p.218.

hedge around the orchard, but eventually came through the large opening in it near the southeast corner. A running battle ensued as the defenders were forced to pull back after being out-flanked. Before long, the defenders broke down into small groups desperately trying to disengage and pull back to the safety of the sunken road on the other side of the hedge along the northern edge of the orchard. Lieutenant Ellison leading the 3rd Battalion's Light Company waited too long and was surrounded by the French infantry. He was well liked by his men and when they saw he was in danger of being killed or captured, a group of them raced back and rescued him.[30] Lord Saltoun was able to quickly organize the men to defend the northern hedge, but their casualties were heavy especially among the officers. Captain William Milnes, the commander of the 2nd Battalion's Light Company was missing and presumed dead. Lieutenant Francis Luttrell was seriously wounded in the face and had to be evacuated to the ridge. Sixteen-year-old Ensign Algernon Greville, who had been in the regiment only fourteen months, was now in command of the much-reduced company. Lieutenant Charles Ellis of the 3rd Battalion's Light Company was also seriously wounded. The 3rd Foot Guards did not get off lightly. Lieutenant Hesketh, commanding the Grenadiers, was hit in the throat.

A French artillery battery, possibly of six 12-pounders and two howitzers, opened fire on the western walls of the chateau. The bombardment was intense and effective. The trees in the vicinity were mown down and soon the buildings caught fire. Private Johann Leonhard of the Nassau Battalion's No.3 Company wrote that the "Walls were collapsing … The skies seemed to have been changed into an ocean of fire; all of the farm's buildings were aflame. The soil underneath my feet began to shake and tremble, and large fissures opened up before my very eyes.'[31] Soon the fire spread to all the buildings along the western side of the lower courtyard, including the Great Barn. The flames would eventually jump to the family living quarters and the chapel.

The French 2nd Line Regiment came through the woods and forced Captain Home and his two companies to retreat northward through the kitchen gardens and into the chateau via the North Gate.[32] Chef de Bataillon Jean-Louis Sarrant, commander of the 2nd Battalion of the regiment, noticed a small door that led into the chateau. He ordered Lieutenant Sylvian Toulouse to try to break in. The lieutenant was successful and he

---

30. Gronow, Vol. 1, p.211.
31. *Waterloo Archive*, Vol. 2, p.159.
32. ibid, Vol 1, p.147 & Vol. 3, p.111.

rushed into the upper courtyard with his company of sixty men.[33] Private Clay and other men of the 3rd Foot Guards, still under the command of Ensign Gooch of the Coldstream Guards, began firing down from the upper storey of the family living quarters at the French soldiers as they rushed in. The defenders in the quarters were rightfully concerned about the building being on fire, especially as the floor became hotter from the flames. Ensign Gooch stood near the only entrance to the room and refused to let anyone leave until the room was engulfed in flames. Everyone escaped, however several were injured by the smoke and the flames.[34]

As Lieutenant Toulouse and his men tried to break into one of the buildings they began to take casualties from the musket fire coming from all sides. Lieutenant Toulouse was wounded by this fire, but they continued to fight on. A counter-attack by Ensign Gooch and his band of light infantry, combined with the heavy fire from Captain Büsgen's Nassau troops, finally proved to be too much and they retreated outside. They did capture seven Nassau grenadiers who had been defending the doorway, but left some of their own wounded behind. Among them, was a drummer boy, whom Private Clay moved to one of the buildings that was not on fire and relatively safe from the French artillery fire.[35]

Unable to take the chateau, the French pulled back into the woods. However, they held onto the hedge lining the southern side of the orchard. Within the chateau, it was chaotic. Thick smoke made it difficult to see and several officers' horses broke out of the stable when it caught on fire. Their panic was made worse by the smoke and noise in the courtyard and they rushed back into the burning building. Captain Mackinnon's dun horse escaped the flames, but was badly injured, including losing an eye. It was the third horse he lost in three days.[36] Captain Home ordered Lieutenant William Drummond, the acting commander of the 4th Company, to place some of his men in the upper level of the farmer's house, the building

---

33. Mr. Field mistakenly has these soldiers being from the French 3rd Line Regiment, but a check of Martinien identifies them as being from the French 2nd Line Regiment. Field, *Waterloo*, pp. 127-128; Martinien, Aristide, *Tableaux par Corps et par Batailles des Officiers Tués et Blessés pendant les Guerres de l'Empire (1805-1815)*. Paris: Éditions Militaires, ND, p.120.
34. Clay, p.26.
35. *Waterloo Archive*, Vol. 2, p.158. Clay, p.27.
36. *Waterloo Letters*, p.268-269. Captain Mackinnon's dun horse survived the battle and was still alive on 23 June. In a letter home, he said he was probably going to have to shoot it, *Waterloo Archive*, Vol. 4, p.145.

just to the east of the family living quarters on the south end of the lower courtyard. Their job was to prevent the fire from spreading to the roof. Other soldiers were delegated to bring them water from the well in the courtyard to douse any embers.[37]

The buildings catching fire became a major problem for the wounded. By 15.00 hours an estimated 700 defenders of Hougoumont had been wounded, of which 175 were severely wounded.[38] When possible, the walking wounded were sent back up the ridge, via the North Gate and the sunken road, for treatment. Those who were too seriously wounded to move were placed in the barns and other buildings in the lower courtyard, and the chapel in the upper courtyard. Medical support was limited at best. Initially, only the light company from each battalion was sent to Hougoumont and no surgeon accompanied them. With each battalion on the ridge was its senior assistant surgeon, who provided immediate medical assistance such as controlling bleeding, dressing wounds, and other minor procedures. When possible, the wounded were then sent to a farm at Mont St. Jean about 2km away where the 1st Corps's dressing station was. The battalion's surgeon and other assistant surgeon worked at the dressing station to save the lives of the wounded who were able to get there. It is unknown if an assistant surgeon was in Hougoumont. If there was, it is likely that either Assistant Surgeon George Smith or William Hunter,[39] both of the Coldstream Guards, followed their battalion down to Hougoumont and were there by 14.30 hours. There he would have treated the wounded and possibly performed an amputation or two. The number of patients he might have helped before the buildings caught fire was probably very few.[40]

---

37. *Waterloo Archive*, Vol. 1, p.144.
38. Email discussion with Doctor Michael Crumplin, dated 24 October 2017: 'Any wound was then a risk - from sepsis or bleeding, but in general about 15-30 per cent of wounds during these wars were "serious" or "dangerous". Also, Hodge reckoned that 10 per cent of those wounded would later succumb from their injuries/surgery.'
39. Assistant Surgeon William Hunter was the son of John Hunter, who is known as the Father of British Scientific Surgery and Surgeon General of the Army in the late eighteenth century. Assistant Surgeon Hunter kept a diary during the Waterloo Campaign. Unfortunately, critical pages relating to Waterloo were torn out by his heirs many years later because they violated their sensitive Victorian mores.
40. Crumplin, Michael, *Bloody Fields of Waterloo: Medical Support at Wellington's Greatest Battle*. Godmanchester: Ken Trotman, 2015, p.14.

Soon the fire spread to almost all the buildings in the lower courtyard. The French were still assaulting the complex and the commanders were faced with a dilemma. They were too heavily engaged to pull troops from their positions to fight the fires and evacuate the wounded. Their only options were to weaken the defence by sending men in to get the wounded or to continue to fight and hope the latest assault would be beaten back before the wounded were consumed by the flames. They had no choice but to do the latter. Up until this time, wounded officers had been placed on the ground floor of the chateau's living quarters on the south end of the lower courtyard. The other ranks were placed wherever there was space, including all the buildings in the lower courtyard and the chapel adjoining the living quarters. Major Woodford and Captain Macdonell and several officers attempted to enter the Great Barn, but the heat and the suffocating smoke prevented them from rescuing more than a handful of the wounded.[41] Captain Home went into the burning living quarters to get the wounded officers and men out. There he found Lieutenant George Evelyn who had been shot when the French broke through the North Gate. His orderly was attending the lieutenant and helped him up. The halls and rooms were choked with smoke and they had trouble finding their way out. Not sure where to go, they took a random turn. Fortunately for them, it led to the outside.[42]

Corporal James Graham, the Coldstream soldier who helped closed the North Gate with Captain Macdonell, saw the Great Barn on fire and left his post to rescue his brother John who had been wounded earlier. As he approached the barn, he ran into the captain, who had already witnessed the corporal's bravery, was puzzled about him abandoning his post. Corporal Graham explained that his brother was in the barn and he needed to get him out. Permission was immediately given and the corporal rushed into the inferno. He found his brother and carried him through the smoke and flames into the courtyard. After ensuring his brother was safe, the corporal immediately returned to his position on the wall.[43] The wounded who had taken shelter in the small chapel, which measured less than 4m by 4m, were soon caught by the conflagration. Most perished and legend has it that those who survived were seated with their backs

---

41. *Waterloo Letters*, pp.262 & 264.
42. *Waterloo Archive*, Vol. 3, p.111.
43. Paget, p.63; Wellington, Duke of, *Supplementary Dispatches* ... Vol. 11, p.121; Paget, p.63; *WSD*, Vol. 11, p.121.

to a wall, underneath a large crucifix. The flames burned the right foot of Christ, but then the flames miraculously went out.[44]

Wellington, who was in the centre of the Allied line, could see Hougoumont burn and was concerned that the Guards would abandon the position. He hurriedly wrote out a message in pencil for the commander of the chateau, on a piece of ass skin that was used for messages.[45]

> I see that the fire has communicated from the Hay stack to the roof of the Chateau. You must however still keep your Men in those parts to which the fire does not reach. Take care that no Men are lost by the falling in of the Roof or floors – After they both are fallen in occupy the Ruined walls inside the Garden; particularly if it should be possible for the Enemy to pass through the Embers in the inside of the House.[46]

The message was carried by Lieutenant James Hamilton, DAAG. At the time Major Woodford or Captain Macdonell could not be found, so he delivered the message to Captain Home. Knowing that he would be questioned on whom he gave the message to and if the recipient understood it, Lieutenant Hamilton said to Captain Home, 'The Duke considers the defence [of] this post of the last consequence to the success of the operations of the day; do you perfectly understand these orders?' Captain Home told him that he did 'Perfectly, and you may assure the Duke from me that his orders shall be punctually obeyed'. Having successfully delivered the message, Lieutenant Hamilton returned to Wellington.[47]

After bringing the French drummer boy to safety, Private Clay returned to the upper courtyard and was posted with Private Isaac Philpott of Captain Mercer's company at the gate in the western wall, that the French had broken into. French artillery continued to fire at the wall and one of their shots hit the gate and broke it open. Fortunately for the defenders there were no French soldiers in the vicinity to rush through it. The two privates found tree stumps, broken beams, and other pieces of woods to

---

44. Paget, p.96. The crucifix was stolen in 2011 but recovered in 2014.
45. Ass skin was used because the message could be wiped clean and re-used. This and three other messages still survive. The Hougoumont message is in Wellington's home in London, Apsley House, Paget, p.64.
46. Muir, Rory, *Tactics and the Experience of Battle in the Age of Napoleon*. New Haven: Yale, 1998, p.148.
47. *Waterloo Archive*, Vol. 1, p.143.

block the shattered gate. Shortly after making the barricade, Lieutenant Elrington, the senior officer still with the Light Company moved him and Private Philpott to the upper level of the building, above the door. The French artillery had knocked a large hole in the wall and the floor was covered with the bodies of dead defenders. Guarding other side of the opening was Sergeant Joseph Aston, also of the Light Company. The artillery fire finally tapered off and except for an occasional musket shot at their position, no further attack came through their way.[48]

Once the French failed to capture the chateau, they pulled back into the woods. Lord Saltoun and the five companies of Guards re-occupied the southern hedge. Captain Mercer and Lord Saltoun knew that they would have trouble holding out against another French attack. The captain agreed to go back to the ridge and seek reinforcements. Once he got there, he found that Major Hepburn had already sent the 2nd and 5th companies down the hill to reinforce the chateau. Captain Home kept these two companies with him in the kitchen gardens but sent the 1st Company to the orchard. General Byng, after being informed of the critical situation in the orchard, ordered Major Hepburn to send the remaining three companies of the 3rd Foot Guards there. Captain Mercer formed the 6th, 7th, and 8th companies and marched them down to the orchard. There he met Lord Saltoun who said that 'he was about to return to his battalion on the heights we had just quitted, in consequence of his having lost almost all of his men'.[49] Lord Saltoun and the two light companies of the 1st Foot Guards had started the day with six officers and 165 other ranks. In less than two hours they lost half their officers and a third of their men.[50] The senior non-commissioned officer in the 2nd Battalion's Light Company was twenty-five-year-old Corporal Thomas Morgan.[51] Before Lord Saltoun and his men left, Captain Mercer looked around and saw that most of the men in the hedge were from his own battalion.

Captain Mercer now had six companies of the 3rd Foot Guards to defend the orchard: the Grenadiers, 1st, 3rd, 6th, 7th, and 8th companies. The Grenadiers and 3rd Company had been in combat for several hours,

---

48. Clay, p.7.
49. ibid.
50. Captain Milnes's company of the 2nd Battalion had three killed, three who would die of wounds, and twenty-four wounded. Captain Saltoun's company of the 3rd Battalion had two killed, four whom would die of wounds, and twenty-one wounded.
51. Chambers, Vol. 2, p.543.

while the 1st Company had been fighting for about an hour. The Grenadiers were down to 60 per cent of their strength and while the 1st Company had lost about 25 per cent of its men. Despite being at Hougoumont as long as the Grenadiers, the 3rd Company had only taken 10 per cent casualties.[52] Although the 6th, 7th, and 8th companies had only just been committed to Hougoumont, they were not at full strength. The battalion had to provide two officers, ten sergeants, seven drummers, and fifty-seven corporals and privates to guard prisoners. The two officers were Lieutenant Richard Wigston of the 7th Company and Ensign George Anson from the 6th Company. The majority of the corporals and privates, likely came from their companies. So the strength of these three companies was about 250 men.[53]

The orchard was an abattoir, covered with the dead and dying French, British, Hanoverian and Nassau soldiers. Captain Mercer found that the 'dead lay very thick on the whole length of the ground we occupied'.[54] The three companies entered the orchard via an opening near the northeast corner of the wall to the formal garden. The 6th and 7th companies moved through the orchard to take position along the eastern end of the hedge. The 8th Company moved into the open field directly east of the orchard using the large opening in the southeast corner that the French had attacked through. As it was forming into line they encountered French infantry standing in line a short distance away. The French immediately

---

52. By the end of the day, the Grenadier Company would have fifty dead and wounded. The 1st Company would have forty-two dead and wounded, while the 3rd Company lost two dead and ten wounded.
53. The 6th Company began the day with two officers, five sergeants, seven corporals, one drummer and ninety-two privates for a strength of 107. Subtracting those on command (one officer, one sergeant, one corporal and thirty privates), their strength as the marched down the ridge would be about seventy-five men. The 7th Company had four officers, five sergeants, eight corporals, one drummer and eighty-four privates for a strength of 102 all ranks that morning. Subtracting those on command (one officer, one sergeant, one corporal and thirty privates), their strength at Hougoumont would have been about seventy men. The 8th Company had a morning strength of four officers, five sergeants, eight corporals, one drummer, and ninety-one privates for a total of 109 officers and men. They likely only had a sergeant and a corporal on the prisoner detail, thus they had about 107 officers and men.
54. *Letters from the Battle of Waterloo*, p.172.

opened fired and the Guards responded the best they could. They found themselves badly outnumbered and took casualties. They slowly backed into the orchard, but were quickly followed by the French, who forced the 3rd Guards back to the sunken road behind the northern hedge. The French continued to advance through the orchard but were brought under fire by Major Woodford and his Coldstream Guards, who were lining the eastern wall of the formal gardens. This was too much for the French soldiers and they pulled out of the orchard.[55]

For some reason Major Hepburn did not initially go with Captain Mercer and the last three companies of his battalion when they marched down the ridge to the orchard. He re-joined them about the time they were pushed back to the sunken road. There he found Captain Mercer 'reforming stragglers and men who returned from carrying wounded officers to the rear'.[56] Once the six companies of the battalion were re-organized Major Hepburn gave the order to clear the orchard. This time they encountered little resistance. However, the French attacked a third time through the gap in the hedges in the southeast corner and the battalion was forced back again to the sunken road on the other side of the orchard. Once again, the French were decimated from the fire of the Coldstream Guards and pulled back to the woods.

The 3rd Foot Guards had taken heavy casualties, especially among the officers. In the 1st Company, Lieutenant Thomas Craufurd, the twenty-two-year-old grandson of General Thomas Gage,[57] was missing and presumed killed. The 7th Company was commanded by twenty-two-year-old Lieutenant Hon. Hastings Forbes, the son of Lieutenant General George Forbes, the 6th Earl of Granard. The lieutenant carried a miniature of his fiancée in his breast pocket. The bullet that killed him went through the miniature.[58] Lieutenant John Ashton, the commander of the 5th Company that day, had also been killed about this time. Ensign Charles Lake was shot a little above the right temple but was saved by the thick leather of his shako which prevented the bullet from penetrating his skull. It knocked him unconscious. When he awoke he found Captain Charles

---

55. ibid, p.176.
56. ibid.
57. General Gage commanded the British Army in North America during the early years of the American Revolution.
58. Lieutenant Forbes was engaged to Mademoiselle de Ghistelle. Someone, possibly Ensign Lake, returned the damaged miniature to her. Capel, Caroline, *The Capel Letters*. London: Jonathan Cape, 1955. p.131.

West, the commander of the 8th Company, using his own handkerchief to bandage him. The captain offered to have a couple of his men escort the ensign to the rear, but he objected saying he felt fine. He fainted a second time when he tried to stand up. Ensign David Baird was with him when he was shot, and knowing that he would want to keep his sword, put his own back in its sheaf and picked up Ensign Lake's. Soon after, Ensign Baird was shot in the mouth and the bullet lodged in his throat.[59]

Within the chateau itself the fire continued to rage and soon all the buildings in the lower courtyard, were on fire, except for the farmer's house that was connected to the family quarters on the north side. Many of the serious wounded died in the Great Barn and the other buildings from the flame and smoke or crushed to death by the collapsing roofs. The exact number of the wounded who died in the inferno will never be known, because the buildings held not only British soldiers, but Nassau and Hanoverian troops, plus an occasional Frenchman. The names of the British Guardsmen who died in the inferno is unknown, but it is likely they numbered about twenty.[60]

Arrangements were made to send the wounded to the rear. Among those who left, was Captain Daniel Mackinnon, who had been shot in the knee when the Coldstream Guards cleared the kitchen garden a few hours before. He left the wound untreated and was in excruciating pain. Because all his horses had been killed or wounded, he was carried up the ridge

---

59. Lake, pp.68-69.
60. The light companies of the 1st Foot Guards, the Coldstream Guards, and the 3rd Foot Guards had only ninety-eight sergeants and other ranks reported as having died at Waterloo. According to Dr. Michael Crumplin, 15 to 33 percent of all wounds during the Napoleonic Wars were serious. The Coldstream Guards had 242 enlisted soldiers wounded and fifty-four killed, while the 3rd Foot Guards had 188 wounded and thirty-nine killed. If we use a figure of 20 per cent of the wounded were serious, then the number of seriously wounded men for the two battalions was forty-eight and thirty-eight respectively. The killed to seriously wounded ratio for the two battalions was one man killed for every man seriously wounded. Since the number of men reported killed for the two battalions was ninety-three, perhaps about a quarter of those died in the fire, or about twenty men. As the dead to wounded ratio was around one to five, this infers that the fire probably did not destroy a large number of lightly or seriously wounded soldiers. Those in the upper floor of the family living quarters would have been most at risk.

in a makeshift litter.[61] Ensign Lake was ordered to go get some medical help for his head wound. He climbed the ridge and passed the 1st Foot Guards which were in a square. Behind them were the British 23rd Light Dragoons.[62] As he staggered by the cavalry, one of the officers noticed his plight and offered him a spare horse that belonged to a trooper who had wounded. The only thing the officer asked is for him to bring the horse to the cavalry depot in the city. Ensign Lake considered this act of generosity 'a Godsend for how I should have go to my journey's end on foot I know not'.[63]

Lieutenant George Evelyn of the 3rd Foot Guards' Light Company survived the fire and was able to walk on his own, most likely with the help of his servant. He eventually made it to the hospital at the Mont St. Jean farm, where his wound was dressed. He was told by the surgeon that he would have to have his arm amputated. The lieutenant decided to return to Brussels rather than stay in the hospital. He came across a soldier on horseback, who loaned him the horse. Rumours began to fly that the French cavalry was coming and he pushed the horse into a trot, but had to slow down due to the intense pain. He soon came across a carriage that belonged to the Prince of Orange and convinced him to take him part of the way to Brussels. After being dropped off by the carriage driver, he persuaded a boy who was riding on a horse to take him the rest of the way. He was brought to Madame Janti's house, which was occupied by his friend Lieutenant John Godwin of the 81st Foot.[64] The lieutenant immediately sent for his regimental surgeon, Peter Schooles, who told him that it was as 'bad a wound as he ever saw in a limb.'[65]

After Lord Saltoun and the remnants of the two light companies left the orchard, they quickly moved up to the ridge and rejoined their battalions. There they were treated somewhat as returning heroes. General Maitland told him that: 'Your defence saved the army: nothing could be more

---

61. *Waterloo Archive*, Vol. 4, p.145; Thomson, Vol. 9, p.424.
62. Ensign Lake erroneously identifies the regiment as the 24th Light Dragoons which were not at Waterloo. The 23rd Light Dragoons were position on the ridge near the 1st Foot Guards.
63. Lake, p.68.
64. The 81st Foot was part of the Brussels garrison and did not fight at Waterloo.
65. *Waterloo Archive*, Vol.3, pp.111-112.

gallant. Every man of you deserves promotion'. Saltoun replied that it was, 'touch and go – a matter of life and death – for all within the walls had sworn that they would never surrender'.[66]

The situation for their brigade was not good. After Lord Saltoun and his men had moved down the ridge to Hougoumont, the 1st Brigade remained under almost continuous artillery fire while Hougoumont was being attacked. General Maitland stood with his battalions and exuded a cheerful and calm demeanour. Beneath it though he still felt the loss of his ADC, Ensign James Lord Hay, who had died by his side two days before; and the officers in his brigade whom he got to know so well.[67]

The two battalions were formed in squares and almost everyone, except the officers, were lying down. Ensign Richard Master, the 3rd Battalion's King's Colour Bearer, wrote that: 'We were formed 4 deep in square, receiving the balls and shells, twelve men at a time being wounded and two or three blown up in the air'.[68] Since they were on the reverse slope of the ridge, the biggest danger was exploding shells fired by the enemy howitzers. Captain Goodwin Colquitt was standing in the 2nd Battalion's square when a shell landed between him and another officer. He ran to the smoking shell, which weighed about 9kg, and 'picked it up as if it had been a cricket ball and flung it over the heads of both officers and men, thus saving the lives of many brave fellows'.[69]

The casualties were immense. Lieutenant James Nixon, commander of the 2nd Battalion's 7th Company was lying down to avoid the fire. Standing next to his head was his battalion commander, Captain Richard Cooke. The captain was hit in the shoulder with a cannonball and had to be evacuated to the rear.[70] Captain Francis D'Oyly, then took command of the battalion. Lieutenant Somerville Burgess, the commander of the 2nd Battalion's 4th Company, was also severely injured by the artillery fire. The twenty-one-year-old lieutenant, had served only seven months in the Peninsula, but during that time was in four different actions. He was known as a fire-eater, who 'enjoyed soldiering in the real sense of the

---

66. Gronow, Vol. 2, p.31.
67. Lennox, p.242.
68. Master, p.139.
69. Gronow, Vol. 2, p.20.
70. *Waterloo Archive*, Vol. 1, p.136.

word and sought glory on every field of battle ... and his buoyant spirits and athletic frame fitted him for a military life'.[71] He was hit by a cannon ball that shattered his leg. He was evacuated to the dressing station where his leg was amputated. After performing the operation, the surgeon called over a couple of soldiers to help the lieutenant to a cart. He refused to be carried and said, 'I will hop into it'. Surprisingly he was able to do this without further damaging himself.[72]

The situation in the squares was total carnage. Casualties continued to mount during the afternoon. The worst thing for the soldiers was that they could do nothing. They had to lie there and take it without being able to respond because the enemy was too far away. Colour Sergeant Charles Wood, the senior non-commissioned officer in the 3rd Battalion's 7th Company spoke to his men at the beginning of the bombardment telling them to 'be steady and attentive to orders – keep perfect silence – and put your whole trust in God's help, for he is with us'.[73]

Years later, Ensign Rees Gronow left a vivid description what it was like to be in the 3rd Battalion's square: 'Inside we were nearly suffocated by the smoke and smell from burnt cartridges. It was impossible to move a yard without treading upon a wounded comrade, or upon the bodies of the dead; and the loud groans of the wounded and dying were most appalling. At four o'clock our square was a perfect hospital being full of dead, dying, and mutilated soldiers'.[74]

---

71. Gronow, Vol. 2, p.23-24.
72. ibid.
73. *Waterloo Archive*, Vol. 6, p.128.
74. Gronow, Vol. 2, p.18-19.

Chapter 12

18 June 1815
Waterloo 16.00-20.00 Hours

The Great Cavalry Charges

For Napoleon the attack on Hougoumont was supposed to be a diversion. Its mission was to convince Wellington that was where the main attack would be made and force him to take troops from other parts of the line to reinforce it. Once the centre of the line was weakened sufficiently, Napoleon would launch the main assault up the Brussels-Charleroi Road.

While the 6th Division fought for possession of Hougoumont, the French continued to bombard the Allied line. About 13.00 hours Napoleon received word from Colonel Jean-Baptiste Marbot, who was screening the right flank of the army with his 7th Hussars, that he had captured some Prussian hussars. After searching the prisoners, they discovered a message to Wellington from General Friedrich Bülow, the commander of the Prussian 4th Corps. This was the first information that Napoleon received that the Prussians were not retreating away from Brussels but marching to support Wellington.[1]

Consequently, Napoleon ordered Lieutenant General Jean Drouet, Comte d'Erlon, and his 18,000-man 1st Corps to attack the centre of the Allied line. Napoleon believed this portion of the line was its weakest because of the large number of Dutch troops there.[2] Visible on the ridge was the 1st Brigade of the 2nd Netherlands Division. Behind it, protected

---

1. Field; *Waterloo*, pp.80-81.
2. 'As for the Belgians, they had proved to be good soldiers and steadfast allies, and Napoleon believed that at the first reverse they would enthusiastically take up their old alliance with France,' ibid, p.85.

by the reverse slope of the ridge, were the three brigades of Lieutenant General Picton's 5th Division. Both divisions had fought at Quatre Bras and had taken heavy casualties. The four divisions of the French 1st Corps would attack to the east of the Charleroi-Brussels Road. The 1st Division, commanded by Général de Brigade Baron Joachim Quoit, would attack up the road and try to take La Haye Sainte, the farmhouse that served as a strongpoint in front of the Allied line. Lieutenant General François Donzelot's 2nd Division would be to its right, with Lieutenant General Pierre Marcognet's 3rd Division to its right. On the right flank was Général de Brigade Jean Pégot's 1st Brigade of Lieutenant General Pierre Durutte's 4th Division.

The 1st Corps began its attack about 13.30 hours. The area it was advancing through was less than 1.5km wide. The 1st Division became bogged down trying to capture La Haye Sainte. The rest of the corps, proceeded by skirmishers, quickly marched up the hill brushing aside the Dutch skirmishers. As they crested the ridge and pushed through a hedge lined road, they were met by the fire of Major General Sir James Kempt's 8th British Brigade and Major General Sir Denis Pack's 9th British Brigade. The French were not aware that there were British troops behind the Dutch and the heavy fire staggered them. Between forcing their way through the hedge and the many casualties caused by the British fire, the French attack lost its momentum and stalled. They continued to fight in a disorganized manner and a few battalions went forward but were unable to pierce the British line. It was during this fight that General Picton was shot in the head and killed. Shortly after General Picton died, his ADC, Captain Newton Chambers of the 1st Battalion 1st Foot Guards, also was killed.[3] General Kempt, the senior brigade commander in the 5th Division, assumed command of the division after General Picton's death.

As the French officers tried to gain control of their battalions and force them to continue their attack, the British launched the 2nd British Cavalry

---

3. There is contradictory evidence about when Captain Chambers was killed. Ensign Gronow wrote thirty-eight years later that: 'After Picton's death, poor Chambers, in carrying orders to Sir James Kempt to retake at all hazards the farm of La Haye Sainte, advanced at the head of the attacking column, and was in the act of receiving the sword of a French officer who had surrendered to him, when he received a musket ball through the lungs, which killed him on the spot'. This would have placed his death about 18.30 hours. However, Ensign Gronow was not there when he said Captain Chambers was killed; Gronow, Vol. 2, p.21).

Brigade against the disordered French troops. The Brigade, known as the Union Brigade had three regiments, one each of English, Scot, and Irish Dragoons.[4] Commanded by Major General Sir William Ponsonby, it had a strength of 1,300 officers and men. In one of the greatest cavalry charges of the Napoleonic Wars, the three regiments caught the 1st Corps by surprise and shattered it. Thousands of the French were killed or wounded, another 2,000 were taken prisoner, and the eagles of the 45th and 105th line regiments were captured. It would be hours before the remaining officers and men could be re-organized for another attack. The Union Brigade also took heavy casualties, including its commander who was killed by counter-attacking French cavalry. Despite its epic charge, for all practical purposes the Union Brigade was destroyed.[5]

After the 2nd Brigade of the Guards Division moved to Hougoumont, Wellington ordered Colonel Johann Elias Olfermann, the commander of the Brunswick Corps, to send three battalions forward to fill the gap in the line.[6] At 16.00, Lieutenant General Sir Henry Clinton, commander of the 2nd Division, ordered the 1st King's German Legion Brigade, commanded by Brevet Colonel Charles Du Plat, from its position about 500m in the rear of the line, down the ridge, to support the 2nd Guards Brigade in Hougoumont. The rest of the 2nd Division's brigades remained behind the front lines.

By 16.00 hours the forces deployed in the vicinity of the Guards included: to the left of the 3rd Battalion 1st Foot Guards was Major General Sir Colin Halkett's 5th British Brigade of the 3rd Division. To the right rear, about 50m away was the 2nd Battalion 1st Foot Guards. To the right front of the 2nd Battalion were the three Brunswick infantry battalions. To the rear were the two brigades of the 2nd Infantry Division and five Brunswick battalions. On the forward slope of the ridge, between the Brunswick battalions and Hougoumont were the four battalions of Colonel Du Plat's 1st KGL Brigade. In anticipation of a cavalry attack, these twenty-six battalions were in columns that would allow them to quickly move into a square should they be attacked by cavalry. The battalions were arranged in a giant checkerboard pattern that would allow mutual fire support if attacked.

---

4. The 1st (Royal) Dragoons, 2nd (Royal North British) Dragoons, and the 6th (Inniskilling) Dragoons.
5. Adkins, pp.246-247; Field, *Waterloo*, p.121.
6. These were the 2nd and 3rd Light Battalions and the 3rd Line Battalion, *Waterloo Archive*, Vol. 5, p.163.

Left behind on the ridge when the 2nd Battalion 3rd Foot Guards moved to Hougoumont, were the colours, and the 7th and 8th companies of the Coldstream Guards under the command of Captain Henry Dawkins. This detachment had less than 200 officers and men.[7] According to Ensign Charles Short, who carried the battalion's colours they stayed to the immediate right of 2nd Battalion 1st Foot Guards. Too weak to form an effective square, they were ordered by General Byng to retire to the rear should the French cavalry attack.[8]

By 16.00 the 1st Division's situation was not much better. Except for two companies of the 2nd Battalion Coldstreams, all of the 2nd Brigade had been committed to the defence of Hougoumont. The 1st Brigade, which had taken over 25 per cent casualties two days before at Quatre Bras, had been under almost continuous artillery fire for over four hours. Although the two battalions of the 1st Foot Guards were protected by the ridge, their casualties were slowly beginning to climb. They included Captain Henry D'Oyly, the second-in-command of the 3rd Battalion. He had been severely wounded and had to be evacuated.[9] The division command group was mounted on horses in order to maintain command and control. They were one of the few visible targets for the French artillery and they did not go unscathed. Lieutenant Colonel Henry Bradford,[10] the 1st Division's AQMG had two horses wounded, while a cannonball knocked his hat off and another hit his scabbard and bent it.[11] Shortly after 16.00 a shell hit the division's command group and General Cooke was struck in the left arm. Lieutenant Colonel Henry Rooke, the division's AAG, was next to him when he was hit and the general fell into his and Captain

---

7. The 7th Company, commanded by Lieutenant George Bowles, had two officers, three sergeants, six corporals, two drummers, and seventy-eight privates on the morning of 18 June. The 8th Company, commanded by Captain Henry Dawkins, had two officers, six sergeants, four corporals, two drummers, and seventy-five privates. There would have been another two officers carrying the colours, guarded by four sergeants.
8. *Waterloo Letters*, p.265.
9. *Letters from the Battle of Waterloo*, p.346.
10. Lieutenant Colonel Bradford belonged to the 2nd Battalion 1st Foot Guards.
11. Sheardown, W., *Records and Family Notices of Military and Naval Officers Connected with Doncaster and Its Neighbourhood*. Doncaster: Gazette, 1873, p.5.

George Disbrowe's arms. The two of them, along with his extra ADC, Ensign Augustus Cuyler,[12] evacuated him to the field hospital at Mont St. Jean, where his arm was amputated close to the shoulder.[13] Among those assisting General Cooke to the rear was Private Samuel Perkins of the Light Company of the 2nd Battalion 1st Foot Guards.[14]

This effectively decapitated the division's command structure. Three of General Cooke's staff had escorted him to the hospital, leaving only Lieutenant Colonel Bradford to notify General Byng that he was now in command. It did not take him long to find the general, who also did not have much of a staff left. His ADC, Captain Henry Dumaresq, and Brigade Major, Captain William Stothert,[15] had both been seriously wounded, leaving him only his extra ADC, Ensign Hon. Edward Stopford.[16] General Byng had to let Major Hepburn, the commander of the 2nd Battalion 3rd Foot Guards, know that he was now the acting commander of the 2nd Brigade. His only option was to send Ensign Stopford to Hougoumont to inform him. General Byng rode with Lieutenant Colonel Bradford back to the vicinity of the 1st Brigade, arriving there just as Napoleon launched a massive cavalry attack against the Allied army lines between La Haye Sainte and Hougoumont.[17] The 1st Brigade was the centre point of the French attack.

The Great Cavalry Charges

There is much confusion about the French cavalry charges that struck the Allied infantry in the late afternoon. Although most sources agree on which regiments charged, there is no general consensus on what French regiments attacked the different Allied battalions. Almost every account left by British Guards say they were charged by cuirassiers and lancers. The lancers are usually identified as being part of the Imperial Guard, but most called them Polish lancers. As for the cuirassiers, the British accounts only identify them as cuirassiers. Their steel cuirasses and helmets would make them hard to mistake. Compounding the issue of who attacked where, is

---

12. Ensign Cuyler was from the 2nd Battalion Coldstream Guards.
13. *Waterloo Archive*, Vol. 1, pp.3-4.
14. Chambers, Vol. 2, p.595.
15. Captain Stothert was in the 2nd Battalion 3rd Foot Guards.
16. Ensign Stopford was from the 1st Battalion 3rd Foot Guards.
17. *Waterloo Archive*, Vol. 4, p.144.

the question of how many charges were made against the Foot Guards? The French attacked in two separate waves and during each wave the cavalry regiments might have charged up the ridge, fell back, and then charged again several times. The few surviving French accounts usually do not say. A possible exception is that of Fortuné Brack, an officer in the Imperial Guard's 2nd Lancers. He claims his regiment charged five times.[18] In the end, for the two battalions of the 1st Foot Guards, it did not really matter. They had to hold their position until the cavalry stopped coming.

By 16.00, the French infantry attacks against the centre had been unable to capture La Haye Sainte and break the Allied line. Napoleon had received intelligence that the Prussian Army was approaching from the east and would be there in a few hours. He had to break Wellington's army before the Prussians arrived and greatly outnumber his force. He ordered Lieutenant General Edouard Milhaud, the commander of the 4th Reserve Cavalry Corps to attack the Allied line between La Haye Sainte and Hougoumont. His command of 4,000 men,[19] consisted of Lieutenant General Pierre Watier's 13th Cavalry Division and Lieutenant General Jacques Delort's 14th Cavalry Division. Each division had two brigades of two cuirassier regiments. Supporting each of the divisions was a horse artillery battery of six 6-pounder guns and four 5.5-inch howitzers. With the 4th Reserve Cavalry Corps rode the Imperial Guard Light Cavalry Division, commanded by Lieutenant General Charles Lefebvre-Desnouëttes. It consisted of only two regiments, the Guard Chasseurs-à-Cheval and the 2nd Lancers.[20]

The cuirassier regiments were heavy cavalry and were trained to charge and break infantry on the battlefield. The men were selected for their size and were usually at least 177 cm (70 inches) in height. They wore a cuirass of steel[21] and a helmet. Because of their size and equipment, the cuirassier rode large horses, between 156 cm and 160 cm height at the shoulders (61-63 inches). The Norman Cob was the preferred horse, but due to the losses of horses between 1812 and 1814, almost any large, healthy horse was accepted. The Imperial Guard Chasseurs and Lancers were the elite of Napoleon's Light cavalry

---

18. Pawley, Ronald, *The Red Lancers*. Ramsbury: Crowood, 1998, p.108.
19. The 4th Reserve Cavalry Corps had fought at Ligny on 16 June and had several hundred casualties.
20. Adkin, p.56.
21. A cuirass was armour that covered the rider's upper body both in the front and back.

and each of the regiments were as large a cuirassier brigade. Their horses were smaller with a height of between 140 cm and 147 cm at the shoulders (55-58 inches) and horses from Tarbe and Agen were preferred. The light cavalry troopers of the Imperial Guard tended to be smaller with an upper limit of 172 cm in height. What they lacked in size, they made up in experience. All were brought into the Guard after serving several years in line cavalry regiments.[22]

About 18.00, General Kellermann and the 3,600 men of his 3rd Reserve Cavalry Corps was sent in. Its 11th Division, commanded by Lieutenant General Samuel L'Héritier, was the cavalry that wreaked so much havoc on the British infantry two days before at Quatre Bras, but it had taken heavy casualties there. Its cuirassier brigade was down to about 500 mounted men. The dragoon brigade was stronger with about 1,100 men. Lieutenant General Nicolas Roussel d'Hurbal's 12th Division was about the same strength as the 11th Division, but it had seen little combat since the campaign began. It had four regiments of heavy cavalry: the 1st and 2nd Carabiniers in the 1st Brigade and the 2nd and 3rd Cuirassiers in the 2nd Brigade.

The officers of the 1st Foot Guards could see the cavalry moving in the distance and when the French artillery finally stopped its bombardment, they knew that the cavalry would be coming their way. To some they welcomed the cessation of the artillery. Even though they knew that soon they would face some of the best cavalry in the world, they would finally get a chance to hit back at the enemy.[23] Captain Stanhope now felt that possibly all the rain the night before was not at all that bad because there was no 'dust we saw every movement plain and would fire without risk to each other. Nothing daunts the soldier more so much as a charge of cavalry proceeded by a cloud of dust which concealing the force magnifies the peril'.[24]

The Allied artillery opened-up on the French cavalry as soon as it came in range. Despite round shot knocking men and horses down, the cuirassiers closed up their ranks and kept on coming. Timing for the British

---

22. Dawson, Paul L., *Au Gallop! Horses and Riders of Napoleon's Army*. Stockton-on-Tees: Black Tent, 2013, pp.88 & 119. Dawson, Paul L., *Crippled Splendour: the French Cavalry from Valmy to Toulouse*. Stockton-on-Tees: Black Tent, 2016. p.18. For more detailed information on the problems finding mounts in 1815, see Paul Dawson's *Au Pas de Charge!*, pp.22-32.
23. Gronow, Vol. 2 p.19.
24. *Waterloo Archive*, Vol. 6, p.123.

artillery crews was critical. They stayed with their guns to the last possible second and then ran for the safety of the squares. One of the first squares to be hit was that of the 3rd Battalion 1st Foot Guards. They knew it was time to stand up when the artillerymen started running over the ridge. The officers ordered the men to get up and they moved to the crest of the hill. There they saw 'a mass of cuirassiers close to us with thousands of forked pennons waving behind them in all their vanity of colours'.[25] The pennons were on the end of the lances of the 2nd Guard Lancer Regiment. In the centre of the square stood the colour party with the colours unfurled.[26]

French cavalry usually moved at a trot until they got within 50m of their target and then they urged their horses into a gallop. The sudden appearance of an infantry battalion stopped the cuirassiers in their tracks. They were too close to the infantry to build up speed to make their charge effective. Ensign Robert Batty, commander of the 3rd Battalion's 1st Company, whose company was on the face of the square opposite of them, wrote shortly after the battle that a few of the cuirassiers 'with a courage worthy a better cause, rode out of the ranks, and fired at our people and mounted officers with their pistols, hoping to make the face of the square throw its fire upon them, and thus become an easy prey: but our men, with a steadiness no language can do justice to, defied their efforts, and did not pull a single trigger. The French then made a sudden rush, but were received in such a manner, and with a volley so well directed, as at once to turn them'. The regiment retreated down the hill, re-organized itself and then charged again, but this time against the 2nd Battalion's square. They had no luck there either.

The cuirassiers returned again and again. The artillery took a great toll but that did not stop them. After the first charge, they knew what was waiting for them on the other side of the ridge and rode up it at a gallop that caused the earth to shake. The Guards officers told their men not to fire at the cuirassiers but to fire low to hit their horses, because that would dismount them and 'with their cuirasses and big Jack boots they were sure to stick in the muddy field and be knocked over at ease'.[27] Another described the sound of the bullets hitting their cuirasses like the 'the noise of a violent hail-storm beating upon panes of glass'.[28]

---

25. Stanhope, p.176.
26. Master, p.139.
27. ibid.
28. Gronow, Vol. 2, p.19.

A few days after the battle, Captain Stanhope, of the 3rd Battalion, wrote a vivid description of the charges:

> Soon after a cry of cavalry was heard on the crest of the hill & we saw the artillerymen run from their guns & seek protection in our squares. The men stood up; we advanced a few yards & saw a mass of cuirassiers close to us with thousands of forked pennons waving behind them in all their vanity of colours. From the rain there was no dust & it was a most beautiful sight. The square on the left of the 3rd Division opened their fire first and soon from every square issued a steady well directed & destructive fire. For four hours the cavalry never left our front, sometimes retiring a little under the hill to get into order & then charging afresh with all the fury of despair; it is not possible to exaggerate their bravery. They repeatedly rode in upon & got temporary possession of our guns; the instant our fire drove them back, our brave artillerymen returned & poured fresh volleys of grape into their dense masses till successive charges drove them back into our squares. Thus continued our part of the battle & except a momentary impetuosity on first beating off the cavalry, when our men shouted & wished to charge, they were as cool as if in the park. The French cavalry at length sent skirmishers close up to us to fire pistols into our squares to tease us into a volley at these small game, whilst we saw their great masses below laying wait to charge; but we were as cool as they were & allowed only a few of our good shots to pick these fellows off. When we drove the cavalry from the guns many came up to us & shook their sabres at us in rage & some smashed their swords on the guns they had so often ineffectively taken.[29]

A French officer in the 9th Cuirassier Regiment, which might have been one of the regiments that charged the 1st Foot Guards,[30] wrote about what it was like to make the charge:

> My men were restless in their saddles and often fidgeted. I felt excited and eager to gallop in our turn. The cannonade was of unbelievable proportions, I had to shout to make myself heard when I gave the order to tighten the girths on the horses.

---

29. Stanhope, pp.176-177.
30. Adkins, p.357.

Now was the time for us to fight. God be praised! The Division advanced, followed by the mounted chasseurs and red lancers of the Guard. We formed in the hollow of the valley, then we came forward in column of squadrons, in checkerboard formation, towards the road of Ohain, towards Braine-La-Eud [sic – L'Alleud]. The mounted chasseurs and the red lancers were on our left and we ascended the rising ground at the trot. The ground was muddy, churned up and very slippery. Our horses slipped, and every moment seemed as if they were to fall over.

A sea of steel arose. The English projectiles cut down the squadrons at the front and the ranks were somehow reformed. The charge was sounded; cries of Vive l'Empereur vibrated through the smoke. A cannon ball grazed my knee and cut down two riders behind me. We were now on the plateau, amid the guns abandoned by their servants, and the English infantry presented their bayonets into the chests of our horses. Lances, swords, pistols worked best, but there was not enough momentum for a new charge. It stalled from the start. Death, death and still more death and wounded I saw around me. The bullets hit our armour as a ladle on a pot... my blood boiled as I advanced, with my sword in hand, my guard served me as a club, I shouted, I rounded up my men. As in a fog, I thought I saw our quartermaster waving, with an outstretched arm, a kind of floating object that seemed to be red and blue but I could not clearly distinguished.

I rescued, with great sabre cuts, my non-commissioned officer who had become dismounted in the fight against the bayonets; a gray horse that was riderless, with his nostril quivering, his neck affected in two places was mounted by the sergeant with my aid. Suddenly, I felt a shock to the head; a ball had passed through the crest of my helmet, close to the steel comb. At that moment, exhausted, we retreated without success.[31]

The unknown French officer's wound was more serious than he thought. He was captured by the British and died from gangrene in Brussels on 4 July.

When the cuirassiers finally withdrew after being unable to break the Allied squares, it was the 2nd Lancers of the Imperial Guard's turn. They were nicknamed the Red Lancers due to their red, Polish-style uniform. About 800 men strong they surged over the ridge, being hit by cannon

---

31. Dawson; *Au Pas de Charge!*, p.142.

balls and shrapnel the whole way. One lancer officer, who was determined to silence the guns that were taking such a heavy toll of his men rode, straight at the gun immediately before it fired, determined to sacrifice his own life to prevent it from killing his soldiers. Fate intervened, and the round missed him. But he stood by the gun while his men continued their charge and was able to prevent its crew from re-manning it. He was eventually killed by a Brunswick soldier who was just west of the gun.[32]

Twenty years later, Captain Fortuné Brack of the 2nd Lancer Regiment described what it was like to charge the Guards' squares:

> We rode through the batteries, which we were unable to drag back with us. We turned back and threatened the squares, which put up a most honourable resistance. Some of them had such coolness, that they were still firing ordered volleys by rank. It has been said that the Dragoons and Mounted Grenadiers to our left broke several squares; personally I did not see it – and I can state we Lancers did not have the same luck, and that we crossed our lances with the English Bayonets in vain. Many of our troopers threw their weapons like spears into the front ranks to try and open the squares.
>
> The expenditure of ammunition by the English front line and the compact pattern of the squares which composed it mean that the firing was at point blank range, but it was the harm which the artillery and squares in the second line were doing to us, in the absence of infantry and artillery to support our attack, which determined our retreat.
>
> We moved slowly, and faced front again in our position at the bottom of the slope, so that we could just make out the first English line. It was then that Marshal Ney, alone, without a single one of his staff accompanying him, rode along our front and harangued us, calling out to the officers he knew by their names. His face was distracted, and he cried out again and again: "Frenchmen, let us stand firm! It is here that the keys to our freedom are lying!" I quote him word for word.
>
> Five times we repeated the charge; but since the conditions remained unchanged; we returned to our position at the rear five times. There at 150 paces, from the enemy infantry, we were exposed to the most murderous fire. Our men began to lose heart;

---

32. Clarke, Hewson, *History of the War from the Commencement of the French Revolution to the Present Time*. 3 vols. London: Kinnersley, 1816. Vol. 3, p.280.

they were being hit at the same time by bullets from the front and cannonballs from the flank, and by new projectiles (small shells) which exploded above their heads and fell.[33]

Critical to the survival of the squares was the Allied artillery on either side and in front of them. The crews bravely stood by their guns, firing them until the last possible moment and then running as fast as possible to the safety of the squares. Some who were wounded or too tired to move dived beneath the guns hoping that the charging cavalry would ignore them as they rode by. Directly to the west of the 3rd Battalion's square was Captain (Brevet Major) William Lloyd's Brigade of 9-pounders. Ensign Batty watched the captain and another officer who, 'was obliged to take refuge in our square at the time these charges were made, being unable to continue longer at their posts. There was a gun between our battalion and the Brunswickers, which had been drawn back; this major [sic] Lloyd, with his friend, discharged five or six times at the French cavalry, alternately loading it and retiring to the square as circumstances required. We could see the French knocked off their horses as fast as they came up'.[34]

Twenty-year old Lieutenant Basil Jackson, of the Royal Staff Corps, who was serving as a DAQMG was in the 3rd Battalion's square also saw the heroics of Captain Lloyd and said that he never went into the square, but instead he 'found shelter under its lee. When the enemy withdrew, the six guns remained untouched; seeing which, Lloyd ran up to them, followed by the young staff officer in question, and seizing a rammer, tried one of the pieces, which he found loaded; this he fired upon the retiring foe, then not a hundred and fifty yards distant; a second gun was also found loaded, and the cuirassiers treated with another parting salute. This was the work of only a minute or two, and as yet the gunners had not returned'.[35] During one of the charges by the 2nd Lancers, Captain Lloyd stayed too long with the guns. He was run down by a lancer officer and seriously wounded.[36]

About 17.30, the French cavalry attacks petered out and they withdrew down the ridge so they were out of range of the infantry. The 2nd Lancers

---

33. Pawley, pp.108-109.
34. Clarke, Vol. 3, p.280.
35. Jackson, Basil, *With Wellington's Staff at Waterloo: the Reminiscences of a Staff Officer during the Campaign of 1815 and with Napoleon on St. Helena.* Leonaur, 2010. p.37.
36. Captain Lloyd died from his wound in Brussels on 29 July, *Waterloo Letters*, p.235; Dalton, p.224.

dismounted half of their squadrons just inside musket range and 'a voluntary truce, so to speak was reached between the combatants due to the complete exhaustion of the troops'. [37] The British Guards took the time to re-organize their squares, evacuate the seriously wounded, and re-distribute ammunition.

The two companies of the Coldstream Guards, who were to the right of the 2nd Battalion 1st Foot Guards immediately retired to the rear as soon as it was apparent they were about to be charged by cavalry. They moved about 750m to the west northwest across the Nivelles Road towards Braine-l'Alleud. There they found a hollow that provided protection from artillery. To the right was the 51st Foot of the 4th British Brigade of the 4th Division.[38]

The 1st Division's artillery was missing. Most of the guns remained, but their crews were gone. During one of the cavalry attacks both Captain Sandham's Artillery Brigade and Captain Kuhlmann's Horse Artillery Troop disappeared. The ground on the ridge was still heavily saturated with water from the previous night's rain and had been torn up by the hooves of the charging cavalry.[39] Captain Sandham was able to move some of his guns to the rear but left the others.[40] Finding his guns too difficult to move, Captain Kuhlmann chose to leave them and rode away on the troop's limbers and horses. In his after-action report, Captain Kuhlmann justified the abandoning of the position and his guns:

> It then turned out that our position had in effect been broken through because the enemy cavalry moved down behind the said plateau out of our sight. It unexpectedly fell on our left flank and forced us to retreat. It was only at some distance to the rear that my battery was able to locate a somewhat empty space, free of retreating troops and wagons, where other batteries had already halted and where it was possible to put everything in order to the extent circumstances permitted, which was indeed a time consuming process. It was at this time also that Lieutenant Colonel Adye joined us with his English battery, which had retreated further to the rear. Since on the 16th that battery had fired less than ours, it now had to let us have some of its ammunition.[41]

---

37. Pawley, p.109.
38. *Waterloo Letters*, pp.265-266.
39. *Waterloo Archive*, Vol. 4, p.130.
40. *Waterloo Letters*, p.225.
41. *Waterloo Archive*, Vol. 2, p.44.

After the initial attacks by the French cavalry, General Clinton ordered the 3rd British Brigade, commanded by Major General Frederick Adam, to advance from its position in the rear of the 1st Guards Brigade, down the slope to the vicinity of Hougoumont. The battalions marched in a four-deep line and stopped with its right anchored on the northeastern corner of the orchard. There they stood targeted by French skirmishers and artillery fire. In front of the 1st Foot Guards was the 1st Battalion 52nd Foot.[42]

The lull in activity lasted until around 18.00 hours when the cuirassiers of General Kellermann's 3rd Reserve Cavalry Corps charged. This time the French brought up artillery. The cavalry charged again and still could not penetrate the squares: 'The horses of the first rank of cuirassiers, in spite of all the efforts of their riders, came to a stand-still, shaking and covered with foam, at about twenty yards' distance from our squares, and generally resisted all attempts to force them to charge the line of serried steel... In the midst of our terrible fire, their officers were seen as if on parade, keeping order in their ranks, and encouraging them. Unable to renew the charge, but unwilling to retreat, they brandished their swords with loud cries of *'Vive l'Empereur!'* and allowed themselves to be mowed down by hundreds rather than yield. Our men, who shot them down, could not help admiring the gallant bearing and heroic resignation of their enemies.'[43]

The artillery that the French cavalry brought with them began to take its toll. At one point it created a hole in the 3rd Battalion's square. Two French officers charged through the gap into the centre of the square where they were met by Captain Stables and Lieutenant Lonsdale Boldero,[44] the battalion's acting adjutant. The two cuirassier officers were quickly surrounded and killed.[45]

Throughout the French cavalry attacks, Wellington was in the vicinity and moved from square to square to encourage the troops. 'He appeared perfectly composed; but looked very thoughtful and pale. He was dressed in a gray great-coat with a cape, white cravat, leather pantaloons, Hessian

---

42. For more information about their movement, see Chapter 13 of Gareth Glover's *Waterloo: The Defeat of Napoleon's imperial Guard*.
43. Gronow, Vol. 2, p.19-20.
44. Lieutenant Boldero was assigned to the 1st Battalion 1st Foot Guards but was serving as the 3rd Battalion's acting adjutant. Ensign Gronow misidentifies him as Lieutenant Robert Adair who was seriously wounded at Quatre Bras and was not at Waterloo.
45. Gronow, Vol. 2, p.19.

boots, and a large cocked hat à la Russe.'[46] Lieutenant General Lord Uxbridge, was also there, and at one point rode up to the 3rd Battalion and said, 'Well done men, by God we stand on you. If I could only get my fellows to do the same but by God they won't budge; but I'll try again'.[47] General Lord Uxbridge did try to find some cavalry support for the Guards, but the only available British cavalry was Major General Colquhoun Grant's 5th Hussar Brigade but it was already committed in support of General Clinton's 2nd Division.

Around 18.00, the French sent infantry skirmishers with the cavalry of General Kellermann's Corps. Once again, the cuirassiers found that they were unable to break the squares and soon retreated back down the ridge. The French skirmishers however, remained. Their fire proved to be effective especially against the officers. Among those hit, was the division's AQMG, Lieutenant Colonel Henry Bradford, who was severely wounded in the hip, while the DAQMG, Captain Edward Fitzgerald[48] was also wounded. Major General Byng needed help and ordered Captain James Stanhope[49] to take Lieutenant Colonel Bradford's place. Fearing that the enemy would capture the guns which had been abandoned after the previous cavalry attack, General Byng sent Captain Stanhope to the rear to find the missing artillerymen.[50]

It was likely that it was during this fire that Captain Charles Thomas, the commander of the 3rd Battalion's 5th Company was killed. General Maitland was in the 3rd Battalion's square directly behind its front face with Brigade Major Captain James Gunthorpe, and other staff officers. He quickly grew tired of the annoying fire, but there was little he could do because the French cavalry was too close. Captain Horace Seymour,[51] an ADC to Lieutenant General Lord Uxbridge, rode into the square and asked, 'God damn you; don't you see there are French.

---

46. ibid, Vol. 3, p.70.
47. Stanhope, p.177.
48. Of the 25th Foot.
49. Captain Stanhope commanded the 3rd Battalion's 8th Company.
50. *Waterloo Archive*, Vol. 5, p.118.
51. Captain Seymour, of the 60th Foot, was known as 'the strongest man in the British Army'. *The Waterloo Roll Call* mistakenly has him in the 18th Hussars, however he was promoted to captain in the 60th Foot on 6 April 1815. Possibly causing the confusion is that the return of wounded staff for Waterloo, Captain Seymour is recorded as being a lieutenant in the 18th Hussars, Dalton; p.12.

Why don't you fire at them?' Lord Saltoun coolly replied, 'Why damn you; don't you think we know better when to fire than you do?'[52]

After being on the receiving end of their fire for a time, General Maitland decided to force the enemy skirmishers to retreat by moving the 3rd Battalion forward down the ridge. Instead of forming into the traditional two-deep line and thus exposing themselves to the cavalry in the distance, he ordered them into a four-deep line. At this time the 3rd Battalion was in an oblong square with the Grenadier Company facing south towards the French, with the 1st Company directly behind it. The Left Divisions of the 2nd, 3rd, 4th, 5th, and 6th Companies formed the left (or east) face of the square, while the Right Divisions of the 2nd, 3rd, 4th, 5th, and 6th Companies formed the right (west) face of the square. The 7th and 8th Companies formed the rear face of the square.[53]

Gren & 1st	
2L	2R
3L	3R
4L	4R
5L	5R
6L	6R
7th & 8th	

3rd Battalion 1st Foot Guards Oblong Square

When the order was given, the battalion 'opened from the centre of the rear face of the Square that face and the two flank faces bringing their right and left shoulders forward until in line with the front face, thus forming an irregular line of four deep'.[54]

---

52. Stanhope, p.177.
53. *Letters from the Battle of Waterloo*, p.162.
54. *Waterloo Letters*, p.256.

::: _ _ _ _ _ _ _ _ _ _ _ _ _ _ _ _ _ _ ::: LT 8L 7L 6L 5L 4L 3L 2L Gren & 1st 2R 3R 4R 5R 6R 7R 8R LT	

The 3rd Battalion 1st Foot Guards Deployed in a 4 Deep Line

The 3rd Battalion did not stop at driving the skirmishers off. Instead General Maitland ordered his men to march over the ridge and down into the valley below, about 300m further south. As they marched down the ridge, the general could see a large mass of cavalry to their front. He halted the battalion and ordered it back into a square.[55] This left the battalion in an exposed position. The left of the battalion was unprotected, but to its right was a large number of the skirmishers from the 2nd Battalion 95th Rifles. To the right of the rifles was the 1st Battalion 52nd Foot. On the other side of the 52nd Foot was the eastern hedge of the Hougoumont orchard.[56]

The move surprised the French and at first they did not respond. Perhaps they thought that British cavalry was about to charge, because according to Colour Sergeant Charles Wood, they too formed squares.[57] Unfortunately for the British Guardsmen their movement down the slope put them in canister range of the French artillery on the slope on the other side of the valley. They were quickly brought under fire and began to take heavy casualties. General Maitland wrote later that the 'enemy poured on us a heavy fire of his artillery, mowed a passage two or three times through the faces of our square, while the cavalry were prepared on our right to take advantage of the least disorder'.[58] The general was not the only one concerned that the fire might break the square and thus expose them to the enemy cavalry. Colour Sergeant Wood wrote that the French artillery had 'raked us with grape, canister, and horse nails;[59] and our line at two different times was so shattered that I feared they could

---

55. *Waterloo Archive*, Vol. 4, p.132; *Waterloo Letters*, p.247.
56. Glover, Gareth. *Waterloo: The Defeat of Napoleon's Imperial Guard, Henry Clinton, the 2nd Division and the End of a 200-year-old Controversy*. Barnsley: Frontline, 2015, p.141.
57. *Waterloo Archive*, Vol. 6, p.129.
58. ibid, Vol. 4, p.132.
59. The artillery rounds filled with horseshoe nails were called langrage and was basically anything on hand that could be shoved into the muzzle as an anti-personnel round. Email from Kevin Kiley dated 1 November 2017.

not stand'.[60] Among the casualties was Captain Edward Stables, the 3rd Battalion's acting commander, who was hit by canister shot and had to be evacuated. The next surviving senior officer was Captain George Fead who assumed command.

Soon the French regiment[61] came out of its squares and advanced on the Guards. A desperate exchange of fire, unlike the Guards had ever seen, began between the two. Casualties mounted quickly for the men in four ranks and among the officers. Ensign Edward Pardoe was shot in the forehead while standing in the centre of the square next to Ensign Richard Master, who was the King's Colour bearer. The dead ensign was particularly unlucky. He had been shot in both arms and captured at Bergen-op-Zoom the year before and had just returned to the battalion three days before. Ensign Master quickly removed Ensign Pardoe's sash, watch, and other valuables so that they would not be stolen.[62] Those who could fire, began to run out of ammunition and the square began to unravel. 'The sergeants placed their pikes against the men's backs in line … and bore them up by their shoulders by main strength. Some of the men kept up firm in line, but others fell back to get out ammunition, and others were begging ammunition in the rear as all their own was spent, which with our continual loss, quite unsteadied the line, so the pikes were intended to prevent any from falling back for ammunition, as we wanted the men to use the bayonets.'[63]

During a pause in the firing Colour Sergeant Wood noticed that someone had removed Ensign Pardoe's coat. Fearing the battalion would break at any moment and be run down by the French cavalry, he grabbed the bloody coat and forced himself through the ranks of the square and stood about 20m in front of it. He turned to their battered ranks and while waving the coat over his head called to them, that 'while our officers bled

---

60. *Waterloo Archive*, Vol. 6, p.129.
61. Colour Sergeant Wood identified the regiment as the 105th Regiment. However, he was probably mistaken, since it had been shattered by the charge of the Union Brigade a few hours before and lost its eagle. It was most likely the 108th Regiment, which was part of the 2nd Brigade of Lieutenant General Gilbert Bachelu's 5th Division of the 2nd Corps, and in the vicinity.
62. Master, p.140. After the battle Ensign Master delivered these items to Ensign Pardoe's relative, Lieutenant Charles Allix, the adjutant of the 2nd Battalion 1st Foot Guards.
63. *Waterloo Archive*, Vol. 6, p.129.

we should not reckon our lives dear'.[64] This seemed to steady the men and eventually the French infantry withdrew.

The 3rd Battalion was not out of danger though. The French infantry had pulled back because the French cavalry was preparing another charge. This time they avoided the 3rd Foot Guards and charged through the space that had been occupied by the 95th Rifles to their right. The riflemen, seeing the cavalry advancing, quickly dispersed. The cuirassiers continued up the ridge and then out of sight of the 3rd Battalion as they went around Hougoumont.

The disengagement of the French infantry opened the 3rd Battalion to French artillery fire once again. Captain Fead was slightly wounded but did not give up command of the battalion. Nineteen-year-old Ensign Robert Bruce was grazed in the chest by a canister shot and knocked to the ground. Unable to get up, he was afraid that he would be left behind when the battalion pulled back to the ridgeline. The Colour Party[65] also was hard hit. Only two of the six colour sergeants were still standing. Once the cavalry disappeared, General Maitland ordered the 3rd Battalion back up the ridge. After they reached its reverse slope, the order was given to lay down. Many of the men were so exhausted they fell asleep as soon as they hit the ground.[66] Someone ensured that Ensign Bruce was not abandoned when the battalion retreated back up the hill. Ensign Robert Batty, the acting commander of the 1st Company, which had been in the front ranks of the square during the fight, was seriously wounded. The number of casualties in the 3rd Battalion from the fight with the 108th Line Regiment is unknown. However, they were likely very heavy, as high as 150-200 killed and wounded.[67]

---

64. ibid.
65. The Colour Party consisted of two ensigns carrying the battalion's colours, and four to six sergeants to protect them.
66. *Waterloo Letters*, p.247; Master, p.140.
67. The 2nd and 3rd Battalions of the 1st Foot Guard, spent most of the day close to each other on the ridge and thus were exposed to the same amount of the danger. The number of their casualties should have been similar. Yet the 3rd Battalion took almost 250 per cent more casualties than the 2nd Battalion. The only explanation for such a large discrepancy in their casualties is that the 3rd Battalion took heavy casualties when it was ordered down the ridge and fought in a square against the 108th Line.

Captain Stanhope, who had left the 1st Brigade, before the 3rd Battalion moved down the ridge, went to the rear to look for the artillery crews, their limbers, and mounts. Not finding them immediately behind the brigade's formation, he rode east and eventually arrived in the vicinity of the village of Mont St. Jean. During his ride, the French cavalry charged again, and he barely avoided becoming a prisoner.[68] The situation behind the lines was total chaos. There he found 'the whole road was choked with their cavalry of all sorts, wounded on horseback and in blankets, artillery wagons passing and returning.'[69] Near the 1st Corps field hospital he came across the Prince of Orange and Colonel John Elley, the DAG, both wounded. He also found Lieutenant Colonel Lord Fitzroy Somerset, of his regiment's 2nd Battalion, who had been serving as Wellington's Military Secretary. The colonel had been hit by a shot fired from La Haye Sainte right after it fell to the French. After an hour of fruitless searching, Captain Stanhope gave up trying to find the artillery and headed back to the ridge. On his way back he came across 'poor Stables of my own battalion, who had been wounded in my absence with a grape shot through the body. By his looks I saw it was all over, I helped him to an artillery wagon.'[70] He made it back to the 3rd Battalion, but they were no longer on the ridge.

At Hougoumont, the French had given up trying to capture the chateau and its buildings. Instead they brought more troops up to reinforce their position in the orchard, where they held the southern hedge line. Two hundred metres on the other side of the orchard, the 3rd Foot Guards were sheltered by the sunken road and the hedge. Supporting the 3rd Foot Guards was the 1st KGL Brigade, which were standing in squares in the open. The orchard in between the two positions had become a no-man's land, filled with dead and wounded French, British, and German soldiers and French skirmishers who had spread out to take cover among the downed trees and bodies of their enemies and friends. The KGL battalions soon began taking casualties from these skirmishers and from those that came up with the French cavalry.

The situation for the six companies of the 3rd Foot Guards defending the Orchard was grim. The battalion was now commanded by Captain Douglas Mercer. Its original commander, Major Francis Hepburn, had become the commander of the 2nd Brigade about 16.30 hours, when

---

68. *Waterloo Archive*, Vol. 6, p.126.
69. Stanhope, p.177.
70. ibid.

Privates 1st Regiment of Foot Guards circa 1815 by Charles Hamilton Smith. (From the Tony Broughton Collection)

An Officer of the Guards in Full Dress circa 1815 by Charles Hamilton Smith. (From the Tony Broughton Collection)

Coldstream Guards Officer by Jacques Brouillet. (Courtesy of the Anne S.K. Brown Military Collection, Brown University Library)

Sir James Macdonell by unknown artist. (Author's Collection)

Alexander Fraser, 16th Baron Saltoun by William Salter. (© National Portrait Gallery, London)

A View of the western side of Hougoumont. The large structure with the orange roof is the great barn. It was along this stretch of wall that Private Clay fought in the vegetable garden. (From the Gareth Glover Collection)

The view of Hougoumont as seen from the formal garden. The building on the left is the gardener's house, the chapel is in the centre, while the Great Barn is the large structure on the right. Behind the chapel are the farm buildings that lined the western wall of the upper courtyard. (From the Gareth Glover Collection)

South gate of Hougoumont. The gardener's house is over the gate. Circa 2005. (From the Tony Broughton Collection)

South wall of the formal garden. (From the Gareth Glover Collection)

Sous-Lieutenant Legros breaking down the North Gate by L. Sergeant. (From the Tony Broughton Collection)

Six Contre Deux Cents by Eugéne Chaperon, the fight for the formal gardens. (From the Tony Broughton Collection)

Closing the Gates at Hougoumont by Robert Gibb. (© National Museums Scotland)

The interior of Hougoumont during the battle on the glorious 18th of June, 1815, engraved 1816. (Courtesy of the Anne S.K. Brown Military Collection, Brown University Library)

At the Battle of Waterloo a Serjeant of the Coldstream Obtained Permission to Leave the Ranks for a Few Minutes by Francis Lord. Sergeant James Graham's rescue of his brother from the burning barn at Hougoumont. (Courtesy of the Anne S.K. Brown Military Collection, Brown University Library)

Wellington Ordering The Guards to Charge by Captain Richard Jones, Royal Artillery. This sketch was done immediately after the battle was over. (Author's Collection)

Burying the Dead at Hougoumont by William Mudford. (From the Gareth Glover Collection)

The Upper Courtyard of Hougoumont by William Mudford (From the Gareth Glover Collection)

A View of the Hougoumont Woods by William Mudford. (Author's Collection)

'The interior of Hougoumont, reduced nearly to a heap of ruins', by William Mudford engraved by James Rouse, 1816.

The Halt, c. 1815 by Orlando Norie. A party of the Coldstream Guards halted and resting on a march to Paris. (Courtesy of the Anne S.K. Brown Military Collection, Brown University Library)

Hougoumont June 18 (1816) by Elizabeth Stanley. (From the Gareth Glover Collection)

Interior of Hougoumont 1816 by Elizabeth Stanley. (From the Gareth Glover Collection)

General Byng took command of the 1st Division, upon the wounding of General Cooke. None of the 3rd Foot Guard companies were commanded by captains. The 3rd, 6th, and 8th companies were led by lieutenants, while the Grenadiers, 1st, and 7th companies were commanded by teenage ensigns. Seventeen-year-old Ensign Henry Montagu was in the 8th Company during the cavalry attacks, however once the French withdrew, he was ordered to take command of the Grenadier Company which he found 'very well formed, occupying the strong fence above the hollow lane, at the bottom of the orchard'.[71]

The defenders were also running low on ammunition. Captain Mercer ordered the battalion's Adjutant, Ensign Barclay Drummond, to go find some. He rode up the ridge and found Captain Horace Seymour, General Uxbridge's ADC. They went to the rear and Captain Seymour soon ran into 'a private of the Waggon Train in charge of a tumbril on the crest of the position. I merely pointed out to him where he was wanted, when he gallantly started his horses, and drove straight down the hill to the Farm, in the gate of which I saw him arrive. He must have lost his horses, as there was a severe fire kept on him. I feel convinced to that Man's service the Guards owe their ammunition'.[72] The brave waggon driver was likely Private Joseph Brewer of the Royal Waggon Train.[73]

One of the myths that have grown in the re-telling of this story is that Private Brewer delivered the ammunition through the North Gate of the chateau. Even the painting *Powder and Shot* by Charles Stadden shows him doing so. But did he? Major Francis Hepburn, the commander of the 2nd Battalion 3rd Foot Guards states it was he who ordered the ammunition and it was delivered to them. This would have been in the sunken road along the northern hedge of the orchard. It is highly likely that Private Brewer was escorted down ridge by the 2nd Battalion's Adjutant, Ensign Drummond, who would have directed the driver to where the ammunition was needed.[74]

---

71. *Letters from the Battle of Waterloo*, p.176.
72. *Waterloo Letters*, pp.19-20; Maurice, Vol. 2 p.35.
73. Supposedly Private Brewer re-enlisted and joined the 3rd Foot Guards, however this cannot be supported by 3rd Foot Guards or Royal Waggon Train muster rolls, Paget, p.66.
74. Maurice, Frederick, *The History of the Scots Guards from the Creation of the Regiment to the Eve of the Great War*. 2 vols. London: Chatto & Windus, 1934. Vol. 2, p.35.

After the French cavalry attacks tapered off around 19.00, Major Hepburn gave the order to force the French out of the orchard. To do this, in addition to the six depleted companies of the 3rd Foot Guards, he had been given the 2nd and 3rd KGL Line Battalions by General Clinton. With a loud shout, the three battalions surged through the hedge. They quickly pushed the French out of the orchard. Instead of stopping at the southern hedge, Ensign Montagu and his grenadiers continued through the gap between the hedge and the wall of the formal garden in the southwest corner. They and the 2nd KGL Line battalion chased the retreating French across the road and into the woods. According to Private William Pritchard of Captain Edward Bowater's company, they 'could hardly go along for dead bodies'. The British and Germans stayed in the woods for about thirty minutes, when they were attacked on the right flank and forced to retreat back to the hedge.[75]

---

75. Glover, Gareth, *Waterloo: the Defeat of Napoleon's imperial Guard*, p.125; *Letters from the Battle of Waterloo*, p.176.

Chapter 13

18 June 1815
Waterloo 20.00-21.00 Hours

The Defeat of the Imperial Guard

'To do them justice they came on like men but our boys went at them like Britons and drove them off the field in less that than ten minutes.'

Lord Saltoun[1]

Unlike the initial French cavalry charges that were led by Lieutenant General Milhaud, the charges led by Lieutenant General Kellermann were supported by infantry and artillery. While General Kellermann's cuirassiers were attacking the Allied line to the west of La Haye Sainte, the infantry of Lieutenant General d'Erlon's 1st Corps attacked east of the fortified farm. By 18.30 hours the French infantry had captured La Haye Sainte but the attack soon bogged down. The fall of the stronghold allowed the French to bring several batteries of horse artillery close to the Allied lines and they began to blow large gaps in the Allied lines. It was during this time that the commander of the Allied 1st Corps, the Prince of Orange, was seriously wounded and removed to the field hospital at Mont Saint Jean.

For both Napoleon and the Allies, the real question was, where were the Prussians? About 18.00 hours Captain Horace Seymour rode up to Wellington and reported that he had seen the Prussians in the distance. Although this was good news, the Duke needed to know more information, such as how many there were and how soon they could

---

1. Letter from Lord Saltoun to his wife Catherine dated 22 June 1815, *Waterloo Archive*, Vol. 6, p.109.

get there. He sent his ADC, Lieutenant Colonel John Fremantle of the 1st Battalion Coldstream Guards, to find them and ask them for 3,000 men to replace his losses. Lieutenant Colonel Fremantle rode east and then south and eventually found Lieutenant Generals Hans von Ziethen and Friedrich Bülow in the vicinity of Plancenoit, a village 2km south of the French lines. Lieutenant Colonel Fremantle passed the request on to the two generals and was told 'that the whole Army was coming up, and that they could not make a detachment. I said I could return to the duke with such a message.'[2] On his way back to Wellington, Lieutenant Colonel Fremantle came across a Prussian artillery battery with eight guns. The battery could not see any French but could see Lieutenant General Perponcher-Sedlnitsky's 2nd Netherlands Division, whom they mistakenly thought were French and had begun firing on them. Lieutenant Colonel Fremantle was able to stop the friendly fire and redirect it to the south.

The arrival of 30,000 Prussians in his rear could not have come at a worse time for Napoleon. He had finally broken the Allied line and by committing his reserves there he could destroy the Allied army and march on Brussels. However, he now had to deal with the Prussians on his flank. His initial move was to send Lieutenant General George Mouton, Count de Lobau's 10,000-man 6th Corps to stop the Prussians. They were able to slow the Prussian advance but had to give up Plancenoit. When Napoleon saw General Lobau's men fall back he knew the situation was critical. He had to do something about the threat on his flank or his army might be destroyed. The logical thing to do would be to immediately order a retreat and hope he could extricate his army before the Prussians cut the road to Charleroi. There were immense political risks with this move. His only chance of remaining in power against the combined forces of a united Europe was to either destroy or inflict such heavy casualties on the Allied and Prussian armies they would no longer be a factor in the war. When Napoleon moved into Belgium on 15 June he was also betting that if he knocked the Allies and Prussians out of the war, the Russians and Austrians would withdraw rather than face him on their own. If Napoleon retreated to France, he would be facing the combined Allied armies of 800,000 men with less than 200,000 of his own men.[3] It

---

2. Fremantle, p.212.
3. Chandler, David, *The Campaigns of Napoleon*. New York: MacMillan, 1966. pp.1014-1015.

would be the winter of 1814 all over again. He might delay their armies but eventually he would lose.[4]

Although the situation looked bleak, Napoleon still had the three infantry divisions of the Imperial Guard which had not been committed to the battle. These 14,000 men included seven battalions of grenadiers and eight battalions of chasseurs in what was known as the Old Guard[5] and four battalions each of tirailleurs and voltigeurs in his Young Guard. Napoleon decided to gamble everything on one last attack. He would send the 4,700 men of the Young Guard under the command of Lieutenant General Philibert Duhesme to retake and hold the village of Plancenoit.

Supporting them were two battalions of the Old Guard: the 2nd Battalion of the 2nd Grenadier Regiment and the 1st Battalion of the 2nd Chasseur Regiment.[6] While they held the right flank, Napoleon would commit nine battalions of the Old Guard to attack the centre of the Allied line. Furthermore, this attack was to be a combined attack with the 1st and 2nd Corps and the remaining French cavalry. About 10,000 men would take part.

---

4. After being defeated at Leipzig and losing most of his army in October 1813, Napoleon was forced to retreat to France, where he fought the combined armies of Russia, Austria, and Prussia. Despite waging a brilliant campaign, he was finally forced to abdicate on 11 April and go into exile on the island of Elba. Over the years there has been much confusion about whether the troops making the attack were from the Old Guard or the Middle Guard. When Napoleon returned to France in March 1815, one of the first things he did was re-organized the Imperial Guard. In the Decree of 11 April 1815, he specifically states that the Grenadiers and Chasseurs would be in the Old Guard and the Tirailleurs and Voltigeurs would be in the Young Guard. There is no mentioned of a Middle Guard. Saint-Hilaire, Emile Marco de, *History of the Imperial Guard*. Translated by Greg Gorsuch. Napoleon Series. 2017.
5. Over the years there has been much confusion about whether the troops making the attack were from the Old Guard or the Middle Guard. When Napoleon returned to France in March 1815, one of the first things he did was re-organized the Imperial Guard. In the Decree of 11 April 1815, he specifically states that the Grenadiers and Chasseurs would be in the Old Guard and the Tirailleurs and Voltigeurs would be in the Young Guard. There is no mentioned of a Middle Guard, Saint Hilaire, Chapter 15.
6. For a good description of the defene of Plancenoit from the French perspective see Chapter 18 of Andrew Field's *Waterloo*.

To meet this attack were twenty-two British, Brunswick, Hanoverian, and Nassau battalions totaling no more than 9,000 men. They were the battered forces of the 1st, 2nd, and 3rd Divisions, a Brunswick Brigade, and the 1st Nassau Regiment. The 2nd Division's 3rd British Brigade, commanded by Major General Frederick Adam, stood to the right of the 1st Guards Brigade. Directly to the east of the Guards was Major General Sir Colin Halkett's 5th British Brigade of the 3rd Division. It had taken heavy casualties at Quatre Bras and its four battalions were combined into two composite battalions.[7] To the left of the 5th Brigade were 3 Brunswick battalions,[8] the 1st Nassau Regiment, and the much depleted 2nd KGL Brigade. Behind the Brunswickers was Major General Friedrich von Kielmansegge's 1st Hanoverian Brigade. Except for the 1st and 3rd British Brigades, all of these units had been involved in the recent fight around La Haye Sainte and probably had no more than 60 per cent of their strength left.

The two battalions of the 1st Foot Guards were not in much better shape. The 2nd Battalion started the morning with 757 officers and men, but by 20.00 hours was down to 600. Captain Francis D'Oyly, who had commanded the 1st Company, was its second commander of the day and while the only other company commander, Captain Goodwin Colquitt, was serving as the battalion's acting major. Seven of the companies were commanded by lieutenants and the other three by ensigns. The oldest of these ensigns was nineteen, while the other two ensigns were eighteen-years-old. In addition to the three ensigns serving as company commanders, the battalion had only nine other ensigns. Two were carrying the colours, leaving only seven to serve with their companies. Ensign Daniel Tighe, of the 8th Company, was slightly wounded in one of his fingers when a musket ball hit it, but he too stayed with his company. The battalion's Light Company had been decimated since the day began. It began the morning with eighty-eight officers and men but were down to fifty-five by that evening. Its leadership had taken heavy casualties. Of the officers, two of them had been severely wounded. Four sergeants and all four of its corporals had been wounded. Among the wounded NCOs was the company's Colour Sergeant, James Draffin, who had been shot in both thighs and in the testicles,[9] while Corporal John Baker had been shot in the

---

7. The 33rd and 69th Foot formed one battalion, while the 30th and 73rd Foot formed the other. By this time the 5th Brigade had probably no more than 1,500 men still with the colours.
8. The 2nd and 3rd Light Battalions and the 3rd Line Battalion.
9. Chambers, Vol. 1, p.209.

left cheek and leg.[10] The company's senior corporal, Thomas Morgan, had multiple wounds, including being bayoneted in the lip and tongue, shot in the knee, and in the back of the neck. Surprisingly, these wounds were listed as slight![11]

The 3rd Battalion 1st Foot Guards was only a shadow of its former self. There were 824 officers and men at the morning roll call, however their casualties had been heavy in the past seven hours. By the time the cavalry attacks had stopped, they could only muster about 500 officers and men. The battalion was now commanded by Captain George Fead, its third commander in three days. Captain Fead was the fifth senior officer in the battalion when it marched from Enghien two days before. There were only two other captains still with the battalion: Lord Saltoun and John Reeve. Both were serving as the battalion's acting majors. Four of the companies were commanded by lieutenants, while the other six companies were led by ensigns. Only two companies had more than one officer assigned to it. Of the six ensigns in command, all were teenagers except for Ensign John Dirom who was the old man at twenty. Ensign Dirom took command of the 1st Company after Ensign Batty had been severely wounded. The Light Company had 25 percent casualties since the day began and was down to sixty-seventy effectives, including one officer, three sergeants, a corporal, a drummer, and sixty-four privates.

Captain Sandham's and Captain Kuhlmann's batteries were still in the rear,[12] leaving the Guards Brigade without their divisional artillery support. However, to the right of the 2nd Battalion was Captain Samuel Bolton's five 9-pound guns;[13] to the left of the 3rd Battalion were Captain Lloyd's six guns.

By this time, the Guards Brigade was beginning to run out of ammunition. Several officers had been sent to the rear to find the ammunition, but the caissons had moved and they returned unsuccessful. General Byng finally sent Lieutenant Colonel Henry Rooke, the 1st Division's AAG. He left right before the Imperial Guard began its advance and did not return until after their attack had been repulsed.[14]

---

10. ibid, Vol. 1, p.107.
11. ibid, Vol. 2, p.543.
12. *Waterloo Archive*, Vol. 2, p.44.
13. Their 5 ½-inch howitzer was inoperable due to it being loaded with a canister round by mistake, *Waterloo Letters*, p.229.
14. *Letters from the Battle of Waterloo*, p.158.

The Guards Brigade was no longer located on the reverse slope of the ridge. When Wellington realized that another infantry attack was coming, he ordered all the battalions to form into a four-deep line, instead of the traditional two deep line that the British Army was known for. This would allow them greater flexibility in the event of another cavalry attack, but it would have several drawbacks. The battalions were in such a compact mass that it created a better target for the enemy's artillery and also reduced their own firepower, since the infantry in the fourth row would not be able to fire. British drill had only privates and corporals standing in a line. The officers, sergeants, and drummers would be standing behind their companies. The officers directed the fire, while the sergeants stood by with their halberds. A common reaction for a soldier when faced with an approaching enemy or being shot at was to step backwards. If enough soldiers did this, the line would be broken and the battalion would run. If their troops began to show signs of backing up, the sergeants stood directly behind the rear rank and held their halberds horizontally against their backs. Most of the time this was enough to stop them. However, if this was not the sergeants would lean into the rear rank and created a solid barrier that stopped further movement.

Although the 2nd Battalion still had 600 men with the colours, seventy-five to eighty were officers, sergeants, and drummers, and were not in the line. This left about 520-550 corporals and privates. In a four-deep line, the 2nd Battalion would have a facing of 130-140 men wide. Each of these soldiers would occupy 60cm (twenty-four inches) in line. Thus, the battalion would have a frontage of about 80-85m. The 3rd Battalion had about 500 officers and men of which about 400-420 were corporals and privates. Their frontage would have been about 100 men wide, or about 60-70m. According to British regulations, the distance between battalions in line was six paces or about 5m. The total width of the 1st Brigade while standing in this four-deep line was no more than 200m wide.

The formation of the Guards Brigade into a four-deep line caused it to move forward so that it crossed the crest of the ridge. Lieutenant Henry Powell, the commander of the Grenadier Company of the 2nd Battalion wrote that the 'Duke of Wellington had but a short time previous rode down to see what was doing at Hougoumont, and in returning had ordered the 1st Brigade of Guards to take ground to its left and form line four deep, which poor Frank D'Oyley [sic] did by wheeling up the sides of the Square, putting the Grenadiers and my Company (1st Battalion

Company)[15] in the centre of our line. What would Dundas have said!!! This brought the Brigade precisely on the spot the Emperor had chosen for his attack.'[16]

The battalions from the Imperial Guard committed to the attack on the British line were the 1st Battalion 2nd Grenadiers, 1st and 2nd Battalions 3rd Grenadiers, the combined 1st and 2nd Battalions 4th Grenadiers, 1st and 2nd Battalions 2nd Chasseurs, 1st and 2nd Battalions 3rd Chasseurs, and the combined 1st and 2nd Battalions 4th Chasseurs. The average strength of the battalions were about 550 officers and men. Supporting the attack were Imperial Guard Horse Artillery batteries under the command of Major Jean Duchand de Sancey.

When the Imperial Guard attacked, the French 2nd Corps on its left and the 1st Corps on its right were also supposed to attack. The problem being these units have been engaged for much of the day and were exhausted. Lieutenant General d'Erlon's 1st Corps was in poor shape. It had been fighting for almost six hours and two of its four divisions had been shattered by the British cavalry in mid-afternoon. Despite taking heavy casualties from the British cavalry, General Nicolas Schmitz's Brigade of Lieutenant General François Donzelot's 2nd Division had taken La Haye Sainte but could do no more. Lieutenant General Pierre Marcognet's 3rd Division was still contesting the ridge to the east of La Haye Sainte, but as a force it was spent. The only brigade of the 1st Corps still in good shape was General Jean Pégot's 1st Brigade of Lieutenant General Pierre Durutte's 4th Division. The brigade was ordered from its position to march through the valley below the ridge that was held by Wellington and attack to the immediate east of La Haye Sainte. The 2nd Corps was in worse condition than the 1st Corps. It had taken heavy casualties at Quatre Bras and then thrown into the meat grinder of the fight for Hougoumont. Lieutenant General Honoré Reille, the 2nd Corps commander, ordered them forward but he wrote later that their attacks were without much vigour.[17]

The Imperial Guard was to attack in two waves. The first wave had about 3,000 men in six battalions. On the far right was the 1st Battalion

---

15. This is an error. Lieutenant Powell was in the Grenadier Company. Because the part in question is in parenthesis it was likely added by the editor of the *Waterloo Letters*.
16. *Waterloo Letters*, pp.254-256.
17. Field, *Waterloo*, p.195.

3rd Grenadiers. To its immediately left was the combined battalions of the 4th Grenadiers. In the center was the 1st Battalion 3rd Chasseurs and to their left was the 2nd Battalion 3rd Chasseurs. Next to them was the 4th Chasseurs and on the left flank was the 2nd Battalion 3rd Grenadiers. In the second wave from east to west, were the 1st Battalion 2nd Grenadiers, the 2nd Battalion 2nd Chasseurs, and the 1st Battalion 2nd Chasseurs. These battalions had about 1,700 men.

Prior to the attack, the French artillery began bombarding the Allied lines. Major Duchand moved his two batteries of Imperial Guard Horse Artillery to the slopes of the ridge and began firing at the enemy formations on the ridge which were within 200m range. How much damage this fire caused to the Guards Brigade depended on where the company was lying down. Lieutenant Powell and the Grenadier Company had some cover: 'There ran along this part of the position a cart road, on one side of which was a ditch and bank, in and under which the Brigade sheltered themselves during the cannonade, which might have lasted three-quarters of an hour. Without protection of this bank every creature must have perished.'[18] Lieutenant James Nixon, the commander of the 5th Company of the 2nd Battalion was on the flanks of Lieutenant Powell's company said that: 'Our squares stood in the face of grape, shell and everything else, which caused the Guards a terrible loss, without being able to return a shot'.[19] According to Ensign Gronow, the 3rd Battalion was better protected by the ridge.[20]

During this bombardment, Captain D'Oyly, the commander of the 2nd Battalion was killed. Although he had ordered his men to lay down, he remained on horseback. The senior officer in the battalion was Captain Colquitt, who had been a company commander for less than a year. General Maitland ordered Lord Saltoun to come over from the 3rd Battalion and take command of the 2nd Battalion.[21] Despite being better protected from the artillery fire, Captain Fead, the commander of the 3rd Battalion was also wounded in the bombardment. His wound was not serious and he remained in command.

---

18. *Waterloo Letters*, pp.254-256.
19. *Waterloo Archive*, Vol. 1, p.135.
20. Gronow, Vol. 3, p.73.
21. Saltoun, Alexander, *Waterloo Letters Written by Lieutenant Colonel Alexander, Lord Saltoun, 1st Foot Guards, 1815*; Gareth Glover (ed.) Godmanchester: Ken Trotman, 2010, p.14; *Waterloo Archive*, Vol. 1, p.135.

The five battalions in the first wave of the attack were formed into squares, due to the possibility of being charged by Allied cavalry. These battalions averaged about 550 men and were organized into four companies. Each face of the square was formed by a company of 135 men in three ranks. The width of each side of the square was about 30m. The assault was top heavy with general officers. Marshal Michel Ney was on the right with the 3rd Grenadiers while the commander of all four grenadier regiments, Lieutenant General Louis Friant, was with the 4th Grenadiers. The 1st Battalion 3rd Grenadiers had its regimental commander, Maréchal de Camp[22] Paul Poret de Morvan, while the 4th Grenadiers were commanded by Maréchal de Camp Louis d'Harlet. Lieutenant General Claude Michel, the second-in-command of the Guard Chasseurs, led the three Chasseur Battalions. In the second wave, the battalions were under the command of Lieutenant General François Rouguet, the second-in-command of the Grenadiers. With them were Maréchal de Camp Joseph Christiani, commander of the 2nd Grenadiers, and Maréchal de Camp Pierre Cambronne, who commanded the 1st Chasseurs.

Between each square was a two-gun section of Imperial Guard Horse Artillery. They would bring their guns within 50m of the Allied line and blast it with canister fire. It was thought that the fire from these guns and from the infantry would be enough to break the enemy line. No skirmishers were sent out in advance to screen the marching squares.

The march down the ridge, across the valley, and then up the slopes of the other ridge would not be easy. It had rained for hours the night before and the ground, especially in the valley was still saturated with water. For the previous three hours, thousands of horses had moved through the valley and charged up the slopes, turning the whole area into a quagmire of mud and trampled crops. The closer they came to the ridge another major obstacle would have to be overcome. There were hundreds and possibly thousands of dead and wounded men and horses that laid between them and the enemy. Ensign Gronow of the 3rd Battalion 1st Foot Guards described the scene near him:

> the ground was strewed with the fallen horses and their riders ... It was pitiable to witness the agony of the poor horses, which really seemed conscious of the dangers that surrounded them: we often saw a poor wounded animal raise its head, as if looking for its rider to afford him aid. There is nothing perhaps amongst the

---

22. A maréchal de camp was the equivalent to a general of brigade.

episodes of a great battle more striking than the debris of a cavalry charge, where men and horses are seen scattered and wounded on the ground in every variety of painful attitude. Many a time the heart sickened at the moaning tones of agony which came from man, and scarcely less intelligent horse, as they lay in fearful agony upon the field of battle.[23]

The impact of so many dead and wounded before them was immense. Initially, there were not too many, but the closer the formations came to the ridge, the more there were. The battalions had to step over or around the corpses, which not only slowed them down, but would also affect the unit cohesion. As three or four files climbed over the bodies the files to their right and left would soon be ahead of them. Eventually the lines would not be straight but broken. Then there was the matter of the sight of so many casualties on the men's morale. The grenadiers and chasseurs were all hardened veterans but knowing that they were marching into a maelstrom of fire that had killed or wounded thousands before them, had to make them re-think what they were about to do.

The Imperial Guard came under Allied artillery fire almost as soon as it started moving down the ridge. The Allied artillery had been ordered to ignore the French artillery and concentrate their fire on the infantry. Most did and the French were shot at almost continuously. Although this fire did cause some casualties, it was not enough to stop their attack.

Within a few minutes of the advance, Napoleon sent an ADC to the 2nd Battalion 3rd Grenadiers which was on the far left. He was afraid that the British in Hougoumont would move out of the orchard and attack the Guard in the flank. He ordered the battalion to halt and not to advance unless the Allies retreated. For some reason, possibly because they had received their orders too late, the three battalions in the second wave did not move forward with the rest of the Imperial Guard. They eventually moved partially down the ridge, but never participated in the attack. The men of the first wave were on their own. Instead of attacking with nine battalions, the main French thrust against the Allied line was down to five battalions and less than 2,600 men.

The 1st Battalion 3rd Grenadiers and the 4th Grenadiers struck the battered remnants of General Halkett's 5th British Brigade, while General Pégot's 1st Brigade swept around La Haye Sainte and attacked the Brunswickers and Nassau battalions. The 1st and 2nd Battalions 3rd

---

23. Gronow, Vol. 3, pp.72-73.

Chasseurs and the 4th Chasseurs were on a direct collision course with the 1st Foot Guards.

As the Imperial Guard moved closer to the top of the ridge, Captain Fead, the commander of the 3rd Battalion decided to send out skirmishers to harass them. Ensign Thomas Swinburne, who commanded the 6th Company while Captain Reeve served as the battalion's acting major, went forward with a handful of men. They came fairly close to the Chasseurs, but their numbers were too small to be effective and had to retreat before they were overrun.[24]

Unlike most of the 1st Foot Guards who were lying down to avoid the French artillery fire, General Maitland was on horseback and watch the whole attack unfold:

> The force employed by the Enemy in this service consisted of two strong Columns of Infantry; a third Corps, consisting of both Cavalry and Infantry being in reserve. The attacking Columns were alike composed of the Infantry of the Imperial Guard, the Grenadiers forming one Column, the Chasseurs of that Corps the other. As the attacking force moved forward it separated, the Chasseurs inclined to their left. The Grenadiers[25] ascended the acclivity towards our position in a more direct course, leaving La Haye Sainte on their right, and moving towards that part of the eminence occupied by the 1st Brigade of Guards. Numerous pieces of ordnance were distributed on the flanks of this Column. The Brigade suffered by the Enemy's Artillery, but it withheld its fire for the nearer approach of the Column. The latter, after advancing steadily up the slope, halted about twenty paces from the front rank of the Brigade.[26]

It was at this point General Maitland gave the order for the Guards Brigade to stand up and fire. One of the myths about Waterloo is that Wellington, who was also with the Guards, turned to General Maitland and called,

---

24. *Waterloo Letters*, p.167.
25. The Grenadiers and Chasseurs of the Old Guard were virtually indistinguishable from each other, because during the attack they wore dark blue greatcoats and bearskin hats. General Maitland mistook the Chasseurs for Grenadiers. This was a common problem among those who left accounts of the attack.
26. *Waterloo Letters*, p.244-245.

'Up Guards and at them'. Whether he actually said that is not known. However, Lord Saltoun wrote to William Siborne in 1838 that: 'I did not hear him, nor do I know of any person, or ever heard of any person that did. It is a matter of no sort of importance, has become current with the world as the cheering speech of a great man to his troops, and is certainly not worth a controversy about.'[27]

Regardless of whether he said it or not, the Foot Guards stood up and open fire on the advancing Chasseurs. The sudden appearance of the concealed troops to their immediate front had to be a total shock, for up until that point, the Chasseurs had not met any real resistance except for artillery fire. The surprise was not all one-sided. The British troops knew that the Imperial Guard was coming but did not fully understand the implications. Ensign Master, carrying the 3rd Battalion's King's Colours, said that after they received the order to stand up, 'what did we behold! A large mass creeping up the declivity *"en Battalion Serré"*,[28] fine stout fellows with huge fur grenadier caps, screaming out *"Vive L'Empereur, en avant en avant"*;[29] we formed a line of 4 deep, the first rank kneeling the second also firing the third and fourth loading and handing on to the front, and kept up such a continued fire into this mass of heaped up Grenadiers'.[30]

Ensign Dirom, commanding the 3rd Battalion's 1st Company, had to keep reminding his men to stay down and wait until the order came to stand up before they fired. But once they did the effect was immediate:

> The Imperial Guard advanced in close Column with ported arms, the Officers of the leading Divisions in front waving their swords. The French Columns showed no appearance of having suffered on their advance, but seemed as regularly formed as if at a field day. When they got within a short distance we were ordered to make ready, present, and fire. The effect of our volley was evidently most deadly. The French Columns appeared staggered, and, if I may use the expression, convulsed. Part seemed inclined to advance, part halted and fired, and others, more particularly towards the centre and rear of the Column, seemed to be turning around.[31]

---

27. ibid, p.248.
28. "in battalion squares".
29. "Long live the Emperor! Forward Forward!"
30. Master, p.140.
31. *Waterloo Letters*, pp.257-258.

Lieutenant Powell of the 2nd Battalion was in the centre of the line had a slightly different perspective:

> A close Column of Grenadiers (about seventies in front) of la Moyenne Garde, about 6,000 strong, led, as we have since heard, by Marshal Ney, were seen ascending the rise au pas de charge shouting 'Vive l'Empereur. They continued to advance till within fifty or sixty paces of our front, when the Brigade were ordered to stand up. Whether it was from the sudden and unexpected appearance of a Corps so near them, which must have seemed as starting out of the ground, or the tremendously heavy fire we threw into them, La Garde, who had never before failed in an attack suddenly stopped. Those who from a distance and more on the flank could see the affair, tell us that the effect of our fire seemed to force the head of the Column bodily back. In less than a minute about 300 were down. They now wavered, and several of the rear divisions began to draw out as if to deploy, whilst some of the men in their rear beginning to fire over the heads of those in front was so evident a proof of their confusion.[32]

The effect of this fire on the two Chasseur battalions was catastrophic. The fire brought down all the senior leadership. Captain-Adjutant-Major Louis Prax, the adjutant of the 3rd Chasseurs noted: 'All our heads were put hors de combat'.[33] Lieutenant General Michel, 'fell from his horse crying out, "Ah, my God! I have broken my arm again!"' His ADC, Captain Guillaume Berthelet des Verges, 'quickly dismounted and unbuttoned his coat to locate his wound. My general dead; a ball had passed through his body'.[34] Maréchal de Camp Antoine Malet, the 3rd Chasseurs regimental commander was wounded in the shoulder, while both battalion commanders, Majors Claude Cardinal of the 1st Battalion and Jean Angelet of the 2nd Battalion were killed.[35]

As the Chasseurs continued to take more and more casualties, their formation began to waver and slowly back-up. In what had to be perfect timing, General Maitland gave the order to charge. The reaction of the 1st

---

32. ibid, pp.254-255.
33. Field, *Waterloo*, p.200.
34. ibid, p.200.
35. ibid, pp.200-201.

Foot Guards was electric. Lord Saltoun 'holloaed [sic] out, "Now's the time, my boys". Immediately the Brigade sprang forward. La Garde turned and gave us little opportunity of trying the steel'.[36] The 3rd Chasseurs had had enough. They turned about and ran as fast as they could go. Their bodies were stacked up like a hedge and the British had to walk on them to get down the ridge.[37] The 3rd Battalion 'rushed on with fixed bayonets, and that hearty hurrah peculiar to British soldiers. It appeared that our men, deliberately and with calculation, singled out their victims; for as they came upon the Imperial Guard our line broke and the fighting became irregular. The impetuosity of our men seemed almost to paralyse their enemies: I witnessed several of the Imperial Guard who were run through the body apparently without any resistance on their parts.'[38]

The cohesion of the 1st Foot Guards began to fall apart and at times it was every man for himself. Some stopped to loot the fallen French soldiers, especially the dead or wounded officers. Colour Sergeant Charles Wood, of the 3rd Battalion was able to pick up a sword belonging to an Imperial Guard colonel.[39] After breaking the 3rd Chasseurs and causing them to run, the impetuous charge was quickly brought to a halt by their officers. To their front was the 4th Chasseurs stilled formed and bristling for a fight. The British Guards backed up the ridge, closely followed by the French. Before it reached the crest of the ridge Lord Saltoun commanded his battalion to '"Halt, front, form up," and it was the only thing that could be done. Any other formation was impossible, and as soon as this order was understood by the men it was obeyed and everything was right again. The left shoulders were then brought forward, and we advanced against the second Column of the Imperial Guards.'[40]

Before the 2nd Battalion could reach the 4th Chasseurs, Lieutenant Colonel Sir John Colborne, commander of the 1st Battalion 52nd Foot, brought his battalion into the fight.[41] On his own initiative he ordered

---

36. *Waterloo Letters*, p.255.
37. *Letters from the Battle of Waterloo*, p.167.
38. Gronow, Vol. 3, p.73.
39. Instead of selling it he kept it as a souvenir and wore in Paris the following month, *Waterloo Archive*, Vol. 6, p.129.
40. *Waterloo Letters*, p.248.
41. The 52nd Foot was part of Major General Frederick Adam's 3rd British Brigade of the 2nd Division. All of the battalions in this brigade were light and rifle battalions and was often referred to as the Light Brigade.

a company of men under Lieutenant Matthew Anderson to form into a skirmish line and bring the advancing French square under fire. While they were doing this, he had the rest of the battalion to pivot left, form an extended line, and fire into the flank of the 4th Chasseurs. The French halted their move up the ridge and turned to face this threat. The Chasseurs stood and fought for several minutes, but they were outnumbered two to one with an enemy battalion to their front and the British Guards rapidly approaching from the ridge. The 4th Chasseurs finally gave up the uneven fight and retreated.[42]

The assault on the Allied line to the left of the Guards Brigade by the two battalions of the 2nd and 3rd Grenadiers had some initial success, but they were greatly outnumbered, and they too fell back. The withdrawal of the Imperial Guard was seen by the exhausted men of the French 1st and 2nd Corps and soon the cry of *'La Garde Recule'*[43] was heard. Panic ensued for the French soldiers, for the unthinkable had happened. The Imperial Guard had never failed before and the sight of so many of them fleeing was too much. Some of the units 1st and 2nd Corps retreated in good order, while many soldiers ignored their officers and ran. Wellington knew the battle was won and ordered a general advance across his front.

The 1st Foot Guards went down the slope and moved south towards the French lines. Like the Imperial Guard, they too found the going slow. In the valley 'there was some ploughed ground but from the rain that had fallen during the night the constant crossing it by the cavalry and the many loose horses that galloped after the advancing and retiring squadrons, the whole was very puddle, and the crops destroyed'.[44] General Maitland soon gave the brigade an order to halt in the valley and the battalions changed from a four-deep line to columns by 'calling out the covering Sergeants and forming Companies'.[45] While they reformed into columns, the brigade was passed by General Adam's 3rd Brigade and the 1st KGL Hussars of Major General Hussey Vivian's 6th British Cavalry Brigade.[46] Once the battalions were reformed they advanced again. They passed a large number of abandoned French artillery pieces and as they approached the village of La Belle Alliance, a staff officer rode up with

---

42. *Waterloo Letters*, pp.284-285.
43. 'The Guard Retreats!'
44. *Letters from the Battle of Waterloo*, p.167.
45. *Waterloo Letters*, p.25.
46. Stanhope, p.178.

orders for the brigade to halt. As they rested a cavalry regiment dressed in dark blue, rode south along the road. Their band was playing *God Save The King* and they saluted the Guards as they passed.[47] The Prussians had arrived, and Wellington had just turned over the pursuit of the defeated French army to them.

While the Imperial Guard attacked the ridge, French troops in the vicinity made another attempt to take Hougoumont, but their attacks were easily turned back. Major Hepburn, who now commanded the 2nd Brigade, was unsure of what was going on elsewhere, but he was confident they would hold Hougoumont. Soon, 'a Staff Officer came from the left at full gallop, with orders for an immediate advance, stating that the whole Army was moving on to the charge. We passed the hedge and moved upon the troops in the cornfield, who retired in no order, and almost without firing'.[48] Clearing the woods was not without its hazards. As the Coldstream Guards moved out of Hougoumont's formal gardens, twenty-two-year-old Lieutenant John Blackman was shot in the head and killed instantly.[49] He was the last Guards officer to be killed outright in the battle. After the 2nd Brigade cleared the French out of the woods, Major Hepburn pulled them back to the fields on the north side of Hougoumont.

The two companies of the Coldstream Guards who had stayed on the ridge with the colours, returned to their original position once the order had been given for the general advance. There they stayed until the eight companies that had defended Hougoumont moved back up the hill. Ensign Charles Short, who had been carrying the battalion's colours throughout the day, was sent down to the woods on the other side of the chateau to picquet the woods.[50]

Captain Stanhope, who had been sent back to find the artillery, arrived back on the ridge after the 1st Brigade had moved from it. He could not find them, so he stayed there and witnessed the attack of the 52nd Foot:

> I hastened back to my battalion, but they had advanced. The first regiment I came up to was the 52nd who were on the flank of the grand attack of the Imperial Guard, who advanced beautifully with their officers in their front waving their swords & hats & cheering them on with *'Vive Napoleon'*. A shout burst from the

---

47. *Waterloo Letters*, p.245.
48. ibid, p.267.
49. Blackman, p.134.
50. *Waterloo Letters*, p.266.

> English line and such a shout of victory never can be forgotten when the fire poured in on them on all sides, stopped them as if turned into stone. The front sections fell like cards; they began to show timidity toward the rear & the English line shouted & moved on. Some cavalry (I believe the old Heavy Germans of Bock's in Spain now turned into light cavalry) swept round the flank of the 52nd and the confusion from that moment & rout were complete.[51]

Captain Stanhope followed the 52nd Foot and somehow passed his brigade in the confusion. Before long, he watched the arrival of the Prussians

> Pausing on the top of the next hill for the first time, I saw that it was not all owing to us. I had heard some time an additional firing in the front of our left, but amid such thunder had thought little about it. It was now getting dusk, but the last gleam showed me a sight all description cannot give an idea of. The plain now dimly seen was dark with a mass of mingled combatants and indistinct from the firing which was still partially kept up on the left towards La Belle Alliance., from the wind setting that way & the ground being wet the smoke of the battle hung low on the ground. Through this at speed came gun after gun & squadron after squadron, who with their lances waving seemed as if they were charging on a cloud. To witness such a glorious soul transporting sight, to feel that I had been able to go through the battle & to be grateful at having survived it, was the work of a moment; but the last feeling of that day.[52]

The divisional artillery eventually sorted out its ammunition re-supply problems and arrived back on the ridge. By the time they got there, the general advance had begun and there were no viable targets.

---

51. Stanhope, p.178.
52. ibid, p.178.

Chapter 14

The Night After Waterloo

'We had 82 officers of the regiment in the field of which 34 have been killed or wounded.'
Lord Saltoun in a letter to His Wife dated 29 June 1815[1]

'I have lost 60 out of 96 and the dreadful number of principal officers killed and wounded exceeds anything we had ever before to lament.'
Captain James Stanhope, commander 8th Company
3rd Battalion 1st Foot Guards[2]

'I lost of my company, killed and wounded, three officers, three sergeants, and 54 rank & file out of 97.'
Colour Sergeant Charles Wood, 7th Company
3rd Battalion 1st Foot Guards[3]

'As one of the 13 guardsmen who were able to muster, being unhurt, I distinctly say that I have been in many a hard fought action and seen many an arduous struggle but to hold the post at Hougoumont was by far the most dreadful I ever witnessed.'
Private Richard MacLaurence, Light Company Coldstream Guards[4]

'It was a very mournful sight the next morning when I was on parade to see but little more than one half the number of men that there were the morning before, and not quite half the officers.'
Ensign Thomas Wedgewood 2nd Battalion 3rd Foot Guards[5]

---

1. *Waterloo Archive*, Vol. 6, p.112.
2. Letter to the 3rd Earl of Mansfield dated 19 June 1815, ibid, p.126.
3. *Waterloo Archive*, Vol. 6, p.130.
4. ibid, p.142.
5. Letter to his mother, dated 24 June 1815, ibid, Vol 1, p.148.

By the time the 1st Brigade had halted in the vicinity of La Belle Alliance it was past sunset. The sun went down at 20.16 hours,[6] but the sky was still light until 22.00 hours when darkness had finally fallen. Even with the onset of night, there sky was relatively light because it was only three days before the full moon.[7] The orders to halt had not come too soon. The division had been fighting for eight hours and had taken heavy casualties at all levels.

The Prince of Orange, the 1st Corps Commander, was wounded about 18.45 hours. Major General Byng, who had assumed command of the 1st Division around 16.00 hours when Major General Cooke was wounded, was the next senior officer in the 1st Corps. The exact time he took command of the corps is unknown, but probably about 19.30 hours at the earliest. Since the 1st Division was split between Hougoumont and the ridge, his absence was not noted by the men of either brigade. It was only after the defeat of the Imperial Guard and the advance of the 1st Brigade did it become important. General Maitland then took command of the division. When he did he found a much-reduced divisional staff. Lieutenant Colonel Henry Bradford,[8] the AQMG assigned to the division had been shot above the left hip,[9] while Captain Edward Fitzgerald, the DAQMG had also been wounded.[10] General Maitland had been using Captain James Stanhope as a temporary replacement for Lieutenant Colonel Bradford, however he had sent the captain to the rear to find the division artillery and he had not returned. He had only his own ADC, Ensign Seymour Bathurst. Major General Cooke's two ADCs were with the wounded general in the rear.

The 1st Brigade's command structure was also in shambles. Its acting commander was Captain George Fead of the 3rd Battalion 1st Foot Guards, who was thirty-three-years-old and had been a captain for less than eighteen months. He had been slightly wounded during the bombardment that preceded the attack of the Imperial Guard but had returned after the 1st Brigade had halted for the night. Fortunately for him, his Brigade Major, James Gunthorpe, had survived. However, he had no ADC. Within the brigade's two battalions, only four captains were still with the colours.

---

6. *Time and Date Online.*
7. ibid.
8. Henry Bradford was assigned to the 2nd Battalion 1st Foot Guards when he was not serving on the staff.
9. Sheardown, p.5.
10. Captain Fitzgerald was assigned to the 25th Foot.

The senior captain was Lord Saltoun who had been given command of the 2nd Battalion 1st Guards right before the attack of the Imperial Guard. He had one captain, six lieutenants, and eight ensigns still with the battalion. The 3rd Battalion 1st Foot Guards was commanded by thirty-one-year-old Captain John Reeve, a veteran who had served almost three years in the Peninsula. The battalion was devastated. Its only captain was now commanding the battalion and he had just three lieutenants and ten ensigns left to lead ten companies.

The 2nd Brigade staff was in worse shape than the 1st Brigade's. Its acting commander, Major Hepburn, had been commanding since Major General Byng had took command of the 1st Division around 16.00 hours. Its Brigade Major, William Stothert, had been seriously wounded, and Lieutenant William Walton, the acting adjutant of the 2nd Battalion Coldstream Guards was serving in his place. Major Hepburn had no ADC, because Major General Byng's surviving ADC, Ensign Edward Stopford, went with him when he moved to the 1st Division and then the 1st Corps. The Coldstream Guards was in the best condition of the four Guards battalions. It was the only battalion that still had its original battalion commander with it. It had three captains, three lieutenants, and ten ensigns present. The 2nd Battalion 3rd Foot Guards was now commanded by Captain Douglas Mercer. Like Captain Fead who commanded the 1st Brigade, Captain Mercer had been a lieutenant only eighteen months before the battle. Only Captain Home,[11] as well as six lieutenants and ten ensigns were still with the colours.

Once the brigade commanders had received the orders to stop the pursuit of the defeated French, Captain Fead ordered the 1st Brigade to stay in the vicinity of La Belle Alliance. After clearing the Hougoumont Woods, Major Hepburn ordered his two battalions to return to the ridgeline overlooking the chateau.[12] Both brigades held formation and before they were dismissed, did a roll call to determine who was still left with the battalion. The initial results were not good. The 3rd Battalion 1st Foot Guards had 40 per cent of its strength killed or wounded while the Coldstream Battalion lost 30 per cent. The 2nd Battalion 3rd Foot Guards had 23 per cent casualties, while the 2nd Battalion 1st Foot Guards had 21 per cent. The official casualty reports were published in *The London Gazette* on 3 July 1815.

---

11. Sometime in the evening Captain Charles West was seriously wounded. The circumstances of his wounding are not known.
12. *Waterloo Letters*, p.267.

The following table is what was reported by the battalions through their chain-of-command to the Army HQ. The numbers for Guards officers killed and wounded was actually much higher, since they did not include those serving on the Army staff. Furthermore, those listed as killed do not include those who died of wounds after the battle. The percent of casualties is based on the strength of each battalion as reported on the morning of 18 June, as shown in Appendix IV. For a complete listing of those who were killed or died of wounds see Appendix VIII (1st Foot Guards Casualties), Appendix IX (Coldstream Guards Casualties), and Appendix X (3rd Foot Guards Casualties).

Table 14.1: Foot Guards Casualties at Waterloo [13]

Battalion	Killed Officers	SGTs	OR[14]	Wounded Officers	SGTs	OR[15]	Missing	Total	%
2nd Bn 1FG	1	-	59	5	7	89	-	161	21%
3rd Bn 1FG	3	5	80	6	7	238	-	339	40%
2nd Bn 2FG	1	1	53	7	13	229	4[16]	308	30%
3rd Bn 3FG	3	2	37	9	10	178	-	239	23%
Total	8	8	229	27	37	734	4	1047	26%

It should be noted that the above figures are only for the casualties at Waterloo and do not reflect their total casualties for the campaign, which were much higher. When the four infantry battalions of the 1st Division left Enghien early in the morning on 16 June, there were 4,333 officers and men marching with the colours. Over the next two days, one man in three would be killed or wounded. The 1st Brigade was hard hit having almost 50 per cent casualties in three days. The 3rd Battalion 1st Foot Guards had 55 per cent casualties, while the 2nd Battalion 1st Foot Guards had 41 per cent. The total casualties for all the battalions since they left Enghien on the morning of 16 June were:

---

13. *The London Gazette*, 3 July 1815, p.1360.
14. Includes drummers and corporals.
15. Includes drummers and corporals.
16. One drummer and three privates were reported missing. They were probably killed in the burning of Hougoumont chateau.

Table 14.2: Total Foot Guards Casualties from 16-18 June 1813[17]

Battalion	Killed			Wounded			Missing	Total	%
	Officers	SGTs	OR	Officers	SGTs	OR			
2nd Bn 1FG	3	1	81	9	13	339		446	41%
3rd Bn 1FG	4	7	96	12	16	464		599	55%
2nd Bn 2FG	1	1	53	7	13	229	4	308	30%
2nd Bn 3FG	3	2	37	9	10	185	-	246	22%
1st Division	11	11	267	37	52	1217	4	1599	37%

Many of the survivors could scarcely believe they were still alive. Ensign Richard Master thought 'all those still alive had drawn a Prize in the lottery of Warfare'.[18] Ensign Rees Gronow examined his clothing and found that the top of his shako as well as one of his coat tails had been shot off.[19] Major Chatham Churchill, of the 1st Battalion 1st Foot Guards, was serving as an ADC to Lieutenant General Rowland Lord Hill, apparently had a death wish and could not believe he survived. He wrote that at one point:

> The French cuirassiers came clean into us. I was on my old brown horse, a grape shot went through his body and a round shot struck my hat at the same moment. He fell dead. I was a good deal stunned and could not get from under my horse. The French cuirassiers rode over me, without my hat off, did not wound me. I lay there till the French were licked back. They again rode by me, one of their cuirassiers was killed passing me, I seized his immense horse and with some difficulty got upon him I rode off and hardly was I clear of them before a round shot struck my horse on the head and killed him on the spot. An officer of the 13th [Light] Dragoons dismounted a man of his regiment and gave me his horse. This was shot in the leg half an hour after. . . I had rather fallen that day as a British infantryman or as a French cuirassier than die ten years hence in my bed. I did my best to be killed, fortune protected me. I was struck by a ball on the side of my thigh, which did not even bleed me. One also struck me on the back of the shoulder, which I did not know of till after the action was over.

---

17. *The London Gazette;* 3 July 1815, pp.1358 & 1360.
18. Master, p.141.
19. Gronow, Vol. 2, p.40.

It was much the same for the enlisted soldiers:

> Now came the time for the distribution of rations, camp kettles all in requisition, and a general cooking along the hedgerows, the issue of rations liquor, and buzz of congratulating interchanges taking place with men of different companies with their townsmen and old acquaintances, sitting or reclining on the ground, each listening to the narrative of his comrade, having been separated from each other during the contest. Had any of our enquiring friends in England been present in this said field in which was our bivouac, they would have listed with the deepest interest to the tales that were told on the night of the 19th of June 1815.
>
> P.S. it should be remembered that a very considerable number of the British force engaged on this memorable occasion were volunteers from the Militia of the United Kingdom, more especially in the year 1813, at which period their services were much required, so that recruits, (with others who had served various periods in the Militia) were in the space of a few weeks after joining their respective regiments in warm contest with the enemy.[20]

Parties were sent out to search for the wounded and missing, especially the officers. Captain William Milnes who fell in the fight for the orchard at Hougoumont was found 'quite naked, having been stripped in the night by the Belgians and thrown in a ditch ... He was shot through the back as he was turning around'.[21] Twenty-one-year-old Lieutenant John Blackman of the Coldstream Guards was buried where he fell in Hougoumont's formal garden. Captain Alexander Craufurd, an officer in 2nd Ceylon Regiment but serving as a volunteer in the 12th Light Dragoons, heard that his brother Lieutenant Thomas Craufurd of the 3rd Foot Guards was missing. He found his body in the orchard and arranged for it to be shipped home and be interred in the family church[22] at Hengrave, St. Edmundsbury, Suffolk. The two brothers were the nephews of Major General Robert

---

20. Clay, p.31.
21. Reid, T. Wemyss, *The Life, Letters, and Friendships of Richard Monckton Milnes*. 2 vols. New York: Cassell, 1891. Vol. 1, p.21.
22. Church of Reconciliation.

Craufurd, who commanded the Light Division in the Peninsular War. He died on 24 January 1812, from wounds received in the assault on Ciudad Rodrigo.

Among the missing was Captain James Stanhope of the 3rd Battalion 1st Foot Guards. After watching the 52nd Foot fight with the French Imperial Guard, went to the Hougoumont Woods where he found the Coldstream Guards. After their advance was called off, he gave up looking for the 1st Brigade and

> dismounted from my horse & laid down upon the ground & in a moment was asleep. The Guards were ordered on and when they came to their bivouac for the night, one of my friends (I believe Major Bowles[23]) missed me & recollected he had seen me lay down. He sent back & after a considerable search I was found still asleep among the dead & the dying, the plunderers & the plundered. If he [had] not remembered me, some kindly hand would probably have spared me the trouble of awaking again. I remained with the Coldstream all the night & next morning rejoined my battalion which was about a mile in front to the left, close to La Belle Alliance.[24]

Ensign Gronow wandered the battlefield and the next morning he came across

> several of our gallant companions in arms who had been wounded. They were lying in waggons of the country, and had been abandoned by the drivers. Some of these poor fellows belonged to our regiment, and, on passing close to one of the waggons, a man cried out, 'For God's sake, Mr. Gronow, give us some water or we shall go mad.' I did not hesitate for a moment, but jumped into the cart, and gave the poor fellow all the water my flask contained. The other wounded soldiers then entreated me to fill it with some muddy water which they had descried in a neighbouring ditch, half filled by the rain of the preceding day. As I thought a flask would be of little use among so many, I took off my shako, and having first stopped up with my belcher handkerchief a hole which a musket ball had made in the top of it,

---

23. Lieutenant George Bowles of the Coldstream Guards.
24. Stanhope, pp.178-179.

filled it with water several times for these poor fellows, who were all too severely wounded to have got it for themselves, and who drank it off with tears of delight.[25]

The parties sent out to find the wounded soon came across soldiers from every army and civilians plundering the dead and wounded. As Captain Stanhope pointed out, many had little compunction about slitting the throats of soldiers who were still alive. The more enterprising officers and NCOs leading the search parties had no problem forcing the looters into 'carrying the sufferers in blankets, which were easily obtained from the knapsacks of the slain'. The 2nd Brigade wounded were generally brought back to the Hougoumont chateau. There the officers were placed in the house that was connected to the eastern wall of the family living quarters that had burned a few hours before. The enlisted wounded were placed in whatever shelter could be found in the chateau. No effort was to segregate the French from the other Allies. Some 'Belgian soldiers with others, who were looking out for their wounded or missing comrades, on seeing Frenchmen amongst the rest began to menace the poor fellows with their bayonets, and would have acted violently towards them had we not have interfered in their behalf'.[26] The 1st Brigade wounded were kept on the ridge where they fell until they could be evacuated to a field hospital.

Once the roll call had been completed and the search parties had been sent out to recover the wounded and the dead, the exhausted Guardsmen's thoughts turned to food. The quartermasters had not caught up with the battalions and the men were hungry. Most had not been eaten since the halt at Nivelles two days before and that had been a very hurried meal. Some troops began to slip away from their bivouacs to see what they could find. Many headed to Hougoumont, while others took the time to search the knapsacks of the dead and wounded. Private Clay was ordered to accompany a corporal to Hougoumont and once there they went looking for food and water. At the well he

> saw numbers of soldiers of different regiments, all surrounding the only well of water known to us on the premises, eagerly striving to obtain a drink of it, which had by this time become a

---

25. Gronow, Vol. 2, pp.32-33.
26. Clay, pp.28-31.

mere puddle, and seeing no chance of obtaining any, we separated in the yard. I proceeded up the yard, where on the heap of ruins lay the body of a comrade of the Coldstreams from whose mess-tin I took some biscuit; and turning to my left, entered the large garden, where I partook of some unripe fruit from a tree by the wall; on proceeding up the shaded avenue or garden walk by the dead body of a Frenchman, I found a small portion of butter in a single-stick basket, which having partaken of, with my biscuit, and being refreshed, returned again to the yard, and on my way was met by a large pig, from the same direction, there immediately appeared in pursuit several English soldiers of different regiments, one of whom fired his musket and shot the pig whilst passing me, and each one in pursuit claimed a share, which I left them to decide.[27]

The officers also went hungry, since many of them lost their baggage to stragglers behind the lines. Ensign Thomas Wedgewood of the 3rd Foot Guards best summed up their situation in a letter to his mother:

The Belgic troops who ran away went to Brussels, where all our baggage was, and said that we were entirely defeated, and that the French were advancing close at their heels. The consequence was that the people of Brussels began to pillage our baggage, but were soon stopped. I understand that my baggage horse is either killed or stolen; but I do not know yet, as we have not seen the baggage since the 15th, and all that time we have been lying on the ground, without any covering and not able to change our clothes.[28]

Some of the officers also took the time to write to their families to let them know that they were still alive. Lieutenant James Nixon wrote a quick note to his father that: 'We are just going to move off in pursuit. I have not taken my clothes off or changed them since I left Enghien and I do not know when I shall. I never was better in my life'.[29] After the 1st Brigade received orders to halt their advance, the officers of the 1st Foot Guards had requisition the hayloft of a barn at La Belle Alliance for their quarters. Ensign Master, was contemplating going to sleep when,

---

27. ibid, pp.29-30.
28. *Waterloo Archive*, Vol. 1, p.147.
29. ibid, Vol. 1, p.135.

Lord March[30] came up to me saying he was going off with the Dispatches, if I wished to write? A scrap of paper from a Sergeant and a Drum for table, I wrote a few words to my Aunt in London, saying I was safe and that we had beaten the French. That scrap of paper was amongst the first news that arrived in London, and as for Aunty dined out in Hill Street, she was delighted to be able to communicate it to those present, also that I was safe (For in 1814, news she received from the Horse Guards after the storming of Bergen-op-Zoom, stated that I was killed or missing, whilst I was a prisoner for a few days only.)[31]

Guards Officers on the Staff

A Guards officer serving on the staff had about the same chance of becoming a casualty as those who served with their battalions. Of the thirty Guards officers serving outside their battalions during the Waterloo Campaign ten were either killed or wounded. Of the wounded, three subsequently died of their injuries.

Table 14.3: Casualties among Guards Officers Serving on the Army Staff from 16 to 18 June 1813

Battalion	Killed	Wounded	Died of Wounds
1st Battalion 1st Foot Guards	1	1	-
2nd Battalion 1st Foot Guards	1	1	1
3rd Battalion 1st Foot Guards	1	-	-
2nd Battalion Coldstream Guards	-	1	-
2nd Battalion 3rd Foot Guards	1	-	2

Among the 1st Division staff officers, Lieutenant Colonel Bradford, the division's AQMG, was severely wounded in the hip around 19.30 hours. There had not been time to evacuate him to the field hospital before the Imperial Guard attacked. When the 1st Brigade was ordered to advance in pursuit of the retreating French, he was left behind.

---

30. Captain Charles Lennox Earl of March.
31. Master, p.141.

Captain William Tomkinson of the 16th Light Dragoons found him and 'put him before one of our dragoons to be taken to the rear. He could not bear the motion of the horse, and was obliged to remain on the field'.[32]

Serving on Wellington's personal staff was very dangerous. Of the five Guards officers on it, three were wounded, two of whom would die of their wounds before the night was over. During the advance of the Allies after the Imperial Guard had been defeated, Lieutenant Colonel Charles Fox Canning,[33] one of the Duke's ADCs, was in the vicinity of La Belle Alliance when he was hit in the stomach by a canister round. As he laid dying he turned to Lord March, an extra-ADC to the Prince of Orange, and said: 'Dear March I cannot live, I owe Campbell some money pray see that paid immediately and let all my debts be paid the first thing'.[34] The Campbell Lieutenant Colonel Canning was referring to was Colonel Sir Colin Campbell of the Coldstream Guards, who was Wellington's HQ Commandant. Lieutenant Colonel Canning was left lying on the field apparently abandoned by the rest of the staff. Soon the British 16th Light Dragoons rode up. He was about to be ridden over by when he called out and Captain William Tomkinson stopped his troop in time:

> My troop moved to the spot he was lying on, when he begged we would not ride over him, saying he was the Duke of Wellington's aide-d-camp. The men opened out, and on my asking him if I could assist him, or leave a man with him, he said he would not live long, being shot in the body with grape. I encouraged him, telling him of our success, and that a surgeon would soon arrive on being sent for. He was quite determined not to allow of anything being done, and on my mentioning my name and his recollecting me, he begged me to dismount to take his sword and watch, to be delivered to his relations.[35]

---

32. Tomkinson, William, *The Diary of a Cavalry Officer in the Peninsular War and Waterloo: 1809-1815* London: Frederick Muller; 1971, pp.314-315.
33. Charles Fox Canning was the commander of the 5th Company 2nd Battalion 3rd Foot Guards.
34. *Waterloo Archive*, Vol. 1, p.145.
35. Tomkinson, p.315.

Lieutenant Colonel Canning was still alive when the 2nd Battalion 73rd Foot arrived at La Belle Alliance. Major Dawson Kelly,[36] was now commanding it when

> one of the men came to me to say that an Aide-de-Camp of the Duke of Wellington was wounded and lying near, when, upon going with him, I found Colonel Canning in the greatest possible agony. He had received a musket shot in the centre of the abdomen, and, although perfectly collected, he could hardly articulate from pain. We raised him, however, to a sitting position by placing knapsacks around him, but a few minutes terminated his existence.[37]

Another of Wellington's ADCs, Lieutenant Colonel Alexander Gordon, was wounded about 18.45 hours. Deputy Inspector of Hospitals John Robert Hume was serving as Wellington's personal physician[38] during the campaign and was there when Lieutenant Colonel Gordon was brought to the rear. He wrote later:

> Sir Alexander Gordon was brought to me [directly off the field] about 7 o'clock in the evening of the 18th by the Sergeant Major[39] & a few of the soldiers of the regiment who were carrying him upon a door, which they had found near the field of battle. I was at that moment occupied in dressing some wounded men near the scene of action [assisting at Mont St Jean Farm] & I suppose I must have seen Colonel Gordon about ten minutes or a quarter of an hour after he had received his wound.

---

36. Major Kelly was a DAQMG assigned to the Army HQ. He took command of the 73rd Foot after the Imperial Guard had been defeated but before the army was ordered to advance.
37. *Waterloo Letters*, p.342.
38. Crumplin, *Bloody Fields of Waterloo*, pp.99-101.
39. Who the sergeant major was is unknown. Michael Crumplin in *Bloody Fields of Waterloo*, p. 153 states it was Sergeant Major Woods 2nd Battalion 30th Foot. Gareth Glover in *Waterloo Archive*, Volume 1, p.252, thinks it was Sergeant Major William Cox of the 3rd Foot Guards. However, the 3rd Foot Guards were at Hougoumont, so it was unlikely Sergeant Major Cox.

A musket ball had entered on the inside of the left thigh and had wounded the femoral artery a little above where it pierces the biceps muscle & going downwards had shattered the femur in several pieces, lodging in [the] knee near the surface of the integument [just under the skin]. The wound was of such a nature that there was no hope of preserving the limb [the femur was shattered in many places and the ball had tracked down to lodge near the knee joint]. He had lost a considerable quantity of blood & complained of excessive pain & as the road was crowded with horses and men in great confusion I thought it was better to, amputate immediately [at Mont St Jean] than to wait till he should reach the Duke's quarters at Waterloo since besides the torture that he was then suffering and which he must necessarily suffer from a broken limb during his removal to a distance of upwards of two miles he would run great risk of sinking should haemorrhage come on in consequence of the wound in the artery. I was assisted in the operation by Dr Kenny of the artillery,[40] which I performed entirely to my own satisfaction and notwithstanding that it was necessary to take off the thigh very high up he bore the operation well & though weak was in tolerable spirits asking me several questions about different officers whom he had seen carried from the field wounded and requesting me to tell him how soon I thought he would get well, whether he should not be able to ride.

He said he felt easy and at his own request was removed slowly by the same soldiers who had carried him from the field to the Duke's house in Waterloo which he unfortunately entered at the moment when Mr Gunning [Deputy Inspector John Gunning] was in the act of amputating Lord Fitzroy Somerset's arm.

From that instant he became very restless and uneasy, sighing frequently and begging for a little wine. I gave him a small quantity with water & as soon as Lord Fitzroy and the Prince of Orange set out for Brussels, had him put to bed [in the Duke's bed] & gave him a few drops of laudanum with a little wine. I was sent for about ten o'clock to see Lord Uxbridge whose leg I found necessary to amputate and whilst I was in the middle of the operation I had a message from Sir Alexander to say that his stump was bleeding & [he was] very uneasy but as I could not

---

40. Second Assistant Surgeon Matthias Kenny of the Ordnance Medical Department.

go to him myself at the moment I sent Mr Cartan[41] surgeon to the 15th Hussars who brought me back word that he was very restless but that nothing appeared amiss with the stump.

As soon as I had finished with Lord Uxbridge I went over to him & as he complained very much of uneasiness & the bandages appeared a good deal tinged with blood. I removed the dressing & examined the face of the wound in the presence of Staff Surgeon Callender[42] and of Mr Cartan the surgeon of the 15th. I found the ligatures on the arteries perfectly secure, but there was very considerable venous oozing [i.e. bleeding from the veins] all over the surface of the stump & particularly from the great femoral vein, round which I had put a ligature cleaning away about 8 or 10 ozs of clotted blood, [250-300 millilitres] which had collected about the ends of the muscles and the integument. I again did up the stump carefully moistening the bandage with cold water & I repeated the anodyne draught [tincture of laudanum]. He said he felt easier and lay for some time more composed but about one o'clock in the morning he became restless as before changing his posture, calling every few minutes for his servant and sitting up and laying down in bed almost every moment and in this manner he continued till he became perfectly exhausted and expired soon after daylight I should think about half past 3 o'clock of the morning.[43]

Lieutenant Colonel Lord Fitzroy Somerset of the 1st Foot Guards, who was serving as Wellington's Military Secretary, was riding near La Haye Sainte about 19.00 hours when he was shot in the right arm.[44] He was able to ride the short distance back to the field hospital at Mont Saint Jean, where Deputy Inspector of Hospitals Dr. John Gunning,[45] who was the senior medical officer assigned to the 1st Corps, amputated his arm above the elbow. Lord Fitzroy's brother, Major General Lord Edward Somerset, wrote to their mother that: 'we have to lament poor Fitzroy's wound, by which he has lost his right arm. I understood the ball entered near the elbow and shattered the bone so much that the surgeons instantly decided to take it off. My friend was in the room with him while the operation was

---

41. Surgeon Thomas Cartan.
42. Surgeon John Callender Medical Staff.
43. Crumplin, pp.99-101
44. Somerset, p.13.
45. Crumplin, *Bloody Fields of Waterloo*, p.152.

performed, and he tells me he bore it manfully, that the Prince of Orange, who lay wounded in the same room, was not aware the amputation had been made.'[46] Legend has it that the Prince was awoken when Lord Fitzroy called out after the surgery when his arm was about to be disposed of: 'Hallo, don't carry away that arm till I have taken off my ring!' The ring had been a gift from his wife.[47]

Aides-de-Camp were vulnerable regardless of the rank of their general. Captain Newton Chambers of the 1st Battalion 1st Foot Guards, who served as the ADC to Lieutenant General Sir Thomas Picton, was shot and killed shortly after his general died. Lieutenant General Rowland Lord Hill had two 1st Foot Guards ADCs, both who were continuously exposed to danger. In addition to Major Churchill having four horses killed under him as mentioned above, Captain Hon. Orlando Bridgeman of the 1st Battalion 1st Foot Guards was also shot. While serving as an extra ADC to the general, he was hit in the back by a canister shot about 20.00 hours. Fortunately for him, it did not penetrate the skin.

The Divisional Artillery

The number of rounds fire by the divisional artillery was immense. After the battle they reported that the expenditure of the following ammunition:

Table 14.4: Return of Ammunition expended by the Guards Division's Artillery on 16, 17, and 18 June, 1815[48]

Unit	16 June 1815		17 June 1815		18 June 1815	
	9-pounder	Howitzer	9-pounder	Howitzer	9-pounder	Howitzer
Kuhlmann's KGL HA	130	31	-	-	314	54
Sandham's RA Brigade	8	-	-	11	1049	78

---

46. *Waterloo Archive*, Vol. 6, pp.16-17.
47. Other versions of his words include, 'Hey, bring my arm back. There's a ring my wife gave me on the finger'; 'Fetch me that hand, it has a ring on it that my wife gave me'; Hello, boy! Look for my arm and bring it to me. Take off my wedding ring, slip it onto my left hand', Sweetman, pp.65-66.
48. Mudford, William, *Historical Account of the Campaign in the Netherlands in 1815*. London: Henry Colburn, 1817, p.337.

These figures are based on the number of rounds it took to re-supply an artillery brigade/troop with their authorized amount of munitions. At first glance it seems that Captain Sandham's guns fired three times the number of rounds that Captain Kuhlmann's guns did. However, Captain Kuhlmann reported that one of the reasons why he abandoned his guns was because they had run out of ammunition. He pulled his crews and limbers back behind the lines in hope that he would be able to re-fill them from the artillery reserve. Captain Kuhlmann eventually found Lieutenant Colonel Adye and Captain Sandham. Once Lieutenant Colonel Adye realized how short of ammunition the KGL Horse Artillery was, he ordered Captain Sandham to re-supply him. This cross-leveling makes it appear that Captain Sandham fired more rounds than Captain Kuhlmann.[49] In reality they probably both fired about 700 rounds or 116 rounds per artillery piece. They began firing around 11.00 hours and had stopped by 17.30 hours. During those six hours, they averaged sixteen rounds per hour or one every three to four minutes.

The Next Morning

At daybreak the full scope of the destruction around Hougoumont was apparent. Ensign Gronow, came down the ridge from La Belle Alliance:

> Early on the morning after the battle of Waterloo, I visited Huguemont [sic], in order to witness with my own eyes the traces of one of the most hotly-contested spots on the field of battle. I came first upon the orchard, and there discovered heaps of dead men, in various uniforms: those of the Guards in their usual red jackets, the German Legion in green, and the French dressed in blue, mingled together. The dead and the wounded positively covered the whole area of the orchard; not less than two thousand men had there fallen. The apple-trees presented a singular appearance; shattered branches were seen hanging about their mother-trunks in such profusion, that one might almost suppose the stiff-growing and stunted tree had been converted into the willow: every tree was riddled and smashed in a manner which told that the showers of shot had been incessant. On this spot I lost some of my dearest and bravest

---

49. *Waterloo Archives*, Vol 2, p.44.

friends, and the country had to mourn many of its most heroic sons slain here.[50]

Ensign Master recalled that:

> Except the battle of Leipsic [sic], never was a there such a slaughter on a field of Battle, frightful to behold; it took five days to clear away the wounded. The well at Belle Alliance all red, all below filled with suffering wounded, agonizing ... I left, fit again, to look after my men, but what a sight to behold, heaps of bodies of all nations, dead and wounded suffering! Asking for help and water, laying about for miles around! This was worse than the Battle itself and I was glad when the orders came to fall in and march off after the enemy.[51]

Private Clay on his foraging expedition to Hougoumont found the buildings still on fire and found it to

> be a more complete picture of destruction than we could have anticipated; (the fire having continued its ravages during the night) ... we proceeded up the wood some distance, which was thickly strewn with the bodies of the slain, many of our comrades being of the number. The heaps of the enemy's slain laying about the exterior of the farm, showed the deadly effect of our fire from within, and on passing near to the site of the circular stack, as stated before, I found that it had been totally destroyed by the enemy's fire and also that many of our comrades had fallen near the spot, and apparently entire, but on touching them, found them completely dried up by the heat. On passing down by the side of the garden we first entered, amongst the numerous bodies of the slain, was a wounded Frenchman in a sitting posture, (having no doubt fallen on the spot the previous evening) being unable to rise, we offered him our assistance, which he refused, and leaving him to his fate, we returned up the hill to our company.[52]

---

50. Gronow, Vol. 1, pp.74-75.
51. Master, p.141.
52. Clay, pp.29-30.

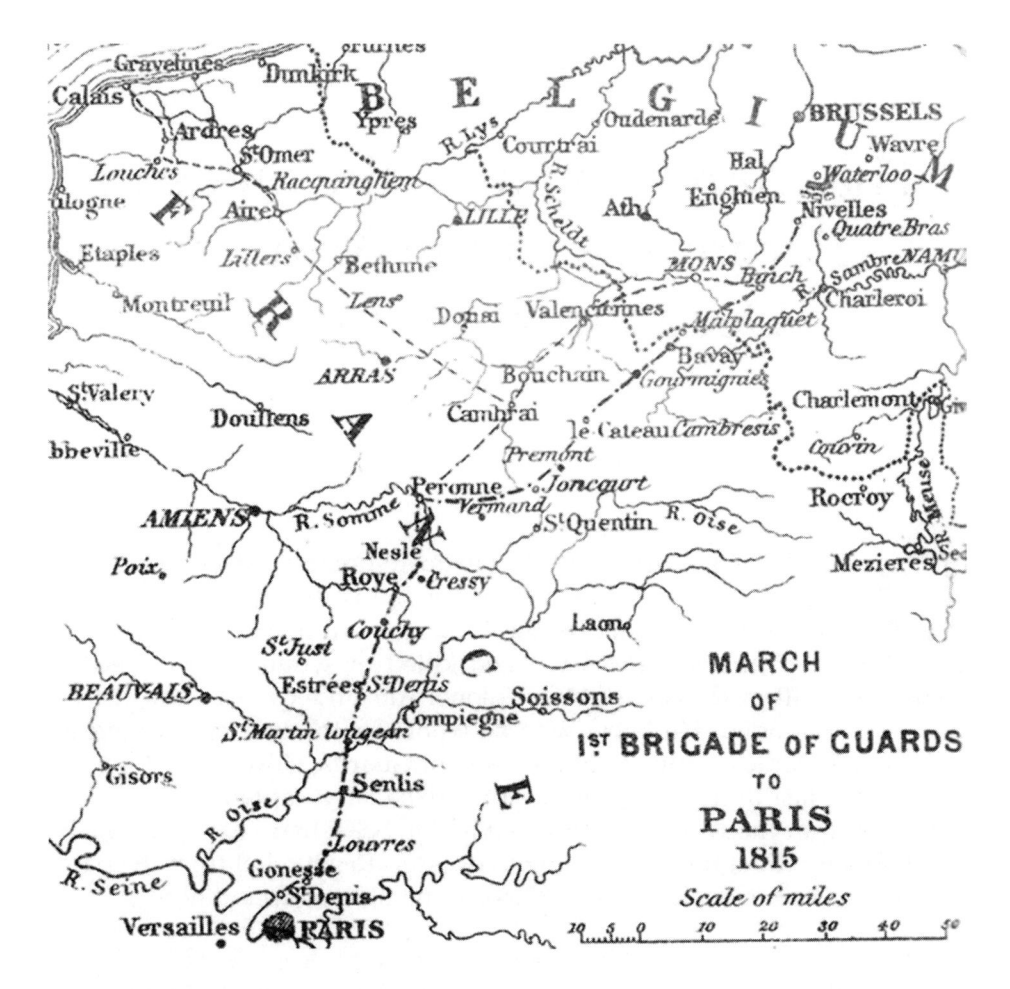

March of the 1st Brigade to Paris
Derived from a map in The Origin and History of the First or Grenadier Guards

Chapter 15

The March to Paris, the Siege of Peronné, and the Army of Occupation of France

During the night the army began to re-organize itself, especially filling vacancies in command and on the staff. Major General Byng remained in command of the 1st Corps but he needed to replace the many staff officers who had been killed or wounded. He needed someone to fill in for his AQMG, Colonel Alexander Abercromby, who had been wounded. He knew who he wanted – the twenty-seven-year-old, Captain James Stanhope of the 1st Foot Guards. However, taking the job was the last thing on the mind of the exhausted captain. He was still suffering from the wound he received at San Sebastian years previously, and had only thoughts about going to Brussels to get relief from the pain. Before he could make his escape, Major General Byng found him:

> In the morning of the 19th I prepared to go to Brussels when Sir John Byng now commanding 1st Corps, urged me so strongly to take if but for a day the duty of Quarter Master General as Abercromby QMG of the 1st Corps & Bradford of the 1st Division were both wounded, but I determined at all risks to attempt it; but it was an arduous undertaking for any one from the ranks with no knowledge of previous arrangements without sufficient horses & with no maps, in my state of health to take such a responsibility, as the charge of the 1st Corps then amounting I suppose to 15,000 men. At Nivelles the same evening I begged him to write to get someone else, but the orders arrived in the middle of the night and it was impossible. The exertion & fatigue began to absorb the abscess, my appetite returned & I was evidently better. In three days I no longer thought of leaving the army & I was rejoiced in

being joined by my servant & favourite mare. He had been taken but had escaped in the confusion of the retreat.[1]

Considering what it had begun the campaign with, the 1st Division staff was seriously undermanned. It had no AQMG or DAQMG and none appeared to be forthcoming. No Guards officer currently serving with his battalion had any staff experience. The logical choice was Captain Stanhope, but he had already been tapped to be the acting AQMG of the 1st Corps.

Guards officers were still in high demand to serve on the staff, but because of their heavy losses none were allowed to go. Lieutenant General Sir Henry Clinton, the commander of the 2nd Division was still waiting for an Assistant Adjutant General to be assigned to his division. He had Captain Charles Bentinck of the Coldstream Guards serving as his DAAG, but felt

> the want of an officer of greater experience in the Adjutant General's duties than Captain Bentinck, in spite of the assiduity with which he endeavours to do every part of his duty. Lt. Colonel Miller,[2] the officer whom I formerly recommended for this appointment has died of his wounds, and I now beg leave to name in his place Lt. Colonel [Henry] Dawkins of the Coldstream Guards of whose zeal and punctuality in the performance of his duty I have a high opinion & as he discharged the duty of Brigade Major during the former five last campaigns in Spain and France and occasionally that of the Assistant Adjutant General to the First Division. I have no doubt of his being sufficiently qualified, from the good opinion which I have every reason to entertain of Captain Bentinck and the desire I have to retain him with me, I hope that if your Grace should find it expedient to comply with my request in favour of Lt. Colonel Dawkins you will allow Captain Bentinck to hold his present post with this division.[3]

Wellington refused Lieutenant General Clinton's request despite Captain Dawkins being Clinton's nephew. His brother, Captain Francis Dawkins of the 1st Foot Guards, was already serving as Clinton's ADC.

---

1. Stanhope, p.179.
2. Captain William Miller 3rd Battalion 1st Foot Guards died of the wounds he received at Quatre Bras on 19 June.
3. Clinton, Vol. 2, p.115.

Changes were made to move officers to company commands within each battalion. In the 2nd Battalion 1st Foot Guards, Lieutenant James Nixon, who commanded Captain Lord Fitzroy Somerset's company at Quatre Bras and Waterloo was given command of the Light Company. Captain Thomas Hill's Company had no officers still with the colours. Who took command is not known. However, the senior surviving officer without a command was Ensign Algernon Greville, who was temporarily assigned to the Light Company during Waterloo. He was probably given command of the company. In the 3rd Battalion 1st Foot Guards, only four lieutenants and ten ensigns were left with the battalion. Lieutenant Lonsdale Boldero continued to serve with as the adjutant, while the other three remained in command of their companies. The battalion was fortunate with its ten ensigns, since they were the ten senior ensigns in the regiment at Waterloo. Surprisingly all three subalterns assigned to Captain Fead's company had come through unscathed: Ensigns Richard Master, Henry Vernon, and James Butler. As the senior ensign, Richard Master would have relinquished his duties as the King's Colour Bearer and taken command of the company. No officers from Captain Thomas's company were still with the battalion, so as the senior ensign without a command, Henry Vernon would likely have been given it.

In the Coldstream Guards, Lieutenant George Bowles got his wish and was given command of the Light Company. Ensign Mark Beaufoy was appointed the acting Adjutant. Neither Captain Mackinnon's Grenadier Company nor Captain Dawkins's company had any subalterns. Who replaced them is unknown. Ensign Gooch was the senior ensign without a command and probably took the Grenadiers. Captain Dawkins was serving as an acting major and would still command the company as they marched. However, should the battalion go into combat he would turn over command to one of the senior ensigns while he took up his duties of an acting major. Who the designated ensign was is unknown, however the next senior ensign was George Buckley. In the 2nd Battalion 3rd Foot Guards, Lieutenant William Drummond, would have commanded Captain Keate's company, but he was too sick to march with the regiment. As the senior lieutenant without a command, Charles Barnet would have been given the company. Ensign Whitwell Butler was ordered to remain behind in Brussels to oversee the care of the sick.

Appendix VI shows how the 1st Division was re-organized on the morning of 19 June.

Dawn came about 03.45 hours the next morning. Yet no orders came to move from the battlefield. While they waited, Lord Saltoun sent the 2nd

Battalion's 1st Foot Guards Adjutant, Lieutenant Allix, and Lieutenant Charles Lascelles back to Brussels to look for the battalion's missing baggage.[4] Family members arrived in the encampments looking for their relatives. Lord Apsley[5] found his younger brother, Ensign Seymour Bathurst who had become Major General Maitland's ADC after Quatre Bras. Lord Aspley wrote to his father, Henry Earl Bathurst, the Secretary of State for War and the Colonies that he had, 'saw Seymour before I went to bed and also Algernon Greville; he is safe. I took him a bottle of brandy this morning to comfort him after three nights bivouacking without baggage'.[6] Missing baggage was not just a problem for the 1st Division. Very few officers in the army had theirs, and that included those on the staff. Lieutenant Colonel William Gomm of the Coldstream Guards who was serving as the AQMG of the 5th Division wrote: 'I have been four days without washing face or hands, but am in hourly expectation of my lavender water, etc., etc. etc.'[7]

Eventually the word came to march. The Prussian army was pursuing the fleeing French army south along the main road towards Quatre Bras and then to Charleroi, so Wellington ordered his army to head southwest on the road to Nivelles. This permitted the division to avoid the congestion on the other road and hopefully link up with its baggage train which was still in the vicinity of Enghien. Lieutenant James Nixon, who commanded the Light Company of the 2nd Battalion 1st Foot Guards, was glad to be leaving the battlefield:

> After our bivouac on the night of the 18th after the battle, we marched to Nivelles over the terrible field, so horrible a scene scarcely ever any man witnessed. The ground for the space of a league was covered with bodies absolutely lying in ranks, horses wandering about most terribly wounded and grouped in heaps with their riders. Towards the right was a chateau which during the battle took fire from the enemy's shells and was in that state most heroically defended by Saltoun and afterwards by the 2nd Brigade of Guards. Its appearance

---

4. ibid, p.114.
5. Henry George Bathurst, the oldest son of the 3rd Earl Bathurst. He was attached to Wellington's staff as a civilian.
6. *Report on the Manuscripts of Earl Bathurst*, p.357.
7. *Waterloo Archive*, Vol. 6, p.15.

brought to my mind San Sebastian, it was equally horrid, though on a smaller scale.[8]

The 12km march to Nivelles along a good road would have been very easy if the troops had not been exhausted. Once there in their bivouacs food and rest was foremost on their minds. The baggage had still not come up and the officers had to rough it with their men. Many took the time to write home to let their families know that they were still alive. Lord Saltoun, still in the command of the 2nd Battalion 1st Foot Guards began what he considered the most difficult duty of being a commander 'of writing to the families of all our poor officers who fell an account of their death, which as commanding officer I am obliged to do'.[9]

After the 1st Corps Headquarters and the 1st Division had arrived in Nivelles for the night, major generals Byng and Maitland took the opportunity to write to the Duke of York who was the Commander-in-Chief of the British Army. As the senior surviving officer in the 1st Division, Major General Byng wrote to tell of the action of not only the division, but of the 2nd Brigade. He also took time to recognize the senior officers who distinguished themselves:

> I have the authority of the Duke of Wellington to say that they highly distinguished themselves; that from the commencement to the end of the action their conduct was most excellent ... Lieutenant Colonel Macdonell of the Coldstream with the two light companies occupied the house and the wood by the light companies of the 1st Brigade and some battalion companies of the Coldstream, the whole under Lieutenant Colonel Lord Saltoun's command. Against this post the first attack of the enemy was made and was successfully resisted; as were the numerous efforts made to close of the day by the enemy to get possession. The Duke of Wellington himself in the early part of the day gave his particular attention to that point and when called to the left by a serious attack on that point, he confided it to my care with directions to keep the house to the last moment, relieving the troops as they required it and the whole of the brigade, except two companies

---

8. ibid, Vol. 1, p.136. Lieutenant Nixon was referring to the siege of San Sebastian, Spain which took place from 7 July-8 September *1813. Wellington's Army took the city but suffered over 3,700 casualties in doing so.*
9. Saltoun, p.14. He finished writing the letters on 25 June.

were required before the action ceased. Colonel Hepburn and Woodford affording me every assistance and giving a fine example to their battalions. The conduct of Lieutenant Colonel Macdonell in defending the house even when it was on fire and maintaining it as ordered, has I have no doubt been particularly noticed to you by the commander of the forces. It was admirable; as was that of Lieutenant Colonel Lord Saltoun. About four o'clock the command of the division devolved upon me; and having rode over to see the first brigade just at the time of the attack was made by the enemy's cavalry, I had an opportunity of witnessing the steady manner in which they received the several charges made to their front. I had also to witness the gallantry with which they met the last attack made by the Grenadiers of the Imperial Guard ordered on by Bonaparte himself. The destructive fire they poured in and the subsequent charge which together completely routed the enemy. A second attempt met with a similar reception and the loss they caused to the French of the finest troops I ever saw was immense. I beg you Sir to understand that my presence or advice to General Maitland never was required. I merely staid [sic] with him as an humble individual when the assistance of every one was required. His judgement and gallantry directed everything was necessary. I cannot say too much in his praise or in that of the several commanders his battalions had. The conduct Sir of every officer and man of both brigades was everything I could wish, the officers on every occasion being conspicuous for their gallantry. Sincerely do I regret the loss of so many valuable officers, such excellent men. I hope I have not trespassed too far on your Royal Highness in my wish to do justice to my gallant friends and soldiers. I believe everyone who witnessed their conduct will confirm my statement.[10]

Major General Maitland, who initially commanded the 1st Brigade, but then the 1st Division when General Byng took command of the 1st Corps, focused most of his letter on the deeds of the 1st Foot Guards, whom the Duke of York was the regimental colonel. The letter covered the performance of the brigade at Quatre Bras and Waterloo. He ended it by endorsing what Major General Byng had to say about the conduct of the officers and men. He did not endorse any officer by name other

---

10. *Waterloo Archive*, Vol. 4, pp.143-144.

than 'Of the conduct of Lord Saltoun and of all their officers and men, General Byng speaks in the highest terms ... I need hardly comment on the splendid conduct of the officers and men. Your Royal Highness has lost many valuable officers, I, many dear and excellent friends.'[11]

There is a strong possibility that the battalion commanders also wrote to their regimental colonels,[12] but if they did the letters have disappeared. Captain James Stanhope of the 3rd Battalion 1st Foot Guards also took the time to write to the Duke of York. He had served as an extra-ADC to the Duke since July 1814. His letter was on Waterloo – mostly on the French cavalry charges and the defeat of the Imperial Guard. Because the Foot Guards were like a close-knit family he also passed on word of some of their officer casualties:

> The loss of the Guards, particularly in officers, Y.R.H. will see by the returns, has been most severe. Poor Stables died this morning as universally regretted as he was by every one loved. I hope Wyndham's wound is not a serious one and I trust the rest of the wounded officers will do well. I fear much however for Miller but have heard nothing of him since the 15th.[13]

The division continued its march on the morning of 20 June. Its destination was the town of Binche about 30km away. The officers' baggage had still not caught up with them. The smart uniforms of garrison duty were only a distant memory. They and their soldiers had the look of battle-hardened soldiers. Most were dirty and unkempt. This was not to be permitted, regardless of the circumstances. At the noon break:

> Every officer and soldier immediately set to work to get rid of the superabundance of beard which had been suffered to grow for several days. During this not very agreeable duty, a shout was heard from Lord Saltoun, who called to witness a bet he had made with Bob Ellison, that he, Ellison, could not shave off his beard in one minute. Preparations were made, Ellison taking care to bathe his face for a considerable time in water. He then commenced

---

11. ibid, pp.131-132.
12. The regimental colonel of the Coldstream Guards was Field Marshal Prince Adolphus Duke of Cambridge, while General Prince William the Duke of Gloucester was the colonel of the 3rd Foot Guards.
13. *Waterloo Archive*, Vol. 1, pp.132-133.

operations, and in less than a minute, and without the aid of a looking-glass, actually won his bet, (a considerable one,) to the astonishment, and, I must add, the satisfaction of his comrades. This feat appeared to us all perfectly impossible to accomplish, as his face was covered with the stubble of a week's growth of hair, so dark that it had procured for him in the regiment the sobriquet of Black Bob'.[14]

The division arrived in Binche where it spent the night bivouacking in the open. The next day (21 June) they marched another 30km to Bavay, France. They crossed the border near Malplaquet,[15] the site of the famous British victory over the French on 11 September 1709 during the War of the Spanish Succession. As the troops were marching past the battlefield Wellington rode by and they 'cheered him and such a cheer in such a spot it brought tears into my eyes'.[16]

The weather on the march was not good. It rained most days and the division once again bivouacked in the open. Ensign Richard Master of the 3rd Battalion 1st Foot Guards did get some of his personal belongings that day. His horse had been sent to the rear at Waterloo, where it was stolen. He never expected to see it again. An officer coming from Brussels found the ensign and delivered his 'saddle and bridle, sent by a Belgian officer who had taken a liking to my horse!'[17] Ensign Thomas Wedgewood, now commanding Captain Canning's company in the 3rd Foot Guards, wrote to his mother a few days later that they were 'without any baggage tents or anything else, and you have no idea of what we underwent during that time, sleeping in the fields without even a hedge to cover us, generally raining the whole night and the ground ankle deep in mud'.[18]

Supplies were a major problem for the whole army, not just for the 1st Division. Lieutenant General Clinton, the commander of the 2nd Division wrote in his diary that night: 'Rain the greater part of the day, the road from Mons after it ceases to be paved extremely bad. We outmarch our supplies & do not understand the procuring them by requisition'.[19]

---

14. Gronow, Vol. 2, p.47-48.
15. Malplaquet is near Taisnières-sur-Hon, France.
16. Stanhope, p.185.
17. Master, p.141.
18. *Waterloo Archive*, Vol 1, p.148.
19. Clinton, Vol. 2, p.116.

Once the 1st Division was in France the attitude of the officers and men changed. Before they crossed the border they believed that they were in a friendly country, but once in France they did not know what to expect. The nearest French force was at the fortified city of Maubeuge less than 14km away. Now that they were in France, they were taking no chances. That evening, Ensign Richard Master had guard duty and was about to take a picquet beyond the lines. He was approached by Ensign Gronow. To his surprise with him was his brother Captain William Master of the 2nd Battalion 3rd Foot Guards. His brother had missed Waterloo and arrived in Belgium after the 1st Division had marched. He likely joined up with his battalion earlier in the day and had just then had time to track down his brother. Captain Master, the commander of the battalion's Light Company, was the senior officer in the battalion and took command from Captain Douglas Mercer.

The division stopped at Gommegnies for the night, having travelled a distance of 8km. The next day, 23 June, the division stayed in its encampments the whole day. The reason why they halted was the army had out-marched its supplies and Wellington needed his pontoon train to catch up.[20]

Supplies did reach the 1st Division, however the officers' baggage had still not made it by the first night. Lieutenant Nixon wrote the night of 22 June that: 'Our baggage was sent to Antwerp and is not yet arrived. At Brussels some stragglers from the Belgians attacked the bat men and pillaged the horses. How I escaped in this respect I don't know.'[21] Even the senior officers were beginning to become bedraggled. Lord Saltoun wrote to his wife that: 'Our baggage is a long way in the rear and I do not know when I shall get a clean shirt, I have got my toothbrush so I am not quite a beast.'[22] However, at least for the 3rd Foot Guards, the baggage arrived on the second day of their halt. Ensign Wedgewood did write home, 'now we have got our baggage and tents and are much better off'.[23]

Another possible reason for the delay was the state of the roads on which the army travelled. The Prussian army moved along the major roads, while Wellington's army stuck to the back roads. This was a deliberate decision on his part for he believed that by using them he could avoid unnecessary

---

20. Wellington, Duke of, *The Dispatches of Field Marshal the Duke of Wellington* ... Vol. XII, p.517.
21. *Waterloo Archive*, Vol 1, p.137.
22. ibid, Vol. 6, p.109.
23. ibid, Vol. 1, p.148.

casualties. The better roads were protected by forts and fortified cities, while the minor roads avoided them. The thought was that if he by-passed the fortifications their governors would not venture out of them to attack him. They would wait instead to see what happened to Napoleon. They would only be a factor if Napoleon was not deposed. If he was, then the fortifications could be left to the new French government to handle. This strategy was sound, but it did cause problems for the movement of the troops as Lord Saltoun pointed out to his wife: 'The weather is most horrible and resembles more a winter than a summer campaign for it has rained almost every day since the action and the roads (for as yet we have been marching by the cross roads and not the chaussees, to avoid the strong places) are up to the men's knees in mud but as we get nearer to Paris I hope it will be better.'[24]

The division broke camp on the morning of 24 June and their march would be the longest in five days. They marched 25km to the town of Le Cateau-Cambrésis but did not stop. Instead they marched through the town and continued another 10km to Busigny. The division made a leisurely march of less than 10km the next day. The division headquarters stopped at Prémont, but the 1st Brigade marched a few kilometres further and encamped in the vicinity of Serain. It was about this time that Colonel Alexander Abercromby resumed his duties as the AQMG of the 1st Corps after being wounded at Waterloo. Captain Stanhope went back to the 1st Division and became its AQMG.

The army had marched 150km in a week. Not a difficult march under normal conditions, however the weather had been rainy, the roads bad, and food inadequate. No shelter was available except for the senior officers and their nightly camps were more often in muddy fields, exposed to the elements. When these factors combined with the stress of having fought two battles in three days, it is not surprising that the men began to get sick. Compounding the problem was the lack of waggons to carry those too sick to march. The waggons and carts that were part of the battalion's baggage train had been left behind at Waterloo to help evacuate the wounded. Lord Saltoun's batman, forty-two-year-old Private James Hughes took sick at Serain. Lord Saltoun wrote to his wife that he was, 'to leave him in the village where we halted last night for from violent rheumatics he was unable to sit on his horse and the number of our wounded so great added to the confusion that took place in the rear owing to the false alarm the day of the battle that our carts for carrying sick men have never come up,

---

24. Saltoun, p.13.

so I do not know whether I shall ever see him again indeed I much fear I shall not'.[25]

The shortage of transport was an army-wide problem and in the General Orders dated 25 June, Wellington issued a warning about the use of waggons for personal baggage: 'The Commander of the Forces has observed the greatest irregularity among the baggage. Private baggage and women are put upon the carts destined to carry tents and hospital stores, and the consequence is that they cannot get on, and delay everything else. If the Commander of the Forces should observe such a practice again, he will order the private baggage to be burnt, and will bring the officer to whom it belongs to a Court-Martial for disobedience of orders.'[26]

On 26 June the 1st Division marched 30km to Caulaincourt and halted for the night. That afternoon, Major General Byng was passing the village of Vermand and found Wellington. The Duke told him: 'You are the very person I wish to see – I want you to take Peronne. You may as well take with you a brigade of guards, and a Dutch-Belgian brigade.'[27] Peronné was another fortified city that sat on a hill overlooking the Somme River. It was surrounded by marshland and had a garrison of less than 500 men. Its nickname was 'La Pucelle' or 'The Maid' because it had withstood many sieges and never been taken. It was considered the key to northern France. Wellington could not afford to leave it along his line of march and take the chance of its garrison making raids along his lines of communications.

Wellington had known for several days that he would have to take Peronné and that he would use the 1st Division to do it. Without revealing his reasons why, he attached 2nd Captain John Brenchley Harris of the Royal Engineers to the division. His detachment included two other Royal Engineers, 2nd Captain Alexander Thomson and 1st Lieutenant Marcus Waters, and the 2nd Company, 2nd Battalion Royal Sappers and Miners under the command of Sub-Lieutenant William Stratton. If a formal siege had to be undertaken, Captain Harris and his men would direct it.

Captain Stanhope, now the 1st Division's AQMG arrived in Caulaincourt, where he received 'fresh orders for the Guards to attack Peronne'. In addition to the 1st Guards Brigade, Wellington was sending

---

25. ibid, p.14.
26. Wellington, Duke of, *The Dispatches of Field Marshal the Duke of Wellington* ... (enlarged ed.); Vol. 8, p.579.
27. Siborne, *History of the Waterloo Campaign*, p.461.

the 1st Brigade[28] of the 2nd Netherlands Division and the Netherlands Heavy Cavalry Brigade commanded by Colonel Jean de Bruyn,[29] General Maitland ordered the 1st Brigade to march another 17km to Peronné and take the fortress. This was after already marching 30km that day. Wellington rode to the fortress and around 13.45 hours demanded that the governor of the fortress surrender it. In Peronné was General of Brigade Jacques-Polycarpe Morgan, the commandant of the 16th Military District. Although Peronné was in the 15th Military District, General Morgan had been given overall command of the defence of the Somme River. He had arrived the previous day to oversee its defence and refused to surrender the fortress. To defend it, he had the Urban Guard which was an artillery company, an artillery detachment of thirty regular soldiers, a company of veterans, and 293 soldiers of the National Guard of the Department of Oise under the command of Commandant Eugène de Bouteville.[30] Commanding the artillery was Sous Lieutenant Charles-Claude Jeandot. Until General Morgan arrived, the city was commanded by Major Pettit.

The 1st Guards Brigade arrived at Peronné about 15.00 hours and Captain Harris, the Royal Engineer, and Captain Stanhope did a reconnaissance of the fortifications. Captain Harris thought the ditch around the walls was shallow enough to be forded since there were reeds growing there. Captain Stanhope however had his doubts and questioned several locals, who said it was about ten feet deep. Captain Harris also thought that the bridge was mined with explosives and would be set off if they attacked across it.[31]

Wellington decided that he did not have the time for a formal siege and decided to take the fortress by storm. He ordered the attack to go through the suburbs that were between the fortress and the river, hoping the buildings there would provide cover for the troops as they advanced. The

---

28. The brigade was commanded by Lieutenant Colonel Wijbrandus de Jongh of the 8th National Militia Battalion. It consisted of five battalions: 7th Belgian Line Battalion, the 27th Dutch Jaeger Battalion, and the 5th, 7th, and 8th National Militia Battalions.
29. The Netherlands Heavy Cavalry Brigade had four regiments: the 1st Dutch Carabiniers, the 2nd Belgian Carabiniers, the 3rd Dutch Carabiniers, and the 6th Dutch Hussars.
30. Wellington, Duke of, *Supplementary Dispatches* ... Vol. 11, p.14; Dournel, p.505.
31. Stanhope, p.185.

3rd Battalion 1st Foot Guards were to make the assault. The 2nd Company of the Royal Sappers and Miners would go with them, carrying fascines to throw in the ditch and to breach the gate. The 1st Division artillery was not there, so Captain Abraham Petter's Netherlands Horse Artillery Half Battery was ordered to provide support. It consisted of three 6-pounder cannon and a 24-pounder howitzer. It was set up on the hills to the east.[32] Captain Andreas Cleeves' 9-pounder Foot Battery of the King's German Artillery was on the hills south of the fortress and could fire directly on to the walls that would be assaulted.

The plan of attack was for the 3rd Battalion to attack in two columns. The left column would attack across the ditch while the right column would cross the bridge and enter the fortress after blowing up the gate. The right column would be preceded by the remnants of the 1st Brigade's light companies under the command of the Lord Saltoun. The news that the battalion was ordered to assault the fortress was not well received. Ensign Master wrote that he 'was walking up and down with some brother officers, in a French Avenue of the Chaussee; we looked at one another when the order came, and thought it hard to run the risk of being killed at this miserable town having escaped Waterloo!'[33] This did not keep him from volunteering to join a forlorn hope made up mostly from the Light Company and 'commanded by Capt. Bob Ellison, Light Company, Lt. Davies and myself'.[34]

The attack began well but the left-hand column that was to cross the ditch and assault the wall soon found that Captain Stanhope was right. When they got to the ditch they threw in the fascines and one of the Royal Engineers was the first to cross them. He 'sank like a float with a bite'.[35] The Forlorn Hope, with some men from the Sappers and Miners Company who were carrying ladders that had been confiscated from houses, raced from the suburbs and across the bridge while under fire. They reached the safety of the gate, but somehow the sappers did not bring explosive charges, sledgehammers or any other tools to break in the gate. Instead, Lieutenant Stratton and Lance Corporal Edward Council of the Sappers and Miners used the ladders to climb to the top of the gate and squeezed

---

32. Hamilton, Vol. 3, p.56; Wellington, Duke of, *The Dispatches of Field Marshal the Duke of Wellington* ... (enlarged edition), Vol. 8, p.176.
33. Master, p.142.
34. ibid.
35. Stanhope, p.185. Who the officer was is not known.

over its spikes and jumped to the ground on the other side. They quickly opened the gate and the Forlorn Hope swept into the city.[36] Ensign Master was hit by a canister shot which bruised his thigh.[37] Although the British were in the fortress, they still had not cleared the walls and the French continued to fire on those on the outside. Lord Saltoun was crossing the bridge when he was hit in the groin by a canister round. He was saved by a coin purse that was in his pocket. He wrote to his wife the next day that:

> I have heard an old saying that everything is made for some purpose, but I do not suspect you had the least idea when you made my little purse that it would ever be put to the use that it was yesterday during the storm of Peronne. A grape shot hit me full in the thigh, fortunately I had a little purse in the pocket full of small gold pieces called ducats which so stopped the ball that although it knocked me down it lodged in the purse and given me a slight bruise not half so bad as a blow with a stick. Had it not been for the purse it would have been very near a finish, so you will see my dear Kate I owe you something. The purse is cut right open by the ball but I shall not have it mended till it comes into your hands what is rather odd [that] the little heart I had in it is the only thing not hurt, for all the gold pieces are bent and twisted about properly.[38]

Most letters downplay the danger they were in to keep their loved ones from worrying. Lord Saltoun was only married less than two months before he went to Belgium in April 1815. He took a different tact in his letters, promising his bride 'to write exactly what had happened and next because they are always so fond of killing people in reports especially if they have been hit in the slightest manner'.[39] Wellington and Captain Stanhope closely followed Lord Saltoun and his men. They were on the bridge and 'we were covered with a shower of grape but escaped'.[40]

The civilian population was neutral about surrendering the city, however once the city began to be bombarded by the Allies, their attitude

---

36. Connelly, Vol. 1, pp.237-238.
37. Master, p.142.
38. Saltoun, p.15.
39. ibid.
40. Stanhope, p.186.

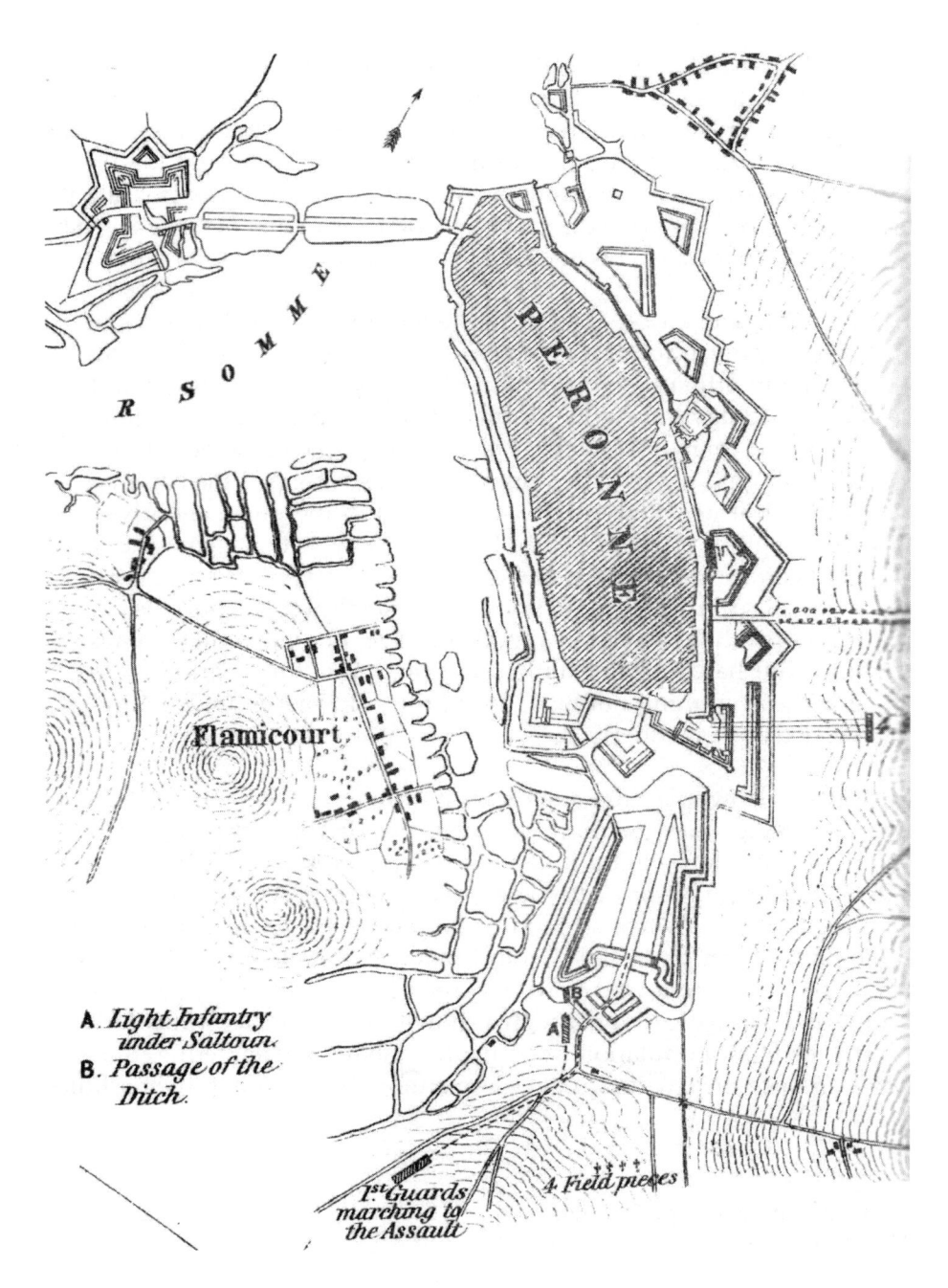

The Storming of Peronné 26 June 1815
Derived from a map in *The Origin and History of the First or Grenadier Guards*

change. Its former mayor, a lawyer named Jean-Baptiste Hiver, approached General Morgan with several demands, including the troops stop firing at the British and the general surrender the city immediately. The general ignored him and Mayor Hiver took matters in his own hands. He had made a white flag in anticipation of the general agreeing to his demands and stirred up the crowd who had followed him to the meeting. General Morgan, realizing that he could do no more, turned command back over to the fortress' commandant, Major Pettit, and escaped the city.

Major Pettit knew he had no options except to surrender.[41] He sent orders to the artillery crews to cease firing, but they refused to do so. So he, Eugène de Bouteville, Mayor Hiver and a large number of civilians climbed the ramparts to appeal directly to the soldiers. They were able to convince them that continuing to fire would expose the city to danger, that they had already done everything that honour would demand, and that to continue to resist meant that they were fighting their legitimate sovereign, the king.

While this was going on in order to avoid further bloodshed, Wellington sent Captain Stanhope in to negotiate a surrender. He walked forward waving a white handkerchief right about the time the firing stopped. He approached the defenders by himself and soon the surrender was arranged. Unbeknownst to him or Wellington, the 2nd Carabiniers from the Netherlands Heavy Cavalry Brigade, took the initiative to enter the fortress through another gate and came charging down the streets. Captain Stanhope tried to stop them, but they mistook him for a French officer since he was standing with Major Pettit. He narrowly avoided being run down and sabred. In the process he lost twenty gold Napoleons that fell out of his pocket.[42] The garrison consisted mostly men of the national guard and had very few full-time soldiers. The surrender terms stipulated that they would be allowed to return to their homes and not become prisoners. The surrender of the city to the British would happen at 20.00 hours.

One of the traditions of the Napoleonic Wars was that soldiers were allowed to sack and loot any city or fortress that they took by storm. The men of the Forlorn Hope felt it was their right and as soon as the city surrendered they quickly disappeared to see what they could find. Ensign Master went looking for them to bring them back and when he went into

---

41. de Calonne, Albéric, *Histoire de la ville d'Amiens*. Paris: Alphonse Picard, 1906, pp.92-93; Dournel, pp.350 & 506.
42. Stanhope, p.186.

one of the shops he found the 'Gardes Nationales who had half changed their uniform into Bourjeois [sic] again pretending to be very civil and glad to see us; who upon my addressing them in French and telling them that having fired on us we were not such fools as to believe all those compliments, so that if they did not disappear immediately (instead of trying to make my men drunk,) I would carry them off as prisoners – they disappeared like lighting.'[43]

As assaults on fortifications went, Péronne was relatively bloodless. 2nd Captain Alexander Thomson of the Royal Engineers was wounded, as well as Sub-Lieutenant William Stratton, the commander of the Royal Sappers and Miners. The 2nd Battalion 1st Foot Guards had one man wounded,[44] while the 3rd Battalion 1st Foot Guards had one private killed and one sergeant and six privates wounded. Twenty-six-year-old Private William Broomfield of Lord Saltoun's light company was the last British Guardsman to be killed in action during the Napoleonic Wars. He was a former cordwainer[45] who volunteered from the Cheshire Militia in 1810.[46]

After successfully taking Péronne, the Guards were not allowed to rest on their laurels. Major General Byng was ordered to have them march at 07.00 hours the next morning to Nesle and then on to Cressy-Omencour where they would join the rest of the 1st Corps. The 5th and 7th National Militia Battalions were ordered to garrison Péronne.[47]

The 1st Brigade marched the 30km to Cressy-Omencour and spent the night there. Division Headquarters was at Billancourt about 5km away. It was the ninth day since Waterloo and officers who had been wounded and left behind when the army advanced into France began arriving. Captain Orlando Bridgeman, an extra-ADC to Lieutenant General Rowland Lord Hill, the commander of the 2nd Corps, was badly contused by a canister shot late in the day and left 'Brussels on the 24th & after a very tedious journey I joined the Duke of Wellington's headquarters at Nesle on the 27th proceeded to Lord Hill the following day'.[48]

---

43. Chambers, Vol. 1, pp.167-168.
44. Private William Pateman of the Light Company.
45. A cordwainer made shoes, while a cobbler repaired them.
46. Chambers, Vol. 1, pp.167-168.
47. Wellington, Duke of, *The Dispatches of Field Marshal the Duke of Wellington* ... (enlarged edition), Vol. 8, p.172.
48. *Waterloo Archive*, Vol. 4, p.29.

Even the 1st Division's Chaplain, Reverend Stonestreet, made an effort to join the troops, after initially staying in Brussels.

> I was busily employed in procuring quarters, doctors and food for the wounded as they arrived and in writing letters by the bedside of officers, to their friends. I consulted General Barnes, then wounded, on the propriety of my remaining at least a few days more at Brussels, where nearly half of my division were brought into the hospitals. But he said it would be more regular and creditable to keep the field with my corps and I rejoined them a little before we broke the French frontier, between Mons and Maubeuge ... Our march was usually from 18 to 22 miles a day.[49]

The march on 28 June was about 25km and the division bivouacked in the vicinity of Choncy-les-Pots. On 29 June the initial plans was to have them march to Ponte-de-Maxence where they would cross the Oise River. Before they marched word had been received that the bridge had been destroyed during the 1814 invasion of France and had not been repaired. After marching 30km they stayed the night in the village of Choisy-la-Victoire waiting for the pontoon bridge to arrive. Lord Saltoun took the time to write to his wife that night that they were only 37 miles (60km) from Paris and expected to be there by next Sunday (2 July) if they were able to get across the river. Word had also been received that replacements for the officers and men killed during the campaign were on the way, but no one was optimistic that they would arrive soon. Lord Saltoun had mixed feelings about them arriving. He recognized that, despite his performance at Quatre Bras, Waterloo, and Peronné, he was too junior to be kept in command of the battalion. He was hoping though that if enough replacement officers did arrive he would be able to go home on leave.[50]

The pontoons arrived the next morning and the 1st Division crossed the river within a few hours. They encamped at La Chapelle-en-Serval after marching 32km. Over the past few days, the Allied army's route-of-march was very close to that of the Prussian army and the attitude of the two armies towards the French populace was the difference between night and day. Wellington wanted to ensure that his troops did not abuse the civilians, fearing that if they did, the countryside would rise up against him and he would be faced with a similar situation that the French had

---

49. Stonestreet, p.54.
50. Saltoun, pp.17-18.

in Spain, a vicious guerrilla war that tied up troops and resources. On 20 June he issued a General Order that stated

> As the army is about to enter the French territory, the troops of the nations which are present under the command of the Field Marshal the Duke of Wellington, are desired to recollect that their respective sovereigns are the Allies of His Majesty the King of France, and that France ought, therefore, to be treated as a friendly country. It is therefore required that nothing should be taken either by officers or soldiers, for which payment be not made. The commissaries of the army will provide for the wants of the troops in the usual manner, and it is not permitted either to soldiers or officers to extort contributions. The commissaries will be authorized either by the Field Marshal or by the generals who command the troops of the respective nations, in cases where their provisions are not supplied by an English commissary, to make the proper requisitions for which regular receipts will be given; and it must be strictly understood that they will themselves be held responsible for whatever they obtain in way of requisition from the inhabitants of France, in the same manner in which they would be esteemed accountable for purchases made for their own government in the several dominions to which they belong.[51]

To enforce this general order, every division had a sergeant assigned to it as a provost marshal. The Guards were no exception. Five Guards sergeants were on command serving as provost marshals. Sergeant Christopher Garman of the Coldstream Guards was the 1st Division's provost marshal. Sergeant James Williamson of the 3rd Battalion 1st Foot Guards was his assistant. Sergeant Josiah Phetheon of the 2nd Battalion 1st Foot Guards was the provost marshal of the 3rd Division. Major cities in Belgium also had provost marshals. Sergeants John Fractwell was in Ostend, while Charles Lloyd served in Ghent. Both were from the 3rd Foot Guards.

The British and their Allies usually followed the general order regarding looting. However, the Prussians were not under Wellington's command. The desire for revenge on the French was strong among them and they descended upon France like a plague of locusts. They raped, looted, and

---

51. Wellington, Duke of, *The Dispatches of Field Marshal the Duke of Wellington* ...Vol. XII, pp.493-494.

THE MARCH TO PARIS, THE SIEGE OF PERONNÉ

pillaged from the time they crossed the border until they reach Paris. What they did not take they vandalized and if the farmers and villagers resisted they were killed, regardless of their sex. Captain Stanhope asked a Prussian officer why and,

> the only answer given to remonstrance is that the French did the same in Prussia. Never saw their army in Spain commit ravages more systematically than these fellows. I am now in a beautiful chateau, all the furniture of which is broken, fine glasses smashed, books torn to rags, linens & curtain cut up to adorn the Prussian amazons. The wine vats broke & the wine wasted, all the poultry killed & left in the fields, and in short every village is the same.[52]

Ensign Master confirmed this. He saw:

> when we got on the line where the Prussians had been before us, we found the villages deserted! In one of those quarters a poor fellow opened the door and peeped out. I called him in; all trembling he said the others being gone he came to see what was left; I assured him he might remain, no harm would come to him or his goods and chattels. He then told me that all the inhabitants were hid in a wood some way off since several days, half starving ... our discipline was so strict, that I had to punish a man for getting up a cherry tree.[53]

Lord Saltoun wrote to his wife on 29 June that:

> We have fallen into the line of a column of Prussians who have been plundering at such a rate that all the villages are entirely deserted and I may almost say destroyed. To be sure they are only paying off old scores but it is rather a bore for us. We have great difficulty in purchasing any articles of provision for the people are afraid of returning to their houses as they do not know that they will be protected by us. However it can't last long and at Paris we shall be able to get anything that we want.[54]

---

52. Stanhope, p.187.
53. Master, p.143.
54. *Waterloo Archive*, Vol. 6, p.111.

Ensign Gronow told of his running into a Prussian plunderer near Ponte-de-Maxence:

> I was sent by the adjutant to look out for quarters for myself and servant. In the neighbourhood of a small wood, I perceived a mill, and near it a river, and on looking a little further, saw a large farmhouse; this I entered, but could not discover any living being. My servant, who had gone upstairs, however, informed me, that the farmer was lying in bed dreadfully wounded from numerous sabre cuts. I approached his bed, and he appeared more dead than alive; but on my questioning him, he said the Prussians had been there the night before, had violated and carried off his three daughters, had taken away his cart-horses and cattle, and because he had no money to give them, they had tied him to his bed and cut him with their swords across the shin-bones, and left him fainting from pain and loss of blood. After further inquiries, he told me that he thought some of the Prussians were still in the cellar; upon which, I ordered my batman to load his musket, struck a light, and with a lantern proceeded to the cellar, where we found a Prussian soldier drunk, and lying in a pool of wine which had escaped from the casks he and his comrades had tapped. Upon seeing us, he, with an oath in German, made a thrust at my batman with his sabre, which was parried; in an instant we bound the ruffian, and brought him at the point of the bayonet into the presence of the poor farmer, who recognised him as one of the men who had outraged his unfortunate daughters, and who had afterwards wounded him. We carried our prisoner to the provost-sergeant, who, in his turn, took him to the Prussian head-quarters, where he was instantly shot.[55]

Captain Bridgeman perhaps summed it up the best: 'I defy the power of man to stop the Prussians, every place they have been at is plundered, what they cannot carry away they break & the inhabitants all fly.'[56] The destruction that the Prussian Army inflicted on the French was well known and its reasons were addressed by Lieutenant Colonel Henry Hardinge of the 2nd Battalion 1st Foot Guards, who was serving as a liaison officer to the Prussian Army. He had lost his left hand at Ligny on 16 June, but

---

55. Gronow, Vol. 1, pp.202-203.
56. *Waterloo Archive*, Vol. 4, p.29.

a month later was in Paris. He wrote Lieutenant General Charles Lord Stewart, the British Ambassador to the Austrian Court on 19 July the following justification the Prussians gave for their behaviour:

> It may be worth while to give your Lordship the Prussian sentiments on this and other points. I am assured that the discipline of the troops has much improved since they have been stationary, and that in most instances safeguards have been given when required: at the same time it is acknowledged that the conduct of their soldiery towards the inhabitants, when contrasted with the British troops, but bear a disadvantageous comparison, resulting from the difference of system in feed the troops. Besides, the Prussian Corps have received no pay for three months, which of course much prejudices the best attempts to enforce discipline. On the general question of the propriety of their measures everything is justified on the plea of retaliation, and which they assert the French who were in Prussia will admit to be moderate retaliation. The policy of immediate requisitions and strong measures at the outset they state to be necessary, because the experience of last year proved that there was no confidence to be placed in the promises of the new government when once reestablished; that in every instance of promised restitution the faith of the French government was evaded or broken. With much admiration and cordiality towards the British during military operations, they are not well pleased that every French protest against Prussian measures finds advocates and protectors against them among British authorities.[57]

When seeing the misery of the inhabitants, some officers tried to help. Captain Stanhope wrote that:

> in the several villages we have passed, I have given trifling sums to poor wretches who had crawled back to their desolate cottages, particularly 2 old sisters of about 70 to 80 each to whom I took a great partiality from their resemblance to my old nurse and I never saw people so grateful in my life. In all the towns, the moment the English uniform is seen, confidence in the usual occupations are resumed.[58]

---

57. Wellington, Duke of, *Supplementary Dispatches* ... Vol. 11, pp.39-40.
58. Stanhope, p.188.

The discipline of Wellington's army was appreciated by the populace and his ADC, Lieutenant Colonel John Fremantle believed that: 'the Prussians are doing themselves a great deal of mischief, by allowing their army to commit every excess on the country. However it raises our character in proportions; as our people are in the most perfect order, and just as quiet as if in England'.[59]

On 1 July Wellington's army moved closer to Paris and the 1st Division stopped at Le Bourget after marching 30km. They were about 12km from Montmarte. As they moved into the positions they were greeted by Prussians and the 'regiments all cheered us with their bands playing "God Save the King" & crying out "Brave English". It is our discipline that most astonishes them.'[60] Ensign St. John said the relationship between the two armies was quite good:

> I was on out picquet yesterday evening when we got here, the picquet was at a wind mill 1 mile and a quarter from Montmartre. They sent a few cannon balls at our heads, but I got well behind the mill with the party. When first we got there was a Prussian picquet of the 2nd Pomeranian Regiment & I never was treated more civilly than by them, we had just come in from a long march & they shared everything they had with us, the colonel was a very gentlemanlike sort of a man. Whenever I went near the place where they were sitting, they all rose up & the colonel handed me a chair & insisted that I should take it, saying 'Brave Anglais'. On the march we passed several Prussian regiments & they all drew up playing 'God Save the King' and cheering us. Nothing can equal their joy at seeing the English.[61]

Lord Saltoun, a harsh critic of the Prussian lack of discipline, gave them a back-handed compliment: 'Today we had a division of Prussian Guards 13,000 strong, the finest body of men I ever saw in my life, the only horrid thing is ere that the French have licked them like sacks'.[62]

The Guards waited the next four days while the Allies negotiated the surrender of Paris. Napoleon was back in Paris on 21 June and abdicated the following day. A provisional government was formed and on 24

---

59. Fremantle, pp.214.
60. Stanhope, p.188.
61. St. John, unpublished letter to his mother dated 2 July 1815.
62. Saltoun, p.41.

June it sent emissaries to Marshal Blücher with their position on ending hostilities. They demanded that King Louis XVIII not be restored, that Napoleon's son (Napoleon II) be recognized as the sovereign of France, and Napoleon not be prosecuted or imprisoned. Needless to say, the Prussians rejected the offer and continued to march on Paris. Napoleon, realizing that all was lost offered to help defend Paris, but this was rejected by the provisional government. He left Malmaison on 29 June to head for Rochefort to escape capture. The French continued to resist the Prussians, but generally avoided the British. On 30 June the French informed the Allies that Napoleon had left Paris and the government wanted a cease-fire. Again, the Prussians rejected the offer while Wellington said that the French Army had to leave Paris before a cease-fire would be granted. On 1 July the French asked Wellington for his terms for the cease fire. A de facto cease fire between the British and the French went into effect. The Prussians ignored it and engaged in some minor battles with the French over the next several days.[63]

While the British Guards waited the outcome of the negotiations, some had mixed feelings about a possible negotiated surrender. Lieutenant Colonel Fremantle wrote: 'We are now in a very unpleasant state for military people "treating and marching". They are very anxious to save Paris, and as they are very strongly fortified, and it will cost a number of lives, I think it is better we should treat.'[64] Lord Saltoun was more sanguinary:

> I almost regret that they did not defend the heights of Montmartre. To be sure we should have lost 2 or 3 thousand men in taking them but then we should have burned the town and that would have been some satisfaction for I hate these rascals almost as much as I love you and that is more than they can be hated by any other. Poor Grose and myself were brothers in that hatred and if the brave fellow were alive, he would have gone half mad to suppose that we came victorious to the gates of Paris and did not show the natives that we were so. So much for national indignation; our chief has most probably good reasons, for my own part I would not give a straw to march through it when the Russians come up.[65]

---

63. For a detailed examination of the negotiations see John Hussey's *Waterloo: The Campaign of 1815*, Vol. 2, Chapters 48, 49, and 50.
64. Fremantle, p.213.
65. Saltoun, p.27.

Sergeant William Tennant of the 3rd Battalion 1st Foot Guards was a bit more philosophical: 'It is a very fine town, very fine buildings, particularly the palace, but the streets in general is very narrow. It would have been glorious sport for our army if we had taken it by storm, there would have been plenty of plunder and we should all have been rich as Jews, but I believe it is better as it is as many thousand would have lost their lives.'[66]

About this time Ensign Master received word that his stolen horse had been spotted in the Dutch-Belgian encampment. He was on picquet duty when Ensign St. John 'rode up from Le Bourget to let me know, that my lost horse had been found and seen in the Belgian camp. I begged him to let Col. Master 3rd Guards[67] know it and try to get the horse again, as he knew him well for he was embarked from England with the Col's horses.'[68] His brother intervened on his behalf and the exact sequence of events is unknown. Ensign Master said that he had some difficulty which implies that the officer refused to give up the horse. Lieutenant Colonel John Waters, the army's acting Adjutant General wrote directly to the Dutch officer on 3 July:

> I am informed by Gen. Maitland that you have a horse in your possession the property of Lieut. Masters, of the 1st Guards. I understand that this horse was violently taken possession of and forced away from Lieut. Masters' servant. I desire that the horse may be sent without delay to head quarters, and that you do appear yourself in order to account for such an irregular proceeding; and I have further to inform you that I shall take the commands of his Excellency the Commander of the Forces on the subject if you do not appear forthwith.[69]

The horse was returned to Ensign Master. Unfortunately, no record exists of what happened to the Dutch captain.

On 4 July terms of surrender were signed. Wellington's army was given the Bois de Boulogne to encamp in. Instead of marching the next day, the

---

66. *Waterloo Archives*, Vol. 3, p.95.
67. His brother, Captain William Master, the acting commander of the 2nd Battalion 3rd Foot Guards.
68. Master, p.143.
69. Wellington, Duke of, *Despatches, Correspondence, and Memoranda of Field Marshal Arthur, Duke of Wellington* [new edition], Vol. 8, p.6.

THE MARCH TO PARIS, THE SIEGE OF PERONNÉ

Guards did not move until 7 July. Lord Saltoun hoped that they would be able to march through 'Paris with laurels in our caps as we deserve to do, but the heads think otherwise'.[70] Instead the army was marched around the city because they were there to restore the rightful ruler of France to his throne and not as conquerors.

The Bois de Boulogne was a former Royal Hunting Preserve and in 1815, despite being so close to Paris, was still heavily wooded. The park was over 850 hectares (8.5 square kilometres), but Wellington's army would have to share it with the Russian Army when it arrived. The troops were in tents just inside the north gate, called Porte Maillot,[71] and the officers were mostly in buildings. Ensign Master found himself a building by 'taking possession of a whole abandoned country restaurant at the gates of Porte Maillot and turned the covered front, where people used to sit at tables, into my stables – which with packhorses amounted to several, mostly sore backs from the campaign.'[72] Senior officers were given a little more latitude and Lord Saltoun was in a house three km from the Bois de Boulogne at the Barrier de Roule near the Faubourg Sainte Honore.[73]

Captain Stanhope settled in to two houses:

> I have une Maison de Campagne near the Bois de Boulogne where the division is, where I go early to settle what business there may be and I have une belle quartier here at Count Castellan's house who is very civil through his maître d'hotel. They seem so astonished at my wanting nothing, at having no 8 or ten people to dine with me, that their hay & corn are not consumed by my horses. I think they think us great fools for it.[74]

The 1st Division Chaplain, Reverend Stonestreet was assigned quarters:

> at the house of the Grand Chamberlain, who after two days has taken himself off. I suspect by order to his country house and I have therefore a good comfortable residence to myself. He has left his cook & butler, but none of his keys. Very greatly

---

70. Saltoun, pp26-27.
71. St. John, unpublished letter to his mother dated 15 July 1815.
72. Master, p.143.
73. Saltoun, p.30.
74. Stanhope, p.194.

> am I disappointed in Paris as a city. The palaces are superb, but the streets have nothing to recommend them. Of all places I ever was in, it is by far the dearest. The mode of living is very much a restaurateurs (coffee houses) but you cannot dine comfortable at less than a guineas expense. I have therefore set up housekeeping.[75]

Making it to Paris could not have come sooner for many of the officers and men. They left their cantonments early in the morning on 16 June and over the next twenty days fought in two major battles, stormed a fortress, and marched over 400km in horrible weather. Through much of it, they camped out with no shelter from the rain and little food. It had begun to take a toll on them by the time they reached Paris. Ensign Wedgewood described the ordeal in a letter home to his mother.

> This 3 weeks campaigning has only affected me in one way, it made my legs very sore. For the first 3 days I did [not] take off my boots and they got wet several times and dried again on my feet, and when I got them off at last, I could not get them on again without cutting the leather half way down my foot, the consequence was that the insteps of my feet were made quite raw. There is also another thing which I cannot account for in the least. My face quite contracted on one side; and when I smile my mouth gets quite to the left side of my face, and when I eat my upper jaw does not come exactly on my under one, and I cannot shut one of my eyes without the other, which I could do before; however I do not feel it quite so much as before.[76]

For one officer, seventeen-year-old Ensign George Buckley of the Coldstream Guards, it broke his health and he died from fatigue in Paris on 16 August. He was the younger brother of Lieutenant Edward Buckley of the 1st Foot Guards.

The 3rd Battalion 1st Foot Guards was particularly hard hit. The other battalions in the division saw an average decrease of 12 per cent of hospitalized soldiers, the 3rd Battalion 1st Foot Guards did not. It had an increase of 15 per cent of its number of soldiers in the hospital.[77]

---

75. Stonestreet, p.55.
76. *Waterloo Archive*, Vol. 1, p.149.
77. For the number of soldiers hospitalized each month see Appendix II.

THE MARCH TO PARIS, THE SIEGE OF PERONNÉ

The horses and pack animals also began to die from the conditions. Lord Saltoun reported on 27 June, after only 12 days of campaigning that:

> The baggage and horses begin to feel it especially from the want of shoeing. I have lost two, one that was stolen in the row and confusion of the false alarm and the other died yesterday; that added to the two that were shot has decreased my stud much. I have however bought two so I can get on and that is all, for the large horse has just fallen lame and got a sore back.[78]

Once they were settled in their new quarters, life was very good for the officers and men. Guards were mounted twenty-four hours a day at the various barriers in the city to ensure order. Captain Stanhope wrote that: 'a squadron of two guns (horses harnessed & matches lighted) & 100 men are at each of the multitudinous barriers and under these we beg the free people of Paris to choose their own government!'[79]

King Louis XVIII entered Paris on 8 July and his arrival was watched with some interest by the Guards officers. On the surface his reception by the people was enthusiastic, but several officers said it was faked. Lieutenant Colonel Fremantle wrote that: 'all the people were dancing for joy in the streets till a late hour, quelle canaille'.[80] Ensign St. John was even more sceptical:

> I saw the entrée of Louis into Paris and if hollowing and crying 'Vive le Roi' proves that the people are attached to the king, he may reckon upon their acceptance for I never heard such a shouting. The old gentleman sat in his carriage so pleased; as a beef eater at Exeter change. If Bonaparte was to come again tomorrow they [would] turn again over to him, there are almost as many for him as for Louis XVIII, the whole army are for Boney. I went into Paris on the day Louis entered & the tricoloured flag was flying half an hour before he came in. I saw it struck on the pillar on the Place de Vendome. He made a speech from the balcony in [the] Tuilleries facing the car[riages] and horses, the only words that we could hear (& I believe the only words he said) were 'Mon Amies' we cheered him royally.[81]

---

78. Saltoun, pp.16-17.
79. Stanhope, p.194.
80. Fremantle, p.214.
81. St. John, unpublished letter to his mother dated 15 July 1815.

On 24 July a grand review of Wellington's army by the Emperor of Russia took place on the Champs Elysées. Lord Saltoun was not too happy about it because they had to be lined up by 10.00 hours and it would take almost all day to pass in review. Furthermore, he believed that the British soldiers in their battle worn uniforms would 'not be able to show such fine men as those emperors and kings have but yesterday as the Prussians were marching by'.[82] Lord Saltoun was right. The review did not finish until 17.00 hours.[83]

The Russian Army was also encamped in the Bois de Boulogne and the British Guards were occasionally given the honour of guarding the Russian Emperor. This went on well into September and possibly the troops were becoming tired of doing so. Colour Sergeant William Tennant of Captain Henry D'Oyly's company of the 3rd Battalion 1st Foot Guards wrote to his wife on 24 September that: 'I come off the Emperor of Russia's guard this morning, I wish it had been the King's Guard at Saint James'.[84] Lord Saltoun was also tapped to be the officer of the Guard. He wrote to his wife:

> You may see by the paper that I am not at home, the fact is I am on guard over HM The Emperor of all the Russias and as he gives nothing but long paper I am obliged to manoeuvre it as well as I possibly can. We have just done dinner six o'clock ... it is very well this hour for His Majesty's household who can go out and walk in the cool of the evening, but for us who have to remain here rather too early; however I will do him the justice to say that the dinner was a very good one and by fortunate accident we had a clean table cloth, for the waiter, a regular ruffian of a fellow had put such a beastly thing on the table that it was even too much for us who of late days have not been much used to luxury. However I had the satisfaction to make the most unfortunate mistake in the world, just as he put some wine down by breaking a bottle of it which so sluiced the tablecloth that we were perforce obliged to have another which was clean.[85]

---

82. Saltoun, p.41.
83. Clinton, Vol. 2, p.171.
84. *Waterloo Archive*, Vol. 3, p.98.
85. Saltoun, pp.37-38.

THE MARCH TO PARIS, THE SIEGE OF PERONNÉ

When not on duty the officers, as well as the NCOs, were allowed to wander around Paris.[86] Within a week of arriving at the Bois de Boulogne, Ensign St. John wrote that:

> I like Paris very much although it is not to be compared to London, excepting in some of the buildings. The Louvre is the handsomest building that I ever saw, the gallery beats everything that you can imagine. Although I am no judge of pictures, I must say that there were a few which I liked very much. One of the finest things in Paris is the pillar in the Place de Vendome, composed of the cannon taken at Austerlitz & Jena, the workmanship is beautiful.[87]

Captain Stanhope did not waste much time before he started exploring Paris. By 12 July he had visited the Louvre, the Hôtel des Invalides, and the Palais de Luxembourg:

> I have been to Les Invalides, where I could not refuse the impulse of my curiosity of asking where such legs had been carried off, those eyes lost *'cet coup de sabre gagne'*[88] and a vast number were our old Spanish friends. I am delighted with the whole institution which (though inferior in size to it & in architecture to Greenwich) in some points is superior to Chelsea as it furnishes a comfortable retirement to nearly 300 officers, who were setting own to dinner when I went in & a very good one it appeared to be ... I then went to the Palais de Luxembourg where I saw some good Rubens but I think most heterodoxically [sic] I fear all his great pictures are vulgar. There are one or two beautiful ones of David & a whole gallery of Vernet's sea ports, as for the Louvre, I dedicated 2 hours a day to it & examine so many pictures otherwise the eye is bewildered and a headache is acquired instead of pleasure.[89]

---

86. *Waterloo Archive*, Vol. 3, p.95.
87. St. John; Unpublished Letter to His Mother dated 15 July 1815.
88. The blow of the sword wins.
89. Stanhope, pp.193-194.

For the officers and men who were left in Brussels either too wounded or sick to march with the army many would languish there for months. Although successfully evacuated from the battlefield, many died from the wounds over the next six months. An average of thirteen per battalion died in July, but as the months went by fewer and fewer succumbed. In the 3rd Foot Guards, four soldiers were reported as dying on 24 September. This could have been a clerical error. The last soldier reported to have died in 1815 was Private Adam Allen on Christmas Eve. He was a member of the Light Company of the 3rd Foot Guards.

Captain Charles Dashwood, who commanded the Light Company of the 3rd Foot Guards, even with his serious wound, was up and about by 2 July. He was feeling good enough to go on a horseback tour of Waterloo with Robert Milnes who was a cousin of Captain William Milnes of the 1st Foot Guards.[90] Captain Dashwood was reported to be with his battalion in Paris on the 25 August 1815 Regimental Returns.

On hearing of his son, Lieutenant George Evelyn of the 3rd Foot Guards, being wounded, his father John, immediately went to Brussels. On 6 July, he wrote home to George's mother that their son

> continues to improve, no bad symptom has appeared and the surgeon speaks with confidence of his recovery. I deferred writing today until he had dressed the wound that I might give you the latest report, he told me George was going on as well possible and that as far as human skill and science could judge, there was no doubt of his recovery. This is very consoling, he's still confined to his bed but I hope he will be able [to] get up in a few days; he now begins to sit up in it, with a support to his back. I am glad I came over, for though I cannot accelerate his recovery, my being with him is a comfort; I sit with him, chat and talk over the battle with him and by this means draw his attention from the present situation … it is doubtful whether his arm will ever recover its former strength, but as he observed to me, an arm of any kind looks better than the sleeve of a coat.[91]

Ensign Thomas Croft of the 2nd Battalion 1st Foot Guards had been shot in the foot, but for some reason the doctors refused to remove the musket ball. He was allowed to return to England and was in London by 27 July.

---

90. Reid, p.25.
91. *Waterloo Archive*, Vol. 3, pp.110-112.

He carried some of Ensign Barrington's personal belongings back with. His aunt wrote that:

> my nephew is better than we could have expected and has not suffered from his removal. His wound is going on so favourably that we are encouraged to hope his recovery will ultimately be complete, but the ball is not yet extracted and we must prepare ourselves for a very tedious confinement and occasionally great suffering. But he is very good and very patient.[92]

Lieutenant John Cowell of the Coldstream Guards had come down with dysentery on 17 June and had to be evacuated to Brussels. By 24 June he was feeling better and decided to rejoin his regiment on their march to Paris. He informed the Commandant of Brussels, Lieutenant Colonel Leslie Jones of the 3rd Battalion 1st Foot Guards, of his intentions. Lieutenant Colonel Jones insisted he stay because he wanted to use him for garrison duties. Lieutenant Cowell left Brussels with two other officers without notifying the commandant and linked up with his regiment on 29 June.[93]

Replacements

Wellington's Waterloo dispatch announcing the victory arrived in London on 21 June, however the number of casualties incurred by the Guards regiments would not be known for several days. Each of the regiments faced the same problem. Where do they get the replacements from? They normally came from the battalion that was left at home, which for the Guards battalions were the 1st Battalions. However, these battalions had been stripped of their healthiest men to strengthen the battalions in Belgium. The 1st Guards sent their 2nd Battalion seventy-five replacements in April and May, while the 3rd Battalion received thirty in May. The 2nd Battalion Coldstream Guards and the 2nd Battalion 3rd Foot Guards each received 250 replacements by early June. Theoretically, the regiments would actively recruit more men to fill up their 1st Battalions. They fell far short. Between April and June 1815, the 1st Foot Guards were able to recruit eighty, the Coldstream Guards 104, and the 3rd Foot Guards fifty-three. Bringing in the recruits was only part of the problem. They had to be trained, which would take several months.

---

92. ibid, Vol. 4, pp.138-139.
93. Harrison, p.66.

The shortage of new men was ignored. The three regiments identified and equipped the replacements by taking as many of the healthy men remaining with the 1st Battalions as possible. On 28 June they departed London. The following figures do not include officers.

Table 15.1: Replacements for the Foot Guards Sent to France on 28 June 1815

Battalion	Number
2nd Battalion 1st Foot Guards	89
3rd Battalion 1st Foot Guards	140
2nd Battalion Coldstream Guards	221
2nd Battalion 3rd Foot Guards	224

Thirty officers were also sent out.

Table 15.2: Officer Replacements for the Foot Guards Sent to France on 28 June 1815

1st Foot Guards	Coldstream Guards	3rd Foot Guards
Captain James West	Lieutenant Patrick Sandilands	Captain Willoughby Cotton
Captain Henry Packe	Lieutenant John Prince	Captain John Clitherow
Captain John Hanbury	Lieutenant Windham Anstruther	Lieutenant Arnold Burrowes
Captain Thomas Dorville	Lieutenant Charles Shirley	Lieutenant Charles Hornby
Lieutenant Thomas Brooke	Lieutenant Charles Girardot	Ensign Thomas Northmore
Lieutenant Benjamin Charlewood	Ensign Henry Salwey	Ensign William Forster
Lieutenant George Higginson		Ensign William Knollys
Lieutenant Robert Thoroton		Ensign Henry Colville
Lieutenant Thomas Barratt		Ensign Thomas Berry
Lieutenant Philip Perceval		Ensign Digby Murray
Ensign Edward Burrard		
Ensign John Grant		
Ensign Richard Fletcher		
Ensign Sackville Fox		

When the replacements actually sailed to Belgium is unknown, however by 6 July they had left Ostend. They probably took barges the 60km to Ghent and from there marched to Paris.

THE MARCH TO PARIS, THE SIEGE OF PERONNÉ

Table 15.3: The Replacements Route to Paris[94]

Date	Start Point	End Point	Distance marched
6 July	Ostende	Ghent	60 km
7 July	Ghent	Oudenaarde	30 km
8 July	Oudenaarde	Ath	45 km
9 July	Ath	Mons	26 km
10 July	Mons	Bavay	14 km
11 July	Bavay	Le Cateau-Cambrésis	29 km
12 July	Le Cateau-Cambrésis	Rest	
13 July	Le Cateau-Cambrésis	Péronne	59 km
14 July	Péronne	Roye	30 km
15 - 19 July	Roye	Bois de Boulogne	111 km

The replacements took five days to march the last 111km to the Bois de Boulogne, arriving there on 19 July. The exact route took is not recorded, but it probably followed that of the 1st Division. Upon arrival at the Bois de Boulogne Captain James West took command of the 2nd Battalion 1st Foot Guards, Captain John Hanbury took command of the 3rd Battalion 1st Foot Guards, and Captain Willoughby Cotton took command of the 2nd Battalion 3rd Foot Guards. Upon being relieved of his command, Lord Saltoun immediately applied for home leave and on 27 July he 'was ordered to send in my reasons in writing so I went this morning to Barnes[95] the Adjutant general and told him my reason was not one that could well be sent upon paper but I would be much obliged to him to tell the Duke that I had been married a fortnight and I wish to go home to bring you out here'.[96] His appeal was granted and he returned to England to be with his wife. He brought his wife back to Paris before the end of the year.[97]

Immediately after Waterloo there were questions concerning who was to command both the 1st Corps and the 1st Division. The 1st Corps was normally commanded by the Prince of Orange but after he was seriously wounded at Waterloo, Major General Byng took command. He led it through the advance to Paris until mid-July when the Prince of Orange

---

94. Packe, p.96-102.
95. Major General Edward Barnes.
96. Saltoun, p.42.
97. Fraser, p.283.

arrived in Paris and resumed command. Upon the arrival of the prince, Major General Byng returned to commanding the 1st Division. Major General Maitland resumed command of the 1st Brigade.

Who was to command the 1st Division also needed to be decided. This involved politics at the highest level. Major General Henry Torrens wrote to Wellington on 24 June that the Duke of York was quite content with leaving Major General Byng in command, 'but there are so many senior claimants for such a command as to render it impossible'.[98] Keeping with tradition of the Guards only being commanded by a Guards general, Major General Sir Kenneth Howard was selected.[99] On 2 July he was placed on the staff of Wellington's army and arrived in Paris in mid-July. He assumed command of the 1st Division by 23 July. He was not in command for long, as the Prince of Orange decided to return to Belgium, relinquishing command of the 1st Corps. On 8 August Major General Howard was promoted to local lieutenant general, with the date-of-rank back dated to 6 July. He officially took command of the 1st Corps on 22 August. Major General Byng was once again given command of the 1st Division and kept it until he went on leave in early October. While on leave he was appointed to command the Eastern District in Essex. Major General Maitland took over command of the 1st Division upon the departure of Major General Byng.

During the march to Paris, the 1st Brigade was commanded by Lieutenant Colonel George Fead of the 3rd Battalion 1st Foot Guards. About the time the replacements had arrived Major General Maitland resumed command of the brigade. There is some question regarding when Major Henry Askew, the commander of the 2nd Battalion, returned to his command. He had been seriously wounded at Quatre Bras and in early July was recuperating in Antwerp. It is possible that he had rejoined his battalion by October. If so, he would have taken command of the 1st Brigade when Major General Maitland took command of the 1st Division in October. The chain-of-command for the 2nd Brigade was straight forward. Except for the short time in July when Major General Byng resumed command of the brigade, it was commanded by Brevet Colonel Francis Hepburn of the 3rd Foot Guards.

---

98. Wellington, Duke of, *Supplementary Dispatches* ... Vol. 10, p.573.
99. Major General Howard was a former Coldstream Guards officer who commanded the Guards Brigade and the 1st Division in the Peninsula.

THE MARCH TO PARIS, THE SIEGE OF PERONNÉ

In September the regimental bands were sent to Paris. The band of the 1st Foot Guards left Brighton on 10 September aboard the *Duke of Wellington* and sailed for Dieppe.[100] September also saw the expansion of the 1st Division with the addition of a KGL Brigade.[101] Its commander was Lieutenant Colonel Lewis Baron Bussche, Lieutenant Colonel Commandant of the 5th Line Battalion KGL. This brigade was formed after the Battle of Waterloo by the amalgamation of the 1st and 2nd KGL Brigades in the 3rd Division by a General Order dated 24 August 1815. The KGL Brigade had eight battalions: the 1st and 2nd Light Battalions, and the 1st, 2nd, 3rd, 4th, 5th & 8th Line Battalions.

Throughout the autumn the 1st Division was kept in tents in the Bois de Boulogne. No reason was given, but there was speculation that they would be moving to Normandy. At the end of October orders were received to move into barracks. Colour Sergeant William Tennant wrote to his wife on 11 November that: 'we left camp on the 30th of last month and we are now in barracks in Paris but the barracks is not very good but still they are better than camp. We have no rooms for Pay Sergeants as we have in London, there is 4 of us in one small room, Sergeant Bell's wife and little boy is come over, she came about 3 days before we left camp, they have got a small place up in the garret.'[102]

A General Ordered issued in Paris 30 November formed the British Contingent of the Army of Occupation of France. This would have a major impact on the Foot Guards. The new 1st Brigade consisted of the 3rd Battalion 1st Foot Guards and the 2nd Battalion Coldstream Guards. Major General Maitland would command it. The brigade was placed in the 1st Division, which in a break from tradition, would be commanded by a non-Guards officer, Lieutenant General Sir Galbraith Lowry Cole. The 1st Brigade would remain in Paris until January 1816 when it was moved to Cambrai. As foreign service went, the next three years was relatively quiet. Senior officers brought over their families and leaves of absences were quite generous. In November 1818, the Army of Occupation of France was disbanded, and the Guards returned home.

The 2nd Battalion 1st Foot Guards and the 2nd Battalion 3rd Foot Guards were not needed in the Army of Occupation of France and they

---

100. Hamilton, Vol. 3, p.60.
101. The exact date the brigade joined the 1st Division is unknown. It was probably around 7 September.
102. *Waterloo Archive*, Vol. 3, p.99.

were ordered home. They had been on active service since December 1813. For the return to England they were brigaded together and placed under the command of Colonel Henry Askew. The 3rd Foot Guards left Paris on 15 December heading for their embarkation point at Calais. Their route was as follows:

Table 15.4: The Route home of the 2nd Battalion 3rd Foot Guards, 15-24 December 1815[103]

Date	Start Point	End Point	Distance marched
15 December	Paris to	Beaumont	30km
16 December	Beaumont to	Noailles	28km
17 December	Noailles to	Beauvais	15km
14 - 18 December	Beauvais to	Abbeville	108km
19 December	Abbeville	Rest	
20 December	Abbeville	Montreuil-sur-Mer	50km
23 December	Montreuil-sur-Mer	Boulogne-sur-Mer	40km
24 December	Boulogne-sur-Mer	Calais	35km

The 2nd Battalion 1st Foot Guards left Paris a few days after the 3rd Foot Guards and spent Christmas Day at Abbeville.[104] Both battalions were back in England by the New Year. Thus, came to a finish a tumultuous year for the Foot Guards who had done so much to defeat Emperor Napoleon and bring an end to the Napoleonic Wars.

---

103. Maurice, Vol. 2, p.37. The exact route is unknown. The table reflects what is in Maurice plus other sources.
104. Hamilton, Vol. 3, p.61.

Chapter 16

What Happened to Them After Waterloo?

For many officers their participation in the Napoleonic Wars and especially at the Battle of Waterloo was the high point of their military career. With the end of the war, the reduction of the Army and the 'Long Peace', promotion in the regiments stagnated. Officers languished in junior ranks for years with only active service in colonial wars offering the chance of advancement and reward. However, for the Guards officers, after both returning home at the end of 1815 and with the disbandment of the Army of Occupation of France in 1818, they were not sent overseas except for two battalions sent to Portugal 1826-1828[1] and two battalions sent to Canada 1838-1842.[2] Neither of these services afforded real opportunities for reward or advancement. Therefore, the only options available were to remain in the Guards and wait for promotion, to exchange to a line regiment, to go on half pay or to leave the Army altogether.

Further to the concise biographies provided for the eight officers who commanded the Guards Division, the brigades and the four battalions, we take a look at the subsequent military careers of a number of other Guards officers who figured in the battles of Quatre Bras and Waterloo. They include those who died of wounds, those who were wounded and survived, as well as those who succeeded to the command of formations or who left memoirs, journals and letters, passages of which are quoted in the text. In addition, we include a 1st Division ADC whose exploit at Waterloo is recorded in the text, a staff officer who was wounded,

---

1. 1st Battalion 1st Foot Guards and 2nd Battalion 3rd Foot Guards.
2. 2nd Battalion Grenadier Guards and 2nd Battalion Coldstream Guards.

as well as, the commanding officers of the Royal Artillery and Royal Engineers attached to the 1st Division. The Guards officers are listed by their regimental seniority in 1815 with the highest rank which they held in the Army. We will also look at the careers of some prominent Other Ranks.

Staff

Brevet Lieutenant Colonel **Henry Dumaresq** retired by sale of an unattached captain's commission 21 March 1834. Brevet Major 18 June 1815 and Brevet Lieutenant Colonel 21 June 1817. Was Military Secretary to Lieutenant General Sir Ralph Darling on Mauritius 1818-1824. Was ADC to Lieutenant General Darling Governor of New South Wales 1825-1834. Placed on half pay 9th Foot 25 February 1816. Appointed, on full pay, to command a New South Wales Royal Veteran Company 24 September 1825. Placed on half pay of a New South Wales Royal Veteran Company in 1831. Died 5 March 1838.

Brevet Lieutenant Colonel **Edward Thomas Fitzgerald** placed on half pay 12th Foot 25 January 1818. Exchanged to 12th Foot 3 April 1817. Brevet Major 21 June 1817.[3] Brevet Lieutenant Colonel 22 July 1830. Died 19 September 1845.

1st Foot Guards

Brevet Colonel Sir **Horatio George Townshend** Kt retired on half pay unattached 12 February 1830. Regimental Lieutenant Colonel 25 July 1821. Brevet Colonel 12 August 1819. Died 24 May 1843.

Lieutenant Colonel **Richard Harvey Cooke** CB retired by sale of his commission 26 March 1818. Granted a temporary pension of £300 for a wound suffered at the Battle of Waterloo commencing 19 June 1816. Died 8 October 1856.

Lieutenant Colonel **Edward Stables** Captain 1st Foot Guards. Died 19 June 1815 from complications of a wound suffered at the Battle of Waterloo 18 June 1815.

---

3. Antedate to 17 March 1814 on 11 May 1821.

Brevet Colonel **James Dawson West** retired by sale of his commission 20 November 1823. Regimental Major 25 July 1821. Brevet Colonel 25 July 1821. Died 3 August 1831.

General **Sir John Hanbury** KCB. Regimental Colonel 99th Foot 6 October 1851. Regimental Major 25 July 1821. Brevet Colonel 25 July 1821, Major General 22 July 1830, Lieutenant General 23 November 1841 and General 20 June 1854. Commanded 1st Battalion 1st Foot Guards in the Guards Brigade[4] of Lieutenant General Sir William Clinton's force sent to Portugal 1826-1828. Died 7 June 1863.

General **Henry D'Oyly** Regimental Colonel 33rd Foot 28 September 1847. Regimental Major 12 February 1830. Regimental Lieutenant Colonel 10 January 1837. Brevet Colonel 12 February 1830. Major General 28 June 1838. Lieutenant General 11 November 1851 and General 30 January 1855. Died 26 September 1855.

Major General Sir **John George Woodford** KCB retired by sale of an unattached lieutenant colonel's commission 26 October 1841. Regimental Major 20 November 1823. Regimental Lieutenant Colonel 12 February 1830. Brevet Colonel 20 November 1823. Major General 10 January 1837. An AQMG on the staff of the AOOF 1815-1818. When Woodford died at age ninety-four, he was one of the last officers still living who had fought at Waterloo. Died 22 March 1879.

Lieutenant Colonel **George Fead** CB retired by sale of his commission 27 March 1828. Died 13 September 1847.

Lieutenant General **Sir Alexander George Fraser, 16th Lord Saltoun** KCB. Regimental Colonel 2nd Foot 7 August 1846. Regimental Major 17 November 1825. Brevet Colonel 27 May 1825, Major General 10 January 1837 and Lieutenant General 9 November 1846. ADC to King George IV 27 May 1825. Commanded the 1st Brigade in Lieutenant General Sir Hugh Gough's Expeditionary Force against China in the 1st Opium War, 1841-1842 and then commanded in Hong Kong 1844. Died 18 August 1853.

---

4. Commanded by Major General Sir Henry Bouverie from Coldstream Guards.

General **John Reeve** Regimental Colonel 61st Foot 11 October 1852. Exchanged to half pay unattached 14 April 1825. Brevet Colonel 22 July 1830, Major General 23 November 1841, Lieutenant General 11 November 1851 and General 7 December 1859. Died 3 October 1864.

Lieutenant Colonel **William Miller** Captain 1st Foot Guards. Died 19 June 1815 from complications of a wound suffered at the Battle of Quatre Bras 16 June 1815.

Lieutenant Colonel Hon. **James Hamilton Stanhope** exchanged to half pay. Portuguese Service 28 February 1822. Exchanged to 29th Foot 14 February 1822. An AQMG in the AOOF 1815-1816. ADC to Field Marshal Prince Frederick Duke of York, Commander-in-Chief 1816 - 1825. Died 5 March 1825.

Lieutenant Colonel **Goodwin Colquitt** CB retired by sale of his commission 26 October 1820. Died in the year 1828.

Lieutenant Colonel **William Henry Milnes** Captain 1st Foot Guards. Died 20 June 1815 from complications of a wound suffered at the Battle of Waterloo 18 June 1815.

Lieutenant Colonel Sir **Henry Hollis Bradford** KCB Captain 1st Foot Guards. An AQMG in the AOOF 1815-1816. Died 7 December 1816 from prolonged complications of a wound suffered at the Battle of Waterloo 18 June 1815.

Captain **Robert Adair** Lieutenant 1st Foot Guards. Died 23 June 1815 from complications of a wound suffered at the Battle of Quatre Bras 16 June 1815.

Lieutenant Colonel **Thomas Streatfield** retired by sale of his commission 26 December 1821. Captain and Lieutenant Colonel 2 July 1815. Died 26 September 1852.

Lieutenant Colonel **James Gunthorpe** retired by sale of his commission 27 December 1833. Brevet Major 18 June 1815. Captain and Lieutenant Colonel 26 December 1821. Brigade Major to 1st Guards Brigade in the AOOF 1815-1818. Died 28 July 1853.

Brevet Colonel **Chatham Horace Churchill** CB. Lieutenant Colonel commanding 31st Foot. Brevet Lieutenant Colonel 18 June 1815. Exchanged to 18th Foot 26 December 1822. Appointed to Ceylon Regiment 22 May 1823. Major half pay unattached 27 July 1826. Lieutenant Colonel half pay unattached 16 July 1830. Restored to full pay 31st Foot 20 April 1832. Brevet Colonel 10 January 1837. Local Major General in the East Indies only 10 January 1837. ADC to Lieutenant General Lord Hill in the AOOF 1815-1818. Military Secretary and ADC to Lieutenant General Sir Edward Barnes, Commander of the Forces on Ceylon 19 January 1824. Military Secretary and ADC to General Sir Edward Barnes, Commander-in-Chief of India, January 1832 – October 1833. Appointed a Brigadier on the staff at Cawnpore, Bengal Presidency 24 December 1833. Appointed Quartermaster General to the Queen's Troops in India 11 August 1837. Served as the Quartermaster General to General Sir Hugh Gough's Army of Gwalior 1843. Died of a wound suffered at the Battle of Maharajpore 29 December 1843.

Lieutenant Colonel Hon. **Robert Clotworthy Clements** Captain 1st Foot Guards. Brevet Major 18 June 1815. Captain and Lieutenant Colonel 6 November 1823. Died in July 1828.

Captain **Sir John Hely-Hutchinson 3rd Earl of Donoughmore**[5] KP exchanged to half pay 1st Foot Guards 27 May 1819. Tried for treason in France 22 - 24 April 1816 for helping Antoine Chamant Comte de Lavalette, Napoleon's Postmaster, to escape from prison. Found guilty and sentenced to three months in prison. Died 14 September 1851.

Brevet Colonel **Robert Ellison** Major 1st Foot Guards. Brevet Major 18 June 1815. Lieutenant Colonel half pay unattached 15 April 1824. Exchanged to full pay Captain and Lieutenant Colonel 1st Foot Guards 27 May 1824. Regimental Major 9 January 1838. Brevet Colonel 9 January 1838. Died 3 July 1843.

Captain **Henry Weyland Powell** retired by sale of his commission 11 October 1821. Died 17 July 1840.

Lieutenant Colonel **William Gordon Cameron** retired by sale of his commission 20 April 1832. Brevet Major 21 January 1819. Lieutenant Colonel 95th Foot 7 July 1825. Exchanged to half pay unattached 8 July 1825. Exchanged to full pay Captain and Lieutenant Colonel Coldstream Foot Guards 13 April 1832. A DQMG in the AOOF 1815-1816. Granted a

---

5. Succeeded as Earl of Donoughmore 29 June 1832.

pension of £100 for loss of his right arm suffered at the Battle of Waterloo commencing 19 June 1816. Died 26 May 1856.

Captain Hon. **Orlando Henry Bridgeman** exchanged to half pay 1st Foot Guards 25 February 1819. ADC to Lieutenant General Lord Hill in the AOOF 1815-1817. Died 28 August 1827.

Brevet Colonel **Charles Parker Ellis** exchanged to half pay Roll's Regiment 10 May 1831. Lieutenant Colonel half pay unattached 16 February 1826[6]. Exchanged to full pay Captain and Lieutenant Colonel 1st Foot Guards 18 May 1826. Brevet Colonel 23 November 1841. Died 6 August 1850.

General Sir **James Simpson** GCB. Regimental Colonel 29th Foot 27 July 1863. Lieutenant Colonel half pay unattached 28 April 1825. Exchanged to full pay 29th Foot 10 June 1826. Exchanged to half pay unattached 31 May 1839. Exchanged to full pay 29th Foot 8 April 1842. Exchanged to half pay unattached 8 December 1846. Brevet Colonel 28 June 1838. Major General 11 November 1851. Local Lieutenant General in the Crimea 16 August 1854 and Local General in the Crimea 29 June 1855. Lieutenant General 29 June 1855 and General 8 September 1855. An ADC to the Lord Lieutenant of Ireland 1840-1841. On the staff Bengal Presidency India 1844-1846 and saw service as a Major General in India only and second-in-command under Major General Sir Charles Napier against the Mountain Tribes on the Indus and in Scinde 1845, also acting governor and commanding in Scinde 1846. Commandant of Chatham 1846-1851. Lieutenant Governor of Portsmouth and commanding South West District 1852-1854. DAG at Headquarters 1854-1855. Served in the Eastern Army[7] in the Crimean War as Chief of Staff and then as Commander-in-Chief 1855. Died 18 April 1868.

Lieutenant Colonel **Philip Joshua Perceval** retired by sale of his commission 30 December 1845. Brevet Major 10 January 1837. Captain and Lieutenant Colonel 10 January 1837. Died 10 September 1847.

---

6. Dated 22 April 1826. On 12 May 1826 it was antedated to 16 February 1826.
7. Commanded by Field Marshal Fitzroy Somerset, 1st Baron Raglan, late Grenadier Guards 1854-1855.

WHAT HAPPENED TO THEM AFTER WATERLOO?

Captain **Francis Fownes Luttrell** retired by sale of his commission 28 April 1825. Appointed Lieutenant Colonel 2nd Somersetshire Militia 4 June 1839. The wound to his face caused him to lose his right eye. Died 4 January 1862.

Brevet Major **James Lock Nixon** retire by sale of his commission 22 June 1847. Exchanged to 60th Foot 15 June 1820. Exchanged to half pay 60th Foot 6 July 1820. Exchanged to full pay 1st West India Regiment 22 June 1847. Brevet Major 22 June 1847 to date from 10 January 1837. Died in the year 1859.

Brevet Colonel **Charles Lascelles** retired by sale of his commission 27 December 1850. Captain and Lieutenant Colonel 21 February 1828. Regimental Major 4 July 1843. Regimental Lieutenant Colonel 10 April 1849. Brevet Colonel 23 November 1841. Died 8 November 1860.

Captain **Somerville Waldemar Burgess**[8] exchanged to half pay 5th West India Regiment 8 May 1817. Granted a pension of £100 for the loss of his left leg suffered at the Battle of Waterloo commencing 19 June 1816. Died 7 March 1869.

Captain **Rees Howell Gronow** retired by sale of his commission 24 October 1821. Lieutenant and Captain 28 June 1815. Died 22 November 1865.

Lieutenant Colonel **Robert Batty** retired by sale of his commission 1 November 1839. Lieutenant and Captain 29 June 1815. Lieutenant Colonel half pay unattached 30 December 1828. Restored to full pay Captain and Lieutenant Colonel 3rd Foot Guards 1 November 1839. Served as ADC to Lieutenant General Sir William Clinton in Portugal 1826-1828. Died 20 November 1848.

Captain **Richard Thomas Master** exchanged to half pay 1st Foot Guards 25 February 1819. Lieutenant and Captain 1 July 1815. Died 8 July 1873.

Captain **William Barton** retired by sale of his commission 5 July 1833. Lieutenant and Captain 3 July 1815. Exchanged to half pay unattached 4 October 1827. Exchanged to full pay 99th Foot 21 June 1833. Died 14 May 1874.

---

8. In Dalton's *Waterloo Roll Call* as Samuel W. Burgess. In Army Lists as either Samuel Wm. Burges or Somerv. Waldeman Burges.

Captain Hon. **Henry Vernon** retired by sale of his commission 28 March 1822. Lieutenant and Captain 5 July 1815. Placed on half pay 1st Foot Guards 25 December 1818. Exchanged to full pay Lieutenant and Captain 1st Foot Guards 25 February 1819. Died 12 December 1845.

Lieutenant General **Thomas Robert Swinburne** Major half pay unattached. Lieutenant in the Army 29 July 1815 to date from 24 June 1813. Lieutenant and Captain 26 December 1816. Placed on half pay 1st Foot Guards 25 December 1818. Exchanged to full pay Captain 3rd Dragoon Guards 27 February 1823. Major half pay unattached 10 September 1825. Brevet Lieutenant Colonel half pay unattached 28 June 1838. Brevet Colonel 11 November 1851. Major General 4 June 1857 and Lieutenant General 31 January 1864. Died 28 February 1864.

Lieutenant Colonel John Pasley Dirom retired by sale of his commission 1 July 1836. Ensign and Lieutenant in the regiment 29 July 1815 to date from 18 November 1813. Lieutenant and Captain 6 January 1820. Captain and Lieutenant Colonel 27 March 1828. Died 2 June 1857.

Ensign **Frederick Thoroton Gould** resigned his commission 20 July 1815. Date of death is unknown, perhaps in the year 1874.

Captain **Robert Bruce** retired by sale of his commission 8 July 1824. Lieutenant in the Army 29 July 1815 to date from 9 December 1813. Captain 60th Foot 25 May 1820. Exchanged to become Lieutenant and Captain 1st Foot Guards 15 June 1820. Died 13 August 1864.

Lieutenant Colonel **George Fludyer** retired by sale of his commission 9 May 1834. Lieutenant in the Army 29 July 1815 to date from 13 January 1814. Lieutenant and Captain 15 March 1821. Captain and Lieutenant Colonel 19 November 1830. Died in February 1856.

Brevet Lieutenant Colonel **William Frederick Tinling** retired by sale of his commission 12 May 1848. Lieutenant in the Army 29 July 1815 to date from 27 January 1814. Lieutenant and Captain 26 December 1821. Major half pay unattached 10 December 1825. Brevet Lieutenant Colonel half pay unattached 28 June 1838. Exchanged to full pay Major 68th Foot 12 May 1848. Died 7 April 1850.

Captain **Algernon Frederick Greville** retired and left the Army 16 March 1830. Lieutenant in the Army 29 July 1815 to date from 1 February 1814.

Lieutenant and Captain 28 February 1822. Exchanged to half pay 2nd West India Regiment 7 November 1822. Restored to full pay in 48th Foot 26 February 1830. ADC to Major General Sir John Lambert in the AOOF 1818. ADC to Duke of Wellington when the Master General of the Ordnance 1819 to 1827. Private Secretary to Duke of Wellington when the Commander-in-Chief 1842. Died 15 December 1864.

Lieutenant Hon. **Henry Lascelles**[9] received a commuted allowance for his half pay commission and left the Army 26 August 1831. Lieutenant in the Army 29 July 1815 to date from 7 April 1814. Exchanged to half pay 1st Foot Guards 24 August 1820. Served in the Yorkshire Hussar Yeomanry: Lieutenant 28 October 1820, Captain 18 November 1823 and Major 8 October 1839. Resigned 22 April 1843. Died 22 February 1857.

Lieutenant **George Mure** exchanged to half pay 1st Foot Guards 15 June 1820. Lieutenant in the Army 29 July 1815 to date from 14 April 1814. Died 16 March 1868.

Lieutenant Sir **Thomas Elmsley Croft**[10] 7th Baronet received a commuted allowance for his half pay commission and left the Army 29 March 1831. Lieutenant in the Army 29 July 1815 to date from 28 April 1814. Exchanged to half pay 1st Foot Guards 2 March 1820. Three years after he was wounded at Quatre Bras he still had not fully recovered from his wound.[11] In 1821 he visited Quatre Bras and Waterloo and wrote a poem about his friend Samuel Barrington, who was killed at Quatre Bras. The poem and others were published in 1827 in a book called *Belgic Charity*. Died 29 October 1835.

Lieutenant **Joseph Henry St. John** received a commuted allowance for his half pay commission and left the Army 27 March 1832. Lieutenant in the Army 29 July 1815 to date from 25 November 1814. Exchanged to half pay 19th Light Dragoons 3 January 1822. Date of death is unknown.

Lieutenant **Daniel Tighe** exchanged to half pay 1st Foot Guards 15 February 1821. Lieutenant in the Army 29 July 1815 to date from 26 November 1814. Died 16 March 1874.

---

9. Succeeded as 3rd Earl of Harewood 7 December 1839.
10. Succeeded as a Baronet in February 1818.
11. *Waterloo Archive*, Vol. 4, page 138.

Coldstream Foot Guards

General **Sir James Macdonell** GCB. Regimental Colonel 71st Light Infantry 8 February 1849. Regimental Major 25 July 1821 and Regimental Lieutenant Colonel 27 May 1825. Brevet Colonel 12 August 1819, Major General 22 July 1830, Lieutenant General 23 November 1841 and General 20 June 1854. Commanded the Ulster District Ireland 1831-1838. On the staff in Canada commanding the Brigade of Guards[12] and second-in-command under Lieutenant General Sir John Colborne 1838-1839 and under Lieutenant General Sir Richard Jackson 1839-1842. Saw active service in the Rebellions of Upper and Lower Canada. Died 15 May 1857.

Brevet Colonel **Daniel Mackinnon** Lieutenant Colonel commanding Coldstream Foot Guards. Regimental Major 22 June 1826 and Regimental Lieutenant Colonel 22 July 1830. Brevet Colonel 22 June 1826. He never regained full use of his leg after the wound to his knee, although he remained with the regiment.[13] He was the author of *Origin and Services of the Coldstream Guards* a two-volume history of his regiment. Died 22 June 1836.

Brevet Colonel **Henry Dawkins** retired by sale of his commission 8 May 1846. Brevet Colonel 10 January 1837. Exchanged to half pay unattached 31 August 1826. Restored to full pay Captain and Lieutenant Colonel Coldstream Foot Guards 8 May 1846. Died 13 November 1864.

Brevet Colonel Hon. **Alexander Abercromby** CB retired by sale of an unattached lieutenant colonel's commission 7 February 1822. Placed on half pay Coldstream Foot Guards 25 October 1821. An AQMG on the staff of the AOOF 1815-1818. Died 27 August 1853.

Brevet Colonel Hon. **Edward Acheson** CB retired by sale of his commission 1 April 1824. Brevet Colonel 19 July 1821. Placed on half pay Coldstream Foot Guards 25 December 1823. Died 24 July 1828.

Field Marshal **Sir William Maynard Gomm** GCB. Regimental Colonel Coldstream Guards 15 August 1863. Regimental Major 16 May 1829 and

---

12. Composed of 2nd Battalion Grenadier Guards and 2nd Battalion Coldstream Guards.
13. MacInnes, p.207.

Regimental Lieutenant Colonel 23 June 1836. Brevet Colonel 16 May 1829, Major General 10 January 1837, Lieutenant General 9 November 1846, Local General in India 24 September 1850, General 20 June 1854 and Field Marshal 1 January 1868. An AQMG in the AOOF 1815-1816. He commanded the forces in Jamaica in 1839, then was appointed to the command of the Northern District in England March 1842 and later that year was appointed Governor and Commander-in-Chief on Mauritius until May 1849. He served as Commander-in-Chief of India 6 December 1850 to 23 January 1856. Died 15 March 1875.

General **Sir Henry Wyndham** KCB. Regimental Colonel 11th Hussars 19 February 1847. Brevet Colonel 27 May 1825, Major General 10 January 1837, Lieutenant General 9 November 1846 and General 20 June 1854. Exchanged to 19th Light Dragoons 11 July 1816. Placed on half pay 19th Light Dragoons 10 November 1821. Exchanged to full pay 10th Light Dragoons 18 March 1824. Exchanged to half pay 9th Light Dragoons 22 March 1833. ADC to King George IV 27 May 1825. Commanded the Cavalry Brigade in Lieutenant General Sir William Clinton's force sent to Portugal 1826-1828. Commanded the Dublin District, Ireland 1843 -1846. Granted a temporary pension of £300 for a wound suffered at the Battle of Waterloo commencing 19 June 1816. He possibly suffered from PTSD for the rest of his life. A family legend states that after Waterloo he could never stay in a room with a closed door. Died 2 August 1860.

General **Sir George Bowles** KCB. Regimental Colonel 1st West India Regiment 9 September 1855. Brevet Major 18 June 1815. Brevet Lieutenant Colonel 14 June 1821. Captain and Lieutenant Colonel 27 May 1825. Regimental Major 31 December 1839. Brevet Colonel 10 January 1837, Major General 9 November 1846, Lieutenant General 20 June 1854 and General 9 November 1862. Went on half pay unattached 30 May 1843. Served as the DAG to the Troops in Jamaica 14 June 1821-18 August 1825. Served in the Brigade of Guards in Canada 1838-1842 during the Rebellions there and then succeeded to the command of the Brigade when General Macdonell left in June 1842. The Brigade left for Britain in October and November 1842. He proved prophetic in his estimate of it taking eight to ten years to be promoted captain commanding a company in his regiment. He was finally promoted, without purchase, in May 1825. This was due to slow promotion in the regiment and junior officers purchasing the rank of captain over his head. Died 21 May 1876.

Major General **John William Fremantle**[14] CB retired by sale of his unattached commission 25 August 1843. Captain and Lieutenant Colonel 1 August 1822. Regimental Major 23 June 1836. Regimental Lieutenant Colonel 8 August 1837. Went on half pay unattached 31 December 1839. Brevet Colonel 22 July 1830. Major General 23 November 1841. ADC to the Duke of Wellington in the AOOF 1815-1818. DAG to the forces in Jamaica 25 August 1819 – 14 June 1821. ADC to the Duke of Wellington when Commander-in-Chief 1827. ADC to both King William IV and Queen Victoria 22 July 1830. Died 6 April 1845.

General **William Lovelace Walton** Regimental Colonel 5th Fusiliers 20 February 1856. Captain and Lieutenant Colonel 20 February 1823. Regimental Major 10 January 1837 and Regimental Lieutenant Colonel 31 December 1839. Brevet Colonel 10 January 1837, Major General 9 November 1846, Lieutenant General 20 June 1854 and General 13 February 1863. Went on half pay unattached 8 May 1846. Died 11 January 1865.

Lieutenant Colonel **John Stepney Cowell**[15] retired by sale of his commission 22 June 1832. Brevet Major 17 February 1820. Captain and Lieutenant Colonel 15 June 1830. Died 15 May 1877.

Captain **Edward Sumner** Lieutenant Coldstream Foot Guards. Died 26 June 1815 from complications of a wound suffered at the Battle of Waterloo 18 June 1815.

Captain **John Edward Rous Viscount Dunwich**[16] disposed of his half pay commission and left the Army 8 April 1826. Exchanged to 93rd Foot 6 November 1817. Exchanged to half pay Nova Scotia Fencibles 15 January 1818. Appointed Colonel East Suffolk Militia 24 May 1830-6 February 1844. Died 27 January 1886.

Captain Windham Carmichael Anstruther[17] retired by sale of his commission 26 February 1817. Major 1st Royal Lanarkshire Militia 23

---

14. Also spelled Freemantle.
15. Took additional surname of Stepney after Cowell 29 December 1857 and created a Baronet 22 September 1871.
16. Became Viscount Dunwich 18 July 1821 and succeeded as 2nd Earl of Stradbroke and a Baronet 17 August 1827.
17. Succeeded as a Baronet November 1831.

March 1846. Resigned his militia commission by April 1869. Died 7 September 1869.

Lieutenant Colonel Hon. **Robert Moore** placed on half pay Coldstream Foot Guards 1 April 1824. Captain and Lieutenant Colonel 1 April 1824. Died 2 November 1856.

Brevet Colonel **Thomas Chaplin** retired by sale of his commission 22 August 1851. Lieutenant Colonel half pay unattached 15 August 1826. Exchanged to full pay Captain and Lieutenant Colonel Coldstream Foot Guards 31 August 1826. Regimental Major 8 May 1846. Regimental Lieutenant Colonel 25 April 1848. Brevet Colonel 23 November 1841. Died 10 May 1863.

Lieutenant Colonel **Henry Gooch** retired by sale of his commission 11 June 1841. Lieutenant in the Army 29 July 1815 to date from 23 July 1812. Lieutenant and Captain 28 October 1819 and Captain and Lieutenant Colonel 26 November 1832. Died 18 January 1867.

Lieutenant **Henry Frederick Griffiths** Ensign Coldstream Foot Guards. Lieutenant in the Army 29 July 1815 to date from 25 January 1814. Died 19 January 1821.

Lieutenant **James Frederick Buller** Ensign Coldstream Foot Guards. Lieutenant in the Army 29 July 1815 to date from 26 January 1814. Died 4 January 1816.

Lieutenant Colonel Hon. **John Montagu** retired by sale of his commission 27 January 1832. Lieutenant in the Army 29 July 1815 to date from 27 January 1814. Lieutenant and Captain 25 October 1821. Captain and Lieutenant Colonel 13 August 1829. Died 12 December 1843.

Lieutenant **George Buckley** Ensign Coldstream Foot Guards. Lieutenant in the Army 29 July 1815 to date from 17 February 1814. Died of 'battle' fatigue at Paris on 16 August 1815.

Captain **James William Hervey**[18] retired by sale of his commission 2 September 1837. Lieutenant in the Army 29 July 1815 to date from 15

---

18. Also spelled Harvey.

March 1814. Exchanged to half pay Coldstream Foot Guards 15 April 1819. Exchanged to full pay 24th Foot 11 January 1821. On half pay 24th Foot 1823. Appointed to full pay Cape Corps (Infantry) 6 November 1823. Exchanged to half pay 60th Foot 27 May 1824. Exchanged to full pay 6th Dragoon Guards 16 December 1824. Captain half pay unattached 3 December 1825. Exchanged to full pay 51st Foot 1 September 1837. He too helped close the North Gate at Hougoumont. Died in the year 1873.

Captain **Henry Vane** Lieutenant Coldstream Foot Guards. Lieutenant in the Army 29 July 1815 to date from 16 March 1814. Lieutenant and Captain 1 August 1822. Died 9 August 1829.

Lieutenant General **Lord Frederick FitzClarence**[19] Regimental Colonel 36th Foot 23 July 1851. Lieutenant in the Army 29 July 1815 to date from 12 May 1814. Captain Cape Corps (Infantry) 23 February 1820. Appointed Captain 11th Foot 10 August 1820. Major 11th Foot 10 January 1822. Lieutenant Colonel 11th Foot 1 April 1824. Appointed Lieutenant Colonel 7th Foot 2 June 1825. Brevet Colonel 6 May 1831. Exchanged to half pay unattached 24 August 1832. Major General 23 November 1841 and Lieutenant General 11 November 1851. ADC to both King William IV and Queen Victoria 6 May 1831. An AAG at Headquarters 1832 -1841. Lieutenant Governor of Portsmouth and commanded South West District 1847-1851. Commander-in-Chief Bombay Presidency India 22 November 1852-30 October 1854. Died 30 October 1854.

Lieutenant Colonel **Charles William Short** retired by sale of his commission 24 February 1837. Lieutenant in the Army 29 July 1815 to date from 13 October 1814. Lieutenant and Captain 17 April 1823 and Captain and Lieutenant Colonel 21 September 1830. Died 19 January 1857.

3rd Foot Guards

General Sir **Willoughby Cotton** GCB. Regimental Colonel 32nd Foot 17 April 1854. Brevet Colonel 25 July 1821. Major General 22 July 1830. Lieutenant General 23 November 1841 and General 20 June 1854. Exchanged to 47th Foot 17 May 1821. Appointed Lieutenant Colonel 14th Foot 13 October 1828. ADC to King George IV 25 July 1821. Commanded

---

19. Illegitimate son of King William IV. Granted Courtesy Title of Lord, 24 May 1831.

at Poona, Bombay Presidency, India 1822. Commanded as Brigadier General, the Madras Division of Major General Sir Archibald Campbell's Army in the 1st Burma War 1824 – 1826. Officiating Quartermaster General of the King's Troops in India 1827. Acting Adjutant General of the King's Troops in India 1828. Lieutenant Governor and commanding the Forces in Jamaica 1831 – 1833. Commanded Western District Home Staff and Lieutenant Governor of Plymouth 1834-1836. Commanded Presidency Division Bengal Presidency, India 1838-1841. Commanded the Army of the Indus formed for service in Afghanistan 1838. Commanded 1st Bengal Division in General Sir Henry Fane's Army of the Indus 1839 and the Bengal Division under Lieutenant General Sir John Keane in the invasion of Afghanistan 1839-1840. Commanded Northern Command in Afghanistan 1840. Commander-in-Chief Bombay Presidency, India 8 April 1847-30 December 1850. Died 4 May 1860.

Major General Sir Henry Willoughby Rooke Kt CB retired by sale of an unattached commission 26 October 1832. Regimental Lieutenant Colonel 25 July 1821. Brevet Colonel 25 July 1821. Exchanged to half pay unattached 15 September 1825. Restored to full pay as Major General unattached 31 August 1830 to date from 22 July 1830. An AAG in the AOOF 1815-1816. Died 2 May 1869.

Lieutenant Colonel **William Chester Master** retired by sale of his commission 28 December 1820. Died 20 November 1868.

Lieutenant General **Douglas Mercer-Henderson**[20] CB. Regimental Colonel 68th Light Infantry 31 January 1850. Regimental Major 22 July 1830. Regimental Lieutenant Colonel 10 January 1837. Brevet Colonel 22 July 1830, Major General 23 November 1841 and Lieutenant General 11 November 1851. Retired on half pay unattached 11 August 1837. Died 21 March 1854.

Lieutenant Colonel **Sir Alexander Gordon** KCB Captain 3rd Foot Guards. Died 19 June 1815 from complications of a wound suffered at the Battle of Waterloo 18 June 1815.

Lieutenant Colonel **Charles Dashwood** CB disposed of his half pay commission and left the Army 14 January 1826. Exchanged to half pay 4th West India Regiment 8 May 1823. Died 20 April 1832.

---

20. Took additional surname of Henderson after Mercer 14 January 1853.

Lieutenant Colonel **Francis Home** retired by sale of his commission 2 April 1818. Died 28 April 1859.

Lieutenant Colonel **Charles Fox Canning** Captain 3rd Foot Guards. Died 18 June 1815 from complications of a wound suffered at the Battle of Waterloo 18 June 1815.

General Sir **Edward Bowater** Kt. Regimental Colonel 49th Foot 24 April 1846. Regimental Major 12 October 1826. Regimental Lieutenant Colonel 20 May 1836. Brevet Colonel 12 October 1826. Major General 10 January 1837. Lieutenant General 9 November 1846 and General 20 June 1854. Died 14 December 1861.

Lieutenant Colonel **Charles Edward West** retired by sale of his commission 30 August 1821. Died 11 October 1872.

Captain **William Stothert** Lieutenant 3rd Foot Guards. Died 23 June 1815 from complications of a wound suffered at the Battle of Waterloo 18 June 1815.

Brevet Colonel **William Drummond** retired by sale of his commission 6 December 1844. Brevet Major 18 June 1815. Captain and Lieutenant Colonel 4 July 1816. Regimental Major 1 November 1839. Brevet Colonel 10 January 1837. Date of death is unknown, possibly in 1862.

Brevet Major **Robert Bamford Hesketh** retired by sale of his commission 12 June 1823. Brevet Major 4 December 1815. Died 15 September 1828 from prolonged complications of a wound suffered at the Battle of Waterloo 18 June 1815.

Lieutenant Colonel **Richard Henry Wigston** retired by sale of his commission 3 August 1820. Captain and Lieutenant Colonel 31 December 1819. Died in September 1843.

Lieutenant Colonel **Charles John Barnet**[21] retired by sale of his commission 26 October 1826. Captain and Lieutenant Colonel 26 October 1820. British Consul General in Egypt 1841-1846. Died 4 August 1856.

---

21. Also spelled Barnett.

WHAT HAPPENED TO THEM AFTER WATERLOO?

Captain **Joseph William Moorhouse** Captain 65th Foot. Placed on half pay 3rd Foot Guards 25 February 1819. Exchanged to full pay Captain 65th Foot 18 November 1819. Died 4 May 1821.

Captain **George Evelyn** disposed of his half pay commission and left the Army 1 October 1825. Exchanged to half pay 60th Foot 29 March 1821. The severe wounding of his arm disabled him from further active service. Received a temporary pension of £100 for the wound suffered at the Battle of Waterloo commencing 19 June 1816. Died 15 February 1829.

Lieutenant Colonel **John Hamilton Elrington** retired by sale of his commission 6 July 1830. Lieutenant Colonel half pay unattached 14 November 1826. Restored to full pay Captain and Lieutenant Colonel 3rd Foot Guards 16 November 1826. Died 26 November 1843.

Captain **Hugh Montgomerie** Lieutenant 3rd Foot Guards. Died 2 May 1817 from prolonged complications of a wound suffered at the Battle of Waterloo 18 June 1815.

Captain **Charles Lake** resigned his commission 26 June 1817. Lieutenant and Captain 2 July 1815. Died 7 December 1863.

Lieutenant Colonel **George Douglas Standen** retired by sale of his commission 18 May 1841. Lieutenant and Captain 6 July 1815 and Captain and Lieutenant Colonel 12 July 1827. Died 16 December 1842.

Captain **Henry Paxton** retired by sale of his commission 6 November 1817. Lieutenant and Captain 13 July 1815. Date of death is unknown.

Captain **David Baird**[22] retired by sale of his commission 9 August 1821. Lieutenant in the Army 29 July 1815 to date from 18 June 1811. Lieutenant and Captain 4 July 1816. Died 20 December 1851.

Captain **William James** exchanged to half pay 3rd Foot Guards 25 February 1819. Lieutenant in the Army 29 July 1815 to date from 4 March 1813. Lieutenant and Captain 8 May 1817. Died 13 October 1854.

---

22. Succeeded as 2nd Baronet 18 August 1829.

Major General Hon. **George Anson** Regimental Colonel 55th Foot 8 December 1856. Lieutenant in the Army 29 July 1815 to date from 8 January 1814. Lieutenant and Captain 20 January 1820. Exchanged to 52nd Foot 26 September 1822. Exchanged to 14th Light Dragoons 1 May 1823. Major 7th Dragoon Guards 1 April 1824. Lieutenant Colonel half pay unattached 19 May 1825. Brevet Colonel 28 June 1838. Major General 11 November 1851. Local Lieutenant General in India 20 June 1854 and Local General in India 20 November 1855. ADC to the Duke of Wellington when Commander-in-Chief 1828 and 1842-1852. Commander-in-Chief Madras Presidency India 23 September 1854 – 23 January 1856. He served as Commander-in-Chief of India 23 January 1856 - 27 May 1857. Died 27 May 1857.

Lieutenant Colonel **Thomas Wedgewood**[23] retired by sale of his commission 10 November 1837. Lieutenant in the Army 29 July 1815 to date from 11 January 1814. Lieutenant and Captain 28 December 1820 and Captain and Lieutenant Colonel 31 December 1830. He never fully recovered from the facial paralysis brought on by exhaustion and exposure during the march to Paris. Died 7 November 1860.

Lieutenant **Whitwell Butler** exchanged to half pay 3rd Foot Guards 25 February 1819. Lieutenant in the Army 29 July 1815 to date from 12 January 1814. Died 11 June 1877.

Ensign **Charles Simpson** died 18 June 1815 from complications of a wound suffered at the Battle of Waterloo 18 June 1815.

General Sir **Henry Robinson-Montagu 6th Baron Rokeby**[24] GCB. Regimental Colonel Scots Guards 13 May 1875. Lieutenant in the Army 29 July 1815 to date from 21 April 1815. Lieutenant and Captain 12 June 1823, Captain and Lieutenant Colonel 21 September 1832, Regimental Major 28 June 1850, Regimental Lieutenant Colonel 17 February 1854. Brevet Colonel 9 November 1846, Major General 20 June 1854, Local Lieutenant General in the Crimea 30 July 1855, Lieutenant General 20 September 1861 and General 8 March 1869. Placed on the Retired List 1 October 1877. Commanded the Guards Brigade and then the 1st Division of the Eastern

---

23. Also spelled Wedgwood.
24. Succeeded as Baron Rokeby and a Baronet 7 April 1847.

Army[25] in the Crimean War 1855-1856. Inspecting General attached to the Foot Guards 1856-1861. Died 25 May 1883.

Royal Artillery/Royal Engineers

Major General **Stephen Galway Adye** CB. Major General unattached late RA. Regimental Colonel 29 July 1825. Major General 10 January 1837. Served in the AOOF 1815. Appointed Superintendent of the Royal Laboratory 15 June 1835. Died 13 September 1838.

Brevet Major **Charles Freeman Sandham** RA was placed on half pay 7 June 1822. Brevet Major 12 August 1819. Died 14 February 1869.

Brevet Major **Henry Jacob Kuhlmann**[26] CB, KGA was placed on half pay 24 February 1816. Died 19 March 1830.

Brevet Major **John Brenchley Harris** RE retired on full pay 6 November 1834. Captain 7 February 1817 and Brevet Major 22 July 1830. Placed on Temporary half pay 1 April 1817. Restored to full pay 8 March 1825. Died 26 October 1835.

Other Ranks

Corporal **James Graham** Light Company Coldstream Foot Guards. Discharged as a sergeant about.1822. Re-enlisted in the 12th Lancers and served as a private for 9 and a half years. Pensioned in 1830 and died 28 April 1845. In August 1815, Reverend John Norcross wrote to Wellington saying he wished to award an annual pension of £10 to the 'bravest man in the British Army at Waterloo'. Corporal Graham was nominated for his actions of closing the gate at Hougoumont and the rescue of his brother from the burning barn. The pension ceased to be awarded after two years because the Reverend Norcross went bankrupt.

Corporal **John Graham** Light Company Coldstream Foot Guards: Died of wounds according to June 1815 muster roll.

---

25. Commanded by Field Marshal Fitzroy Somerset, 1st Baron Raglan late Grenadier Guards 1854-1855.
26. Heinrich Jacob Kuhlmann continued to serve as a major and brevet lieutenant colonel in the Hanoverian Artillery.

Sergeant **Ralph Fraser** Mercer's Company 3rd Foot Guards received silver medal for actions at the North Gate. Born St. Margarets, London and Middlesex. Discharged aged thirty-nine in December 1818. A bedesman in Westminster Abbey.

Private **Matthew Clay** Born Blidworth, Nottinghamshire Served in 3rd Foot Guards; Bedfordshire Militia. Discharged aged fifty-seven.

Sergeant **Brice McGregor** 3rd Foot Guards: Discharged in 1821 with a pension. Appointed a Yeoman of the Guard. Died 27 November 1846.

Sergeant **Joseph Aston** 3rd Foot Guards. Promoted Quartermaster Sergeant after Waterloo. Promoted a Regimental Quartermaster 9 August 1833. Died 27 June 1853.

Colour Sergeant **Charles Wood.** Born Putley, Herefordshire. Served in 1st Foot Guards. Discharged age thirty-nine.

Biographical Sketches of Senior Officers in the 1st Guards Division

The Division Commanders

George Cooke recuperated for his wound in Brussels for a month and in July went to Britain. He stayed there for the next four months and was removed from the staff of Wellington's army in November. He received a pension for the loss of his left arm suffered at the Battle of Waterloo of £350 commencing 19 June 1816. He was appointed to command the Kent District on the Home Staff in late 1815 and became the Lieutenant Governor of Portsmouth and commander of the South-West District from 1819 until his promotion to Lieutenant General on 19 July 1821. Over the years he served as the Regimental Colonel of two regiments: the 77th Foot from 23 June 1815 to 23 December 1834 and then the 40th Foot from 23 December 1834 to 3 February 1837.

Cooke was rewarded for his service in the Waterloo Campaign. He was made a KCB 22 June 1815 and received the Thanks of Parliament. He also received the Waterloo Medal along with two Foreign Awards: the Russian Order of St. George 3rd Class and the Dutch Military Order of William 3rd Class. He died 3 February 1837.

Kenneth Alexander Howard was born 29 November 1767. He entered the Army as an Ensign in the Coldstream Foot Guards 21 April 1786. All of his service was in the regiment except when on the staff. He was promoted to Lieutenant & Captain 25 April 1793 and to Captain & Lieutenant Colonel 25 July 1799. He was promoted to Brevet Colonel 1 January 1805 and became the 2nd Major 4 August 1808. Colonel Howard was promoted to Major General 25 July 1810, but, remained a member of the Coldstream Foot Guards until he was removed from the regiment as a General Officer unattached 25 July 1814.

He saw active service in Flanders February 1793-May 1795 and wounded at St. Amand in May 1793. Served as Brigade Major to the Guards Brigade during the Irish Rebellion 1798. He went with his regiment to the Helder 1799. He had a series of staff appointments in the early 1800s, including on the Home Staff as the acting Inspector General Foreign Troops from 1801 to1802, then the Deputy Inspector General Foreign Troops from 1802 to 1805 and finally as commander of the Foreign Depot from 1805 to 1810.

During the Peninsular War he saw extensive action, as he commanded a brigade 1st Division February-June 1811, a brigade 2nd Division June - October 1811 and November 1811- November 1812 and a brigade 1st Division November 1812 -March 1813. He temporarily commanded the 2nd Division October-November 1811 and was the acting commander of the 1st Division March 1813-April 1814. He fought at Fuentes d'Onoro in May 1811, Arroyo de Molinos in October 1811, Bridge at Almaraz in May 1812, Crossing the Bidassoa in October 1813, Nivelle in November 1813, Nive in December 1813, Crossing the Adour in February 1814 and siege of Bayonne from February to April 1814. He returned to England in June 1814 and was appointed to command the South West District as the Lieutenant Governor of Portsmouth on the Home Staff from 1814 to 1815.

Howard missed the battle of Waterloo as he only came from Britain as a replacement for the wounded Major General Cooke. He was placed on the staff of Wellington's army as a local Lieutenant General on the continent 6 July 1815 to command the 1st Guards Division. He temporarily commanded I Corps in France, but, returned to Britain when the AOOF was formed in November 1815.

He served on the Home Staff resuming his appointment as Lieutenant Governor of Portsmouth and commanding the South West District from 1816 to 1819. He was promoted to Lieutenant General 12 August 1819 and to General 10 January 1837. Howard was appointed the Regimental Colonel of the 70th Foot from 24 October 1816 to 1832 when he was appointed the Regimental Colonel of the 3rd Foot on 30 January 1832. He remained the Regimental Colonel of the 3rd Foot until his death on 13 February 1845.

Throughout his career Howard received numerous awards. He was appointed an ADC to the King on 1 January 1805, a KCB on 2 January 1815 and a GCB on 17 March 1820. He succeeded to a Peerage as 11th Baron Howard of Effingham on 10 December 1816. He was created Earl of Effingham on 27 January 1837. He was awarded the AGM with clasp for Vitoria and the Nive. He received a Foreign Award of Portuguese Commander of the Tower and Sword in May 1815.

The Brigade Commanders

John Byng went to Britain on leave in October 1815. While there he was appointed to command the Eastern District on the Home Staff. He commanded the district until 1816 and then commanded the Northern District for twelve years. In 1828, General Byng was appointed the Commander of the Forces in Ireland and held that post until 1831. He was promoted a Lieutenant General 27 May 1825, a General 23 November 1841 and a Field Marshal 2 October 1855.

Byng was appointed the Regimental Colonel of the York Light Infantry Volunteers 26 December 1815-1816 and subsequently the Regimental Colonel of the 4th West India Regiment 12 December 1816-1819, the 2nd West India Regiment 26 July 1822 – 23 January 1828, the 29th Foot 23 January 1828-15 August 1850 and then the Coldstream Foot Guards 15 August 1850-3 June 1860.

He became a KCB 2 January 1815, a GCB 6 June 1831 and a GCH 1826. He was created a Peer as Baron Strafford of Harmondsworth, on 12 May 1835 and then created Earl of Strafford and Viscount Enfield on 28 August 1847. He received the AGC with clasp for Vitoria, Pyrenees, Nivelle, Nive, and Orthes and the MGSM with clasp for Toulouse. He received the Thanks of Parliament for Peninsula and Orthes. For his service at Waterloo, he received the Waterloo Medal, the Thanks of Parliament and two Foreign Awards: the Russian Order of Saint George and made a Knight of the Austrian Order of Maria Theresa. He died 3 June 1860.

Peregrine Maitland was appointed on the staff of the AOOF and given command of the 1st Guards Brigade on 30 November 1815. He commanded the Guards Brigade until January 1818, when he was appointed the Lieutenant Governor and Commander of the Forces of Upper Canada January 1818 until November 1828. On 21 August 1828, he was promoted to local Lieutenant General in North America. He was then appointed Lieutenant Governor of Nova Scotia November 1828. He returned to England in 1832 because of poor health. He never went back to Nova Scotia, but continued to govern through correspondence until July 1834. He was promoted to Lieutenant General 22 July 1830 and to General 9 November 1846.

Maitland was appointed the Commander-in-Chief of the Madras Presidency in India October 1836 until December 1838. He was appointed the Governor and Commander-in-Chief of the Cape of Good Hope December 1843. He commanded during the 7th Kaffir War 1846. He returned to England October 1846.

He was appointed Regimental Colonel of the 1st West India Regiment 22 February 1830 -19 July 1834 and subsequently Regimental Colonel of the 76th Foot 19 July 1834-2 January 1843 and then 17th Foot 2 January 1843-30 May 1854.

He received the KCB 22 June 1815 and GCB 6 April 1852. He received the AGM for the Nive and the MGSM with clasp for Corunna. For his service at Waterloo, he received the Waterloo Medal, the Thanks of Parliament and two Foreign Awards: the Russian Order of Saint Vladimir 3rd Class and the Dutch Military Order of William 3rd Class. He died 30 May 1854.

The Battalion Commanders

Henry Askew returned to Britain when the AOOF was formed in November 1815. He left the regiment upon promotion to Major General 19 July 1821 and was promoted Lieutenant General 10 January 1837. Despite being promoted, Askew saw no further employment.

He was made a CB on 4 June 1815 and a Kt on 25 July 1821. For his service in the Peninsula he received the AGM for the Nive and for his service at Quatre Bras he received the Waterloo Medal. He died 25 June 1847.

Francis Ker Hepburn returned to Britain when the AOOF was formed in November 1815. He left the regiment upon promotion to major general on 19 July 1821. Despite being promoted, Hepburn was not further employed.

Hepburn was made a CB on 4 June 1815. He received the AGM with clasp for Vitoria and the Nive. For his service at Waterloo he received the Waterloo Medal and two Foreign Awards: the Dutch Military Order of William 4th Class and the Russian Order of Saint Vladimir 4th Class. He died 7 June 1835.

Hon. William Stuart recuperated for his wound in Britain and rejoined his battalion by the end of the year. He commanded the 3rd Battalion 1st Foot Guards serving in the 1st Guards Brigade of the AOOF formed in

November 1815 until November 1818.

He left the regiment upon promotion to Major General 19 July 1821 and was promoted Lieutenant General 10 January 1837. Despite being promoted, Stuart was not further employed.

Stuart was made a CB 22 June 1815. He received the AGM for the Nive. For his service at Quatre Bras he received the Waterloo Medal and a Foreign Award: the Dutch Military Order of William 4th Class. Granted a pension of £300 for the loss of his left arm suffered at the Battle of Quatre Bras commencing 17 June 1816. He died 15 February 1837.

Alexander George Woodford commanded the 2nd Battalion Coldstream Foot Guards serving in the 1st Guards Brigade of the AOOF formed in November 1815 until November 1818. He had temporary command of the 1st Guards Brigade on a number of occasions when its commander was absent.

He was promoted to be the 1st Major commanding the 1st Battalion Coldstream Foot Guards on 18 January 1820 and was promoted the Regimental Lieutenant Colonel commanding the Coldstream Foot Guards 21 July 1821. He left the regiment upon promotion to Major General 27 May 1825. He was subsequently promoted Lieutenant General 28 June 1838, General 20 June 1854 and Field Marshal 1 January 1868. He was appointed Regimental Colonel of the 40th Foot 25 April 1842 and Regimental Colonel of the Scots Fusilier Guards 15 December1861.

He served on the staff of Malta and acted as Lieutenant Governor 1825-1826. He was on the staff as Commander-in-Chief in the Ionian Islands 1827-1835. He commanded on Gibraltar as Lieutenant Governor 1835 and as Governor 1836. He became the Lieutenant Governor of the Royal Chelsea Hospital 26 September 1856 and its Governor 3 August 1868.

Woodford was made a CB 4 June 1815, a KCB 13 September 1831, a GCB 6 April 1852, a GCMG 30 June 1832. He received the AGM with 2 clasps for Salamanca, Vitoria and the Nive and the MGSM with clasps for Ciudad Rodrigo and Nivelle. For his service at Waterloo he received the Waterloo Medal and two Foreign Awards: the Russian Order of Saint George 4th Class and was made a Knight of the Austrian Order of Maria Theresa. He died 26 August 1870.

Appendix I

Organization of the Foot Guard Regiments in 1815

1st Foot Guard Regiment[1]

# of Companies	Colonel, Lieutenant Colonel	Majors	Captains	Lieutenants	Ensigns	Adjutants	Quartermaster	Surgeon	Assistant Surgeon	Solicitor	Drum Major	Deputy Marshal	Sergeant Major	Quarter-Master Sergeant	Armor Sergeant	Hautbois	Fifers	Schoolmaster Sergeant	Sergeants	Corporals	Drummers	Privates	# In Each Company	Total
32	2	3	32	48	48	3	3	3	6	1	1	1	3	3	3	3	8	3	192	192	62	3648	114	4271

2nd and 3rd Battalions 1st Foot Guards

# of Companies	Majors	Captains	Lieutenants	Ensigns	Adjutants	Quartermaster	Surgeon	Assistant Surgeon	Drum Major	Sergeant Major	Quarter-Master Sergeant	Armorer Sergeant	Fifers	Schoolmaster Sergeant	Sergeants	Corporals	Drummers	Privates	# In Each Company	Total
10	1	10	15	15	1	1	1	2	1	1	1	1	2	1	60	60	20	1140	114	1331

---

1. Hamilton, Vol. 3, p.363.

1st Foot Guards Centre Companies

Rank	Number
Captain	1
Lieutenant	1
Ensigns	2
Sergeants	6
Corporals	6
Drummers	2
Privates	114
Total	132

1st Foot Guards Grenadier Companies

Rank	Number
Captain	1
Lieutenants	3
Sergeants	6
Corporals	6
Drummers	2
Fifers	2
Privates	114
Total	134

1st Foot Guards Light Companies

Rank	Number
Captain	1
Lieutenants	3
Sergeants	6
Corporals	6
Drummers	2
Privates	114
Total	132

ORGANIZATION OF THE FOOT GUARD REGIMENTS IN 1815

Coldstream and 3rd Foot Guards Regiments[2]

# of Companies	Colonel, Lieutenant Colonels	Majors	Captains	Lieutenants	Ensigns	Adjutants	Quartermaster	Surgeon	Assistant Surgeon	Solicitor	Drum Major	Deputy Marshal	Sergeant Major	Quarter-Master Sergeant	Armorer Sergeant	Schoolmaster Sergeant	Sergeants	Corporals	Drummers & Fifers	Privates	# In Each Company	Total
20	2	2	20	28	32	2	2	3	4	1	2	1	2	2	2	2	120	120	43	2280	114	2670

2nd Coldstream and 3rd Foot Guards Battalions

Majors	Captains	Lieutenants	Ensigns	Adjutants	Quartermaster	Surgeon	Assistant Surgeon	Drum Major	Sergeant Major	Quarter-Master Sergeant	Armor Sergeant	Schoolmaster Sergeant	Sergeants	Corporals	Drummers	Privates	# In Each Company	Total
1	10	14	16	1	1	1	2	1	1	1	1	1	60	60	20	1140	114	1331

2nd Coldstream and 3rd Foot Guards Centre Companies

Rank	Number
Captain	1
Lieutenant	1
Ensigns	2
Sergeants	6
Corporals	6
Drummers	2
Privates	114
Total	132

---

2. Mackinnon, Daniel, Vol. 2 p.404.

2nd Coldstream and 3rd Foot-Guards Grenadier and Light Companies

Rank	Number
Captain	1
Lieutenants	3
Sergeants	6
Corporals	6
Drummers	2
Privates	114
Total	132

Pioneers

In 1811, the Army decreed that every infantry battalion would have one corporal and ten privates designated as pioneers. The battalions were not authorized an increase in personnel nor did the regulations specify which company the men were to come from. In all likelihood there was one man per company. The task of the pioneers was to give the battalion men who had the skills and tools to construct field fortifications and obstacles out of existing buildings and terrain; or to remove or demolish anything that would prevent the battalion from achieving its mission. They were equipped with ten saws, five axes, eight spades, three mattocks, and three pick-axes.[3]

---

3. *General Regulations,* pp.65-66; Fosten, Vol. 3, page 80.

Appendix II

Monthly Strength Returns for the Foot Guards Battalions in 1815

Every infantry battalion in the British Army was required to submit a report to the Horse Guards of its strength on the 25th of each month. For those battalions in Great Britain, the strength return was submitted by the regiment. For battalions on active service, the return was sent up through its chain-of-command to the headquarters of the theatre where the battalion was assigned. A return was also sent to its regiment in Great Britain. The regimental returns usually did not contain as much information as those from the theatre headquarters. Furthermore, because of the delay of receiving the returns from the theatre, the information in the regimental returns could be one or two months out-of-date.

The returns are divided into four separate categories:

- Officers Present: this reflected the officers who were present for duty with the battalion. It did not include the officers who were assigned to the battalion, but were on the army staff.
- Staff Officers: like Officers Present, this section only included the officers who were present for duty with the battalion and not those who were performing temporary duty on the staff of the army.
- NCOs: this included sergeants, but not corporals. Additionally, drummers were also included in this section.
- Rank and File: this section included all soldiers who were not officers, sergeants, or drummers. It did not differentiate by rank.
  o Fit for Duty: the total number of soldiers who were available to perform their duty. Some returns have this category as Present or Present Fit for Duty
  o Sick in Hospital: the number of soldiers who were incapacitated due to injury, illness, or wounds. The returns did not break the numbers

down by why the soldiers were incapacitated. In some returns it was further divided by those who were sick in their quarters and those who were hospitalized.
- o On Command: the number of soldiers who were assigned to the battalion but were detached for duty in another location.
- o Total: the total of rank and file soldiers assigned to the battalion, regardless of their status.
- Changes from the Previous Month
  - o Joined: the rank and file soldiers assigned to the battalion who had been left in Great Britain but had rejoined the battalion on active service.
  - o Transfers: "Transfer In" is the number of soldiers who joined the battalion as replacements or to bring the battalion back up to strength. "Transfer Out" are those who had been returned to Great Britain. This usually included those soldiers whose term of enlistment had expired or those who were too badly injured, sick, or wounded to continue on active service. This section also included those discharged from the army.
  - o Died: the number of soldiers who died from disease, injury, or combat.
  - o Deserted or PW: despite their elite status, desertion did occur in the Foot Guards. This section shows the number of deserters since the previous month. It also listed those soldiers thought to have been taken prisoner.

Abbreviations:

Adj	Adjutant
CPT	Captain
Dr	Drummer
Ens	Ensign
LT	Lieutenant
Maj	Major
NCO	Non-Commissioned Officer
Pay	Paymaster
PW	Prisoner of War
QM	Quarter-master
SGT	Sergeant

2nd Battalion 1st Foot Guards

Date	Officers Present Maj	CPT	LT	Ens	Staff Officers Pay	Adj	QM	Surgeon	Assistant Surgeon	NCOs SGT	Dr	Rank and File Fit for Duty	Sick In Hospital	On Command	Total	Changes from Previous Month Joined	Transfers In	Out	Died	Deserted or PW
25 Jan 15	1	4	9	8	-	1	-	1	2	54	22	915	56	6	977	-	1	9	2	-
25 Feb 15	1	7	8	13	1	1	-	1	2	56	22	916	55	3	974	-	2	-	3	2
25 Mar 15	1	5	6	16	1	1	-	1	2	52	22	906	51	18	973	-	4	7	-	-
25 Apr 15	1	4	9	18	1	1	-	1	2	55	22	910	60	24	998	-	41	6	1	-
25 May 15	1	4	10	16	1	1	-	1	2	55	24	924	60	53	1017	-	34	15	1	1
25 Jun 15	-	2	9	15	-	1	-	-	2	57	22	552	361	12	925	1	-	21	73	-
25 Jul 15	-	4	8	10	-	-	-	-	3	59	22	637	321	30	988	12	89	27	9	-
25 Aug 15	1	7	12	14	-	1	1	1	3	58	22	714	210	26	950	1	7	31	14	2
25 Sep 15	1	6	10	15	-	1	1	1	3	57	22	756	170	27	953	2	36	51	5	-
25 Oct 15	1	8	15	15	-	1	1	1	3	52	23	810	94	23	927	1	3	26	-	-
25 Nov 15	1	8	10	16	-	1	1	1	3	55	22	749	144	54	947	-	3	7	2	2
25 Dec 15	1	9	9	15	-	1	1	1	2	52	21	-	-	-	924	-	-	2	-	-

3rd Battalion 1st Foot Guards

Date	Officers Present Maj	CPT	LT	Ens	Staff Officers Pay	Adj	QM	Surgeon	Assistant Surgeon	NCOs SGT	Dr	Rank and File Fit for Duty	Sick in Hospital[1]	On Command	Total	Joined	Changes from Previous Month Transfers In	Out	Died	Deserted or PW
25 Jan 15	1	9	10	12	-	1	1	-	2	69	22	739	69	180	988	1	-	13	3	3
25 Feb 15	1	7	11	12	1	1	1	-	2	68	22	797	49	131	978	-	1	7	1	3
25 Mar 15	1	9	11	13	1	1	1	-	2	68	22	885	48	48	981	14	2	1	1	4
25 Apr 15	1	8	7	13	1	-	-	1	-	54	22	966	32	11	1009	-	-	-	-	-
25 May 15	1	9	9	13	1	1	-	1	2	55	22	980	42	15	1037	0	30	-	-	-
25 Jun 15	-	6	8	13	-	-	1	1	2	55	22	562	295	44	967	-	3	0	74	-
25 Jul 15	-	7	11	12	-	-	1	1	2	54	21	686	347	27	1060	-	140	33	16	-
25 Aug 15	-	10	13	14	-	-	1	1	2	52	21	765	232	13	1012	6	0	43	13	-
25 Sep 15	-	10	14	12	-	-	1	1	2	53	21	804	149	9	962	1	9	50	8	1
25 Oct 15	-	9	14	13	-	-	1	1	2	52	20	823	92	10	925	-	1	35	-	-
25 Nov 15	-	9	13	13	-	-	1	1	2	52	21	767	144	47	958	-	2	5	2	-
25 Dec 15	1	8	14	15	-	-	2	1	2	63	22	1136	65	8	1209	-	449	151	1	-

1. For February and March 1815, the figures also include sick in quarters.

2nd Battalion Coldstream Guards

Date	Officers Present Maj	CPT	LT	Ens	Staff Officers Pay	Adj	QM	Surgeon	Assistant Surgeon	NCOs SGT	Dr	Rank and File Fit for Duty	Sick In Hospital	On Command	Total	Changes from Previous Month Joined	Transfers In	Out	Died	Deserted or PW
25 Jan 15	-	4	8	10	-	-	1	1	2	61	22	702	57	5	764	-	3	8	2	-
25 Feb 15	1	6	10	12	-	-	1	1	2	61	22	720	40	5	765	1	1	1	-	-
25 Mar 15	1	5	10	12	-	-	1	-	2	61	22	708	61	17	766	0	3	1	1	-
25 Apr 15	1	5	12	15	-	-	1	1	2	69	22	947	50	13	1010	-	258	1	1	-
25 May 15	1	5	12	15	-	-	1	1	2	55	22	922	80	8	1010	1	3	-	4	-
25 Jun 15	1	5	8	14	-	-	1	1	2	63	21	609	295	44	948	-	-	3	56	6[2]
25 Jul 15	1	4	10	16	1	-	1	1	2	69	22	866	246	30	1142	8	221	18	10	-
25 Aug 15	1	6	11	13	1	1	-	1	2	65	22	936	168	25	1129	2	3	18	4	-
25 Sep 15	1	5	12	13	1	1	1	1	2	61	22	963	100	20	1083	3	-	49	4	-
25 Oct 15	1	5	12	14	1	1	1	1	2	59	22	915	106	53	1074	-	6	-	5	-
25 Nov 15	1	6	12	13	1	1	1	1	2	61	22	953	97	14	1064	1	2	8	3	-
25 Dec 15	1	6	11	15	1	1	1	1	2	68	22	1108	87	58	1253	-	210	3	11	-

2. Two were listed as deserters and four as 'Taken Prisoner'.

2nd Battalion 3rd Foot Guards

Date	Officers Present Maj	CPT	LT	Ens	Staff Officers Pay	Adj	QM	Surgeon	Assistant Surgeon	NCOs SGT	Dr	Rank and File Fit for Duty	Sick in Hospital	On Command	Total	Joined	Changes from Previous Month Transfers In	Out	Died	Deserted or PW
25 Jan 15	-	5	11	15	-	-	1	1	2	61	15	798	32	5	835	-	11	-	2	-
25 Feb 15	-	5	9	15	-	-	1	1	2	60	16	798	28	7	833	-	2	2	2	-
25 Mar 15	-	6	10	15	-	-	1	1	2	60	16	783	28	22	833	-	1	1	-	-
25 Apr 15	-	6	13	15	-	-	1	1	1	69	17	1018	61	11	1090	-	270	1	2	-
25 May 15	1	5	12	15	-	-	1	1	1	58	17	992	53	19	1064	-	3	29	1	-
25 Jun 15	-	6	11	15	-	-	1	1	2	65	17	731	215	58	1004	-	-	4	59	20[3]
25 Jul 15	1	7	11	15	-	-	1	1	2	71	16	972	194	29	1195	16	224	25	19	-
25 Aug 15	1	8	11	15	1	-	1	1	2	70	16	993	137	14	1149	2	2	34	17	-
25 Sep 15	1	8	11	15	-	1	1	1	2	65	16	1024	85	11	1120	7	-	50	6	-
25 Oct 15	1	8	11	14	1	1	1	1	2	65	16	992	70	47	1109	-	7	-	4	-
25 Nov 15	1	9	11	14	-	1	1	1	2	63	16	1032	2	12	1O96	-	-	10	5	-
25 Dec 15	1	8	11	14	-	1	-	1	2	64	16	-	-	-	1105	-	-	1	5	-

3. Listed as 'Taken Prisoner'.

Appendix III

The 1st Division Officers at Quatre Bras (16.00 Hours)

Division Headquarters

Position	Name
Commander	Major General George Cooke
AAG	Lieutenant Colonel Henry Willoughby Rooke
AQMG	Lieutenant Colonel Henry Bradford
DAQMG	Captain Edward Fitzgerald (25th Foot)
Artillery Commander	Lieutenant Colonel Stephen Adye
Assistant Commissary General	John Wood
Aide-de-Camp	Captain George Disbrowe (1FG)
Extra Aide-de-Camp	Ensign Augustus Cuyler (2nd Bn Coldstream)
Chaplain	Reverend George Stonestreet
Staff Surgeon	Thomas Kidd
Hospital Assistant	John Hutchinson Walsh
Provost Marshal	Sergeant Christopher Garman (2nd Bn Coldstream Guards)
Assistant Provost Marshal	Sergeant James Williamson (3rd Bn 1st Foot Guards)

1st Brigade Headquarters

Position	Name
Commander	Major General Peregrine Maitland
Brigade Major	Captain James Gunthorpe (3rd Bn)
DACG	Robert Cotes
Aide-de-Camp	Ensign James Lord Hay (3rd Bn)

2nd Battalion 1st Foot Guards
Headquarters

Position	Name
Commander	Second Major Henry Askew
Acting Major	Captain Richard Cooke
Acting Major	Captain Francis D'Oyly
Adjutant	Lieutenant Charles Allix
King's Colour Bearer	Ensign Henry Lascelles
Sergeant Major	Sergeant Major John Smith
Surgeon	William Curtis
Assistant Surgeon	John Harrison
Assistant Surgeon	John Gardner

Company	Commander	Actual Commander	Subalterns
Grenadier	Captain Richard Cooke	Lieutenant Henry W. Powell	Ensign Hon. Seymour Bathurst
			Ensign Samuel Hurd
			Ensign Fletcher Norton
1st	Captain Francis D'Oyly	Lieutenant Edward Clive	Ensign Joseph St. John
			Ensign James Talbot
2nd	Captain Goodwin Colquitt	Captain Goodwin Colquitt	Ensign George Fludyer
			Ensign William Tinling
3rd	Captain Henry Bradford	Lieutenant William Johnstone	Ensign George Mure
			Ensign Thomas E. Croft
4th	Captain Henry Hardinge	Lieutenant Somerville Burgess	Ensign George T. Jacob
			Ensign Hon. Samuel Barrington
5th	Captain Thomas Hill		Ensign Henry Lascelles
6th	Captain Delancey Barclay	Lieutenant James Simpson	Lieutenant Edward Buckley
7th	Captain Lord Fitzroy Somerset	Lieutenant James Nixon	Ensign George Allen
			Ensign Algernon Greville
8th	Captain Ulysses Burgh	Lieutenant Charles Lascelles	Ensign Donald Cameron
			Ensign Daniel Tighe
Light	Captain William Milnes	Captain William Milnes	Lieutenant Francis Luttrell
			Lieutenant Thomas Brown

THE 1ST DIVISION OFFICERS AT QUATRE BRAS (16.00 HOURS)

3rd Battalion 1st Foot Guards
Headquarters

Position	Name
Commander	Third Major Hon. William Stuart
Acting Major	Captain Horatio Townshend
Acting Major	Captain Edward Stables
Acting Adjutant	Lieutenant Lonsdale Boldero
King's Colour Bearer[1]	Ensign Richard Master
Regimental Colour Bearer	Ensign James Butler
Acting Sergeant Major	Colour Sergeant Francis Dixon
Quartermaster / Paymaster	Robert Colquhoun[2]
Surgeon	Samuel Watson
Assistant Surgeon	Andrew Armstrong
Assistant Surgeon	Frederick Gilder

Company	Company	Actual Commander	Subalterns
Grenadier	Captain Hon. Horatio Townshend	Lieutenant Thomas Streatfield	Ensign Charles Vyner
1st	Captain Edward Stables	Lieutenant Robert Adair	Ensign John Dirom
2nd	Captain Henry D'Oyly	Captain Henry D'Oyly	Ensign William Barton
3rd	Captain Leslie Jones	Lieutenant Thomas Davies	Ensign Edward Pardoe
4th	Captain George Fead	Captain George Fead	Ensign Hon. Henry Vernon Ensign Robert Bruce
5th	Captain Charles Thomas	Captain Charles Thomas	
6th	Captain John Reeve	Captain John Reeve	Ensign Thomas Swinburne Ensign John Erskine
7th	Captain William Miller	Captain William Miller	Lieutenant Hon. Robert Clements Ensign Hon. Ernest Edgcombe

1. The 1807 Major's Colour.
2. Was appointed paymaster for both 1st Foot Guard Battalions when the brigade was formed. Hamilton; Vol. 3, p.12.

289

8th	Captain Hon. James Stanhope	Captain Hon. James Stanhope	Lieutenant Robert Phillimore Ensign Robert Batty Ensign Frederick Swann
Light	Captain Alexander Lord Saltoun	Lieutenant Robert Ellison	Lieutenant Edward Grose Lieutenant Charles Ellis

2nd and 3rd Battalion 1st Foot Guards Serving outside the Battalion

Name	Position
LTC Delancey Barclay (2nd Bn)	AAG
LTC Henry Bradford (2nd Bn)	AQMG
Captain Augustus Viscount Bury (2nd Bn)	ADC to the Prince of Orange
Captain William Cameron (3rd Bn)	DAQMG
Captain Francis Dawkins (2nd Bn)	ADC to General Henry Clinton
Captain Lord Charles Fitzroy (3rd Bn)	DAAG 2nd Corps
Captain James Gunthorpe (3rd Bn)	Brigade Major to General Maitland
LTC Henry Hardinge (2nd Bn)	Attached to Prussian Army
Captain Lord James Hay (3rd Bn)	Extra ADC to General Colville
Ensign James Lord Hay (3rd Bn)	ADC to General Maitland
LTC Sir Thomas Hill (2nd Bn)	AAG
LTC Leslie Jones (3rd Bn)	Commandant of Brussels
Captain William George Moore (2nd Bn)	DAQMG
LTC Lord Fitzroy Somerset (2nd Bn)	Military Secretary to Wellington

1st Battalion 1st Foot Guards

Name	Position
Captain Hon. Orlando Bridgeman	Extra ADC to General Rowland Lord Hill
Captain Newton Chambers	ADC to General Thomas Picton
Major Chatham Churchill	ADC to General Rowland Lord Hill
Captain George Disbrowe	ADC to General George Cooke
Ensign Rees Gronow	Was in Brussels until after the battle
LTC John Woodford	AQMG assigned to 4th Division.

THE 1ST DIVISION OFFICERS AT QUATRE BRAS (16.00 HOURS)

2nd Brigade
Headquarters

Position	Name
Commander	Major General Sir John Byng
Brigade Major	Captain William Stothert (1st Bn 3FG)
Aide-de-Camp	Captain Henry Dumaresq (9th Foot)
Extra Aide-de-Camp	Ensign Hon. Edward Stopford (1st Bn 3FG)

2nd Battalion Coldstream Guards
Headquarters

Position	Name
Commander	Second Major Alexander G. Woodford
Acting Major	Captain James Macdonell
Acting Major	Captain Daniel Mackinnon
Acting Adjutant	Lieutenant William Walton
Sergeant Major	Sergeant Major Thomas Baker
Quartermaster	Benjamin Selway
Surgeon	William Whymper
Assistant Surgeon	George Smith
Assistant Surgeon	William Hunter

Company	Commander	Actual Commander	Subalterns
Grenadier	Captain Daniel Mackinnon	Lieutenant John Blackman	
1st	Captain James Macdonell	Lieutenant Thomas Sowerby	Ensign John Montagu
2nd	Captain Hon. Alexander Abercromby	Ensign Hon. James Forbes	Ensign Francis Douglas
3rd	Captain Sir William Gomm	Lieutenant John Cowell	Ensign Henry Vane Ensign Hon. Walter Forbes

4th	Captain Hon. Edward Acheson	Captain Hon. Edward Acheson	Ensign Alexander Gordon
5th	Captain Hercules Pakenham	Lieutenant Edward Sumner	Ensign Robert Bowen Ensign Charles Short
6th	Captain Henry Wyndham	Lieutenant Beaumont, Lord Hotham	Ensign Henry Gooch Ensign George Buckley
7th	Captain Robert Arbuthnot	Lieutenant George Bowles	Ensign James Hervey
8th	Captain Henry Dawkins	Captain Henry Dawkins	Ensign Mark Beaufoy Ensign Henry Griffiths
Light	Captain Hon. John Walpole	Captain Henry Wyndham	Lieutenant Hon. Robert Moore

Coldstream Guards
Serving outside of the Battalion

Name	Position
Colonel Hon. Alexander Abercromby	AQMG
Captain Charles Bentinck	DAAG 2nd Division
Colonel Sir Colin Campbell (1st Bn)	HQ Commandant
Ensign Augustus Cuyler	Extra ADC to General Cooke
LTC Sir William Gomm	AQMG 5th Division
LTC John Fremantle (1st Bn)	Wellington's ADC

2nd Battalion 3rd Foot Guards
Headquarters

Position	Name
Commander	Second Major Francis Hepburn
Acting Major	Captain Douglas Mercer
Acting Major	Captain Charles Dashwood
Acting Adjutant	Ensign Barclay Drummond
Sergeant Major	Sergeant Major William Cox
Quartermaster	John Skuce
Surgeon	Samuel Good
Assistant Surgeon	Francis Hanrott

THE 1ST DIVISION OFFICERS AT QUATRE BRAS (16.00 HOURS)

Company	Commander	Actual Commander	Subalterns
Grenadier	Captain Francis Home	Captain Francis Home	Lieutenant Robert Hesketh Lieutenant Henry Hawkins Lieutenant Charles Barnet
1st	Captain Edward Bowater	Captain Edward Bowater	Lieutenant Thomas Craufurd Ensign Hugh S. Blane
2nd	Captain Charles Dashwood	Lieutenant Edward Fairfield	Ensign William James Ensign William Hamilton
3rd	Captain Douglas Mercer	Lieutenant Joseph Moorhouse	Ensign Whitwell Butler
4th	Captain William Keate	Lieutenant William Drummond	Ensign Charles Simpson
5th	Captain Charles Fox Canning	Lieutenant John Ashton	Ensign Thomas Wedgewood Ensign Andrew Cochrane
6th	Captain Henry Rooke	Lieutenant Hon. Hastings Forbes	Ensign Hon. George Anson
7th	Captain Hon. Alexander Gordon	Lieutenant Richard Wigston	Ensign Charles Lake Ensign David Baird
8th	Captain Charles West	Captain Charles West	Lieutenant Hugh Montgomerie Ensign Jeffery Prendergast Ensign Henry Montagu
Light	Captain William Master	Captain Charles Dashwood	Lieutenant George Evelyn Lieutenant John Elrington Ensign George Standen

2nd Battalion 3rd Foot Guards
Serving outside the Battalion

Name	Position
LTC Charles Fox Canning	ADC to Wellington
LTC Hon. Alexander Gordon	ADC to Wellington
LTC William Keate	AAG in Hanover
LTC Henry Willoughby Rooke	AAG 1st Division
Ensign Hon. Edward Stopford	ADC to General Byng
Captain William Stothert	Brigade Major for General Byng

Divisional Artillery

Division Artillery Commander	Lieutenant Colonel Stephen Adye
Sandham's Foot Brigade, 3rd Battalion RA	Captain Charles Sandham
	2nd Captain William Stopford
	1st Lieutenant George Foot
	1st Lieutenant George Baynes
	2nd Lieutenant Darell Jago
2nd Horse Artillery KGA	Captain [Brevet Major] Henry Jacob Kuhlmann
	2nd Captain George Wiering
	1st Lieutenant Theodore Speckmann
	1st Lieutenant George Meyer
	2nd Lieutenant Lewis de Wissell

Appendix IV

Strength of the Foot Guards Regiments on 18 June 1815

Each British infantry battalion and cavalry regiment sent in a strength report to the Army Headquarters on the morning of 18 June 1815. It is a list of the officers and men assigned to the battalion at the time. It does not mean the battalions actually had all those listed as present with them on the morning of 18 June 1815. For more information see Chapter 8.

Battalion	Officers				Sergeants						Drummers						Other Ranks					
	Majors	Captains	Subalterns	Staff	Present	Sick Present	Sick Absent	On Command	Total	Present	Sick Present	Sick Absent	On Command	Total	Present	Sick Present	Sick Absent	On Command	Total
2nd Bn 1st FG	-	4	21	4	43	-	8	5	56	21	-	1	-	22	688	-	276	12	976
3rd Bn 1st FG	-	8	17	5	40	-	8	5	53	20	-	2	-	22	758	-	255	8	1021
2nd Bn 2nd FG	1	5	25	3	55	3	1	6	65	15	1	-	6	22	939	49	4	11	1003
2nd Bn 3rd FG	1	4	26	3	55	2	-	10	67	9	1	-	7	17	937	41	6	57	1061

Source: Wellington, Duke of, *The Dispatches of Field Marshal the Duke of Wellington ... WD*, Vol. 12, p.486.

Appendix V

The 1st Division Officers at Waterloo (08.00 Hours)

Division Headquarters

Position	Name
Commander	Major General George Cooke
AAG	Lieutenant Colonel Henry Willoughby Rooke
AQMG	Lieutenant Colonel Henry Bradford
DAQMG	Captain Edward Fitzgerald (25th Foot)
Artillery Commander	Lieutenant Colonel Stephen Adye
Assistant Commissary General	John Wood
ADC	Captain George Disbrowe (1FG)
Extra ADC	Ensign Augustus Cuyler (2nd Bn Coldstream)
Chaplain	Reverend George Stonestreet
Staff Surgeon	Thomas Kidd
Hospital Assistant	John Hutchinson Walsh
Provost Marshal	Sergeant Christopher Garman (2nd Bn Coldstream Guards)
Assistant Provost Marshal	Sergeant James Williamson (3rd Bn 1st Foot Guards)

1st Brigade Headquarters

Position	Name
Commander	Major General Peregrine Maitland
Brigade Major	Captain James Gunthorpe (3rd Bn 1FG)
DACG	Robert Cotes
ADC	Ensign Seymour Bathurst (2nd Bn 1FG)

THE 1ST DIVISION OFFICERS AT WATERLOO (08.00 HOURS)

2nd Battalion 1st Foot Guards
Headquarters

Position	Name
Commander at Waterloo	Captain Richard Cooke
Acting Major	Captain Francis D'Oyly
Acting Major	Captain Goodwin Colquitt
Adjutant	Lieutenant Charles Allix
King's Colours Bearer	Ensign Henry Lascelles
Sergeant Major	Sergeant Major John Smith
Surgeon	William Curtis
Assistant Surgeon	John Harrison
Assistant Surgeon	John Gardner

Company	Commander	Actual Commander	Subalterns
Grenadier	Captain Richard Cooke	Lieutenant Henry W. Powell	Ensign Samuel Hurd; Ensign Fletcher Norton
1st	Captain Francis D'Oyly	Lieutenant Edward Clive	Ensign Joseph St. John; Ensign James Talbot
2nd	Captain Goodwin Colquitt	Ensign William Tinling	
3rd	Captain Henry Bradford	Lieutenant William Johnstone	Ensign George Mure
4th	Captain Henry Hardinge	Lieutenant Somerville Burgess	Ensign George T. Jacob
5th	Captain Thomas Hill		
6th	Captain Delancey Barclay	Lieutenant Edward Buckley	
7th	Captain Lord Fitzroy Somerset	Lieutenant James Nixon	Ensign George Allen
8th	Captain Ulysses Burgh	Lieutenant Charles Lascelles	Ensign Donald Cameron; Ensign Daniel Tighe
Light	Captain William Milnes	Captain William Milnes	Lieutenant Francis Luttrell; Ensign Algernon Greville

3rd Battalion 1st Foot Guards
Headquarters

Position	Name
Commander	Captain Edward Stables
Acting Major	Captain Henry D'Oyly
Acting Major	Captain George Fead
Acting Adjutant	Lieutenant Lonsdale Boldero
King's Colour Bearer	Ensign Richard Master
Regimental Colour Bearer	Ensign James Butler
Acting Sergeant Major	Colour Sergeant Francis Dixon
Quartermaster / Paymaster	Robert Colquhoun
Acting Quartermaster	Quartermaster Sergeant J. Smith
Surgeon	Samuel Watson
Assistant Surgeon	Andrew Armstrong
Assistant Surgeon	Frederick Gilder

Company	Company	Actual Commander	Subalterns
Grenadier	Captain Hon. Horatio Townshend		Ensign Charles Vyner Ensign Rees Gronow
1st	Captain Edward Stables	Ensign Robert Batty	Ensign John Dirom
2nd	Captain Henry D'Oyly		
3rd	Captain Leslie Jones	Lieutenant Thomas Davies	Ensign Edward Pardoe
4th	Captain George Fead	Ensign Hon. Henry Vernon	Ensign Robert Bruce
5th	Captain Charles Thomas	Captain Charles Thomas	
6th	Captain John Reeve	Captain John Reeve	Ensign Thomas Swinburne Ensign John Erskine
7th		Lieutenant Hon. Robert Clements	Ensign Hon. Ernest Edgcombe
8th	Captain Hon. James Stanhope	Captain Hon. James Stanhope	Lieutenant Robert Phillimore Ensign Frederick Swann
Light	Captain Alexander Lord Saltoun	Lieutenant Robert Ellison	Lieutenant Charles Ellis

298

THE 1ST DIVISION OFFICERS AT WATERLOO (08.00 HOURS)

2nd and 3rd Battalion 1st Foot Guards Serving Outside the Battalion

Name	Position
LTC Delancey Barclay (2nd Bn)	AAG
LTC Henry Bradford (2nd Bn)	AQMG
Captain Augustus Viscount Bury (2nd Bn)	ADC to the Prince of Orange
Captain William Cameron (3rd Bn)	DAQMG
Captain Francis Dawkins (2nd Bn)	ADC to General Henry Clinton
Captain Lord Charles Fitzroy (3rd Bn)	DAAG 2nd Corps
Captain James Gunthorpe (3rd Bn)	1st Brigade's Brigade Major
Captain Lord James Hay (3rd Bn)	Extra ADC to General Colville
LTC Sir Thomas Hill (2nd Bn)	AAG
LTC Leslie Jones (3rd Bn)	Commandant of Brussels
Captain William George Moore (2nd Bn)	DAQMG
LTC Lord Fitzroy Somerset (2nd Bn)	Military Secretary to Wellington

1st Battalion 1st Foot Guards

Name	Position
Captain Hon. Orlando Bridgeman	Extra ADC to General Rowland Lord Hill
Captain Newton Chambers	ADC to General Picton
Major Chatham Churchill	ADC to General Rowland Lord Hill
Captain George Disbrowe	ADC to General Cooke
LTC John Woodford	AQMG assigned to 4th Division.

2nd Brigade Headquarters

Position	Name
Commander	Major General Sir John Byng
Brigade Major	Captain William Stothert
DACG	John Henry Edwards
ADC	Captain Henry Dumaresq (9th Foot)
Extra ADC	Ensign Hon. Edward Stopford (1st Bn 3FG)

2nd Battalion Coldstream Guards
Headquarters

Position	Name
Commander	Second Major Alexander G. Woodford
Acting Major	Captain James Macdonell
Acting Major	Captain Daniel Mackinnon
Acting Adjutant	Lieutenant William Walton
Colour Bearer	Ensign Charles Short
Sergeant Major	Sergeant Major Thomas Baker
Quartermaster	Benjamin Selway
Surgeon	William Whymper
Assistant Surgeon	George Smith
Assistant Surgeon	William Hunter

Company	Commander	Actual Commander	Subalterns
Grenadier	Captain Daniel Mackinnon	Lieutenant John Blackman	Ensign Henry Griffiths
1st	Captain James Macdonell	Lieutenant Thomas Sowerby	Ensign John Montagu
2nd	Captain Hon. Alexander Abercromby	Ensign Hon. James Forbes	Ensign Francis Douglas
3rd	Captain Sir William Gomm	Ensign Henry Vane	Ensign Hon. Walter Forbes
4th	Captain Hon. Edward Acheson	Captain Hon. Edward Acheson	Ensign Alexander Gordon
5th	Captain Hercules Pakenham	Lieutenant Edward Sumner	Ensign Robert Bowen
6th	Captain Henry Wyndham	Lieutenant Beaumont, Lord Hotham	Ensign George Buckley
7th	Captain Robert Arbuthnot	Lieutenant George Bowles	Ensign James Hervey
8th	Captain Henry Dawkins	Captain Henry Dawkins	Ensign Mark Beaufoy
Light	Captain Hon. John Walpole	Captain Henry Wyndham	Lieutenant Hon. Robert Moore Ensign Henry Gooch

THE 1ST DIVISION OFFICERS AT WATERLOO (08.00 HOURS)

1st and 2nd Battalion Coldstream Guards
Serving outside of Their Battalion

Name	Position
Colonel Hon. Alexander Abercromby	AQMG
Captain Charles Bentinck	DAAG 2nd Division
Colonel Colin Campbell (1st Bn)	HQ Commandant
Ensign Augustus Cuyler	Extra ADC to Major General Cooke
LTC Sir William Gomm	AQMG 5th Division
LTC John Fremantle (1st Bn)	Wellington's ADC

2nd Battalion 3rd Foot Guards
Headquarters

Position	Name
Commander	Second Major Francis Hepburn
Acting Major	Captain Douglas Mercer
Acting Major	Captain Charles Dashwood
Acting Adjutant	Ensign Barclay Drummond
Sergeant Major	Sergeant Major William Cox
Quartermaster	John Skuce
Surgeon	Samuel Good
Assistant Surgeon	Francis Hanrott

Company	Commander	Actual Commander	Subalterns
Grenadier	Captain Francis Home	Captain Francis Home	Lieutenant Robert Hesketh Lieutenant Henry Hawkins Lieutenant Charles Barnet
1st	Captain Edward Bowater	Captain Edward Bowater	Lieutenant Thomas Craufurd Ensign Hugh S. Blane
2nd	Captain Charles Dashwood	Lieutenant Edward Fairfield	Ensign William James Ensign William Hamilton

301

3rd	Captain Douglas Mercer	Lieutenant Joseph Moorhouse	Ensign Whitwell Butler
4th	Captain William Keate	Lieutenant William Drummond	Ensign Charles Simpson
5th	Captain Charles Fox Canning	Lieutenant John Ashton	Ensign Thomas Wedgewood Ensign Andrew Cochrane
6th	Captain Henry Rooke	Lieutenant Hon. Hastings Forbes	
7th	Captain Hon. Alexander Gordon	Ensign Charles Lake	Ensign David Baird
8th	Captain Charles West	Captain Charles West	Lieutenant Hugh Montgomerie Ensign Jeffery Prendergast Ensign Henry Montagu
Light	Captain William Master	Captain Charles Dashwood	Lieutenant George Evelyn Lieutenant John Elrington Ensign George Standen

2nd Battalion 3rd Foot Guards
Serving outside the Battalion

Name	Position
LTC Charles Fox Canning	ADC to Wellington
LTC Hon. Alexander Gordon	ADC to Wellington
LTC Henry Willoughby Rooke	AAG 1st Division
Ensign Hon. Edward Stopford	ADC to General Byng
Captain William Stothert	Brigade Major for General Byng

THE 1ST DIVISION OFFICERS AT WATERLOO (08.00 HOURS)

Divisional Artillery

Division Artillery Commander	Lieutenant Colonel Stephen Adye
Sandham's Foot Brigade, 3rd Battalion RA	Captain Charles Sandham
	2nd Captain William Stopford
	1st Lieutenant George Foot
	1st Lieutenant George Baynes
	2nd Lieutenant Darell Jago
2nd Horse Artillery KGA	Captain [Brevet Major] Henry Jacob Kuhlmann
	2nd Captain George Wiering
	1st Lieutenant Theodore Speckmann
	1st Lieutenant George Meyer

Appendix VI

The 1st Division Officers on the March to Paris

Note: this reflects the organization as of the morning of 19 June 1815. As replacements arrived, the organization changed.

Division Headquarters

Position	Name
Commander	Major General Peregrine Maitland
AAG	Lieutenant Colonel Henry Willoughby Rooke
Artillery Commander	Lieutenant Colonel Stephen Adye
ADC	Ensign Seymour Bathurst
Chaplain	Reverend George Stonestreet
Staff Surgeon	Thomas Kidd
Hospital Assistant	John Hutchinson Walsh
Provost Marshal	Sergeant Christopher Garman (2nd Bn Coldstream Guards)
Assistant Provost Marshal	Sergeant James Williamson (3rd Bn 1st Foot Guards)

1st Brigade
1st Brigade Headquarters

Position	Name
Commander	LTC George Fead
Brigade Major	Captain James Gunthorpe (3rd Bn)
DACG	Robert Cotes

THE 1ST DIVISION OFFICERS ON THE MARCH TO PARIS

2nd Battalion 1st Foot Guards
Headquarters

Position	Name
Commander	Captain Alexander Lord Saltoun
Acting Major	Captain Goodwin Colquitt
Adjutant	Lieutenant Charles Allix
Sergeant Major	Sergeant Major John Smith
Quartermaster Sergeant	John Payne
Surgeon	William Curtis
Assistant Surgeon	John Harrison
Assistant Surgeon	John Gardner

Company	Commander	Actual Commander	Subalterns
Grenadier	Captain Richard Cooke	Lieutenant Henry W. Powell	Ensign Samuel Hurd Ensign Fletcher Norton
1st		Lieutenant Edward Clive	Ensign Joseph St. John Ensign James Talbot
2nd	Captain Goodwin Colquitt	Ensign William Tinling	
3rd	Captain Henry Bradford	Lieutenant William Johnstone	
4th	Captain Henry Hardinge	Ensign George Jacob	
5th	Captain Thomas Hill	Ensign Algernon Greville	
6th	Captain Delancey Barclay	Lieutenant Edward Buckley	
7th	Captain Lord Fitzroy Somerset	Ensign George Allen	
8th	Captain Ulysses Burgh	Lieutenant Charles Lascelles	Ensign Donald Cameron Ensign Daniel Tighe
Light	Captain William Milnes	Lieutenant James Nixon	

3rd Battalion 1st Foot Guards
Headquarters

Position	Name
Commander	Captain John Reeve
Acting Adjutant	Lieutenant Lonsdale Boldero
Quartermaster / Paymaster	Robert Colquhoun
Acting Quartermaster	Quartermaster Sergeant J. Smith
Surgeon	Samuel Watson
Assistant Surgeon	Andrew Armstrong
Assistant Surgeon	Frederick Gilder

Company	Company	Actual Commander	Subalterns
Grenadier	Captain Hon. Horatio Townshend	Ensign Charles Vyner	Ensign Rees Gronow
1st		Ensign John Dirom	
2nd	Captain Henry D'Oyly		
3rd	Captain Leslie Jones	Lieutenant Thomas Davies	
4th	Captain George Fead	Ensign Richard Master	Ensign James Butler
5th		Ensign Hon. Henry Vernon	
6th	Captain John Reeve	Ensign Thomas Swinburne	Ensign John Erskine
7th		Ensign Hon. Ernest Edgcombe	
8th	LTC Hon. James Stanhope (3rd Bn)	Lieutenant Robert Phillimore	Ensign Frederick Swann
Light	Captain Alexander Lord Saltoun	Lieutenant Robert Ellison	

THE 1ST DIVISION OFFICERS ON THE MARCH TO PARIS

2nd and 3rd Battalion 1st Foot Guards Serving Outside the Battalion

Name	Position
LTC Delancey Barclay (2nd Bn)	AAG
Captain Augustus Viscount Bury (2nd Bn)	Aide-de-Camp to the Prince of Orange
Captain Francis Dawkins (2nd Bn)	Aide-de-Camp to General Henry Clinton
Captain Lord Charles Fitzroy (3rd Bn)	DAAG to Lieutenant General Lord Hill
Captain James Gunthorpe (3rd Bn)	1st Brigade's Brigade Major
Captain Lord James Hay (3rd Bn)	Extra ADC to General Colville
LTC Sir Thomas Hill (2nd Bn)	AAG
LTC Leslie Jones (3rd Bn)	Commandant of Brussels
Captain William George Moore (2nd Bn)	DAQMG
LTC Hon. James Stanhope	AQMG 1st Corps

1st Battalion 1st Foot Guards

Name	Position
Captain Hon. Orlando Bridgeman	Extra Aide-de-Camp to General Rowland Lord Hill
Major Chatham Churchill	Aide-de-Camp to General Rowland Lord Hill
Captain George Disbrowe	Aide-de-Camp to General Cooke
Ensign Rees Gronow	Captain Leslie Jones' Company 3rd Battalion
LTC John Woodford	AQMG 6th Division.

2nd Brigade
2nd Brigade Headquarters after Waterloo

Position	Name
Commander	Colonel Francis Hepburn 3rd Foot Guards
Brigade Major	Lieutenant William Walton Coldstream Guards

WELLINGTON'S FOOT GUARDS AT WATERLOO

2nd Battalion Coldstream Guards
Headquarters

Position	Name
Commander	Second Major Alexander G. Woodford
Acting Major	Captain James Macdonell
Acting Major	Captain Henry Dawkins
Acting Adjutant	Ensign Mark Beaufoy
Sergeant Major	Sergeant Major Thomas Baker
Quartermaster	Benjamin Selway
Surgeon	William Whymper
Assistant Surgeon	George Smith
Assistant Surgeon	William Hunter

Company	Commander	Actual Commander	Subalterns
Grenadier	Captain Daniel Mackinnon	Ensign Henry Gooch	
1st	Captain James Macdonell	Lieutenant Thomas Sowerby	
2nd	Captain Hon. Alexander Abercromby	Ensign Hon. James Forbes	Ensign Francis Douglas
3rd	Captain Sir William Gomm	Ensign Hon. Walter Forbes	
4th	Captain Hon. Edward Acheson	Captain Hon. Edward Acheson	Ensign Alexander Gordon
5th	Captain Hercules Pakenham	Ensign Robert Bowen	Ensign Charles Short
6th	Captain Henry Wyndham	Lieutenant Beaumont, Lord Hotham	Ensign George Buckley
7th	Captain Robert Arbuthnot	Ensign James Hervey	
8th	Captain Henry Dawkins		
Light	Captain Hon. John Walpole	Lieutenant George Bowles	

THE 1ST DIVISION OFFICERS ON THE MARCH TO PARIS

2nd Battalion Coldstream Guards Serving outside of the Battalion

Name	Position
Colonel Hon. Alexander Abercromby	AQMG
Captain Charles Bentinck	DAAG 2nd Division
Colonel Sir Colin Campbell	HQ Commandant
Ensign Augustus Cuyler	Extra ADC to Major General Cooke
LTC Sir William Gomm	AQMG
LTC John Fremantle	Wellington's ADC was in 1st Battalion

2nd Battalion 3rd Foot Guards
Headquarters

Position	Name
Commander	Captain Douglas Mercer
Acting Major	Captain Francis Home
Acting Adjutant	Ensign Barclay Drummond
Sergeant Major	Sergeant Major William Cox
Quartermaster	John Skuce
Surgeon	Samuel Good
Assistant Surgeon	Francis Hanrott
Assistant Surgeon	John Warde

Company	Commander	Actual Commander	Subalterns
Grenadier	Captain Francis Home	Lieutenant Henry Hawkins	
1st	Captain Edward Bowater	Ensign Hugh S. Blane	
2nd	Captain Charles Dashwood	Lieutenant Edward Fairfield	Ensign William James Ensign William Hamilton
3rd	Captain Douglas Mercer	Lieutenant Joseph Moorhouse	
4th	Captain William Keate	Lieutenant Charles Barnet	

5th		Ensign Thomas Wedgewood	Ensign Andrew Cochrane
6th	Captain Henry Rooke	Ensign Hon. George Anson	
7th		Lieutenant Richard Wigston	Ensign Charles Lake
8th	Captain Charles West	Ensign Jeffery Prendergast	Ensign Henry Montagu
Light	Captain William Master	Lieutenant John Elrington	Ensign George Standen

2nd Battalion 3rd Foot Guards
Serving outside the Battalion

Name	Position
LTC Henry Willoughby Rooke	AAG 1st Division
Ensign Hon. Edward Stopford	ADC to General Byng

Divisional Artillery

Division Artillery Commander	Lieutenant Colonel Stephen Adye
Sandham's Foot Brigade, 3rd Battalion RA	Captain Charles Sandham
	2nd Captain William Stopford
	1st Lieutenant George Foot
	1st Lieutenant George Baynes
	2nd Lieutenant Darell Jago
2nd Horse Artillery KGA	Captain [Brevet Major] Henry Jacob Kuhlmann
	2nd Captain George Wiering
	1st Lieutenant Theodore Speckmann
	1st Lieutenant George Meyer
	2nd Lieutenant Lewis de Wissell

THE 1ST DIVISION OFFICERS ON THE MARCH TO PARIS

Divisional Royal Engineers and Royal Sappers and Miners
Note: On 24 June 1815, the division was given engineer support.

Divisional Royal Engineer Commander	2nd Captain John Brenchley Harris
Royal Engineers	2nd Captain Alexander Thomson
	1st Lieutenant Marcus Waters
2nd Company, 2nd Battalion Royal Sappers and Miners	Sub-Lieutenant William Stratton

Appendix VII

Guards Officers on the Staff of Wellington's Army from June 1815 to November 1818

June 1815: Waterloo Campaign

Aides-de-Camp

Colonel Sir Colin Campbell Coldstream Foot Guards – Commandant at HQ

Lieutenant Colonel Lord Fitzroy Somerset 1st Foot Guards – Military Secretary to Duke of Wellington

Lieutenant Colonel Sir Ulysses Burgh[1] 1st Foot Guards – Duke of Wellington

Lieutenant Colonel John Fremantle Coldstream Foot Guards – Duke of Wellington

Lieutenant Colonel Charles Fox Canning 3rd Foot Guards – Duke of Wellington

Lieutenant Colonel Hon. Sir Alexander Gordon 3rd Foot Guards - Duke of Wellington

Captain Hon. Arthur De Ros[2] 1st Foot Guards – General the Hereditary Prince of Orange

Captain Augustus Viscount Bury 1st Foot Guards – General the Hereditary Prince of Orange

Major Chatham H. Churchill 1st Foot Guards – Lieutenant General Rowland Lord Hill

---

1. Not at either Quatre Bras or Waterloo.
2. Not at either Quatre Bras or Waterloo.

Captain Hon. Orlando Bridgeman 1st Foot Guards – Lieutenant General Rowland Lord Hill
Captain Newton Chambers 1st Foot Guards – Lieutenant General Sir Thomas Picton
Captain Francis Dawkins 1st Foot Guards – Lieutenant General Sir Henry Clinton
Captain Lord James Hay 1st Foot Guards – Lieutenant General Sir Charles Colville
Captain George Disbrowe 1st Foot Guards - Major General George Cooke
Ensign Augustus Cuyler Coldstream Foot Guards – Major General George Cooke
Ensign Hon. Edward Stopford 3rd Foot Guards – Major General Sir John Byng
Ensign James Lord Hay 1st Foot Guards – Major General Peregrine Maitland

Brigade Major

Captain William Stothert 3rd Foot Guards – Major General Sir John Byng's 2nd Brigade
Captain James Gunthorpe 1st Foot Guards – Major General Peregrine Maitland's 1st Brigade

Adjutant General Department

Lieutenant Colonel Sir Thomas Noel Hill 1st Foot Guards – AAG
Lieutenant Colonel Delancey Barclay 1st Foot Guards – AAG
Lieutenant Colonel Henry Rooke 3rd Foot Guards – AAG
Captain Lord Charles Fitzroy 1st Foot Guards – DAAG
Captain Charles Bentinck Coldstream Foot Guards – DAAG

Quartermaster General Department

Colonel Hon. Alexander Abercromby Coldstream Foot Guards - AQMG
Lieutenant Colonel John Woodford 1st Foot Guards – AQMG
Lieutenant Colonel Sir William Gomm Coldstream Foot Guards –AQMG
Lieutenant Colonel Sir Henry Bradford 1st Foot Guards – AQMG
Captain William Moore 1st Foot Guards –DAQMG
Captain William Cameron 1st Foot Guards – DAQMG

Liaison Officer with Prussian Army

Lieutenant Colonel Sir Henry Hardinge 1st Foot Guards[3]

Commandant of Brussels

Lieutenant Colonel Leslie Jones 1st Foot Guards

Liaison Officer to King Louis XVIII's Minister of War[4]

Captain Philip Clarke 1st Foot Guards

December 1815[5]

Aides-de-Camp

Colonel Sir Colin Campbell Coldstream Foot Guards – Commandant at HQ
Colonel Lord Fitzroy Somerset 1st Foot Guards – Military Secretary to Duke of Wellington
Lieutenant Colonel Sir Ulysses Burgh 1st Foot Guards – Duke of Wellington
Lieutenant Colonel John Fremantle Coldstream Foot Guards - Duke of Wellington
Captain Hon. Arthur De Ros 1st Foot Guards – General the Hereditary Prince of Orange
Captain Augustus Viscount Bury 1st Foot Guards – General the Hereditary Prince of Orange
Lieutenant Colonel Chatham H. Churchill 1st Foot Guards – Lieutenant General Rowland Lord Hill
Captain Hon. Orlando Bridgeman 1st Foot Guards – Lieutenant General Rowland Lord Hill
Captain Francis Dawkins 1st Foot Guards – Lieutenant General Sir Henry Clinton
Captain Lord James Hay 1st Foot Guards – Lieutenant General Sir Charles Colville

---

3. Serving with rank of Brigadier General.
4. Henri Clarke, Duc de Feltre.
5. Although dated for December 1815, the list represents the final appointments on the staff of Guards officers prior to the formation of the Army of Occupation of France on 30 November 1815.

Lieutenant Hon. Thomas Seymour Bathurst 1st Foot Guards – Major General Sir Peregrine Maitland

Commanding Brigade
Colonel Francis Hepburn 3rd Foot Guards

Brigade Major
Major James Gunthorpe 1st Foot Guards – Major General Sir Peregrine Maitland's 1st Brigade
Captain William Walton Coldstream Foot Guards – Colonel Francis Hepburn's 2nd Brigade[6]

Adjutant General Department
Lieutenant Colonel Sir Thomas Noel Hill 1st Foot Guards – AAG
Lieutenant Colonel Delancey Barclay 1st Foot Guards – AAG
Lieutenant Colonel Henry Rooke 3rd Foot Guards – AAG
Major Lord Charles Fitzroy 1st Foot Guards – AAG
Major Charles Bentinck Coldstream Foot Guards – AAG
Captain Philip Clarke 1st Foot Guards – DAAG

Quartermaster General Department
Colonel Hon. Alexander Abercromby Coldstream Foot Guards - AQMG
Lieutenant Colonel John Woodford 1st Foot Guards - AQMG
Lieutenant Colonel Sir William Gomm Coldstream Foot Guards –AQMG
Lieutenant Colonel Sir Henry Bradford 1st Foot Guards – AQMG
Lieutenant Colonel James Stanhope 1st Foot Guards - AQMG
Captain William Moore 1st Foot Guards – DAQMG
Captain William Cameron 1st Foot Guards - DAQMG

January 1816: Army of Occupation of France
Aides-de-Camp
Colonel Sir Colin Campbell Coldstream Foot Guards – Commandant at HQ

---

6. Major General Sir John Byng had been removed to the Home Staff.

Colonel Lord Fitzroy Somerset 1st Foot Guards – Military Secretary to Duke of Wellington
Lieutenant Colonel Sir Ulysses Burgh 1st Foot Guards – Duke of Wellington
Lieutenant Colonel John Fremantle Coldstream Foot Guards - Duke of Wellington
Lieutenant Colonel Chatham H. Churchill 1st Foot Guards – Lieutenant General Rowland Lord Hill
Captain Hon. Orlando Bridgeman 1st Foot Guards – Lieutenant General Rowland Lord Hill
Captain Francis Dawkins 1st Foot Guards – Lieutenant General Sir Henry Clinton
Captain Lord James Hay 1st Foot Guards – Lieutenant General Sir Charles Colville
Lieutenant Hon. Thomas Seymour Bathurst 1st Foot Guards – Major General Sir Peregrine Maitland

Brigade Major

Major James Gunthorpe 1st Foot Guards - Major General Sir Peregrine Maitland's 1st Brigade

Adjutant General Department

Lieutenant Colonel Sir Thomas Noel Hill 1st Foot Guards – AAG
Lieutenant Colonel Delancey Barclay 1st Foot Guards – AAG
Lieutenant Colonel Henry Rooke 3rd Foot Guards – AAG
Major Lord Charles Fitzroy 1st Foot Guards – AAG
Major Charles Bentinck Coldstream Foot Guards – AAG
Captain Philip Clarke 1st Foot Guards – DAAG

Quartermaster General Department

Colonel Hon. Alexander Abercromby Coldstream Foot Guards – AQMG
Lieutenant Colonel John Woodford 1st Foot Guards – AQMG
Lieutenant Colonel Sir William Gomm Coldstream Foot Guards –AQMG
Lieutenant Colonel Sir Henry Bradford 1st Foot Guards – AQMG
Lieutenant Colonel James Stanhope 1st Foot Guards – AQMG
Captain William Moore 1st Foot Guards – DAQMG
Captain William Cameron 1st Foot Guards – DAQMG

December 1816

Aides-de-Camp

Colonel Sir Colin Campbell Coldstream Foot Guards – Commandant at HQ
Lieutenant Colonel Sir Ulysses Burgh 1st Foot Guards – Duke of Wellington
Lieutenant Colonel John Fremantle Coldstream Foot Guards - Duke of Wellington
Lieutenant Colonel Chatham H. Churchill 1st Foot Guards – Lieutenant General Rowland Lord Hill
Captain Hon. Orlando Bridgeman 1st Foot Guards – Lieutenant General Rowland Lord Hill
Captain Francis Dawkins 1st Foot Guards – Lieutenant General Sir Henry Clinton
Captain Lord James Hay 1st Foot Guards – Lieutenant General Sir Charles Colville
Lieutenant Hon. Thomas Seymour Bathurst 1st Foot Guards – Lieutenant General Sir George Murray
Captain James Lindsay 1st Foot Guards – Major General Sir Peregrine Maitland

Brigade Major

Major James Gunthorpe 1st Foot Guards – Major General Sir Peregrine Maitland's 1st Brigade

Adjutant General Department

Lieutenant Colonel Sir Thomas Noel Hill 1st Foot Guards – AAG
Major Lord Charles Fitzroy 1st Foot Guards – AAG
Major Charles Bentinck Coldstream Foot Guards – AAG
Captain Philip Clarke 1st Foot Guards – DAAG

Quartermaster General Department

Colonel Hon. Alexander Abercromby Coldstream Foot Guards - AQMG
Lieutenant Colonel John Woodford 1st Foot Guards – AQMG
Lieutenant Colonel Sir Henry Bradford 1st Foot Guards – AQMG
Lieutenant Colonel Sir Henry Hardinge 1st Foot Guards - AQMG
Captain William Moore 1st Foot Guards – DAQMG

Commandant of Valenciennes
Lieutenant Colonel Sir Robert Arbuthnot Coldstream Foot Guards[7]

January 1817
Aides-de-Camp
Colonel Sir Colin Campbell Coldstream Foot Guards – Commandant at HQ
Lieutenant Colonel Sir Ulysses Burgh 1st Foot Guards – Duke of Wellington
Lieutenant Colonel John Fremantle Coldstream Foot Guards - Duke of Wellington
Lieutenant Colonel Chatham H. Churchill 1st Foot Guards – Lieutenant General Rowland Lord Hill
Captain Hon. Orlando Bridgeman 1st Foot Guards – Lieutenant General Rowland Lord Hill
Captain Francis Dawkins 1st Foot Guards – Lieutenant General Sir Henry Clinton
Captain Lord James Hay 1st Foot Guards – Lieutenant General Sir Charles Colville
Lieutenant Hon. Thomas Seymour Bathurst 1st Foot Guards – Lieutenant General Sir George Murray
Captain James Lindsay 1st Foot Guards – Major General Sir Peregrine Maitland

Brigade Major
Major James Gunthorpe 1st Foot Guards – Major General Sir Peregrine Maitland's 1st Brigade

Adjutant General Department
Lieutenant Colonel Sir Thomas Noel Hill 1st Foot Guards – AAG
Major Lord Charles Fitzroy 1st Foot Guards – AAG
Major Charles Bentinck Coldstream Foot Guards – AAG
Captain Philip Clarke 1st Foot Guards – DAAG

---

7. From 25 December 1816. G.O. 14 May 1817.

Quartermaster General Department
Colonel Hon. Alexander Abercromby Coldstream Foot Guards - AQMG
Lieutenant Colonel John Woodford 1st Foot Guards - AQMG
Lieutenant Colonel Sir Henry Hardinge 1st Foot Guards - AQMG
Captain William Moore 1st Foot Guards – DAQMG

Commandant of Valenciennes
Lieutenant Colonel Sir Robert Arbuthnot Coldstream Foot Guards

April 1817

Aides-de-Camp
Colonel Sir Colin Campbell Coldstream Foot Guards – Commandant at HQ
Lieutenant Colonel Sir Ulysses Burgh 1st Foot Guards – Duke of Wellington
Lieutenant Colonel John Fremantle Coldstream Foot Guards - Duke of Wellington
Lieutenant Colonel Chatham H. Churchill 1st Foot Guards – Lieutenant General Rowland Lord Hill
Captain Hon. Orlando Bridgeman 1st Foot Guards – Lieutenant General Rowland Lord Hill
Captain Francis Dawkins 1st Foot Guards – Lieutenant General Sir Henry Clinton
Captain Lord James Hay 1st Foot Guards – Lieutenant General Sir Charles Colville
Lieutenant Hon. Thomas Seymour Bathurst 1st Foot Guards – Lieutenant General Sir George Murray
Captain James Lindsay 1st Foot Guards – Major General Sir Peregrine Maitland

Brigade Major
Major James Gunthorpe 1st Foot Guards – Major General Sir Peregrine Maitland's 1st Brigade

Adjutant General Department
Lieutenant Colonel Sir Thomas Noel Hill 1st Foot Guards – AAG

Major Lord Charles Fitzroy 1st Foot Guards – AAG
Major Charles Bentinck Coldstream Foot Guards – AAG
Captain Philip Clarke 1st Foot Guards – DAAG

Quartermaster General Department

Colonel Hon. Alexander Abercromby Coldstream Foot Guards – AQMG
Lieutenant Colonel John Woodford 1st Foot Guards – AQMG
Lieutenant Colonel Sir Henry Hardinge 1st Foot Guards – AQMG
Captain William Moore 1st Foot Guards – DAQMG

Commandant of Valenciennes

Lieutenant Colonel Sir Robert Arbuthnot Coldstream Foot Guards

September 1818

Aides-de-Camp

Colonel Sir Colin Campbell Coldstream Foot Guards – Commandant at HQ
Lieutenant Colonel Sir Ulysses Burgh 1st Foot Guards – Duke of Wellington
Lieutenant Colonel John Fremantle Coldstream Foot Guards – Duke of Wellington
Lieutenant John Hobart Cradock 1st Foot Guards – Duke of Wellington
Lieutenant Colonel Chatham H. Churchill 1st Foot Guards – Lieutenant General Rowland Lord Hill
Captain Francis Dawkins 1st Foot Guards – Lieutenant General Sir Charles Colville
Lieutenant Hon. Thomas Seymour Bathurst 1st Foot Guards – Lieutenant General Sir George Murray
Lieutenant Algernon Greville 1st Foot Guards – Major General Sir John Lambert

Brigade Major

Major James Gunthorpe 1st Foot Guards – Major General Sir John Lambert's 1st Brigade

Adjutant General Department

Lieutenant Colonel John Waters Coldstream Foot Guards – AAG[8]
Lieutenant Colonel Sir Thomas Noel Hill 1st Foot Guards – AAG
Major Lord Charles Fitzroy 1st Foot Guards – AAG
Major Charles Bentinck Coldstream Foot Guards – AAG
Captain Philip Clarke 1st Foot Guards – DAAG

Quartermaster General Department

Colonel Hon. Alexander Abercromby Coldstream Foot Guards – AQMG
Lieutenant Colonel John Woodford 1st Foot Guards – AQMG
Lieutenant Colonel Sir Henry Hardinge 1st Foot Guards – AQMG
Captain William Moore 1st Foot Guards – DAQMG

Commandant of Valenciennes

Lieutenant Colonel Sir Robert Arbuthnot Coldstream Foot Guards

November 1818

Aides-de-Camp

Colonel Sir Colin Campbell Coldstream Foot Guards – Commandant at HQ
Lieutenant Colonel Sir Ulysses Burgh 1st Foot Guards – Duke of Wellington
Lieutenant Colonel John Fremantle Coldstream Foot Guards - Duke of Wellington
Lieutenant John Hobart Cradock 1st Foot Guards – Duke of Wellington
Lieutenant Colonel Chatham H. Churchill 1st Foot Guards – Lieutenant General Rowland Lord Hill
Captain Francis Dawkins 1st Foot Guards – Lieutenant General Sir Charles Colville
Lieutenant Hon. Thomas Seymour Bathurst 1st Foot Guards – Lieutenant General Sir George Murray

---

8. Lieutenant Colonel John Waters, half pay, served on staff of the Adjutant General's Department of Wellington's army at Waterloo in the Campaign of 1815 and subsequently in the AOOF. He only became a Guards officer on 15 May 1817 by exchange.

Brigade Major

Major James Gunthorpe 1st Foot Guards – Major General Sir John Lambert's 1st Brigade

Adjutant General Department

Lieutenant Colonel John Waters Coldstream Foot Guards – AAG
Lieutenant Colonel Sir Thomas Noel Hill 1st Foot Guards – AAG
Major Lord Charles Fitzroy 1st Foot Guards – AAG
Major Charles Bentinck Coldstream Foot Guards – AAG
Captain Philip Clarke 1st Foot Guards – DAAG

Quartermaster General Department

Colonel Hon. Alexander Abercromby Coldstream Foot Guards – AQMG
Lieutenant Colonel John Woodford 1st Foot Guards – AQMG
Lieutenant Colonel Sir Henry Hardinge 1st Foot Guards – AQMG
Captain William Moore 1st Foot Guards – DAQMG

Commandant of Valenciennes

Lieutenant Colonel Sir Robert Arbuthnot Coldstream Foot Guards

Appendix VIII

1st Foot Guards Casualties in the Waterloo Campaign

1st Foot Guards Sergeants, Trumpeters, Drummers, and Other Ranks Casualties (16-18 June 1815) as of 13 April 1816[1]

Battalion	Killed	Died of Wounds	Amputees	Discharged	Rejoined Regiment	Still in Hospital	Total	Missing Rejoined Battalion	MIA
2/1FG	61	29	6	44	197	26	302	10	38
3/1FG	71	30	14	48	361	33	486	3	32
Total	132	59	20	92	558	59	788	13	70

2nd Battalion 1st Foot Guards Losses by Company

Company	Officers	Sergeants	Corporals	Drummers	Privates	Total
Staff	2					2
Grenadier			2		13	15
1st	1	1			4	6
2nd			1		7	8
3rd					8	8
4th	1				14	15
5th					9	9
6th					14	14
7th			1		12	13
8th			1		8	9
Light	2				11	13
Total	6	1	5		100	112

1. WSD, Wellington, Duke of, Supplementary Dispatches .... Vol. 14, p.633. Many soldiers were listed as wounded and missing after the battles. It was only after this report was published in 1816 were they declared dead. Thus the numbers reported here will occasionally conflict with the numbers of soldiers we have identified by name.

2nd Battalion 1st Foot Guards Officers Killed at Quatre Bras

Name	Position	Date of Death	Cause of Death
Ensign Samuel Barrington	4th Company	16 June 1815	Shot in the head
Lieutenant Thomas Brown	Light Company	16 June 1815	
Ensign James Lord Hay	ADC to General Maitland	16 June 1815	Shot

2nd Battalion 1st Foot Guards Officers Wounded at Quatre Bras on 16 June 1815

Name	Position	Type of Wound
Major Henry Askew	Commander 2nd Battalion	Severely
Ensign Thomas E. Croft	3rd Company	Severely; Shot in the foot.
Ensign George Fludyer	2nd Company	Severely
Lieutenant Francis Luttrell	Light Company	Slightly
Lieutenant James Nixon	7th Company	Slightly[2]
Lieutenant James Simpson	6th Company	Severely

2nd Battalion 1st Foot Guards Enlisted Soldiers Killed at Quatre Bras

Company	Commander	Name
Grenadier	Captain Cooke	CPL George Fogg
		Private Samuel Beswick
		Private Thomas Dillworth
		Private Thomas Kellet
		Private John Moorhouse
		Private James Rushworth
		Private Alexander Taylor
		Private Charles Tyson
		Private William Whatmore
1st	Captain D'Oyly	SGT John Ford
		Private David Jarvis
		Private John Taylor
2nd	Captain Colquitt	Private Edmond Edmunds
		Private George Harris
		Private William King

---

2. Contusion in right instep and cut by a bayonet by own soldiers.

1ST FOOT GUARDS CASUALTIES IN THE WATERLOO CAMPAIGN

3rd	Captain Bradford	Private George Bridgeford
		Private William Clarke
		Private Abraham Hewlett
		Private James Payne
		Private John Stride
4th	Captain Hardinge	Private William Adams
		Private Simon Brown
		Private John Dryden
		Private John Firth
		Private John Lewis
		Private James Musson
5th	Captain Hill	Private Henry Forster
		Private William Haywood
6th	Captain Barclay	Private Andrew Anderson
		Private John Bamber
		Private William Bell
		Private Richard Broadbent
		Private Samuel Hopkins
		Private Charles Sheppard
7th	Captain Somerset	Private David Jenkins
		Private Hugh Riley
		Private James Tompkins
		Private William Walker
8th	Captain Burgh	Private James Bacon
		Private John Hunter
		Private John Jones
Light	Captain Milnes	Private John Butcher
		Private John Hood
		Private John Kershaw
		Private Barnett Mimmick

2nd Battalion 1st Foot Guards Serving Outside the Battalion Wounded at Ligny on 16 June 1815

Name	Position	Type of Wound
Lieutenant Colonel Henry Hardinge	Attached to Prussian Army	Lost his left hand

2nd Battalion 1st Foot Guards Officers Killed at Waterloo

Name	Position	Date of Death	Cause of Death
Captain Francis D'Oyly	1st Company	18 June 1815	Shot
Captain William Milnes	Light Company	20 June 1815	Died of Wounds

2nd Battalion 1st Foot Guards Officers Wounded at Waterloo 18 June 1815

Name	Position	Type of Wound
Captain Richard Cooke	Grenadier Company	Severely in the shoulder by canister round
Lieutenant Somerville Burgess	4th Company	Lost left leg with canister round
Ensign Henry Lascelles	King's Colours Bearer	Severely; in right side by exploding shell
Lieutenant Francis Luttrell	Light Company	Severely
Ensign George Mure	3rd Company	Severely
Ensign Daniel Tighe	8th Company	Slightly; finger on right hand by a musket ball

2nd Battalion 1st Foot Guards Enlisted Soldiers Killed at Waterloo

Company	Commander	Name
Grenadier	Captain Cooke	Private Isaac Helps
		Private Robert MacDonald
		Private Jacob Norris
		Private Edward Winpenny
1st	Captain D'Oyly	Private Nathaniel Stevens
2nd	Captain Colquitt	Private Henry Bolton
		Private John Guttridge
		Private John Rook
		Private Francis Sheppard
3rd	Captain Bradford	Private James May
4th	Captain Hardinge	Private John Allwright
		Private John Blythe
		Private John Green
		Private George Ingles
		Private Richard Lewis
		Private Watkin Williams
		Private Thomas Woodcock

1ST FOOT GUARDS CASUALTIES IN THE WATERLOO CAMPAIGN

5th	Captain Hill	Private William Thomas
		Private James Williams
		Private Peter Jones
		Private John Pritchett
		Private George Shepherd
6th	Captain Barclay	Private William Abraham
		Private Andrew Brown
		Private Abraham Crane
7th	Captain Somerset	Private CPL Thomas Johnson
		Private Adam Hood
		Private Richard Key
		Private George Pavior
		Private William Thorpe
8th	Captain Burgh	CPL Dan Lewis
		Private William Trescott
Light	Captain Milnes	Private Edward Cooper
		Private William Harrison
		Private John Smee

2nd Battalion 1st Foot Guards Serving Outside the Battalion Died of Wounds Received at Waterloo

Name	Position	Date of Death	Cause of Death
LTC Henry Bradford	AQMG	7 December 1816	At La Vachiere, near Lillière, France from wounds.

2nd Battalion 1st Foot Guards Enlisted Soldiers Who Died from Wounds[3]

Company	Commander	Name	Date of Death
Grenadier	Captain Cooke	CPL James Evans	9 July 1815
1st	Captain D'Oyly	Private Jonathan Rumbold	5 July 1815
2nd	Captain Colquitt	CPL Barnett Balintine	26 June 1815
3rd	Captain Bradford	Private John Newton	21 August 1815
		Private William Holding	1 September 1815
4th	Captain Hardinge	Private Thomas Hawkins	2 July 1815
		Private John Canney	14 July 1815
		Private Thomas Daniels	4 August 1816
5th	Captain Hill	Private George Hawkes	2 July 1815
		Private John Bannister	2 August 1815

3. Includes those wounded at Quatre Bras and Waterloo.

6th	Captain Barclay	Private Charles Curran	20 June 1815
		Private Zacharia Betts	26 June 1815
		Private John Clarke	27 June 1815
		Private David Davis	4 July 1815
		Private William Bate	29 August 1815
7th	Captain Somerset	Private Robert Young	2 July 1815
		Private Adam Ransom	14 July 1815
		Private William Punter	25 July 1815
		Private Robert Crowther	30 September 1815
8th	Captain Burgh	Private John Kirton	6 July 1815
		Private John Rossiter	6 July 1815
		Private James Moulcock	12 July 1815
		Private John Booth	27 July 1815
Light	Captain Milnes	Private Thomas Pring	17 June 1815
		Private John Revitt	2 July 1815
		Private Thomas Hickman	13 July 1815
		Private Thomas Ralphs	19 July 1815

3rd Battalion 1st Foot Guards Losses by Company

Company	Officers	Sergeants	Corporals	Drummers	Privates	Total
Staff	1					1
Grenadier		2		1	8	11
1st	2	1	1		11	15
2nd		1			9	10
3rd	1	1	1	13	16	17
4th		1	2		15	18
5th	1		2		15	18
6th					4	4
7th	1	1	1		8	11
8th			2		11	13
Light	1		1	1	16	18
Total	7	7	10	2	109	135

1ST FOOT GUARDS CASUALTIES IN THE WATERLOO CAMPAIGN

3rd Battalion 1st Foot Guards Officers Killed at Quatre Bras

Name	Position	Date of Death	Cause of Death
Lieutenant Robert Adair	1st Company	23 June 1815	Died of Wounds
Lieutenant Edward Grose	Light Company	16 June 1815	
Captain William Miller	7th Company	19 June 1815	Died of Wounds

3rd Battalion 1st Foot Guards Officers Wounded at Quatre Bras on 16 June 1815

Name	Position	Type of Wound
Ensign William Barton	2nd Company	Severely
Lieutenant Charles Ellis	Light Company	Severely contused
Lieutenant Thomas Streatfield	Grenadier Company	Severely
Major William Stuart	Battalion Commander	Severely lost his left arm
Captain Horatio Townshend	Grenadier Company	Severely

3rd Battalion 1st Foot Guards Enlisted Soldiers Killed at Quatre Bras

Company	Commander	Name
Grenadier	Captain Townshend	SGT Benjamin Verity
		Drummer Samuel Taylor
		Private John Clarke
		Private James Redyard
		Private Joseph Marshall
		Private Daniel Thomas
1st	Captain Stables	Private George Curtis
		Private James Taylor
2nd	Captain D'Oyly	SGT William Boulcott
		Private James Davies
		Private William Hutchins
		Private James Moore
3rd	Captain Jones	SGT James Brown
		Private Samuel Davies
4th	Captain Fead	SGT William Crews
		Private Bartholomew Doyle
		Private Richard Jones
		Private Joseph Lewis
		Private John Nutter
		Private John Sawkings

5th	Captain Thomas	CPL William Huntington
6th	Captain Reeve	None
7th	Captain Miller	Private James Cornthwaite
		Private George Jones
8th	Captain Stanhope	Private James Barnett
		Private Thomas Fowles
		Private Thomas Reece
Light	Captain Saltoun	CPL James Nixon
		Drummer Edward Smee
		Private John Chappell
		Private Robert Dethick
		Private Jonathan Fawcett
		Private John Gooday
		Private James Harbour
		Private John Pearson
		Private Robert Pegg
		Private Samuel Rogers

3rd Battalion 1st Foot Guards Officers Killed at Waterloo

Name	Position	Date of Death	Cause of Death
Captain Newton Chambers	ADC General Picton	18 June 1815	
Ensign Edward Pardoe	3rd Company	18 June 1815	Shot in the forehead
Captain Edward Stables	1st Company	19 June 1815	Died of Wounds
Captain Charles Thomas	5th Company	18 June 1815	

3rd Battalion 1st Foot Guards Officers Wounded at Waterloo 18 June 1815

Name	Position	Type of Wound
Ensign Robert Batty	Captain Stables's Company	Severely
Ensign Robert Bruce	4th Company	Severely. Grapeshot grazed his chest
Captain William Cameron	DAQMG	Lost his right arm
Lieutenant Robert Clements	7th Captain Miller's Company	Severely
Lieutenant Charles Ellis	Light Company	Severely
Captain George Fead	4th Company	Slightly
Captain Henry D'Oyly	2nd Company	Severely

3rd Battalion 1st Foot Guards Enlisted Soldiers Killed at Waterloo

Company	Commander	Name
Grenadier	Captain Townshend	Private James Allen
		Private James Collar
		Private William Pike
1st	Captain Stables	CPL William Thornhill
		Private Thomas Barnett
		Private John Boyle
		Private John Heritage
		Private John Hible
		Private Richard Morgan
2nd	Captain D'Oyly	Private Thomas Able
		Private Edward Horsley
		Private William Porter
		Private Joseph Young
3rd	Captain Jones	CPL Henry Nicholls
		Private Thomas Barker
		Private Stephen Clough
		Private William Dowling
		Private Moses Hilton
		Private William Musgrove
		Private William Nicholls
		Private Thomas Rease
		Private William Stackwood
		J Private James Walters
4th	Captain Fead	CPL Thomas Haywood
		CPL William Murray
		Private Jeremiah Cope
		Private William Asher
		Private Paul Gregory
		Private Thomas Heath
		Private William Hemsley
		Private Robert Howe
		Private William Oldham
		Private Benjamin Smith

5th	Captain Thomas	CPL John Lowder
		Private Symon Christian
		Private Thomas Cockett
		Private John Farrance
		Private John Hicks
		Private Thomas James
		Private William Payne
		Private John Protherow
		Private Francis Smith
		Private James Watson
6th	Captain Reeve	Private John Bridge
		Private Thomas Dunn
7th	Captain Miller	SGT Nathaniel Wilson
		CPL John Turner
		Private Richard Lathwood
		Private Evan Owen
		Private John Pritchard
		Private William Rippingale
		Private James Shedden
		Private Benjamin Thomas
8th	Captain Stanhope	Private CPL David Reece
		Private CPL William Swann
		Private James Dickinson
		Private Daniel Finch
		Private Samuel Harwood
		Private Thomas Nicholls
		Private William Rose
		Private Robert Walpole
		Private Edward Walker
		Private James Wilson
Light	Captain Saltoun	Private John Bigsworth
		Private David Liversage

3rd Battalion 1st Foot Guards Enlisted Soldiers Killed at Peronne

Company	Commander	Name
Light	Captain Saltoun	Private William Broomfield

3rd Battalion 1st Foot Guards Enlisted Soldiers Who Died from Wounds[4]

Company	Commander	Name	Date of Death
Grenadier	Captain Townshend	SGT John Wood	25 July 1815
		Private Robert Dorcey	1 July 1815
		Private Bartholomew Johnson	12 July 1815
1st	Captain Stables	SGT William Thomas	16 July 1815
		Private Francis Gray	19 June 1815
		Private Thomas Stevens	23 July 1815
		Private James Finlow	24 July 1815
		Private Matthew Jenkins	20 August 1815
2nd	Captain D'Oyly	Private Thomas Barratt	18 June 1815
		Private Samuel Beadle	27 June 1815
3rd	Captain Jones	Private Richard Morgan	17 June 1815
		Private Peter Hampson	24 June 1815
		Private Joseph Pickles	26 July 1815
		Private Orr McFarlane	24 August 1815
4th	Captain Fead	Private John Walker	10 July 1815
		Private James Byers	28 November 1815
5th	Captain Thomas	Private John Petty	2 July 1815
		Private John Sweeper	9 July 1815
		Private George Smith	15 July 1815
		Private Donald Swaffer	16 July 1815
		Private Joseph Walter	3 August 1815
		Private Joseph Brown	26 August 1816
6th	Captain Reeve	Thomas Goodwin	12 July 1815
		Thomas Lockwood	18 July 1815
7th	Captain Miller		
8th	Captain Stanhope		
Light	Captain Saltoun	Private Samuel Hatton	7 July 1815
		Private William Halliday	9 July 1815
		Private Richard Rogers	14 Jul 1815
		Private William Hall	16 August 1815

4. Includes those wounded at Quatre Bras and Waterloo.

1st Foot Guards Officers Serving Outside Their Battalions Wounded at Waterloo

Name	Position	Type of Wound
Captain Orlando Bridgeman (1st Bn)	Extra ADC to Lieutenant General Hill	Badly bruised by canister round
Captain William Cameron (3rd Bn)	DAQMG	Lost right arm
LTC Lord Fitzroy Somerset (3rd Bn)	Wellington's Military Secretary	Lost right arm

Appendix IX

Coldstream Guards Casualties in the Waterloo Campaign

Sergeants, Trumpeters, Drummers, and Other Ranks Casualties (16 – 18 June 1815) as of 13 April 1816[1]

Killed	Died of Wounds	Amputees	Discharged	Rejoined Regiment	Still in Hospital	Total	Missing Rejoined Rgt	MIA
47	26	6	0	208	1	241	4	0

Killed or Died of Wounds

Company	Officers	Sergeants	Corporals	Drummers	Privates	Total
Grenadier	1	1	1	-	13	16
1st					7	7
2nd		2			7	9
3rd					5	5
4th					11	12
5th	1				6	6
6th					3	3
7th					3	3
8th					2	2
Light		1	3		8	12
Total	2	4	4		65	75

1. *WSD*, Wellington, Duke of, *Supplementary Dispatches* ...Vol. 14, p.633.

2nd Battalion Coldstream Guards Officers Killed at Waterloo on 18 June 1815

Name	Position	Date of Death	Cause of Death
Lieutenant John Blackman	Grenadier Company	18 June 1815	Shot in head
Lieutenant Edward Sumner	5th Company	26 June 1815	Died of Wounds

2nd Battalion Coldstream Guards Officers Wounded at Waterloo on 18 June 1815

Name	Position	Type of Wound
Colonel Alexander Abercromby	AQMG	Slightly
Ensign Henry Griffiths	8th Company	Severely
Captain Daniel Mackinnon	Grenadier Company	Severely
Ensign John Montagu	1st Company	Severely
Lieutenant Robert Moore	Light Company	Severely
Ensign Henry Vane	3rd Company	Severely
Captain Henry Wyndham	6th Company	Severely

COLDSTREAM GUARDS CASUALTIES IN THE WATERLOO CAMPAIGN

2nd Battalion Coldstream Guards Enlisted Soldiers Killed at Waterloo on 18 June 1815

Company	Commander	Killed 18 June	Died of Wounds	Date of Death
Grenadier	CPT Mackinnon	Sergeant Abraham Harris	Private James Watson	5 July 1815
		Corporal Robert Bradley	Private Christopher David	15 August 1815
		Private William Carpenter	Private John Lomax	4 September 1815
		Private John Evan	Private Robert Pooley	25 September 1815
		Private John Lewis	Private Joseph Batsevin	26 November 1815
		Private Richard Masham	Private Charles Lancaster	13 December 1815
		Private William Martin		
		Private George Read		
		Private John Stewart		
1st	CPT Macdonell	Private John Edward	Private Aldous Norman	22 July 1815
		Private Thomas Evans		
		Private John London		
		Private William Leach		
		Private Andrew Russell		
		Private Joseph Smith		
2nd	CPT Abercromby	Private James Hilton	Sergeant Thomas James	29 July 1815
		Private John Lampey	Sergeant Henry Maule	26 September 1815
		Private John Milwood	Private Joseph Bevens	21 July 1815
		Private William Rathbone	Private Frank Chappelle	21 July 1815
		Private John Trelores		

3rd	CPT Gomm	Private William Williams	
		Private John Murray	6 July 1815
		Private Charles Talbott	11 July 1815
		Private John Sterling	21 October 1815
		Private Adam Belshaw	7 November 1815
4th	CPT Acheson	Private Thomas Davidson	23 June 1815
		Private Henry Dukes	29 July 1815
		Private Samuel Lacey	
		Private Thomas Petty	
		Private Thomas Richards	
		Private James Ratcliffe	17 September 1815
		Private Isaac Swain	26 November 1815
5th	CPT Pakenham	Private Thomas Morgan	
		Private James Philipan	
		Private John Robson	
		Private Charles Smith	
		Private James Thurlow	
		Private David Williams	
6th	CPT Wyndham	Private John Brown	
		Private William Card	
		Private George Gordon	
		Private David Morgan	
		Private John Pipes	
		Private John Till	
		Private William Anster	15 July 1815
		Private John Ineson	26 July 1815

COLDSTREAM GUARDS CASUALTIES IN THE WATERLOO CAMPAIGN

7th	CPT Arbuthnot	Private Edward Hughes	
		Private Patrick Thompson	
8th	CPT Dawkins	None	
Light	CPT Walpole	Corporal Joseph Dobinson	
		Corporal Thomas Henderson	
		Private John Beckey	
		Private John Frost	
		Private Richard Sharman	
		Private John Webster	
		Private Edward Mann	
		Private Thomas Smith	
		Private Carsoff Thomas	
		Private John Cooke	5 September 1815
		Private John Woodson	7 July 1815
		Private William Middleton	7 July 1815
		Sergeant Richard Seabury	25 October 1815
		Corporal Joseph Graham	23 June 1815
		Private Henry Hudson	26 October 1815

339

Appendix X

3rd Foot Guards Casualties in the Waterloo Campaign

2nd Battalion 3rd Foot Guards Sergeants, Trumpeters, Drummers, and Other Ranks Casualties (16 – 18 June 1815) as of 13 April 1816[1]

KIA	DoW	Amputees	Discharged	Rejoined Regiment	Still in Hospital	Total	Missing Rejoined Rgt	MIA
39	47	12	21	96	19	195	17	1

Killed or Died of Wounds

Company	Officers	Sergeants	Corporals	Drummers	Privates	Total
Staff	3					1
Grenadier	2		1		9	12
1st	1	1			8	10
2nd					5	5
3rd			1		4	5
4th	1				4	5
5th					3	4
6th	1	2	2		8	12
7th					6	8
8th	1	1			19	21
Light			1		10	11
Total	9	4	5		76	94

---

1. *WSD*, Wellington, Duke of, *Supplementary Dispatches...* Vol. 14, p.633.

2nd Battalion 3rd Foot Guards Officers Killed at Waterloo

Name	Position	Date of Death	Cause of Death
Lieutenant John Ashton	Grenadier Company	18 June 1815	Shot
LTC Charles Canning	ADC to Wellington	18 June 1815	Died of Wounds
Lieutenant Thomas Craufurd	1st Company	18 June 1815	Shot
Lieutenant Hasting Forbes	6th Company	18 June 1815	Shot
LTC Alexander Gordon	ADC to Wellington	19 June 1815	Died of wounds
Lieutenant Robert Hesketh	Grenadier Company	15 September 1828	Died of wounds
Lieutenant Hugh Montgomerie	8th Company	2 May 1817	Died of Wounds
Ensign Charles Simpson	4th Company	18 June 1815	Died of Wounds
Captain William Stothert	Brigade Major 2nd Brigade	23 June 1815	Died of wounds

2nd Battalion 3rd Foot Guards Officers Wounded at Waterloo 18 June 1815

Name	Position	Type of Wound
Ensign David Baird	7th Company	Severely
Captain Edward Bowater	1st Company	Severely
Captain Charles Dashwood	Light Company	Severely
Lieutenant George Evelyn	Light Company	Severely
Ensign Charles Lake	7th Company	Slightly
Captain Charles West	8th Company	Severely

2nd Battalion 3rd Foot Guards Enlisted Soldiers Killed at Waterloo on 18 June 1815

Company	Commander	Killed 18 June	Died of Wounds	Date of Death
Grenadier	CPT Home	Private James Allsop	Corporal William Vincent	9 July 1815
		Private John Cassett	Private Donald McBeth	25 June 1815
		Private Thomas Gawkers	Private John Brooks	25 June 1815
		Private Thomas Gange	Private Henry Baineslough	25 June 1815
		Private George Green	Private James Famous	25 June 1816
		Private William Landers	Private William Reed	9 July 1815
			Private William Hickam	14 July 1815
			Private Benjamin Merrick	8 October 1815
			Private Robert Watts	2 December 1815
			Private John Burrows	16 December 1815
1st	CPT Bowater	Sergeant Thomas Selwyn	Private John Williams	24 July 1815
		Private William Clayton	Private William Hipkiss	5 August 1815
		Private William Brook		
		Private Benjamin Boyer		
		Private Abraham Hunter		
		Private James Kent		
		Private William Lister		
2nd	CPT Dashwood	Private John Lee	Private Charles Edgards	1 July 1815
			Private Michael M'Kenley	5 August 1815
			Private Joseph Shaw	9 August 1815
			Private Thomas Wynne	24 August 1815

3RD FOOT GUARDS CASUALTIES IN THE WATERLOO CAMPAIGN

3rd	CPT Mercer	Private Benjamin Blizzard	
		Corporal William Woodward	14 December 1815
		Private Isaac Philpott	4 July 1815
		Private Stephan Hunt	5 August 1815
		Private Douglas West	20 November 1815
4th	CPT Keate	Private Stephen Grigsby	
		Private James Arnoth	
		Private John Hawkins	2 December 1815
		Private James Baker	7 December 1815
5th	CPT Canning	None	
		Private George Asborne	25 July 1815
		Private John Symington	29 July 1815
		Private John Worthing	21 November 1815
6th	CPT Rooke	Sergeant James Laing	
		Corporal John Elwell	
		Private George Russell	
		Private Charles Newmann	
		Private Michael Connelly	
		Corporal Charles Anderson	29 July 1815
		Private John Kirk	25 June 1815
		Private John Day	4 July 1815
		Private William Bramley	5 July 1815
		Private Nugent Bishop	22 July 1815
		Private Richard Brennan	21 August 1815
7th	CPT Gordon	Private John Bainbridge	
		Private Edward Bambridge	
		Private Henry Hubbard	
		Private Isaac Houselander	29 June 1815
		Private Elijah Tugdy	9 October 1815
		Private Benjamin Briscoe	21 November 1815

8th	CPT West	Sergeant Alexander Sutherland	24 September 1815
		Private William Brunton	25 June 1815
		Private Richard Holmes	30 June 1815
		Private Thomas Dickman	3 July 1815
		Private Thomas Gale	5 July 1815
		Private Thomas Harvett	15 July 1815
		Private James William	22 July 1815
		Private Peter Deanne	22 July 1815
		Private Thomas Peters	24 September 1815
		Private George Golding	24 September 1815
		Private John Jones	24 September 1815
		Private William Robinson	24 September 1815
		Private John Tomkinson	
		Private Richard Scudder	
		Private John Walker	
		Private Thomas Butler	
		Private John Jackson	
		Private Ralph Mitchell	
		Private William Cartwright	
		Private Alexander Hickham	
Light	CPT Master[2]	Corporal James Twigg	10 July 1815
		Private George Aspinall	22 July 1815
		Private John Birch	16 October 1815
		Private Richard Cleevesley	21 November 1815
		Private Joseph Peate	24 December 1815
		Private Samuel Landiford	
		Private Henry Shaw	
		Private Thomas Morgan	
		Private John Caddock	
		Private William Drury	
		Private Adam Allen	

2. Commanded by Captain Dashwood at Waterloo.

Appendix XI

British Awards

Dual Rank

All of the ensigns at the time **in** the three Guards Regiments, **and those subsequently appointed,** were granted a step in substantive rank in the Army becoming ensign and lieutenant in the regiment. This was similar to the dual rank held by the lieutenants and captains in the regiments. This was granted by the Prince Regent on 29 July 1815.

Battle Honour

The three Guards regiments were granted the battle honour of Waterloo to be worn on their colours and appointments. This was granted on 23 November 1815 and announced by the War Office on 23 December 1815.

Regimental Distinction

On 29 July 1815, the Prince Regent approved of the 1st Foot Guards being made a Regiment of Grenadiers and styled as 'The 1st or Grenadier Regiment of Foot Guards'. This was in commemoration of their having defeated the Grenadiers of the French Imperial Guards at Waterloo. This was, of course, an error as they defeated the Chasseurs and not the French Grenadiers.

Rewards For Service

By Circular Letter No. 287, of 31 July 1815, the Prince Regent ordered a number of rewards be given to the officers and men of the British Army for their services on the 16th, 17th and 18th of June.[1]

---

1. Written as 'who served in the Battle of Waterloo, or in any of the actions which immediately preceded it'.

They included increasing the amount of a wound pension for loss of an eye or limb or equivalent wound to loss of a limb awarded to the officers by allowing the pension to increase with the subsequent progressive promotion of the officers in Army rank. Officers already on the pension list were to have their augmentation dated 18 June 1815.[2]

The next was to allow every subaltern in the army and every ensign in the Foot Guards, who fought on the days specified, to add two years to his length of service in determining his pay as a lieutenant of seven years' standing; and to receive an additional 1 shilling per day once he had served five years as a lieutenant.

Lastly, the soldiers who served on the days specified would be carried on the muster rolls and pay lists of their Corps as 'Waterloo' men and to add two years service in determining an increase in pay or for a pension when discharged.

Waterloo Medal

In a Memorandum of 10 March 1816, it was announced that a medal to commemorate the battle would be awarded to every officer, non-commissioned officer and soldier present. This was announced on 23 April 1816. The award of the medal was expanded to include those present at the battles of Quatre Bras and Ligny, the retreat on 17 June, and to those stationed at Hal and Tubize. The medal was awarded to the next of kin of those who died before the medal was distributed.

The 1st Foot Guards sent in all of the names and had 2,141 recipients. Both the Coldstream Foot Guards and the 3rd Foot Guards sent in only the names of the survivors. The Coldstream Foot Guards had 907 recipients and the 3rd Foot Guards had 1,061 recipients.

Officers who received the medal would have a 'W' placed before their name in the Army Lists.

Brevet Promotion

The following officers were promoted to brevet rank in the Army for their service in the campaign of 1815. The promotions dated 18 June 1815.

---

2. Parsimonious as all governments are, this provision was rescinded by Circular Letter No. 362, 30 July 1817 for all subsequent wounds.

Brevet Lieutenant Colonel in the Army:
>Brevet Major Chatham Churchill 1st Foot Guards

Brevet Major in the Army[3]:

>Captain James Gunthorpe 1st Foot Guards
>Captain Robert Clements 1st Foot Guards
>Captain Lord Charles Fitzroy 1st Foot Guards
>Captain Robert Ellison 1st Foot Guards
>Captain George Bowles Coldstream Foot Guards
>Captain Charles Bentinck Coldstream Foot Guards
>Captain William Drummond 3rd Foot Guards

Lieutenant Colonel Lord Fitzroy Somerset 1st Foot Guards was promoted a brevet colonel in the Army as an Extra ADC to the Prince Regent 28 August 1815.

Captain Robert Hesketh 3rd Foot Guards promoted brevet major in the Army 4 December 1815.

Knight Commander of the Order of the Bath

Major General George Cooke was made a Knight on 20 June 1815. Major General Peregrine Maitland was made a Knight on 22 June 1815.

Companion of the Order of the Bath

The following officers were made a Companion of the Order of the Bath being nominated by the Duke of Wellington for their service on 16 and 18 June 1815. The award was dated 22 June 1815.

>*Brevet Colonel Henry Askew 1st Foot Guards
>*Brevet Colonel Hon. William Stuart 1st Foot Guards[4]
>Lieutenant Colonel Richard Cooke 1st Foot Guards
>Lieutenant Colonel George Fead 1st Foot Guards

---

3. Captain Henry Dumaresq, 9th Foot, ADC to General Byng was promoted brevet major 18 June 1815.
4. Although nominated a CB for 4 June 1815, Stuart's CB was dated 22 June 1815.

Lieutenant Colonel Alexander Lord Saltoun 1st Foot Guards
Lieutenant Colonel Goodwin Colquitt 1st Foot Guards[5]
Lieutenant Colonel Delancey Barclay 1st Foot Guards
*Brevet Colonel Hon. Alexander Abercromby Coldstream Foot Guards
*Brevet Colonel Alexander Woodford Coldstream Foot Guards
Lieutenant Colonel James Macdonell Coldstream Foot Guards
Brevet Lieutenant Colonel John Fremantle Coldstream Foot Guards
*Brevet Colonel Francis Hepburn 3rd Foot Guards
Lieutenant Colonel Henry Rooke 3rd Foot Guards
Lieutenant Colonel Douglas Mercer 3rd Foot Guards
*Lieutenant Colonel Stephen Adye RA
Brevet Major Henry Kuhlmann King's German Artillery

---

* Already awarded a CB 4 June 1815 for former service. This was not known when Wellington made his nominations.

Prize Money

Prize money was awarded on 24 June 1817.
    General officers - £1274 10s 10d
    Colonels and field officers - £433 2s 5d
    Captains - £90 7s 4d
    Subalterns - £34 14s 9d
    Sergeants - £19 4s 4d
    Corporals, drummers, privates - £2 11s 4d

---

5. Although nominated a CB for 22 June 1815, Colquitt's CB was dated 4 June 1815.

Appendix XII

Foreign Awards

A number of foreign sovereigns awarded their Orders of Knighthood to British officers to commemorate their service at Waterloo. The decision of who were to receive the awards was left to the Duke of Wellington to decide. He awarded a number to Guards officers. Although the officers received permission to wear the insignia of the Orders of Knighthood, they were not permitted to be considered as British Knights or be addressed as 'Sir'.

Austria: Knight of the Order of Maria Theresa

Colonel Lord Fitzroy Somerset 1st Foot Guards
Lieutenant Colonel Alexander Lord Saltoun 1st Foot Guards
Colonel Hon. Alexander Abercromby Coldstream Foot Guards
Colonel Sir Colin Campbell Coldstream Foot Guards
Colonel Alexander Woodford Coldstream Foot Guards
Lieutenant Colonel James Macdonell Coldstream Foot Guards

Bavaria: Knight of the Order of Maximilian Joseph

Colonel Lord Fitzroy Somerset 1st Foot Guards
Lieutenant Colonel Sir Thomas Hill 1st Foot Guards
Colonel Sir Colin Campbell Coldstream Foot Guards
Lieutenant Colonel John Fremantle Coldstream Foot Guards

Colonel Hon. Arthur Upton 1st Foot Guards was awarded the Order for his service with the Bavarian Army in the campaign of 1815.

Netherlands: Military Order of William 4th Class

Colonel Hon. William Stuart 1st Foot Guards
Lieutenant Colonel Sir Henry Bradford 1st Foot Guards
Colonel Francis Hepburn 3rd Foot Guards

Russia: Order of Saint Anne 2nd Class

Lieutenant Colonel Sir William Gomm Coldstream Foot Guards

Russia: Order of Saint George 4th Class

Colonel Lord Fitzroy Somerset 1st Foot Guards
Lieutenant Colonel Alexander Lord Saltoun 1st Foot Guards
Colonel Hon. Alexander Abercromby Coldstream Foot Guards
Colonel Sir Colin Campbell Coldstream Foot Guards
Colonel Alexander Woodford Coldstream Foot Guards

Russia: Order of Saint Vladimir 4th Class

Lieutenant Colonel Richard Cooke 1st Foot Guards
Lieutenant Colonel Sir Henry Bradford 1st Foot Guards
Lieutenant Colonel James Macdonell Coldstream Foot Guards
Colonel Francis Hepburn 3rd Foot Guards

Appendix XIII

Promotions within the Guards Regiments Caused by Deaths

By long-standing tradition, promotions to fill vacancies caused by deaths in battle were filled by regimental seniority. The patronage to fill these vacancies belonged to the Commander-in-Chief of the Army. In 1815, this office was held by Field Marshal HRH Prince Frederick Duke of York. The Duke was also the senior regimental colonel of the Foot Guards. This would doubly ensure that the promotions to fill the vacancies in the Foot Guards went in the regiment per tradition.

The Guards suffered heavy losses in the ranks of its officers with a total of twenty-one officers killed or died of wounds at the battles of Quatre Bras and Waterloo. The following officers were promoted in rank in the regiment to fill these vacancies. With 'dual' rank they were also promoted in higher rank in the Army. The date given is the date of the promotion.

1st Foot Guards

Lieutenant to captain
    Alexander Higginson vice Edward Stables KIA 1 July
    Thomas Streatfield vice William Miller DoW 2 July
    Thomas H. Davies vice William Milnes DoW 3 July
    Charles Allix vice Francis D'Oyly KIA 4 July
    Thomas Brooke vice Charles Thomas KIA 5 July

Ensign to lieutenant
    Rees Gronow vice Edward Grose KIA 28 June
    Robert Batty vice Newton Chambers KIA 29 June
    John Home vice Thomas Brown KIA 30 June
    Richard Master vice Robert Adair DoW 1 July

Augustus Dashwood vice Alexander Higginson 2 July
William Barton vice Thomas Streatfield 3 July
John Honyman vice Thomas Davies 4 July
Henry Vernon vice Charles Allix 5 July
Courtney Chambers vice Thomas Brooke 6 July

Ensign
Edmund Bridgeman vice James Lord Hay KIA 30 June
Ferrars Loftus vice Samuel Barrington KIA 1 July
Henry Wombwell vice Edward Pardoe KIA 2 July
John Law vice Rees Gronow 3 July
Charles Blane vice Robert Batty 4 July
Henry Langrishe vice John Home 5 July
Felix Manners vice Richard Master 6 July
John Hobart Cradock vice Augustus Dashwood 13 July
George Harrington Hudson vice William Barton 19 July
Arthur Manners vice John Honyman 24 August
Edward Douglas vice Henry Vernon 31 August
Montagu Chambers vice Courtney Chambers 9 November

Adjutant: Lieutenant Lonsdale Boldero vice Charles Allix promoted 6 July

Coldstream Foot Guards

Lieutenant to captain
   None

Ensign to lieutenant
   Edward Clifton vice John Blackman KIA 6 July
   Henry Salwey vice Edward Sumner DoW 20 July

Ensign
   John Jenkinson vice Edward Clifton 6 July
   William Cornwall vice Henry Salwey 10 August
   Henry Murray vice George Buckley deceased 21 September[1]

---

1. Ensign Buckley died of 'battle' fatigue at Paris on 16 August.

3rd Foot Guards

Lieutenant to captain
William Scott vice Alexander Gordon DoW 5 July
Hugh Seymour vice Charles Canning DoW 6 July

Ensign to lieutenant
Charles Lake vice Hastings Forbes KIA 2 July
Edward Stopford vice Thomas Craufurd KIA 3 July
Barclay Drummond vice John Ashton KIA 4 July
William Grant vice William Scott 5 July
George Standen vice Hugh Seymour 6 July
Henry Paxton vice William Stothert DoW 13 July

Ensign
Lieutenant George L'Estrange vice Charles Lake 2 July[2]
Ensign Charles Fraser vice Edward Stopford 3 July[3]
Frederick Turner vice Barclay Drummond 4 July
Henry Leach vice William Grant 5 July
Charles Fairfield vice George Standen 6 July
Thomas Gordon vice Charles Simpson DoW 13 July
Robert Gordon vice Henry Paxton 14 July

Adjutant: Lieutenant Charles Sandes vice William Stothert DoW 13 July

---

2. From h.p. 31st Foot.
3. From 14th Foot.

Appendix XIV

Other Officer Promotions in the Guards Regiments in 1815

During the course of 1815, officers were promoted into, or joined, the Foot Guards regiments in addition to those promoted to fill the death vacancies of Quatre Bras and Waterloo. Only one of these officers served in those two battles.[1]

Where an officer was promoted in 1814 and his subsequent vacant position was filled in 1815, only the newly promoted officer's date in 1815 is given. [e.g. James Talbot was promoted in 1815 filling the vacant position created by the promotion of Ensign Charles Lascelles which was dated 9 June 1814.]

1st Foot Guards

Captain Francis John Davies[2] to be lieutenant and captain by exchange with Lieutenant and Captain Sir Henry Lambert, Baronet 13 April.

James Talbot to be ensign, without purchase, vice Ensign Charles Lascelles promoted lieutenant and captain 16 February.

Philip Spencer Stanhope to be ensign, without purchase, vice Ensign Somerville Burgess promoted lieutenant and captain 30 March.

Francis Glanville to be ensign, without purchase, vice Ensign William Johnstone promoted lieutenant and captain 20 April.

---

1. Ensign James Talbot 1st Foot Guards.
2. From 69th Foot.

John Lyster to be ensign, without purchase, vice Ensign James Nixon promoted lieutenant and captain 27 April.

Geoffrey Nightingale to be ensign, without purchase, vice Ensign Frederick Gould resigned his commission 20 July.

Quartermaster Sergeant John Payne to be quartermaster vice George Hodder placed on the Retired List 31 August.

Coldstream Foot Guards

Joseph Henry Blake 1st Baron Wallscourt to be ensign, without purchase, vice Ensign Thomas Chaplin promoted lieutenant and captain 5 January.

Jasper Hall to be ensign, by purchase, vice Ensign Francis Eyre retired by sale of his commission 1 June.

Ensign and Lieutenant George Gould Morgan to be lieutenant and captain, without purchase, vice Lieutenant and Captain Edward Lascelles deceased 26 October.

Edward John Duke to be ensign and lieutenant, without purchase, vice Ensign and Lieutenant George Gould Morgan promoted lieutenant and captain 26 October.

Lieutenant and Captain John Prince to be adjutant vice Lieutenant and Captain Edward Lascelles deceased 26 October.

Ensign and Lieutenant Thomas Duncombe to be lieutenant and captain, without purchase, vice George Percival deceased 23 November.

Joseph Tharp to be ensign and lieutenant, without purchase, vice Ensign and Lieutenant Thomas Duncombe promoted lieutenant and captain 23 November.

Ensign and Lieutenant James Forbes to be lieutenant and captain, without purchase, vice Lieutenant and Captain William Stothert, retired 14 December.

Percy Ashburnham[3] to be ensign and lieutenant, by purchase, vice Ensign and Lieutenant James Forbes promoted lieutenant and captain 28 December.

---

3. Ashburnham was a Gentleman Cadet of the Royal Military College.

3rd Foot Guards

Richard Armit to be ensign, by purchase, vice Ensign James Poingdestre retired by sale of his commission 2 March.

Swindal Norval[4] to be ensign, by purchase, vice Ensign George Tuffnell promoted lieutenant and captain 13 April.

Quartermaster Sergeant Charles Weston to be quartermaster vice John Skuce deceased 28 December.

---

4. Norval was a Gentleman Cadet of the Royal Military College.

Appendix XV

The Waterloo Dispatch

In the early morning of 19 June 1815, Wellington sat in his headquarters in the village of Waterloo and penned his 'Waterloo Dispatch'. In it he summarized the course of the fighting over the last three days for the British Government ending with the victory in the Battle of Waterloo. He took the time to mention the Guards Division and its actions during the fighting. The dispatch was published in its entirety in *The London Gazette* on Thursday 22 June 1815.[1]

He praised the general officers by name for their conduct at Quatre Bras, 'highly distinguished themselves, Lieutenant-General Cooke,[2] and Major-Generals Maitland and Byng, as they successively arrived.'[3]

He followed this by describing the defence of Hougoumont. The French, 'commenced a furious attack upon our post of Hougoumont. I had occupied that post with a detachment from General Byng's brigade, which was in position in its rear; and it was for some time under the command of Lieutenant Colonel Macdonel [sic] and afterwards of Colonel Home; and I am happy to add, that it was maintained throughout the day by the utmost gallantry, by these brave troops, notwithstanding the repeated efforts of large bodies of the enemy to obtain possession of it.'[4]

Wellington did not mention the Guards nor any other regiments in the defeat of the Imperial Guard [which he also did not mention by name].

---

1. *The London Gazette*, issue 17028, pp.1213-1215.
2. Wellington was incorrect, Cooke was only a major general during the campaign.
3. *The London Gazette*, issue 17028, p.1214.
4. ibid.

He ended by again praising the general officers commanding and the Guards at Waterloo. 'The division of Guards, under Lieutenant General Cooke, who is severely wounded; Major General Maitland and Major General Byng, set an example which was followed by all; and there is no Officer, nor description of troops, that did not behave well.'[5]

---

5. ibid, p.1215.

Bibliography

Adkin, Mark, *The Waterloo Companion*. Mechanicsburg: Stackpole, 2001.

Army Lists, various years.

Bamford, Andrew, *A Bold and Ambitious Enterprise: the British Army in the Low Countries 1813 – 1814*. Barnsley: Frontline, 2013.

Blackman, John, *'It all Culminated at Hougoumont': the Letters of Captain John Lucie Blackman, Coldstream Guards 1812-15*. Gareth Glover (ed.), Godmanchester: Ken Trotman, 2009.

Booth, John, *The Battle of Waterloo: Containing the Accounts Published by Authority, British and Foreign*. London: J. Booth, 1815.

Bowles, George, *A Guards Officer in the Peninsula and at Waterloo: the Letters of Captain George Bowles, Coldstream Guards. 1807-1819*. Gareth Glover (ed.), Godmanchester: Ken Trotman, 2008.

Bridgeman, Orlando, *A Young Gentleman at War: the Letters of Captain Orlando Bridgeman 1st Foot Guards in the Peninsula and at Waterloo 1812 – 15*. Gareth Glover (ed.). Godmanchester: Ken Trotman, 2008.

Burnham, Robert and McGuigan, Ron, *The British Army against Napoleon: Facts, Lists, and Trivia 1805-1815*. Barnsley: Frontline, 2010.

Caldwell, George and Cooper, Robert, *Rifles at Waterloo*. Bugle Horn, 1995.

Capel, Caroline, *The Capel Letters*. London: Jonathan Cape, 1955.

Chambers, Barbara, *The Men of the 1st Foot Guards at Waterloo and Beyond*. 2 vols. Letchworth Garden City: Privately Published; 2003.

Chandler, David, *The Campaigns of Napoleon*. New York: MacMillan, 1966.

Charras, Jean, *Histoire de la Campagne de 1815*. Brussels: Meline, 1857.

Clarke, Hewson, *History of the War from the Commencement of the French Revolution to the Present Time*. 3 vols. London: Kinnersley, 1816.

Clay, Mathew, *Narrative of the Battle of Quatre Bras & Waterloo with the Defence of Hougoumont*. Gareth Glover (ed.). Godmanchester: Ken Trotman; 2006.

Clinton, Henry, *The Correspondence of Sir Henry Clinton in the Waterloo Campaign*. 2 vols. Gareth Glover (ed.). Godmanchester: Ken Trotman, 2015.

Connolly, T., *History of the Royal Sappers and Miners*. 2 vols. London: Longman, Brown, Green, Longmans and Roberts, 1857.

Cook, John, and Burnham, Robert, 'Nicknames of British Units during the Napoleonic Wars' The Napoleon Series Website. June 2013.

Cotton, Edward, *A Voice from Waterloo*. East Ardsley: EP, 1974.

Crumplin, Michael, *Bloody Fields of Waterloo: Medical Support at Wellington's Greatest Battle*. Godmanchester: Ken Trotman, 2015.

Crumplin, Michael, *Guthrie's War: a Surgeon of the Peninsula & Waterloo*. Barnsley: Pen & Sword, 2010.

Dalton, Charles, *The Waterloo Roll Call*. London: Arms and Armour, 1971.

Dawson, Paul L., *Au Gallop! Horses and Riders of Napoleon's Army*. Stockton-on-Tees: Black Tent, 2013.

Dawson, Paul L., *Au Pas de Charge! Napoleon's Cavalry at Waterloo*. Stockton-on-Tees: Black Tent, 2015.

Dawson, Paul L., *Crippled Splendour: the French Cavalry from Valmy to Toulouse*. Stockton-on-Tees: Black Tent, 2016.

de Calonne, Albéric, *Histoire de la ville d'Amiens*. Paris: Alphonse Picard, 1906.

De Fonblanque, Edward, *Administration and Organization of the British Army, with Especial Reference to Finance and Supply*. London: Longman, Brown, Green, Longmans, and Roberts, 1858.

Dournel, Jacques, *Histoire générale de Péronne*. Péronne: J. Quenton, 1879.

Du Fresnel, Henri, *Un Régiment à Travers l'Histoire: le 76e, ex-ler Léger*. Paris: E. Flammarion, 1894.

Field, Andrew, *Grouchy's Waterloo: the Battles of Ligny and Wavre*. Barnsley: Pen & Sword, 2017.

Field, Andrew, *Prelude to Waterloo: Quatre Bras – The French Perspective*. Barnsley: Pen & Sword, 2014.

Field, Andrew, *Waterloo: the French Perspective*. Barnsley: Pen & Sword, 2015.

Fletcher, Ian and Pouler, Ron, *'Gentlemen's Sons' the Guards in the Peninsula and Waterloo, 1808-1815*. Tunbridge Wells: Spellmount, 1992.

Floud, Roderick and Harris, Bernard, 'Health, Height, and Welfare: Britain, 1700 – 1980', *Health and Welfare during Industrialization*. Chicago: University of Chicago, January 1997, pp.91-126

Fortescue, John W., *A History of the British Army*. 18 vols. Uckfield: Naval and Military Press, 2004.

Fortescue, John W., *The County Lieutenancies and the Army: 1803 - 1814* London: MacMillan, 1909.

Fosten, Bryan, *Soldiers of the Napoleonic Wars: British Foot Guards at Waterloo June 1815*. 4 vols. New Malden: Almark, 1967.

Fraser, Alexander, *The Frasers of Philorth*. 3 vols. Edinburgh: Privately printed, 1879.
Fremantle, John. *Wellington's Voice: the Candid Letters of Lieutenant Colonel John Fremantle, Coldstream Guards, 1808-1837*. Glover, Gareth (ed.), Barnsley: Frontline, 2012.
General Orders, Portugal, Spain & France, 1815-1818. London: T. Egerton. 1815-1818.
General Regulations and Orders for the Army. London: Adjutant General's Office, 1811.
Glover, Gareth. 'Defence of Hougoumont'. Project Hougoumont Online, 13 September 2017.
Glover, Gareth. *Waterloo: The Defeat of Napoleon's Imperial Guard, Henry Clinton, the 2nd Division and the End of a 200-year-old Controversy*. Barnsely: Frontline, 2015.
Gomm, William M., *Letters and Journals of Field-Marshal Sir William Maynard Gomm from 1799 to Waterloo 1815*. Francis Carr-Gomm (ed.). London: John Murray; 1881.
Gordon, Alexander, *At Wellington's Right Hand: the Letters of Lieutenant-Colonel Sir Alexander Gordon, 1808-1815*. Rory Muir (ed.). Phoenix Mill: Sutton, 2003.
Gronow, Rees Howell, *The Reminiscences and Recollections of Captain Gronow: being Anecdotes of the Camp, Court, Clubs, and Society 1810-1860*. 2 vols. London: Smith, Elder, 1863.
Gurwood, John, *The General Orders of Field Marshal the Duke of Wellington in the Campaigns of 1809 to 1818*. London: W. Clowes, 1837.
Hamilton, Frederick W., *The Origin and History of the First or Grenadier Guards*. 3 vols. London: John Murray, 1874.
Harrison, Robert, *Some Notices of the Stepney Family*. London: Privately published, 1870.
Haythornthwaite, Philip, *British Napoleonic Infantry Tactics 1792-1815*. Botley: Osprey, 2008.
Haythornthwaite, Philip, *Redcoats: the British Soldiers of the Napoleonic Wars*. Barnsley: Pen & Sword, 2012.
Hime, Henry, *History of the Royal Regiment of Artillery 1815-1853*. London: Longmans, Green, 1908.
Hussey, John, *Waterloo: The Campaign of 1815*. 2 vols. Barnsley: Greenhill, 2017.
Jackson, Basil, *With Wellington's Staff at Waterloo: the Reminiscences of a Staff Officer during the Campaign of 1815 and with Napoleon on St. Helena*. Leonaur, 2010.
Jones, George, *The Battle of Waterloo, with Those of Ligny and Quatre Bras, Described by Eye-Witnesses*. London: L. Booth, 1852.

Jones, John, *The History and Antiquities of Harewood, in the County of York.* London: Simpkin Marshall, 1859.

Journals of the House of Commons

Lake, Charles, 'Waterloo Reminiscences of Ensign Charles Lake, Third Guards'. *Scots Guards Magazine.* 1961. Pages 66-67

Lennox, Lord William Pitt, *Fifty Years' Biographical Reminiscences.* 2 vols. London: Hurst and Blackett, 1863.

Letters from the Battle of Waterloo: Unpublished Correspondence by Allied Offices from the Siborne Papers, Gareth Glover (ed.), London: Greenhill, 2004.

Littell's Living Age, Vol. 180. T.H. Carter & Company, 1889.

Macbride, Mac Kenzie, *With Napoleon at Waterloo and Other Unpublished Documents of the Waterloo and Peninsular Campaigns.* London: Francis Griffiths, 1911.

MacInnes, John. *The Brave Sons of Skye: Containing the Military Records of the Leading Officers, Non-Commissioned Officers and Private Soldiers. . .* Edinburgh: Norman Macleod, 1899.

Mackinnon, Daniel, *Origin and Services of the Coldstream Guards.* 2 vols. Cambridge: Ken Trotman, 2003.

Mackinnon, Donald, *Memoirs of Clan Fingon.* London: Lewis Hepworth, 1899.

Martinien, Aristide, *Tableaux par Corps et par Batailles des Officiers Tués et Blessés pendant les Guerres de l'Empire (1805-1815).* Paris: Éditions Militaires, ND.

Master, Richard, 'An Ensign at War: the Narrative of Richard Master, First Guards'. David Fraser (ed.). *Journal of the Society for Army Historical Research.* Vol. LDVI Number 267 August 1988, pp.127-145.

Maurice, Frederick, *The History of the Scots Guards from the Creation of the Regiment to the Eve of the Great War.* 2 vols. London: Chatto & Windus, 1934.

McGuigan, Ron and Burnham, Robert, *Wellington's Brigade Commanders: Peninsula and Waterloo.* Barnsley: Pen & Sword, 2017.

Medical Times and Gazette, various dates.

Monthly Army Lists, various years.

Mudford, William, *Historical Account of the Campaign in the Netherlands in 1815.* London: Henry Colburn, 1817.

Müffling, Carl von, *The Memoirs of Baron von Müffling: a Prussian Officer in the Napoleonic Wars.* London: Greenhill, 1997.

Muir, Rory, *Tactics and the Experience of Battle in the Age of Napoleon.* New Haven: Yale, 1998.

Nafziger, George. *Imperial Bayonets: Tactics of the Napoleonic Battery, Battalion and Brigade as Found in Contemporary Regulations.* London: Greenhill, 1996.

Near Observer. *The Battle of Waterloo Containing the Series of Accounts Published by Authority, British and Foreign.* London: J. Booth, 1815.

Packe, Henry, *With the 1st Foot Guards in the Peninsular and at Waterloo: the Letters of Lieutenant Colonel Henry Packe, 1806-16.* Godmanchester: Ken Trotman, 2016.

Paget, Julian and Saunders, Derek, *Hougoumont: the Key to Victory at Waterloo.* Barnsley: Pen & Sword, 2001.

Pawley, Ronald, *The Red Lancers.* Ramsbury: Crowood, 1998.

Principles of War, Exhibited in the Practice of the Camp; and as Developed in a Series of General Orders of Field-Marshal the Duke of Wellington. London: Cadell and Davis, 1815.

Reid, T. Wemyss, *The Life, Letters, and Friendships of Richard Monckton Milnes.* 2 vols. New York: Cassell, 1891.

Report on the Manuscripts of Earl Bathurst. London: His Majesty's Stationery Office, 1923.

Return of the Names of the Officers in the Army Who Received Pensions for Loss of Limbs, or for Wounds. London: War Office, 1818.

Robinson, Mike, *The Battle of Quatre Bras 1815.* Stroud: Spellmount, 2008.

Ross-of-Bladensburg, John, *A History of the Coldstream Guards, from 1815 to 1895.* London: A. D. Innes, 1896.

Royal Military Calendar or Army Service and Commission Book. 5 vols. London, 1820

Royal Military Chapel, Wellington Barracks. London: Hatchards, 1882.

Rules and Regulations for the Formations, Field-Exercise, and Movements of His Majesty's Forces. London: War Office, 1792.

Saint-Hilaire, Emile Marco de, *History of the Imperial Guard.* Translated by Greg Gorsuch. Napoleon Series. 2017.

Saltoun, Alexander, *Waterloo Letters Written by Lieutenant Colonel Alexander, Lord Saltoun, 1st Foot Guards, 1815.* Gareth Glover (ed.) Godmanchester: Ken Trotman, 2010.

Scott, Walter, *Paul's Letters to His Kinsfolk.* Edinburgh: Archibald Constable, 1816.

Sheardown, W., *Records and Family Notices of Military and Naval Officers Connected with Doncaster and Its Neighbourhood.* Doncaster: Gazette, 1873.

Shelley, Frances, *The Diary of Frances, Lady Shelley.* Richard Edgecombe (ed.) New York: Charles Scribner, 1912.

Siborne, William, *History of the War in France and Belgium in 1815.* 2 vols. London: T. and W. Boone, 1844.

Siborne, William, *History of the Waterloo Campaign.* London: Greenhill, 1990.

Somerset, Lord Fitzroy, 'Somerset's Account of the Battle of Waterloo'. Gareth Glover (ed.). *Waterloo Association Journal.* Spring 2007, pp.4-19.

St. John, Joseph, 'Letters to His Parents writing during the Waterloo Campaign', various dates. Unpublished.

Stanhope, James H., *Eyewitness to the Peninsular War and the Battle of Waterloo: the Letters and Journals of Lieutenant Colonel the Honourable James Stanhope 1803 to 1825.* Gareth Glover (ed.) Barnsley: Pen and Sword, 2010.

Stonestreet, George G., *Recollections of the Scenes of which I was a Witness in the Low Countries & France in the Campaigns of 1814 and 1815 and the Subsequent Occupation of French Flanders: The Journal and Letters of the Reverend George Griffin Stonestreet 1814-16.* Gareth Glover (ed.). Godmanchester: Ken Trotman, 2009.

'Sunrise and Sunset Calculator'. *Time and Date Online.* 2017.

Surtees, William. *Twenty-five Years in the Rifle Brigade.* London: Greenhill, 1996.

Sweetman, John, *Raglan: From the Peninsula to the Crimea.* Barnsley: Pen & Sword, 2010.

The National Archives (TNA). WO17.

Thomson, Thomas, *A Biographical Dictionary of Eminent Scotsmen.* 9 vols. London: Blackie, 1855.

Tomkinson, William, *The Diary of a Cavalry Officer in the Peninsular War and Waterloo: 1809-1815* London: Frederick Muller; 1971.

Waterloo Archive. 6 vols. Gareth Glover (ed.). Barnsley: Frontline, 2010 – 2014.

Waterloo Letters. Herbert T. Siborne (ed.). London: Greenhill, 1993.

Waterloo Medal Roll. Dallington: Naval and Military Press, 1992.

Wellington, Duke of, *The Dispatches of Field Marshal the Duke of Wellington, During his Various Campaigns in India Denmark, Portugal, Spain, the Low Countries, and France, from 1799 to 1818.* Edited by Lt.-Col. John Gurwood. London: John Murray; 1834-9.

_____. *Despatches, Correspondence, and Memoranda of Field Marshal Arthur, Duke of Wellington, K. G.,* Edited by his son, the Duke of Wellington. 'in continuation of the former series' London: J. Murray 1857-80. *[Referenced as (new edition)].*

_____. *Dispatches of Field Marshal the Duke of Wellington, During his Various Campaigns in India Denmark, Portugal, Spain, the Low Countries, and France.* Edited by Lt.-Col. John Gurwood. London: Parker, Furnivall and Parker, 1844-1847. *[Referenced as (enlarged edition)].*

_____. *Supplementary Dispatches, Correspondence, and Memoranda of Field Marshal Arthur Duke of Wellington, K.G.*, Edited by the 2nd Duke of Wellington. London: John Murray; 1860-1871.

White, Alasdair, 'Of Hedges, Myths and Memories – A Historical Reappraisal of the Château/Ferme de Hougoumont'. Project Hougoumont Online. 13 September 2017.

Name Index

Wellington and Napoleon are not listed as they are mentioned numerous times.

Abercromby, Alexander, 38, 50, 51, 63, 68, 81, 215, 225, 262, 291, 292, 300, 301, 308, 309, 313, 315, 315, 317, 319, 320, 321, 322, 336, 337, 348, 349, 350
Able, Thomas, 331
Abraham, William, 325
Acheson, Edward, 64, 140, 141, 262, 292, 300, 308, 338
Adair, Robert, 95, 172, 256, 289, 329, 351
Adam, Frederick, 105. 172, 184, 194, 195
Adams, William, 325
Adye, Stephen, 48, 100, 171, 213, 271, 287, 294, 296, 303, 304, 310, 348
Alcock, William, 11
Aldin, Thomas, 17
Allen, Adam, 144, 146
Allen, George, 188, 197, 205
Allen, James, 331
Allix, Charles, 11, 63, 68, 176, 219, 288, 297, 305, 351, 352
Allsop, James, 342
Allwright, John, 11, 326
Alten, Charles Baron, 75, 114
Anderson, Andrew, 325
Anderson, Charles, 343
Anderson, Matthew, 195
Angelet, Jean, 193
Anson, George, 106, 112, 153, 270, 293, 310
Anson, William, 2
Anster, William, 338
Anstruther, Windham, 7, 69, 248, 264
Anthing, Karl Baron, 115
Arbuthnot, Robert, 7, 50, 51, 68, 292, 300, 308, 318, 319, 320, 321, 322, 339
Armit, Richard, 356
Armstrong, Andrew, 289, 298, 306
Arnoth, James, 343
Asborne, George, 343
Ashburnham, Percy, 355
Asher, William, 331
Ashton, John, 145, 154, 293, 302, 341, 353
Ashton, Josiah, 30
Askew, Henry, 19, 22, 35, 37, 51, 87, 97, 110, 250, 252, 275, 288, 324, 347
Askew, Thomas, 60
Aspinall, George, 344
Aston, John, 134
Aston, Joseph, 134, 152, 272
Atkins, William, 27

Bachelu, Gilbert, 125, 176
Bacon, James, 325
Bainbridge, John, 343
Baineslough, Henry, 342
Baird, David, 64, 94, 97, 155, 269, 293, 302, 341

NAME INDEX

Baker, James, 343
Baker, John, 184
Baker, Thomas, 291, 300, 308
Balintine, Barnett, 327
Bamber, John, 325
Bambridge, Edward, 343
Bannister, John, 327
Barclay, Delancey, 11, 19, 63, 67, 94, 288, 290, 297, 299, 305, 307, 313, 315, 316, 325, 327, 328, 348, 353
Baring, Georg, 120
Barker, Thomas, 331
Barnes, Edward, 233, 249, 257
Barnet, Charles, 318, 268, 293, 301, 308
Barnett, James, 330
Barnett, Thomas, 331
Barratt, Thomas Private, 333
Barratt, Thomas Lieutenant, 248
Barrington, Samuel, 43, 47, 57, 82, 90, 94, 247, 261, 288, 324, 352
Barton, William, 18, 34, 95, 139, 259, 289, 329, 352
Bate, William, 328
Bathurst, Henry Earl, 219
Bathurst, Henry George Lord Apsley, 219
Bathurst, Seymour, 46, 60, 63, 67, 97, 199, 219, 288, 296, 304, 315, 316, 317, 318, 319, 320, 321
Bathurst, Thomas. See Bathurst, Seymour
Batty, Robert, 12, 17, 18, 78, 82, 166, 170, 177, 185, 259, 290, 298, 330, 351, 352
Bauduin, Pierre-Francis, 81, 127, 128
Baynes, George, 294, 303, 310
Beadle, Samuel, 333
Beane, George, 126
Beaufoy, Mark, 218, 292, 300, 308
Beckey, John, 339
Bell, John, 251
Bell, William, 325
Belshaw, Adam, 338

Bentinck, Charles, 13, 69, 217, 292, 301, 309, 313, 315, 316, 317, 318, 320, 321, 322, 347
Berry, Thomas, 248
Berthelet des Verges, Guillaume, 193
Best, Charles, 75, 85
Beswick, Samuel, 324
Betts, Zacharia, 328
Bigsworth, John, 332
Birch, John, 344
Bishop, Nugent, 343
Blackman, John, 41, 44, 45, 56, 58, 68, 196, 203, 291, 300, 336, 352
Blake, Joseph, 355
Blake, William, 83
Blane, Charles, 352
Blane, Hugh, 293, 301, 309
Blizzard, Benjamin, 343
Bloomfield, John, 137
Blücher, Prince Gebhard, 65, 73, 74, 98, 113, 115, 239
Blythe, John, 326
Boldero, Lonsdale, 34, 46, 60, 172, 218, 289, 298, 306, 352
Bolton, Henry, 326
Bolton, Samuel, 185
Bonaparte, Prince Jerome, 75, 81, 125, 129, 146
Bonnet, Sous-Lieutenant, 133
Booth, John, 328
Boulcott, Joseph, 12. 329
Bouverie, Henry, 35. 38, 51, 255
Bowater, Edward, 64, 135, 145, 180, 268, 293, 301, 309, 341, 342
Bowen, Robert, 292, 300, 308
Bowles, George, 18, 40, 41, 42, 43, 44, 60, 62, 64, 71, 98, 162, 204, 218, 263, 292, 300, 308, 347
Boyer, Benjamin, 342
Boyle, John, 331
Brack, Fortuné, 164, 169

367

Bradford, Henry, 19, 48, 50, 51, 59, 63, 67, 162, 163, 173, 199, 207, 216, 236, 287, 288, 290, 296, 297, 299, 304, 313, 315, 316, 317, 325, 326, 327, 350
Bradley, Robert, 337
Bramley, William, 343
Brennan, Richard, 343
Brewer, Joseph, 179
Bridge, John, 332
Bridgeford, George, 325
Bridgeman, Edmund, 352
Bridgeman, Orlando, 63, 212, 232, 236, 258, 290, 299, 307, 313, 314, 316, 317, 318, 319, 334, 352
Brinkman, Julius, 128
Brinkman, Wilhelm, 128
Briscoe, Benjamin, 343
Broadbent, Richard, 325
Brook, William, 342
Brooke, Thomas, 248, 351, 352
Brooks, John, 342
Broomfield, William, 232, 332
Brown, Andrew, 327
Brown, James, 329
Brown, John, 338
Brown, Joseph, 333
Brown, Simon, 325
Brown, Thomas, 80, 94, 138, 288, 324, 351
Bruce, Robert, 177, 260, 289, 298, 305
Brunton, William, 344
Buckley, Edward, 18, 242, 288, 297, 305
Buckley, George, 218, 242, 265, 292, 300, 308, 352
Buller, James, 69, 255
Bülow, Friedrich, 159, 182
Burgess, Somerville, 18, 19, 157, 259, 288, 297, 326, 354
Burgh, Ulysses, 19, 50, 51, 54, 59, 60, 67, 288, 297, 305, 312, 314, 316, 317, 318, 319, 320, 321, 325, 327, 328
Burrard, Edward, 248

Burrows, John, 342
Burrowes, Arnold, 248
Bury, Augustus Viscount, 17, 67, 290, 299, 307, 312, 314
Buschieb, Andreas, 130
Büsgen, Moritz, 108, 119, 121, 122, 145, 148
Bussche, Lewis Baron, 251
Butcher, John, 325
Butler, James, 46, 80, 218, 270, 293, 302
Butler, Thomas, 344
Butler, Whitwell, 18, 129, 218, 270, 293, 302
Byers, James, 333
Byng, John, 21, 48, 49, 56, 62, 64, 102, 105, 117, 121, 128, 137, 140, 141, 142, 145, 152, 162, 163, 173, 179, 185, 199, 200, 216, 220, 221, 222, 226, 232, 249, 250, 274, 291, 293, 299, 302, 310, 313, 315, 347, 357, 358

Caddock, John, 344
Callender, John, 211
Cambridge, Prince Adolphus Duke of, 69, 222
Cambronne, Pierre, 189
Cameron, Donald, 110, 288, 297, 305
Cameron, William, 52, 67, 257, 290, 299, 313, 315, 316, 330, 334
Campbell, Colin, 19, 50, 51, 59, 63, 208, 292, 301, 309, 312, 314, 315, 317, 318, 319, 320, 321, 349, 350
Campbell, Guy, 104
Canney, John, 327
Canning, Charles, 54, 70, 208, 209, 223, 268, 293, 302, 312, 341, 343, 353
Card, William, 338
Cardinal, Claude, 193
Carpenter, William, 337
Cartan, Thomas, 211
Cartwright, William, 344

NAME INDEX

Cassett, John, 342
Catalani, Angelica, 58
Chambers, Courtney, 352
Chambers, Montagu, 352
Chambers, Newton, 34, 61, 105, 106, 160, 212, 256, 290, 299, 313, 330, 351,
Chaplin, Thomas, 68, 265, 355
Chappell, John 330
Chappelle, Frank, 337
Charlewood, Benjamin, 248
Chassé, David, 114
Christian, Symon, 332
Christiani, Joseph, 189
Churchill, Chatham, 63, 202, 212, 256, 299, 307, 312, 314, 316, 317, 318, 319, 320, 321, 347
Clarke, Henri, Duc de Feltre, 314
Clarke, John 3rd Bn 1FG, 328
Clarke, John 2nd Bn 1FG, 329
Clarke, Philip, 314, 315, 316, 317, 318, 320, 321, 322
Clarke, William Drummer, 138
Clarke, William Private, 325
Clay, Matthew, 86, 89, 90, 92, 93, 94, 103, 107, 108, 131, 132, 142, 144, 148, 151, 203, 214, 272
Clayton, William, 342
Cleeves, Andreas, 228
Cleevesley, Richard, 344
Clements, Robert, 105, 106, 257, 289, 298, 330, 347
Clifton, Edward, 352
Clinton, Henry, 33, 34, 35, 36, 37, 38, 43, 114, 161, 172, 173, 180, 217, 223, 290, 299, 307, 313, 314, 316, 317, 318,319
Clitherow, John, 248
Clive, Edward, 188, 197, 305
Clough, Stephen, 31
Cochrane, Andrew, 18, 293, 302, 310
Cockett, Thomas, 332
Colborne, John, 194, 262

Cole, Galbraith, 251
Collar, James, 331
Colquhoun, Robert, 289, 298, 306
Colquitt, Goodwin, 110, 157, 184, 188, 256, 288, 297, 305, 324, 326, 327, 348
Colville, Charles, 54, 114, 123, 290, 299, 307, 313, 314, 316, 317, 318, 319, 320, 321, 322
Colville, Henry, 248
Connelly, Michael, 343
Cooke, George, 20, 47, 48, 61, 62, 63, 69, 70, 72,76, 80, 162, 163, 179, 199, 272, 273, 287, 290, 296, 299, 301, 307, 309, 313, 347, 357, 358
Cooke, John 3rd Bn 1FG, 12
Cooke, John Coldstream Guards, 339
Cooke, Richard, 11, 37, 97, 110, 135, 157, 254, 288, 297, 305, 324, 326, 327, 347, 350
Cooper, Edward, 327
Cope, Jeremiah, 331
Cornthwaite, James, 330
Cornwall, William, 352
Cotes, Robert, 109, 287, 296, 304
Cotton, Willoughby, 248, 249, 266
Council, Edward, 228
Coventry, John, 338
Cowell, John, 64, 100, 104, 105, 111, 247, 264, 291
Cox, William, 209, 292, 301, 309
Cradock, John, 320, 321, 352
Crane, Abraham, 327
Cranshaw, William, 28
Craufurd, Alexander, 203
Craufurd, Robert, 204
Craufurd, Thomas, 154, 203, 293, 301, 341, 353
Crews, William, 329
Croft, Thomas, 18, 82, 94, 246, 261, 288, 324
Crofts, James, 83, 138
Crooke, John, 27, 30

Crowther, Robert, 328
Curran, Charles, 328
Curtis, George, 329
Curtis, William, 288, 297, 305
Cuyler, Augustus, 13, 48, 62, 69, 163, 287, 292, 296, 301, 309, 313

Daniels, Thomas, 327
Dashwood, Augustus, 352
Dashwood, Charles, 15, 17, 70, 76, 86, 112, 122, 129, 131, 132, 144, 246, 267, 292, 293, 301, 302, 309, 341, 342, 344
Davidson, Thomas, 339
Davies, Francis, 359
Davies, James, 329
Davies, Samuel, 329
Davies, Thomas, 228, 289, 298, 306, 351, 352
Davis, David, 328
Dawkins, Francis, 63, 217, 290, 299, 307, 313, 314, 316, 317, 318, 319, 320, 321
Dawkins, Henry, 14, 55, 162, 217, 218, 262, 292, 300, 308, 319, 320, 321
Day, John, 343
Deanne, Peter, 344
de Bouteville, Eugene, 227, 231
de Bruyn, Jean, 227
de Jongh, Wijbrandus, 227
Delbridge, John, 83, 138
Delort, Jacques, 164
D'Erlon, Jean Comte, 116, 159, 181, 187
De Ros, Arthur, 312, 314
Despans-Cubierès, Amedee, 128, 131, 132, 142, 143
Dethick, Robert, 330
de Wissell, Lewis, 294, 310
d'Harlet, Louis, 189
Dick, Robert, 77
Dickinson, James, 332
Dickman, Thomas, 344
Dillworth, Thomas, 324

Dirom, John, 185, 192, 260, 289, 298, 306
Disbrowe, George, 48, 63, 67, 163, 287, 290, 296, 299, 307, 313
Dixon, Francis, 139, 289, 298
Dobinson, Joseph, 339
Donzelot, Francois, 160, 187
Dorcey, Robert, 333
Dorville, Thomas, 248
Douglas, Edward, 352
Douglas, Francis, 291, 300, 308
Dowling, William, 331
Doyle, Bartholomew, 329
D'Oyly, Francis, 11, 19, 51, 110, 111, 157, 184, 188, 288, 297, 324, 326, 327, 351
D'Oyly, Henry, 56, 95, 162, 244, 255, 289, 298, 306, 329, 330, 333
Draffin, James, 184
Drummond, Barclay, 14, 70, 179, 292, 301, 309, 353
Drummond, John, 7, 69
Drummond, William, 14, 148, 218, 268, 293, 302, 347
Drury, William, 344
Dryden, John, 325
Duchand de Sancey, Jean, 187, 188
Duhesme, Philibert, 183
Duke, John, 355
Dukes, Henry, 338
Dumaresq, Henry, 49, 64, 141, 142, 145, 163, 187, 254, 291, 299, 347
Duncombe, Thomas, 355
Dunn, Thomas, 332
Du Plat, Charles, 161
Durutte, Pierre, 160, 187

Edgards, Charles, 342
Edgcombe, Ernest, 64, 289, 298, 306
Edmunds, Edmond, 324
Edward, John, 337
Edwards, John, 109, 299
Elley, John, 178

NAME INDEX

Ellis, Charles, 60, 82, 95, 139, 147, 258, 290, 298, 329, 330
Ellison, Robert, 46, 103, 119, 138, 146, 147, 222, 228, 257, 290, 298, 306, 347
Elrington, John, 15, 131, 132, 152, 269, 293, 302, 310
Elwell, John, 343
Erskine, John, 34, 289, 298, 306
Estorff, Albrecht von, 114
Evan, John, 337
Evans, James, 327
Evans, Thomas, 337
Evelyn, George, 131, 132, 133, 150, 156, 246, 269, 293, 302, 341

Fairfield, Charles, 353
Fairfield, Edward, 293, 301, 309
Famous, James, 342
Farrance, John, 332
Fawcett, Jonathan, 330
Fead, George, 12, 176, 177, 185, 188, 191, 191, 199, 200, 218, 250, 255, 289, 298, 304, 306, 329, 330, 331, 333, 347
Finch, Daniel, 325
Finlow, James, 333
Firth, John, 325
Fitz Clarence, Frederick, 69, 266
Fitzgerald, Edward, 48, 173, 299, 254, 287, 296
Fitzroy, Lord Charles, 11, 17, 51, 63, 67, 68, 290, 299, 307, 313, 314, 316, 317, 318, 320, 321, 322, 347
Fletcher, Richard, 248
Fludyer, George, 46, 60, 63, 94, 260, 288, 324
Fogg, George, 324
Foot, George, 294, 303, 310
Forbes, George, 154
Forbes, Hasting, 64, 112, 154, 293, 302, 341, 353
Forbes, James, 64, 291, 300, 308, 355
Forbes, Walter, 104, 291, 300, 308

Ford, John Private, 83, 138
Ford, John Sergeant, 95, 324
Forster, Henry, 325
Forster, William, 248
Fowles, Thomas, 330
Fox, Sackville, 248
Foy, Maximilien, 125, 127, 146
Fractwell, John, 234
Fraser, Charles, 353
Fraser, Ralph, 128, 133, 143, 272
Fremantle, John, 19, 50, 54, 63, 182, 238, 239, 243, 264, 292, 301, 309, 312, 314, 316, 317, 318, 320, 321, 348, 349
Friant, Louis, 189
Frost, John, 339

Gage, Thomas, 154
Gale, Thomas, 344
Gange, Thomas, 342
Gann, Robert, 132, 142, 144
Gardner, John, 288, 297, 305
Garman, Christopher, 48, 71, 111, 234, 287, 296, 304
Gawkers, Thomas, 342
Gilder, Frederick, 95, 289, 298, 306
Girardot, Charles, 248
Glanville, Francis, 354
Gloucester, Prince William Duke of, 222
Godwin, John, 155
Golding, George, 344
Gomm, William, 17, 19, 50, 51, 53, 54, 55, 60, 68, 74, 100, 104, 219, 262, 291, 292, 300, 301, 308, 309, 313, 315, 316, 338, 350
Gooch, Henry, 13, 133, 144, 148, 218, 265, 292, 300, 308
Good, Samuel, 292, 301, 309
Gooday, John, 330
Goodwin, Thomas, 333
Gordon, Alexander 3FG, 19, 51, 54, 58, 63, 70, 112, 209, 267, 293, 302, 312, 341, 343, 353

371

Gordon, Alexander
   Coldsteam, 292, 300, 308
Gordon, George, 338
Gordon, Robert, 353
Gordon, Thomas, 353
Gould, Frederick, 46, 60, 68, 260, 355
Graham, James, 133, 134, 150, 271,
Graham, John, 133, 134, 271
Graham, Joseph, 339
Graham, Thomas, 10, 20, 23, 58
Grant, Colquhoun, 173
Grant, John, 248
Grant, William, 353
Gray, Francis, 333
Green, George, 342
Green, John, 326
Gregory, Paul, 331
Greville, Algernon, 18, 63, 110, 147, 218, 219, 260, 288, 297, 305, 320
Griffiths, Henry, 17, 144, 265, 300
Grigsby, Stephen, 343
Grimstead, William, 69
Gronow, Rees, 12, 61, 95, 105, 106, 111, 125, 134, 135, 157, 158, 160, 166, 172, 188, 189, 190, 194, 202, 204, 205, 213, 214, 223, 224, 236, 259, 290, 298, 306, 307, 351, 352
Grose, Edward, 80, 94, 139, 239, 290, 329, 357
Grouchy, Emmanuel de, 115
Guiton, Francois, 85
Gunning, John, 210, 211
Gunthorpe, James, 46, 49, 63, 68, 105, 172, 199, 256, 287, 290, 296, 299, 304, 307, 313, 315, 316, 317, 318, 319, 320, 322, 347
Guthrie, George, 142
Guttridge, John, 224

Halkett, Colin, 25, 85, 161, 184, 190
Hall, William, 333
Halliday, William, 139, 333
Hamilton, James, 151
Hamilton, William, 17, 18, 293, 301, 309
Hampson, Peter, 330
Hanbury, John, 248, 249, 255
Hanrott, Francis, 292, 301, 309
Harbour, James, 330
Harding, George, 338
Hardinge, Henry, 11, 19, 50, 51, 67, 95, 236, 288, 290, 297, 305, 314, 317, 319, 320, 321, 322, 325, 326, 327
Harris, Abraham, 337
Harris, George, 324
Harris, John, 226, 227, 271, 311
Harrison, John, 288, 297, 305
Harrison, William, 327
Harth, Andreas, 130
Harvett, Thomas, 344
Harwood, Samuel, 332
Hatton, Samuel, 333
Hawkes, George, 327
Hawkins, Henry, 293, 301, 309
Hawkins, John, 343
Hawkins, Thomas, 327
Hay, James Lord, 13, 17, 49, 63, 68, 88, 89, 94, 97, 157, 267, 290, 313, 324, 352
Hay, Lord James, 17, 18, 54, 68, 290, 299, 307, 313, 314, 316, 317, 318, 319
Hay, Peter, 26
Haywood, Thomas, 331
Haywood, William, 325
Heath, Thomas, 331
Helps, Isaac, 326
Hely-Hutchinson, John, 68, 257
Hemsley, William, 331
Henderson, Thomas, 339
Hepburn, Francis, 20, 22, 23, 38, 47, 51, 69, 70, 97, 128, 145, 152, 154, 163, 178, 179, 180, 196, 200, 221, 250, 275, 292, 301, 307, 315, 348, 350
Heritage, John, 331

NAME INDEX

Hervey, Felton, 76
Hervey, James, 132, 133, 292, 300, 308
Hesketh, Robert, 14, 64, 69, 129, 139, 147, 268, 293, 301, 341, 347
Hewlett, Abraham, 325
Hible, John, 331
Hickam, William, 342
Hickham, Alexander, 344
Hickman, Thomas, 328
Hicks, John, 323
Higginson, Alexander, 351, 352
Higginson, George, 248
Hill, Rowland Lord, 58, 114, 202, 212, 232, 257, 258, 290, 299, 307, 312, 313, 314, 316, 317, 318, 319, 320, 321, 334
Hill, Thomas, 19, 63, 67, 110, 218, 288, 290, 297, 299, 305, 307, 3133, 315, 316, 317, 318, 319, 321, 322, 325, 227, 349
Hilton, James, 337
Hilton, Moses, 331
Hipkiss, William, 342
Hiver, Jean-Baptiste, 231
Hodder, George, 355
Hogg, Philip, 83, 137
Holding, William, 327
Holmes, Richard, 344
Home, Francis, 15, 112, 126, 129, 134, 145, 147, 148, 150, 151, 152, 200, 268, 293, 301, 309, 342, 357
Home, John, 351, 352
Honyman, John, 352
Hood, Adam, 327
Hood, John, 83, 325
Hope, James, 50, 51
Hopkins, Samuel, 325
Hornby, Charles, 248
Horrocks, John, 27
Horsley, Edward, 331
Hotham, Beaumont Lord, 17, 292, 300, 308
Houselander, Isaac, 343

Howard, Kenneth, 250, 272, 273, 274
Howe, Robert, 331
Hubbard, Henry, 343
Hudson, George, 352
Hudson, Henry, 339
Hughes, Edward, 339
Hughes, James, 225
Hume, John, 209
Hunt, Stephan, 343
Hunter, Abraham, 342
Hunter, John, 149
Hunter, William, 149, 300, 308
Huntington, William, 330
Hurd, Samuel, 110, 288, 297, 305
Hutchins, William, 329

Ineson, John, 338
Ingles, George, 326

Jackson, Basil, 170
Jackson, John, 344
Jacob, George, 288, 297, 305
Jago, Darell, 294, 303, 310
James, Thomas, 332, 337
James, William, 112, 269, 293, 301, 309
Jarvis, David, 324
Jeandot, Charles-Claude, 227
Jenkins, David, 325
Jenkins, Matthew, 333
Jenkinson, John, 352
Jepson, John, 138
Jessop, John, 78
Johnson, Bartholomew, 333
Johnson, Thomas, 327
Johnstone, William, 288, 297, 305, 354
Jolyet, Pierre, 127, 128
Jones, George, 330
Jones, John 2nd Bn 1FG, 325
Jones, John 3FG, 344
Jones, Leslie, 12, 67, 247, 289, 290, 298, 299, 306, 307, 314, 329, 331, 333

Jones, Peter, 327
Jones, Richard, 329

Keate, William, 70, 218, 293, 302, 309, 343
Kellermann, Francois, 85, 165, 172, 173, 181
Kellet, Thomas, 324
Kelly, Dawson, 209
Kempt, James, 75, 160
Kenny, Matthias, 210
Kent, James, 342
Keppel, Frederick, 47
Kershaw, John, 325
Key, Richard, 327
Kidd, Thomas, 48, 288, 297, 304
Kielmansegge, Friedrich Graf von, 75, 122
King, William, 324
Kirk, John, 343
Kirton John, 328
Knollys, William, 248
Kuhlmann, Henry, 62, 70, 72, 84, 85, 86, 100, 117, 126, 127, 171, 185, 212, 213, 271, 294, 303, 310, 348

Lacey, Samuel, 338,
Laing, James, 343
Lake, Charles, 69, 94, 97, 101, 112, 154, 155, 156, 269, 293, 302, 310, 341, 353
Lambert, Henry, 354
Lambert, John, 261, 320, 322
Lampey, John, 337
Landers, William, 342
Landiford, Samuel, 344
Langrishe, Henry, 352
Lascelles, Charles, 219, 259, 288, 297, 305, 354
Lascelles, Edward, 355
Lascelles, Henry, 110, 261, 288, 297, 326
Lathwood, Richard, 332
Law, John, 352
Leach, Henry, 353

Leach, William, 337
Lee, John, 342
Lefebvre-Desnouettes, Charles, 164
Legros, Pierre, 133
Lennox, Lord William, 49, 55, 57, 58, 89, 138,
Leonhard, Johann, 147
Lester, Joseph, 134
L'Estrange, George, 353
Lewis, Dan, 327
Lewis, John Coldstream Guards, 337
Lewis, John 2nd Bn 1FG, 325
Lewis, Joseph, 329
Lewis, Richard, 326
L'Heritier, Samuel, 165
Liester, Joseph, 134
Lindsay, James, 68, 317, 318, 319
Lister, Joseph, 134, 139
Lister, William, 342
Liversage, David, 332
Lloyd, Charles, 234
Lloyd, William, 170, 185
Lobau, Georges Comte de, 116, 182
Lockwood, Thomas, 333
Loftus, Ferrars, 352
London, John, 337
Lowder, John, 332
Luttrell, Francis, 94, 110, 138, 147, 259, 288, 297, 324, 326
Lyster, John, 355

MacDonald, Robert, 326
Macdonell, James, 14, 35, 48, 68, 71, 85, 86, 89, 90, 91, 102, 103, 111, 120, 121, 123, 129, 132, 133, 134, 140, 144, 145, 150, 151, 220, 221, 262, 263, 291, 300, 308, 337, 348, 349, 350
MacKenzey, John, 138
Mackinnon, Daniel, 14, 140, 141, 143, 148, 155, 218, 262, 291, 300, 308, 336, 337
MacLaurence, Richard, 119, 198

NAME INDEX

Maitland, Peregrine, 21, 35, 47, 48, 49, 55, 56, 57, 58, 62, 63, 68, 81, 82, 84, 86, 87, 88, 89, 97, 117, 137, 138, 156, 157, 173, 174, 175, 177, 188, 191, 193, 195, 199, 219, 220, 221, 227, 240, 250, 251, 274, 275, 287, 290, 296, 304, 313, 315, 316, 317, 318, 319, 324, 347, 357, 358
Malet, Antoine, 193
Mann, Edward, 339
Manners, Arthur, 352
Manners, Felix, 352
Marbot, Jean-Baptiste, 159
March, Charles Lord, 207
Marcognet, Pierre, 160, 187
Marshall, Joseph, 329
Martin, William, 337
Masham, Richard, 337
Master, Richard, 59, 77, 80, 157, 176, 202, 218, 223, 224, 289, 298, 306, 352
Master, William, 59, 70, 224, 240, 293, 302, 310
May, James, 326
McBeth, Donald, 342
McFarlane, Orr, 333
McGregor, Brice, 134, 272
Mercer, Douglas, 15, 37, 128, 178, 200, 224, 267, 292, 293, 301, 302, 309, 348
Mercer, Robert, 11, 29
Merlen, Jean Baron, 65
Merrick, Benjamin, 342
Meyer, George, 294, 303, 310
Michel, Claude, 189, 193
Middleton, William, 339
Milhaud, Edouard, 116, 164, 181
Miller, William, 19, 88, 95, 217, 256, 289, 329, 351
Milnes, William, 110, 138, 147, 203, 246, 288, 297, 305, 326, 351
Milwood, John, 337
Mimmick, Barnett, 325
Minchell, Thomas, 107

Mitchell, Ralph, 344
M'Kenley, Michael, 342
Montagu, Henry, 64, 179, 270, 293, 302, 310
Montagu, John, 64, 144, 265, 291, 300, 336
Montgomerie, Hugh, 269, 293, 302, 341
Moore, James, 329
Moore, Robert, 122, 265, 292, 300, 336
Moore, William, 11, 67, 313, 315, 316, 317, 319, 320, 321, 322
Moorhouse, John, 324
Moorhouse, Joseph, 129, 293, 302, 309
Morgan, David, 338
Morgan, George, 355
Morgan, Jacques-Polycarpe, 227, 231
Morgan, Richard 1st Company 3rd Bn 1FG, 331
Morgan, Richard 3rd Company 3rd Bn 1FG, 333
Morgan, Thomas 3rd Bn 1FG, 152, 185
Morgan, Thomas Coldstream Guards, 338
Morgan, Thomas 3FG, 344
Moulcock, James, 328
Muffling, Carl von, 109, 115, 122,
Mure, George, 261, 288, 297, 326
Murray, Digby, 248,
Murray, George, 317, 318, 319, 320, 321
Murray, Henry, 352
Murray, John, 338
Murray, William, 331
Musgrove, William, 331
Musson, James, 325

Needham, Francis, 60
Netherlands, Prince Frederik of, 115
Newmann, Charles, 343
Newton, John, 327
Ney, Michel, 73, 189
Nicholls, Henry, 331
Nicholls, Thomas, 332
Nicholls, William 331
Nightingale, Geoffrey, 355

Nixon, James 2nd Bn 1FG, 94, 104, 157, 188, 206, 218, 219, 220, 224, 259, 288, 297, 305, 324, 355
Nixon, James 3rd Bn 1FG, 330
Norcross, John, 271
Norris, Jacob, 326
Northmore, Thomas, 248
Norton, Fletcher, 110, 288, 297, 305
Norval, Swindal, 356
Nutter, John, 329

Oldham, William, 331
Olfermann, Johann, 161
Ompteda, Christian Baron, 75
Orange, Prince William of, 20, 23, 33, 40, 59, 61, 62, 69, 74, 80, 81, 114, 126, 127, 156, 178, 181, 199, 208, 210, 212, 249, 250, 290, 299, 307, 312, 314
Owen, Evan, 332

Pack, Denis, 75, 160
Packe, Henry, 248
Pakenham, Hercules, 50, 51, 68, 292, 300, 308, 338
Pardoe, Edward, 68, 97, 176, 289, 298, 330, 352
Pateman, William, 232
Pavior, George, 327
Paxton, Henry, 353
Payne, James, 325
Payne, John, 305, 355
Payne, William, 332
Pearson, John, 330
Peate, Joseph, 344
Pegg, Robert, 330
Pegot, Jean, 160, 187, 190
Perceval, Philip, 67, 248, 258
Percival George, 355
Perkins, Samuel, 163
Perponcher Sedlnitsky, Hendrik Baron de, 66, 114, 182

Perry, James, 27
Peters, Thomas, 344
Petter, Abraham, 228
Pettit, Major, 227, 231
Petty, John, 333
Petty, Thomas, 338
Phetheon, Josiah, 234
Philipan, James, 338
Phillimore, Robert, 34, 111, 290, 298, 306
Philpott, Isaac, 151, 152, 343
Pickles, Joseph, 333
Picquet, Cyrille, 87
Picton, Thomas, 61, 75, 85, 104, 105, 114, 160, 212, 290, 299, 313, 330
Pike, William, 331
Pipes, John, 338
Poingdestre, James, 356
Ponsonby, William, 161
Poret de Morvan, Paul, 189
Porter, William, 331
Powell, Henry, 17, 46, 60, 74, 84, 87, 93, 97, 99, 110, 125, 186, 187, 188, 193, 257, 288, 297, 305
Prax, Louis, 193
Prendergast, Jefferey, 293, 302, 310
Prince, John, 248, 355
Pring, Thomas, 328
Pritchard, John, 332
Pritchard, William, 119, 180
Pritchett, John, 327
Protherow, John, 332
Punter, William, 328

Quoit, Joachim Baron, 160

Ralphs, Thomas, 328
Ramdohr, Ludwig von, 85
Ramsay, Norman, 126
Ransom, Adam, 328
Ratcliffe, James, 338
Rathbone, William, 337

NAME INDEX

Read, George, 337
Rease, Thomas, 331
Reden, August von, 108, 122, 127, 128, 130
Redyard, James, 329
Reece, David, 332
Reece, Thomas, 330
Reed, William, 342
Reeve, John, 46, 111, 116, 185, 191, 200, 256, 289, 298, 306, 330, 332, 333
Reille, Honoré, 66, 74, 116, 125, 187
Revitt, John, 328
Richards, Thomas, 338
Riley, Hugh, 325
Rippingale, William, 332
Robinson, William, 344
Robson, John, 338
Rodney, James, 70
Roebuck, Benjamin, 26
Rogers, Richard, 333
Rogers, Samuel, 330
Rook, John, 326
Rooke, Henry, 19, 48, 70, 112, 162, 185, 267, 287, 293, 296, 302, 304, 310, 313, 315, 316, 343, 348
Rose, William, 332
Rossiter, John, 328
Rouguet, Francois, 189
Rous, John, 68, 264
Roussel d'Hurbal, Nicolas, 165
Rowden, William, 338
Rumbold, Jonathan, 327
Rushworth, James, 324
Russell, Andrew, 337
Russell, George, 343

St. John, Joseph, 44, 57, 83, 238, 240, 243, 245, 261, 288, 297, 305
Saltoun, Alexander Lord, 12, 17, 46, 63, 71, 74, 77, 80, 81, 82, 84, 87, 88, 89, 103, 107, 109, 110, 137, 138, 139, 140, 145, 146, 147, 152, 156, 157, 174, 181, 185,
188, 192, 194, 198, 200, 218, 219, 220, 221, 222, 224, 225, 228, 229, 232, 233, 235, 238, 239, 241, 243, 244, 249, 255, 290, 298, 305, 306, 330, 332, 333, 348, 349
Salwey, Henry, 248, 352
Sandes, Charles, 353
Sandham, Charles, 48, 70, 72, 84, 100, 117, 126, 171, 185, 212, 213, 271, 294, 303, 310
Sandilands, Patrick, 248
Sarrant, Jean-Louis, 147
Sawkings, John, 329
Saxe-Weimar, Prince Bernhard von, 122
Schmitz, Nicolas, 187
Schooles, Peter, 156
Scott, William, 47, 353
Scudder, Richard, 344
Seabury, Richard, 339
Selway, Benjamin, 106, 291, 300, 306
Seymour, Horace, 173, 179, 181
Seymour, Hugh, 353
Sharman, Richard, 339
Shaw, Henry, 344
Shaw, Joseph, 342
Shawe, Meyrick, 45, 47, 52, 53
Shedden, James, 332
Shelly, Frances Lady, 137
Shepherd, George, 327
Sheppard, Charles, 325
Sheppard, Francis, 326
Shirley, Charles, 248
Short, Charles, 78, 91, 93, 97, 102, 142, 162, 196, 266, 292, 300, 308
Simpson, Charles, 135, 270, 293, 302, 341, 353
Simpson, James, 94, 258, 288, 324
Skuce, John, 101, 292, 301, 309, 356
Smee, Edward, 330
Smee, John, 327
Smith, Benjamin, 331
Smith, Charles, 338

Smith, Francis, 332
Smith, George Assistant Surgeon, 100, 149, 291, 300, 308
Smith, George Private, 333
Smith, J. Quartermaster Sergeant, 298, 306
Smith, John, 26, 288, 297, 305
Smith, Joseph, 337
Smith, Thomas, 339
Smyth, Sidney, 58
Somerset, Lord Edward, 211
Somerset, Lord Fitzroy, 11, 17, 19, 50, 51, 59, 63, 67, 109, 140, 178, 210, 211, 218, 288, 290, 299, 305, 312, 314, 316, 334, 347, 349, 350
Southgate, John, 107
Sowerby, Thomas, 13, 291, 300, 308
Soye, Jean-Louis, 81, 129, 131, 146
Speckmann, Theodore, 84, 85, 86, 294, 303, 310
Stable, John, 139
Stables, Edward, 12, 95, 97, 110, 172, 176, 178, 222, 254, 289, 298, 330, 331, 333, 351
Stackwood, William, 331
Standen, George, 14, 91, 104, 131, 293, 302, 310, 353
Stanhope, James, 12, 17, 43, 46, 55, 58, 59, 62, 63, 77, 81, 84, 87, 88, 94, 98, 101, 111, 125, 126, 165, 167, 173, 178, 196, 197, 198, 199, 204, 205, 216, 217, 222, 225, 226, 227, 228, 229, 231, 235, 237, 241, 243, 245, 256, 290, 298, 306, 307, 315, 316, 330, 332, 333
Stanhope, Philip, 354
Stanley, Samuel, 338
Stedman, John, 114
Sterling, John, 338
Stevens, Nathaniel, 326
Stevens, Thomas, 333
Stewart, Charles Lord, 54, 237
Stewart, James, 50, 51

Stewart, John, 337
Stone, John, 139
Stonestreet, George, 48, 50, 56, 109, 233, 241, 287, 296, 304
Stopford, Edward, 49, 64, 105, 163, 200, 291, 293, 299, 302, 310, 313, 353
Stopford, William, 294, 303, 310
Stothert, William 3FG, 14, 18, 49, 70, 142, 163, 200, 268, 291, 293, 299, 302, 313, 341, 353
Stothert, William Coldstream Guards, 355
Stratton, William, 226, 228, 232, 311
Streatfield, Thomas, 95, 256, 289, 329, 351, 352
Stride, John, 325
Stuart, Charles, 58, 59
Stuart, William, 22, 46, 51, 88, 97, 110, 275, 276, 289, 329, 347, 350
Sumner, Edward, 13, 144, 264, 292, 300, 336, 352
Sutherland, Alexander, 344
Swaffer, Donald, 333
Swain, Isaac, 338
Swann, Frederick, 290, 298, 306
Swann, Henry, 88
Swann, William, 332
Sweeper, John, 333
Swinburne, Thomas, 111, 191, 260, 289, 298, 306
Symington, John, 343

Talbot, James, 18, 288, 297, 304, 354
Talbott, Charles, 338
Taylor, Alexander, 324
Taylor, James, 329
Taylor, John, 324
Taylor, Samuel, 329
Tennant, William, 240, 244, 251
Tharp, Joseph, 355
Thomas, Benjamin, 332
Thomas, Carsoff, 339

NAME INDEX

Thomas, Charles, 105, 173, 289, 298, 330, 351
Thomas, Daniel, 329
Thomas, William Sergeant, 333
Thomas, William Private, 327
Thompson, Charles, 30
Thompson, Patrick, 339
Thomson, Alexander, 226, 232, 311
Thornhill, William, 331
Thoroton, Robert, 248
Thorpe, William, 327
Thurlow, James, 338
Tighe, Daniel, 126, 184, 261, 288, 297, 305, 326
Till, John, 338
Tinling, William, 18, 110, 260, 288, 297, 305
Tomkinson, John, 344
Tomkinson, William, 208
Tompkins, James, 325
Torrens, Henry, 45, 52, 53, 54, 55, 250
Toulouse, Sylvian, 147, 148
Townshend, Horatio, 12, 95, 110, 254, 289, 298, 306, 329, 331, 333
Trelores, John, 337
Trescott, William, 327
Tuffnell, George, 356
Tugdy, Elijah, 343
Turner, Frederick, 353,
Turner, John, 332
Twigg, James, 344
Tyson, Charles, 324

Upton, Arthur, 45, 349
Uxbridge, Henry Earl of, 59, 114, 172, 179, 210, 211

Vane, Henry, 144, 266, 291, 300, 336
Verity, Benjamin, 96, 329
Vernon, Henry, 68, 218, 260, 289, 298, 306, 352
Vincent, William, 342

Vivian, Hussey, 195
Vyner, Charles, 289, 298, 306

Walker, Edward, 332
Walker, John 3rd Bn 1FG, 333
Walker, John 2nd Bn 3FG, 344
Walker, William, 30, 325
Walpole, John, 7, 68, 292, 300, 308, 339
Walpole, Robert, 332
Walsh, John, 48, 287, 296, 304
Walter, Joseph, 333
Walters, James, 331
Walton, William, 69, 200, 264, 291, 300, 307, 315
Warde, John, 309
Waters, John, 240, 321, 322
Waters, Marcus, 226, 311
Wathiez, Adrien, 74, 75, 87
Watier, Pierre, 164
Watson, James 3rd Bn 1FG, 332
Watson, James Coldstream Guards, 337
Watson, Samuel, 46, 289, 298, 306
Watts, Robert, 342
Webster, John, 339
Wedgewood, Thomas, 125, 198, 206, 223, 224, 242, 270, 293, 302, 310
West, Charles, 112, 155, 200, 268, 293, 302, 310, 341, 344
West, Douglas, 343
West, James, 248, 249, 255
Weston, Charles, 356
Whatmore, William, 324
White, Charles, 69
Whymper, William, 104, 291, 300, 308
Wiering, George, 294, 303, 310
Wigston, Richard, 106, 112, 153, 268, 293, 310
William, James, 344
Williams, David, 338
Williams, James, 327
Williams, John, 342

Williams, Watkin, 326
Williams, William, 338
Williamson, James, 234, 287, 296, 304
Wilson, James, 332
Wilson, Nathaniel, 332
Winpenny, Edward, 326
Wombwell, Henry, 352
Wood, Charles, 57, 83, 158, 175, 194, 198, 272
Wood, George, 114, 138
Wood, John ACG, 48, 109, 287, 296
Wood, John Sergeant, 333
Woodcock, Thomas, 326
Woodford, Alexander, 17, 19, 20, 23, 51, 55, 56, 62, 64, 66, 71, 104, 140, 141, 143, 144, 145, 150, 151, 154, 221, 276, 291, 300, 308, 348, 349, 350
Woodford, John, 53, 54, 55, 123, 255, 290, 299, 307, 313, 315, 316, 317, 319, 320, 321, 322
Woods, Sergeant Major, 209
Woodson, John, 339
Woodward, William, 343
Worthing, John, 343
Wyndham, Henry, 14, 60, 64, 132, 133, 134, 222, 263, 292, 300, 308, 336, 338
Wynne, Thomas, 342

York, Prince Frederick Duke of, 46, 54, 220, 221, 222, 250, 256, 351
Young, Joseph, 331
Young, Robert, 328

Ziethen, Hans von, 182